PESTALOZZI

PESTALOZZI

The Man and his Work

by

KATE SILBER

Routledge and Kegan Paul
LONDON

First published 1960
by Routledge & Kegan Paul Ltd.
Broadway House, Carter Lane, E.C.4

Printed in Great Britain
by Butler & Tanner Ltd.
Frome and London

© *Kate Silber 1960*

Contents

CONTENTS

CONTENTS

Illustrations

The frontispiece, the engravings of Zurich, Neuhof, Burgdorf, and
Yverdon, as well as the Schöner painting, are reproduced by
courtesy of Zentralbibliothek, Zurich. The portraits by Anton
Graff and F. M. Diogg, and the terracotta mask, are by courtesy
of Pestalozzianum, Zurich.

Preface

'WHILE the name of Pestalozzi is known as a familiar household word on the Continent, and his memory . . . is everywhere held in pious veneration, we in this island, from accidental circumstances, are hardly acquainted with its sound, and know not that to him the world stands more deeply indebted than to any other man for the beginning of the sound and benevolent system, . . . the improvement of the poorer classes of the people.'

This was written by Henry Brougham in *The Edinburgh Review* in 1828, one year after Pestalozzi's death, but it might well have been written today. What constituted the accidental circumstances which prevented a better acquaintance with Pestalozzi's work at that time will be mentioned in Appendix I to this book. In our own time they consist mainly in the lack of up-to-date literature on this subject. Yet the name of Pestalozzi is not entirely unfamiliar in this country; it is still quoted in training college courses and histories of education among those of great educators, but it means little more than an acknowledgement of his past existence. His name has recently been revived in England by the 'Pestalozzi Children's Village Trust' and in the United States by the 'Pestalozzi Foundation of America' whose work is carried out in the memory and the spirit of this great children's benefactor.

The lack of adequate information on Pestalozzi in English is probably due less to the foreignness of his thought than to the involved style of his writing. Although at first sight he appears to have written on one theme only and to have varied only in the manner of approach, his works are, on closer investigation, more complex than anticipated and hard to assess. An account of them, even in German, is a bold undertaking, and in translation presents formidable difficulties.

Yet there have always been enthusiasts who thought it worth while to struggle with the task; for the subject is of a quality so fascinating, even uplifting, that the dealing with it yields a rich reward. A wave of interest in Pestalozzi in England and America has usually followed one on the Continent of Europe; the first at the time of the publication by Cotta of his *Collected Writings* (1819–26), associated with Maclure, Synge, Mayo, and Greaves, the second after the edition by Seyffarth of his *Collected Works* (1896–1902), stimulating, among others, Green, Russell, and Holman. English books on Pestalozzi still in use are based on the latter edition and those subsequent German studies now considered outdated by Continental experts. A new English appreciation covering material come to light more recently has therefore long been overdue.

For a third tide of research on Pestalozzi has surged up in Switzerland and Germany with fine results. Since 1927, the centenary of his death, there has been in progress a Critical Edition of his *Collected Works and Letters* which has almost doubled his hitherto published writings and necessitated a new appraisal of his significance. In consequence he is no longer considered to be only a schoolmaster and inventor of a new teaching method, nor merely a kind-hearted lover of children and helper of the poor. He is now seen in a wider context and ranked among social critics, political reformers, and teachers of mankind of a larger stature. In detailed studies scholars such as Bachmann, Barth, Litt, and Spranger have employed modern methods to stress one or the other of these aspects. In my own book *Pestalozzi: Der Mensch und sein Werk*, Heidelberg, 1957, my aim was to give a comprehensive account of the man and his work based on all the material available, including manuscripts, the Critical Edition, and the entire secondary literature.

This book I have rewritten in English with those modifications which were necessary for publication in this country, and now wish to present to the English reader. Not, I confess, without misgivings; for that I whose native tongue is not English should have rushed in 'where angels fear to tread' may appear to be a hazardous undertaking. I chose it because I believe that a book on Pestalozzi, even a translation, requires complete familiarity with the subject matter which can only be achieved through life-long research. In this way I hope to have done full justice to Pestalozzi and to have brought out, in my own text and in my rendering of quotations, the essence rather than the literal meaning of his often obscure writing. I have certainly not completed the work without asking many questions and receiving valuable advice on English usage and terminology.

Two alternatives were open for the method of presentation, the systematic and the genetic. I did not adopt the systematic method because Pestalozzi himself did not succeed in establishing a complete system. His struggles to create one could, I felt, be described more adequately in an historical account, and such system as he had achieved might be traced easily enough in the table of contents. Moreover, a systematic presentation tends to break up too much the story of a life which here is of paramount importance. In my view the ups and downs of Pestalozzi's development, the wide range of his experiences, and the inspiring impact of his personality are of greater interest than what goes by the name of his educational thought. They can only be related in narrative form. A certain repetition of his main ideas is in the process unavoidable, for the content of later works elaborating earlier thoughts must be given to indicate the development. After all, Pestalozzi himself, like every visionary intent on driving home a truth, was very repetitive, and it would give a false impression of his work if it were presented in too abbreviated a form.

I have tried, then, to give a reliable report of Pestalozzi's life, work, and character, his achievements and failures, and his position in his own time and place. Since reading Pestalozzi in the original is a laborious task even for someone acquainted with German, and for the English reader is restricted to the one or two works available in translation, I have thought it advisable to give accounts and interpretations of his main writings. In these I have attempted to reproduce Pestalozzi's own way of thinking and of expressing himself in order to give as true a picture as possible of the manner of man he was. Thus I hope that the book may be of use not only to teachers and students of education, social history, and psychology, but to parents and laymen without any previous knowledge of the subject matter but with a concern for children, and to the general reader interested in human experience and the lives of exceptional men.

While I have endeavoured to follow faithfully the various trends of Pestalozzi's own thought I have, for the sake of conciseness, strictly avoided all controversy. A prolific author like Pestalozzi lends himself to very diverse interpretations. Indeed he has been described as a Christian as well as a humanist, as a representative of the Enlightenment and as a mystic, as a liberal, a socialist, a conservative, and a revolutionary, as an educationist, a social reformer, or a political philosopher. Instead of attacking, or supporting, any one point of view I have chosen to make my criticisms and state my own opinions implicitly in the interpretation of his works and his life's events. For he is something of everything, and the biographer's task is to endow apparently contradictory traits with a measure of unity and thus to bring a historical figure long dead back to life.

Again, while I have indicated correspondences of ideas with contemporary or earlier thinkers and tried to place Pestalozzi in the framework of his time, I have refrained from pointing out similarities to modern theories and movements. I have preferred to write the book in such a way that the reader will be able to draw the parallels himself. He will discover that much of Pestalozzi's thought, though expressed in its historical context, is of perennial, even topical significance. For if it is only natural that some of his views are now considered obsolete— e.g. his notions on children's work and on the static order of social classes—and that others are only of historical interest— e.g. his school teaching method which was so highly esteemed in the nineteenth century—it will be found that in many respects he is astonishingly modern and far ahead of his time.

In recognizing the vital significance of the early relationship between mother and child and in stressing the importance of a smooth transition from the instinctive to the conscious level, he anticipated much of Freudian theory and of recent educational research, e.g. Bowlby's. His conception of a sequence of well-defined developmental stages, his insistence that intuitive perception precedes formal mental operations, his recognition of the interaction of environment with inborn tendencies— these and other ideas have parallels in the theories and experimental findings of his modern compatriot Piaget. By making accurate observations of actual children and keeping a diary recording the behaviour of his own son he created a method which later child psychologists, e.g. Stern, would use.

His demand for inner and outer security as an element in social and economic well-being is of immediate urgency. The connection he pointed out between economic success and Reformed Protestant religion was stated much later by Troeltsch and Weber in Germany and is at present the subject of research in the U.S.A. His mass psychology has been confirmed by the studies of Ortega y Gasset, and his judgment of Napoleon holds true of more recent dictators whose activities are still fresh in peoples' minds. His ideas on penal reform and the after-care of prisoners have not been fully realized even in our own century.

His insight into the evils of his time—progressive mechanization without happy human relations, growing mass demands without correspondingly greater exertion, increasing State control and diminishing individual responsibility—is highly relevant to the problems of our own day. Equally valid are the remedies which he suggests. They consist in an appeal for better education, sustained effort, and good workmanship, for self-reliance, independent judgment, and individual moral decision, but supremely for a healthy family life, inner and outer security, and good will towards all men. These demands spring not from abstract ideals but from a heart filled with love and a life full of sacrifice.

If this book gains for Pestalozzi in the English-speaking world the wider significance which he has attained on the Continent of Europe, and wins for him the love and esteem which are his due, it will have achieved its purpose.

Edinburgh,   KATE SILBER
September 1959

NOTE

All titles and quotations are given in English. Detailed notes and references, which are all in German, can be found in the German edition of this book. A select Bibliography is attached at the end.

I   *The Youth*
(1746–1769)

'ZURICH is really an incomparable place,' wrote a foreign visitor in 1752, 'not only because of her lovely situation which is unique in the world but also because of her good and clever people.' Indeed, the beautiful town by the lake with the Alps in the background was in the middle of the eighteenth century a famous centre of culture, and for literature the capital of the German-speaking world. She produced a number of men of European renown who, again, brought their literary friends home with them from abroad; the galaxy of their talents gave brilliance to the town on the Limmat. If in public and civil life the old code of behaviour established in the Reformation period still prevailed, new ideas were introduced in the spheres of science and arts. Tradition and modernity lived side by side in the Zurich of that time.

The government of the city-state still represented the spirit of old times. Although originating from the democratic right of every citizen to political self-determination, it had over recent centuries come into the hands of a small number of families, and had in the eighteenth century developed a political aristocracy that preserved its privileges right up to the French Revolution. The city-fathers were very jealous of their power; in close association with the leaders of the Zwinglian church they controlled the daily life of everyone. Sumptuary edicts and moral precepts ruled the conduct of the citizens, censors pried into their personal habits. The oligarchic government had become a bureaucracy; repression of freedom was the official policy.

Below the aristocracy of the ruling families there were the middle-class citizens divided into guilds. Every citizen had to be a member of a guild, but not every man born in Zurich was a citizen, for citizenship had been closed for two centuries and was passed on from father to son only in a restricted number of families. Democracy and equality of rights had disappeared.

The inhabitants of the country-district belonging to the city-state, in number almost ten times that of the town proper, were excluded from participation in public life in spite of constitutional declarations to the contrary. They were not allowed to enter the service either of the government or of the church; their children were not admitted to high-schools; the administration of their own communities was carried out by bailiffs appointed by the town. They could not run manufactories on a large scale; the only occupations permitted them were small crafts and agriculture. The country people were not even interested in the improvement of the land, for an increase in production would have meant higher dues to their landlords. It was, however, not merely aristocratic self-interest which tried to preserve the centralized city-state, but also the Mercantile system prevailing everywhere at that time.

Yet in spite of these restrictions a certain stir was caused even in the country parts by the developing cotton manufacture. Through higher wages the cottage worker became conscious of his greater importance in the country and anxious for the improvement of his political status. Some individual entrepreneurs were even wealthy and respected, though for some time they had to trade in the name of a citizen.

Two movements, though very different from each other, were responsible for introducing a new era: Pietism and the Enlightenment. In contrast to the rigid State-church Pietism cultivated personal religious experience and individual Bible-study; instead of worldly success it recommended meditation and the simple life. But the 'Quietists', as they were called, were oppressed by the official church; sects were dissolved. All the same Pietism laid the foundation for a more emotional interpretation of Christianity and a more liberal application of the mind; it prepared the way for the literary movements of Sentimentality and of Storm and Stress.

The Enlightenment which began in Zurich with the introduction of the Leibnizian philosophy brought the town to the height of her glory. Her Moral Weeklies after the fashion of the *Spectator* became the model for a spate of periodicals all over Germany. Bodmer's and Breitinger's victory in their literary contest against Gottsched established the natural against the artificial, feeling against rule, the English against the French style. In his epics Bodmer celebrated the old-testament patriarchs, and his young visitor Klopstock wrote a *Messiah* in the style of Milton. At the same time he extolled the beauty of Lake Zurich, while Salomon Gessner wrote and painted pastoral idylls. 'Nature' in all its significance was being discovered and exalted.

This led to a new interest in country life and to new theories of agriculture and economics. The school of the Physiocrats now saw the wealth of the nation in its soil, not, as the Mercantilists, in its trade. This had far-reaching consequences. Societies for the study of nature were founded; townspeople began to be interested in country-folk. Into this movement there struck like lightning Rousseau's *Emile* (1762) with its attack on society and its call 'Back to Nature!' It made a tremendous impression especially on young people and influenced, at least in one case, their choice of career. Thus a thing happened that would have been unthinkable a decade or two earlier: one of her citizens left Zurich to take up farming.

The Pestalozzi family was one of the few with the right of election to the City Council, though for some generations its members had not taken any active part in the civic administration. Their ancestor had come to Zurich from the vicinity of Chiavenna in the middle of the sixteenth century. His descendants, after first making good in various walks of life, had lost their positions through ill fortunes and early deaths. Pestalozzi's grandfather was a pastor in a small village on the outskirts of Zurich; his father Johann Baptist (1718-51), a surgeon, died at the early age of thirty-three. The family of Pestalozzi's mother Susanna Hotz of Wädenswil (1720-96), on the other hand, was rising in the world and included a number of well-known physicians; but they were country people and therefore without any political rights.

Johann Heinrich Pestalozzi (born January 12th, 1746) was the second of his parents' three surviving children; the others were his elder brother Johann Baptist and his sister Anna Barbara. The early death of his father left the family in straitened circumstances, and the atmosphere of the home which his mother managed to provide was of the greatest significance for his future development. In several autobiographical surveys Pestalozzi describes both the blessings and the shortcomings of his sheltered but restricted childhood. His mother was a shy woman who lived quietly because of her small means and her country origin. She was devoted to her children; yet she could not have brought them up properly without the generous help of a faithful servant. This Babeli (Barbara Schmid of Buchs) had promised her master on his death-bed not to leave his wife and children as long as they needed her; and she served Mrs. Pestalozzi faithfully for over forty years until her death. She declined offers of better posts and of suitable marriage to keep her promise.

The love and devotion of these two women, especially the servant's, made a profound impression on the mind of the child. As he grew up in the security of his home he became early aware that generosity and noble-mindedness can be active even in a poor maid, and that they have the power to draw forth the same qualities in others. Here lie the roots of Pestalozzi's belief in the original goodness of man and of his dedication to the poor; this is the source of his tireless efforts to improve their lot. In later years he compared the unflinching loyalty of this simple woman with the spirit of the Swiss Confederates whose courage and self-sacrifice had saved their country.

Babeli ran the small household with scrupulous care and economy. In order to obtain fruit and vegetables at lower prices she went to the market at a time when the stall-keepers were getting ready to go home. She made the children change their clothes and shoes as soon as they came home and kept them indoors as much as possible so that they should not wear these things out too quickly. At the same time she saw to it that the family obligations were observed meticulously, and presents and tips were given almost beyond their means.

The feminine atmosphere of his surroundings intensified the boy's natural tendencies. Young Heinrich was of a delicate constitution and possessed a lively imagination. His feelings

4

were strong and deep, and they were easily roused. But he was not interested in outside matters and was careless about everyday things. He had no practical abilities and no opportunities for acquiring them. The loss of his father at the age of five deprived him of the male guidance of which with his emotional temperament he stood in exceptional need. So he grew up in a small town house where everything was saved but nothing earned; where his heart was gratified but his mind kept ignorant of the outside world; where sheltered by the care of these devoted women he became an unpractical dreamer.

For reasons of economy the boy was denied the company of other children. He was not allowed to play with them in the street; so he did not know their games, their ways, their secrets. When he met them by chance he behaved awkwardly and was laughed at by them all. When he was about nine or ten they nicknamed him 'Harry Queer of Foolstown'.

'Love, work, and social intercourse,' says Pestalozzi in his educational writings, 'are the natural means of developing our faculties.' In his own upbringing these three factors were not properly balanced. The power of love which he experienced was not offset by a training for practical work nor by a necessity for dealing with people. It was to the one-sidedness of these early influences that he later attributed his life's failures.

School was a wholesome complement to home life, for it gave his eager mind scope for activity. The boy learned easily, but his work was uneven. He quickly got hold of any problem but made incredible howlers in carrying out details. He became keenly interested in matters of the mind in compensation for the lack of manual occupation and of relaxation through games. But no school, no Latin, no reading nor writing, says Pestalozzi, can fill the gaps in a child's education that come from the omission of all practical training and from awkwardness in dealing with people. In these respects the poorest country child, though deprived of schooling, is superior to the educated town child, for he is rich in practical experience. Thus Pestalozzi never set any great store by the teaching given in schools, regarding it at best as a necessary evil.

Elementary school-teaching in his youth was indeed very dull and mechanical. For the most part it took the form of making the children learn passages by heart. All higher education was a preparation for the study of theology; the sciences were not fostered, nor was independent thinking encouraged. The teachers were pitiable creatures, despised and despising their craft. Their corrupt practices filled young Heinrich with disgust. He could never forget the scene during the earthquake of 1755 'when the tall masters leapt down the school stairs over our heads like giants among Lilliputians; when we had all got down I alone of the hundred children risked going up again to fetch hats and books; all the rest including my brother ran home'.

Good-natured and free of guile, Harry Queer always let himself be used for tasks which other boys did not like; it never occurred to him that they could have done them just as well themselves. In this strange lad whom his fellow-pupils teased and for whom his teachers predicted failure there lay a hidden strength of which those around him had not an inkling. His cheerful courage which knew no danger; his unfailing optimism which emerged unimpaired from all misfortunes; his good nature which did not think ill of anybody; his confidence, his light-heartedness, in short, his faith and love were powers capable of moving mountains. He was always guided by his heart. Basically he knew exactly what he wanted. Thus from childhood on he stood apart, an individual confronting the imperturbable uniformity of his fellows.

There was one place, however, where young Heinrich got to know life as it really was: Höngg, the parish of his grandfather. Andreas Pestalozzi (1692-1769) was a pastor of the good old sort. He visited his flock not only when they were ill or dying but regularly during the year. In this way he became the friend of every household and the kind adviser on their moral and religious problems. He also held the schoolmaster and the village children to their duties and saw to it that school-teaching did not lose touch with home life. Heinrich took an active interest in this rural community from his early youth and so got to know country life and country-folk in their old-fashioned patriarchal ways.

It was here he first realized the dissimilarity of country and town conditions and the resulting differences in the ways of looking at things. For though blind to matters outside his interests he was extremely observant of everything concerning them.

He noticed that the rich viewed the world very differently from the poor, the ruler from the ruled; and he began to ask for the reasons why. He compared his well-to-do city schoolfellows with the shabby country children and wondered whether either group was better than the other, and where he stood himself. He found that the ragged village children had lived carefree and healthy lives until the ages of five or six, when 'the double misery of the ABC-one-sidedness and the cotton industry' smothered their vitality. Must this be so? His heart told him that it was his task to find ways and means for the improvement of the village people's lot, and he developed a decided partiality for the poor and the weak of the country. The contrast between their actual conditions and their constitutional rights angered him and turned him into a 'patriot'; he intended becoming an advocate to be in a position to help the disinherited with an expert's skill.

II DEVELOPMENT

After having gone through elementary and grammar school and the Collegium Humanitatis, Pestalozzi studied philology and philosophy at the Collegium Carolinum. This institution had at that time some highly distinguished professors. Breitinger introduced his students to the very spirit of Greek and Hebrew literature; his name was of European renown. Steinbrüchel taught Greek philology; he was a great scholar but a dull teacher. His shortcomings roused Pestalozzi to challenge him in the translation of Demosthenes' Olynthian speeches; and though the professor had the sounder knowledge of grammar, the student showed a higher flow of rhetoric. But the professor with the greatest influence on several generations of Swiss scholars was Johann Jacob Bodmer who taught Swiss history and politics in the Carolinum for almost half a century. He gave his students a passionate love for their country and an enthusiastic interest in their past. Comparing the Swiss city-states with those of antiquity, especially with Sparta, he set forth an example of freedom and justice, of simplicity and self-sacrifice for the common weal. 'Virtue' was the keynote of his moralizing lectures. The young men found in him a kind friend and adviser. They listened to him not only in class but also outside

7

after the manner of Greek students, as they strolled with him by the rivers Limmat and Sihl. Pestalozzi did not take the final class in theology but left the college at the age of nineteen without having sat the examination. He did not after all become an advocate, nor did he enter the Church like his fellow-students; his choice of career was to lie in quite a different direction.

More important for him than his college work was his membership of an historical-political association. In contrast to the solitariness of his school years he now took an active part in the life of a community of like-minded people. A group of brilliant young men called 'Patriots' founded in the 'sixties with Bodmer's support the 'Helvetic Society', a kind of youth movement for the raising of the country's moral standards. The works of Montesquieu and especially of Rousseau had inspired them; to the moral precepts of the Enlightenment they added a strong dash of Spartan asceticism and Stoic ethics. 'Perfection' and 'virtue' were their ideals. They had a strict sense of duty, practised self-denial and restraint, and put the claims of their country before personal desires. They were convinced that they were born for great things.

Pestalozzi's closest friends amongst the members of the Helvetic Society were Johann Caspar Füssli, Caspar Schulthess and Johann Caspar Bluntschli. The best-known to the world was Johann Caspar Lavater. His moral writings and patriotic *Swiss Songs* were already widely read; his masterly rhetoric and emotional style of preaching drew large crowds to his church. If Pestalozzi admired Lavater's genuine religious feeling and his social accomplishments, he disliked his soul-stirring sermons and belief in the miraculous. Lavater, too, was both attracted and repelled by Pestalozzi. Thus no close friendship existed between these two famous contemporaries, but in time of trouble Pestalozzi would readily turn to the more competent Lavater for help which the latter as readily gave.

The Patriot with the greatest influence on the group was Bluntschli, called 'Menalk' by his friends. Himself of absolute integrity, he wished to help others in their struggle for 'moral perfection'. He showed great strength of will in his endeavours to apply his maxim: 'To uproot what is deep-rooted, is virtue.' His intention was eventually to enter the government and thus be in a position to implement his ascetic ideals; indeed he pro-

8

posed to recommend the abolition of meals. Unfortunately, however, he contracted a deadly disease which forced him not only to give up all his ambitious plans but also to conquer a passion for a girl which now could never be gratified.

The untimely death of this promising young man (1767) gave a special importance to his ideas, increasing their significance for his friends. Pestalozzi was destined to be his heir in more than one respect. He shaped his early adult life after Bluntschli's model, but he was not always to recollect in time his friend's parting words. For Menalk, by way of a last bequest, had warned the good-natured Pestalozzi never to enter into a far-reaching enterprise without the considered support of someone with a shrewder knowledge of men and affairs than he. How well Menalk understood the unpractical dreamer! How bitterly Pestalozzi missed this true friend! He was shattered by the loss of Bluntschli, yet his death was the occasion of a new beginning. For in their common grief Menalk's great friend and the girl he had loved found each other and became linked for life.

Since the beginning of 1765 the Patriots had been issuing a Moral Weekly of their own, *The Monitor*. Lavater and Füssli were the editors, Pestalozzi was a contributor. He expressed a number of *Wishes*, the only possible form of public criticism permitted under the strict Zurich censorship; he demanded a 'purification' of literature and art. 'Would that no man of high mental endowment deemed it beneath him to work for the common weal, nor that he despised his lesser yet more industrious fellow creatures!' 'Would that all anacreontic songs of a Gleim, a Lessing, an Uz and all such refined indecencies were prohibited!' 'Would that every conceivable effort were made to teach moral principles to young men devoting themselves to the arts and sciences!'

Another article of Pestalozzi's, *Agis*, recommends to his native town emulation of the Spartan king who wished to renew the laws of Lycurgus to re-establish virtue. Under the guise of discussing ancient history he laments the loss of 'liberty and equality', the decline of the city-state, and the power of the magistrate. What, he asks, was the political danger, then as now? The fact, he answers, that democracy had turned into oligarchy, that the administration had gained absolute control. What if

9

their officials ceased to have the necessary attributes of justice and honesty?

At this juncture the Patriots began to be active in politics. With the rashness of youth they felt called upon to expose shady financial practices and to put an end to abuses. They brought to light several cases of embezzlement without achieving anything, however. In the so-called 'Grebel affair' Lavater and Füssli publicly accused a bailiff of gross injustice. But although his misdemeanour was known all over the town it was they who were treated as the guilty ones and forced to make public apology. In another case concerning a disreputable clergyman Pestalozzi and Bluntschli were summoned and reprimanded for their unwarranted interference. Finally, when a pamphlet was circulated proclaiming the right of the Geneva citizens to set up a constitution of their own choosing, Pestalozzi was suspected of being its author. He was cross-examined several times and kept under arrest in the town hall for three days. On the following Sunday 'the very grievous signs of a rebellious mentality' were condemned from every pulpit, and the infamous document was publicly burnt by the executioner. 'Herr Heinrich Pestalozzi and other Suspects' had to pay for their keep in the town hall and for the three cords of wood for the burning. During the auto-da-fé the young Patriots walked to and fro on the roof of a nearby guild-house, smoking their pipes.

This period of Patriotism certainly influenced Pestalozzi's final choice of a career, but with the sobering experience of practical work he abandoned his 'wild enthusiasm' sooner than did his friends. In later years he was harshly critical of his 'Patriotic' activities. He described Bodmer's teaching, after his restricted home environment and his natural inefficiency, as the third adverse factor in his youthful development. It had merely encouraged his proneness to dream, preparing him ill for real life. The hope to reform a small Swiss canton 'through superficial book-knowledge of the great Greek and Roman civic life' and the impact of *Emile*, 'this equally unpractical dream-book', had dazzled him, he said; they led to words, not to deeds. That, however, was his mature view; at this early stage he obeyed Rousseau and went 'back to Nature'.

Probably several reasons combined to induce Pestalozzi not to take up theology like all his friends, but to go in for agricul-

ture. His strong individuality refused, to the point of physical illness, to be pressed into the mould of rigid church regulations.
Besides, he did not consider his own conviction strong enough
to justify his preaching to others. Again, he early wished to set
up a home of his own and hoped to find a secure livelihood more
quickly in farming than in the church. Further, as already
hinted, the call of the time to lead a 'natural' life impressed
him more deeply than other young men; he took it literally. 'I
wished to do what others only talked about. I was vitally interested in all that concerned men's hearts and was naturally led
to seek honour and love rather in the path of sacrifice and charity than in that of thinking and research.' On the land he
hoped to be able to work for the poor; thus his choice of an occupation was considerably influenced by his determination to
serve his people, or rather mankind, even at the cost of his personal comfort. Pestalozzi's taking up farming meant a lowering
in social status for him as the son of a ruling-class family. It was
the first instance of those unconventional actions so characteristic of him.

Meanwhile love had struck him 'like a thunderbolt'; it had
turned the youth into a man. To this first girl who attracted him
he vowed that he would sooner die than cease in his devotion
for her. Until her death after more than forty years of married
life he kept this promise, and no other woman ever took her
place in his heart. But in his preparations both for work and for
marriage and the bringing up of a family he never lost sight of
his patriotic ideals and his public duties. Indeed in the first long
letter he wrote to his sweetheart asking her to marry him he
tells her at once that he would consider his duties towards a wife
to be subordinate to his country's claims. To this declaration
also he remained faithful throughout his life. Fortunately the
girl who was Caspar Schulthess's sister and Bluntschli's friend
understood and approved of the Patriots' views. Menalk had
made a deep impression on her, too; he had educated her mind
and cultivated her heart. Through him she had become superior
to the ordinary Zurich young women.

Anna Schulthess of 'The Plough' (born 1738) was good-look-
ing, well-to-do, educated, and capable. She belonged to one of
the most respected Zurich families, had all the social graces and

was greatly admired. Yet she was slow in choosing a husband though not happy at home. Her mother, an efficient business woman, ruled the house strictly; her good-tempered father gave way in everything to keep the peace. The grown-up daughter and five younger sons were treated like children. Anna was held firmly to her tasks in house and shop. She performed her duties conscientiously, but her interests were very different from those of her parents. She had never known the tenderness of a loving mother and felt wretched in an environment uncongenial to her.

'Nanette' was approaching her thirtieth year when she met Pestalozzi; he was eight years younger than she. He was plain, poor, and without definite professional prospects; he was generally looked upon as eccentric. Yet she allowed him to take the place of Menalk. When he insisted on being more than a friend she held him at bay for a while. After an exchange of long letters disclosing their respective faults Anna consulted 'her mind more than her heart' and promised herself to him for ever before God. She was well aware of the difficulties ahead of her, especially of the objections from her parents. What then had prompted her decision? She recognized Pestalozzi's great heart and eminent mind; she knew he would guide her towards 'goodness' and 'perfection'; she valued his honesty and appreciated his tender respect for her as a woman. She realized his superiority to her former suitors and to herself; 'I have known nobody like you.' Anna Schulthess is the first person to mention Pestalozzi's large black eyes; in them she saw expressed the kindness of his heart, the greatness of his mind, and the tenderness of his love. She was the first also to recognize the genius in Pestalozzi. On account of it she was willing to join her life to his. Asked later how she had come to marry such an uncouth fellow she answered: 'He has a beautiful soul.'

What attracted the young man in the maturer woman was not in the first place anything specially feminine but rather her essentially human qualities, her moral endeavours, her Patriotism. He admired her dignity and her poise; he believed her capable of bringing up useful citizens. She embodied for him the type of the women of Sparta which at that moment represented his ideal of womanhood.

Immediately after their engagement Pestalozzi had to leave

his betrothed to begin his training in the country. For Anna there began two long years full of worry and difficulties in which she had to confront alone her domineering mother. The voluminous correspondence of the engagement period documents very revealingly every complication of their emotions during that time. It bears witness to their common striving after 'perfection' and reflects their daily struggles with ever-present difficulties; it shows their efforts to prepare themselves for their future life together. Lavater and Füssli were their messengers, for the engagement had to be kept secret. They exchanged, however, a number of 'polite' letters suitable for showing to Anna's parents, in which they discuss in cheerful terms the good progress of Heinrich's affairs.

In September 1767 Pestalozzi, on Lavater's recommendation, went to Johann Rudolf Tschiffeli's experimental farm Kirchberg in the canton of Berne for training in modern farming methods. This Bernese session-clerk and gentleman-farmer specialized in the cultivation of clover for stall-feeding, of madder for the red dye in the newly developed cotton industry, and of potatoes which had only recently been introduced to Switzerland. Tschiffeli was equally up-to-date in the theory of agriculture, being a member of the Berne Economic Society. He let Pestalozzi share all his experience and gave him, like 'the best of fathers', a very profitable time. Pestalozzi intended to concentrate on the cultivation of madder and of vegetables also. He expected good profits from growing the finer kinds of vegetable in his home canton where these were as yet uncommon, and of fruit which he planned to dry or to store over winter so as to obtain a better price for it in spring. He was favourably impressed with the way Tschiffeli's model farm was run; he did not know, however, that Kirchberg was financed largely from Tschiffeli's private income. When he realized this much later he blamed himself for 'dreaming' about agriculture on leaving Kirchberg in the same way as he had been 'dreaming' about public affairs when entering it, and he included Tschiffeli among the idealists responsible for the misdirection of his education.

Pestalozzi hoped to find near Lake Zurich some neglected piece of ground at a reasonable price on which to start experimenting. He demonstrated the soundness of his schemes to Nanette with masses of figures. More experienced in business matters than he she warned him; she advised beginning in a small way rather than to take on too much, though her confidence in Pestalozzi was greater than her anxiety about the future. For his sake she was willing to accept every deprivation. She now had the unpleasant task of telling her parents of her engagement.

To her surprise they did not take too unfavourable a view of Pestalozzi's membership of the 'Patriots'; his character was unimpeachable. But they said he must first give proof of his skill in a profession before they gave their only daughter into his keeping. His training in Kirchberg by no means convinced Anna's parents of his suitability for agriculture; his premature departure—he had intended to stay for at least eighteen months but left after nine—took even his fiancée by surprise. This aggravated the situation. Harsh words were spoken in Nanette's home; Pestalozzi was forbidden the Schulthess house, Anna was sent away from Zurich and ordered to break her engagement. The conflict of feelings aroused in both lovers by these events is movingly expressed in their letters. Anna suffered deeply, torn between loyalty to Pestalozzi and obedience to her parents. Pestalozzi's mood kept changing from firm determination to utter despair. At one time he believed it his duty to rescue his fiancée from the misery of her home; at another he was tormented by self-accusation, asking himself whether he was worth this suffering on her part. Unable to foresee an end to it all he begged her to come to a decision. After her mother had offered him fresh insults, Nanette was almost ready to follow him even against the wishes of her parents. Then the situation improved; through the intervention of influential people—Pestalozzi's cousin Dr. Hotze, Lavater, and the burgomaster Heidegger—the mother's opposition was weakened so that she now demanded only a postponement of the marriage for two years, pending evidence of improvement in Pestalozzi's financial position. How easily Anna's parents could have helped instead of making difficulties! From now on, at least, the young people could appear in public as an engaged couple; the indignity of secret meetings was ended.

Meanwhile Pestalozzi, as enthusiastic as ever, had been conceiving plans and abandoning them, had been making contacts and inspecting farms. He did not find the neglected land he was looking for in the canton of Zurich, however, and so he left the vicinity of his home town, never to live there again. He decided on some land near the village of Birr in the canton of Berne at the foot of the historic castles Brunegg, Wildegg, and Habsburg. The proximity of the rivers Aar and Reuss was a great advantage as goods were mainly carried by water. Pestalozzi found springs for irrigating the dry moor; he planned to dig ditches for draining the damp marshes; a nearby lime pit would supply plenty of fertilizer. In short, he saw that the soil could easily be improved. The only question was, where the capital for the purchase was to come from. He reckoned that he would be able to repay it in a few years' time. As his own family's advances were not enough he entered into an agreement with a Zurich banking-house. This enabled him to rent a house and to settle on the Birrfeld. Within a year he had bought reasonably cheaply about sixty acres of land, a purchase spread over fifty separate transactions through his attempts to connect up individual lots and to round off his estate.

His intentions as to what he should cultivate seem to have changed; there is less talk of vegetables but more of feeding-stuffs. His main interest was still in madder which had been so successful in Kirchberg. It is also interesting to note that already at this point there is talk of introducing cotton-spinning into the neighbourhood as an additional means of earning for the poor villagers as well as for himself. Throughout his correspondence he speaks confidently of his prospects, and he assures Anna's father of the safety of his enterprise. 'I know my business,' he declares. And so he did not wish to wait any longer. Winter was approaching, and he was reluctant to bring Nanette to her new home at the worst time of the year. He also maintained that a farmhouse could not be run without a wife. So father and mother Schulthess at last gave their ungracious permission for a quiet wedding. There was no celebration; the bridegroom was not allowed to meet his bride in her father's house as was the custom; she had to go alone to the home of her 'new mamma'. She brought with her only her personal belongings; Pestalozzi had expressly agreed not to expect anything else. Yet they were thankful to have arrived at their goal after a struggle of more than two years. On the last day of September

1769 they were married in the small village church of Gebens-dorf.

The picture of Heinrich Pestalozzi at the time of his marriage is that of a young man at the beginning of his career, his character not yet fixed. But certain traits, later so prominent, are already discernible: his simplicity amounting sometimes to naïveté; his habit of making straight for a goal perceived to be right; his warm impulsiveness; his unfailing obedience to the dictates of his heart; his spontaneous generosity manifest in offering the house he had not yet secured to poor children and needy relatives. From early youth he had a sensitive social conscience; he considered himself a servant of men. A keen sense of duty speaks from his letters to his betrothed which are full of references to his obligations to society, especially young people. These statements represent more than mere programme points of the Helvetic Society. And this is the difference between Pestalozzi and the other Patriots: he put his patriotism into practice. He left the conventional road of his fellow-students; he was original. In going 'back to Nature' in the true sense of the word by taking up farming he aimed to get back to 'the elements' of human activity, a worthwhile experiment even though this first attempt was to prove a failure. His wish to take poor children into his house came from a heart filled with love; he was conscious of the urge and the power to act and to help. 'It was not in Pestalozzi's nature', he later wrote of himself, 'to limit himself to mere speculation and reasoning. All the teachings of his epoch impelled him to a life of action and could not have affected him in any other way.'

Other qualities, as yet barely evident, were to develop throughout the course of a long life. There was to be no stagnation; even as an old man he was as flexible, impressionable, and unpredictable as in his youth. This perpetual youthfulness is one of Pestalozzi's most outstanding characteristics, setting him in sharpest contrast to Anna Schulthess. At the time of their engagement she was the more mature, but she had already reached her full potentialities, a fact that was to be of importance in his future activities. At this point she had the wider experience of the two in many respects, particularly in religion; here Pestalozzi was inclined to be conventional as yet.

ZURICH

Engraving by F. Hegi after H. Maurer, about 1810

PESTALOZZI

Drawing by Anton Graff
1765

He had grown up in the unbroken tradition of Reformed Protestantism, used to prayer and Bible reading in his mother's home. Ecclesiastical forms were completely spoiled for him by the mechanical catechism instruction in school and the rigidity of the prevailing orthodoxy. His comments on religion show features of Pietism, for example in the consciousness of sin and preparedness for death expressed at the time of his inner conflicts during the engagement period. His 'expectation of eternity' contains something of 'Enthusiasm'; he seems almost to enjoy suffering, welcoming it as a means to self-improvement. Merciless probings into, and prolonged reflections on the self, the exposing and the correcting of faults are all prominent in the notes of both, before and after marriage.

Striving after 'virtue' and 'perfection' is, however, a characteristic trait of the Enlightenment also. Without breaking with his protestant past Pestalozzi had assimilated from Bodmer the doctrines of the Wolffian and Leibnizian philosophies proclaiming a freer, undogmatic, 'natural' religion. The accent shifts from God to man. God gives the strength and the comfort, religion the ways and the means. Man has a duty to realize all the capacities with which he has been endowed. The value of religion lies then for Pestalozzi in its moral implications.

When, finally, it is recalled what a deep impression Rousseau's social criticism had made on the young man it becomes clear how open was his developing mind to the various intellectual currents of the day. Thus far he had not achieved mental harmony, yet from the outset his preoccupation with moral problems had lent a certain unity to his thinking. Man and his destiny were his main concern. To the improvement of man's inner self and his outer lot Pestalozzi's energies were to be devoted.

II The Writer
(1769–1783)

THE young couple now lived according to Rousseau's doctrines in a country cottage. A joint diary which they kept
during their first year together reveals that after the tensions
of the previous two years they dwell less on the happiness of
their union than, in pietistic introspection, on the difficulties of
their new situation. Two such independent characters did not
find it at all easy to fit in with each other in these unfavourable
circumstances. When her husband came home at night hungry
and in wet clothes, the aristocratic lady would succumb to her
'pet failing'; she would lose her hard-won 'composure'. Thus
began her hopeless struggle against Pestalozzi's disregard of
personal tidiness to which even before marriage she had tactfully sought to turn his attention. More significant is the growing divergence of their spiritual attitudes. Since marriage Frau
Pestalozzi had begun to withdraw more and more into herself
and to spend much time in religious meditations. The young
woman, formerly so active, now left the entire management of
their affairs to the younger man. As her share in this marital
division of labour she took over the responsibility of his soul as
well as her own. Her thoughts were taken up increasingly by
'the joyful expectation of the blessing of their union', for the
young couple hoped to have a large family of 'patriotic sons'
and 'virtuous daughters'.

Heinrich and Anna did not find life in the country lonely; on
the contrary they were almost overrun by friends. However
enjoyable this may have been, it was a distraction from medita-

tion and a strain on their budget. For their part they paid calls in the neighbourhood and an occasional visit to town. Their first stay at 'The Plough', intended to last three days, was extended to three weeks. Their relation with her parents improved; they received presents and money. Mother Schulthess came to see them in the country; it was a happy change from the year before.

Pestalozzi threw himself into his work with great zeal. He had a new house built at the foot of the Brunegg and set about scientific cultivation. Agriculture in its old form, the open-field system, had brought little profit to this district. Large stretches of land had never been ploughed and had been used only for grazing. By growing clover and planting potatoes Pestalozzi improved the quality of the soil and the value of the land. This new method of farming had important consequences also in social relations. It interfered with common rights of pasture and brought Pestalozzi into litigation with his neighbours. In their fight to retain their rights of way which cut across his land the people of Birr took Pestalozzi to court. He won the case but lost the villagers' sympathy.

The peasants of Birr viewed the new-fangled ideas of the gentleman-farmer with suspicion and scorn, even with enmity. Unfavourable reports reached the Zurich banking-house; the owner sent two experts to get a reliable opinion. Before one year was up he informed Pestalozzi that he considered the enterprise a failure, and withdrew his support. Pestalozzi's farming experiment had miscarried. What was the cause of this sudden collapse?

Looking back on his failure in the *Swansong*, Pestalozzi distinguishes between his design which was 'perfectly well thought out' and its execution which had involved 'insurmountable difficulties'. Of these he cites his association with an agent who cheated him in his purchases, and the planning of his house which he calls ill-considered and unsuitable. It seems indeed surprising that Pestalozzi started on such a large building, considering his enthusiasm for 'natural' simplicity and Anna's contentment with modest conditions. Was there perhaps the intention at the back of his mind to accommodate the poor and the needy? It is more readily understandable that the careless and credulous young man should entrust his business affairs to a Birr butcher with a bad reputation. This man lined his own pockets by persuading Pestalozzi, to give one example, to exchange his good 'Hummel-acres' for poorer land of his own. In *Leonard and Gertrude* Pestalozzi immortalized him in the wicked character of Bailiff Hummel.

The large house was left unfinished, a roof being put on the first storey; and in the following spring the young couple moved into the Neuhof under unfavourable auspices. With the financial help of friends and relatives they persevered in their agricultural experiment for another year or two, but the seventeen-seventies were particularly hard years everywhere in Europe. Pestalozzi tried by all conceivable means to raise capital but was unable to recover financially.

'He could not keep proper accounts, for he would not be bothered with the trivialities of book-keeping but would only make very general plans,' commented a friend of Pestalozzi's. 'A man who sees and yearns for the stars, who thinks most profoundly, who has the finest moral sense but none for the details of everyday life, who has neither eye nor ear for domestic requirements, who as he contemplates the stars stumbles into the pit yawning at his feet, who cannot address anyone or do anything without making an unfavourable impression through his hasty, uncouth, and thoughtless behaviour—how could such a man ever have reasonable hope of success in the world of action?' This first biographical note written about ten years later, emphasizing as it does the remarkable combination of spiritual greatness and lack of practical ability, indicates in essence all later characteristics.

Pestalozzi blamed no one but himself for the failure. 'The cause of the miscarriage of my enterprise lay not in it but solely in myself and in my pronounced incapacity for any undertaking demanding practical ability.' A heavy sense of responsibility overwhelmed him especially on seeing his wife pregnant. 'You are carrying our beloved child, yet here am I, penniless and without a livelihood,' he exclaimed. On the birth of his son he burst into violent self-accusations doubting his worthiness and fitness for the duties of fatherhood.

During the years of his agricultural experiments Pestalozzi had always kept alive an interest in the affairs of his country, hoping to be able one day to serve it even from his remote village. Nor did he ever consider his work only as a means of supporting his family but always felt responsible for a larger circle of people. In his new surroundings it was the poor rural population for whose welfare he was actively concerned.

The majority of the peasant class were desperately poor. Soil cultivation alone no longer sufficed to sustain the growing population of the latter part of the eighteenth century. So the poor snatched at the new source of income, home industry. This, however, was a double-edged sword, 'like knife and scissors in the hands of children'. For on the one hand it led to greater oppression than had feudalism, on the other it yielded larger earnings which in their turn created more demands. So much was clear: a new era had begun; Europe was on the threshold of an industrial revolution which brought in its wake entirely new conditions and problems. Therefore old customs had to be strengthened, new dangers eliminated; people had to learn how to deal with money; the workers had to be educated. This situation was the starting-point of Pestalozzi's life-long efforts to find ways and means which would enable the people, especially the poorest, to make their own lives worth living.

He may have found it regrettable that the 'natural' ways of bread-winning were being replaced by 'artificial' ones, but he accepted the fact as inevitable. He saw what was needed; and seeing a need and exerting himself to satisfy it was for him one and the same thing. He recognized that 'the more artificial ways of making their living necessitate a better education for the people, and a country can enjoy greater earnings and a wider choice of commodities only when it has been taught how to use them'. 'It is, therefore, an absolute necessity to relate the education of the poor to the spirit of industry.' To achieve this he began at the beginning, i.e. with the children.

That children had to take part in the support of a family was at that time a matter of course and presented no problem for Pestalozzi. But it seemed to him unnecessary, even pitiful, that they should be physically and mentally ruined in the process. Educating poor children for industry, he said, does not mean making them turn a wheel. No, they are human beings, images of God. The purpose of their training must not merely be greater earning capacity; all their human faculties must be developed equally. Here no less than anywhere else it is possible 'to achieve moral ends'. 'No matter what his circumstances or work, man is capable of being guided to the good.'

Having supported the home industry in the neighbouring villages through the supply of cotton to the small peasant families from the beginning of his stay in the Birrfeld, Pestalozzi now started an industrial enterprise in the Neuhof itself (at the end of 1773). The large house was there, his estate provided the basic essentials in food; workers (children!) were available in plenty. His ardent wish to help hurried him on. The idea was to teach poor, neglected, sometimes even physically unfit children to earn their living by their own work as cotton spinners or weavers. While working, they would learn arithmetic and the catechism by repeating together what they had been told. In the evenings, by way of recreation, the boys would do gardening, the girls cooking and sewing. Pestalozzi placed great hopes in the possibility of realizing his plans.

Two pairs of contrasting thoughts occupied Pestalozzi's mind all through his life; the relation of work to education or the necessity of education for a specialized occupation against that of man as a moral being; and the differences or similarities between the education fitting man for a particular condition of living (i.e. poverty) and that appropriate for the general condition of humanity. As regards the first, Pestalozzi had made the observation that it was not the working from morning till night, but the lack of essentials and the surplus of non-essentials which obstruct the child's development. If harmful factors could be removed and replaced by favourable conditions, children in spite or rather because of their work could be brought from a state of deprivation to one of full humanity in which their practical abilities for a useful life as well as their capacities for confidence and love would be developed and cultivated. On the question of class-education against general education Pestalozzi put the emphasis differently at different periods of his life; in fact the two run parallel and support each other. When he was running his first industrial school, to educate the poor for their particular place in life seemed to him the necessary pre-condition for educating them for manhood and womanhood. 'Each class should train their young to meet the limitations, restrictions, and difficulties of their adult days,' he writes; the educator of the poor ought therefore to train those faculties 'on which their support will probably depend at various points in their future lives'. Therefore institutions for the poor must be centres of industry. The poor child should not receive alms but must learn how to work.

In the course of the next few years his house for the poor became an institution accommodating about fifty people. It employed several master-spinners and weavers as well as men and women servants. The children were a very mixed lot of boys and girls whose ages ranged from six to eighteen years. Some did well, others were lazy; some were strong and lively, others showed an astonishing combination of faults and gifts. One was sickly but had a decided talent for drawing, another was backward but possessed an extraordinary ear for music. The state of health of all was surprisingly good. Their output of work was favourably affected by their living as a community.

The institution was neither a manufactory nor a school; it was a big family. The head of such a community, says Pestalozzi, should be father of his house; he should rejoice in the progress of his children in their work, their increasing earnings, and the improvement in their behaviour. The purpose of such houses should be the true cultivation of the human heart; this being granted they would 'meet both the needs of humanity and the circumstances of the poor'. Religious education should not be a matter of formal instruction but the turning to spiritual advantage of the daily happenings in the shared lives of the house father and the children.

It soon became clear, however, that the growing institution could not support itself after all. So Pestalozzi, convinced that he was pursuing a matter of public interest, felt justified in asking 'humanitarians and benefactors' for help. He received small subscriptions which would have tided him over in normal years. But his difficulties increased. They were to some extent inherent in the enterprise itself, but were also caused by a combination of unfortunate circumstances.

Not all the children had reacted to his unselfish devotion with a corresponding gratitude. Many of them were so used to begging and loafing that they could not refrain from pilfering nor control their greed; they could not be brought to order.

An even greater obstacle lay in the attitude of their parents. They behaved as if they were doing Pestalozzi a favour in leaving their children with him; as soon as a boy had been given new clothes and had learned something useful they inveigled him into running away. 'Oh, you poor child, must you now work all day long? Do you get enough to eat? Is it well cooked? Wouldn't you rather come home?' The confusion in his accounts and Pestalozzi's general lack of experience were disastrous. In an excess of zeal he did not confine his efforts to the workshop but set up a retail business in home-produced cotton cloths which he himself sold at the fairs. Further misfortunes added to his worries: the poor crops during the 'seventies and two hail-storms in one summer destroyed his harvest. On top of this his wife became seriously ill. All this was more than one man alone could bear. Financial disaster could no longer be averted.

With a heavy heart Pestalozzi had to send most of the children away. His attempts to build up a self-supporting industrial school for poor children had failed in a lamentable way. However, the institution had been in existence for over five years (1774–9), and those orphans who had nowhere else to go remained in the Neuhof for some time. But the large-scale enterprise planned by Pestalozzi had broken down. Its collapse shattered him even more violently than the failure of his first agricultural experiment, for it touched his personal vocation, the ardent desire of his heart.

Although, as before, he was ready to admit mistakes and to take the blame for the failure upon himself he was yet convinced that his idea for the education of the poor was practicable and right. He again distinguished between 'accidental details' and 'the essence of the matter'; among the first he quoted his unfortunate tendency 'always to reach for the top of the ladder before having secured a firm footing on the bottom'. He had attempted too much in combining a retail business with the workshop; he should, as he realized too late, have kept things as simple as possible in his education of the poor. His onetime neighbour, the governor Tscharner, passed a similar judgment. 'The plan was too ambitious, his enthusiasm carried him too far. . . . With wings often singed or lost he always tried to reach the sun.' Pestalozzi's future assistant Niederer hits the nail on the head with his remark that 'the immensity of his enterprise was utterly opposed to the accepted views of his time and place'. That he was attempting something quite new for which his time was not yet ripe, Pestalozzi knew himself. All the more tormenting, therefore, was his fear that for many people the soundness of his ideas might depend on the success or failure of this particular institution, and that in consequence a matter of importance to mankind might be spoilt through his personal shortcomings. For he was convinced that the scheme was of great public concern and that attention should be drawn to it. Despite his explicit opposition to State-controlled charity organizations he yet wanted the protection and the approval of the government. But the Bernese aristocrats still thought in Physiocratic terms and despised manufacture. The main reason for their allowing Pestalozzi's experiment to fail was simply the fact that it was not a charitable institution; his advanced ideas about the natural equality and fraternity of men were quite alien to them.

The poorer Pestalozzi grew and the more remote the possibility of carrying out his ideas became, the more firmly did he believe in the necessity for putting them into effect and in his own duty to do it. He had found his true vocation: 'to bring light to the people' in order to improve their way of life, and he was determined to persevere in this task 'until his last breath'. 'If I had to work years for this end on bread and water and to live in a thatched cottage, I should smile at the deprivation and be confident of succeeding and of not giving up even in the most wretched conditions.' If the Swiss cantons could not be won over to his ideas there would surely be somewhere in the world a humane king or minister desirous of being a father to his people. Pestalozzi was ready to leave Switzerland if there was a chance of realizing his plans elsewhere. 'My life is devoted to the education of the poor; this is what I seek and nothing else.' Twenty years were to elapse, however, before he was given the opportunity of putting his idea into practice.

The spiritual enrichment gained through this experience was as great as the despair about its failure. Pestalozzi had learned 'immeasurable truths'; the enormous stimulation given to thought and emotion kept his mind occupied for years and enlivened his solitude. Many problems still required clarification, but he had tested the truth of his idea and proved the power of his love.

The family in the Neuhof was now utterly destitute and often lacked the barest essentials. Pestalozzi later told the story of how, when other people were sitting down to a meal, he would wander about in the fields, eating a piece of dry bread and drinking water from the brook with it. He did not dare to go either to town or to church because he had no decent clothes. He became 'the laughing-stock of the people'; the mob called him 'Pestilence' or 'Scarecrow', jeering 'wherever he goes, the birds fly away'. With the loss of his money he had also forfeited public confidence in himself and in his true capacity. His Zurich friends avoided him; when they espied him at the top of one street they would go down another, for to have been obliged to speak to a man so far beyond help would only have embarrassed them and been of no use to him. Pestalozzi relates in his *Swansong* how Caspar Füssli the bookseller 'told me at that time to my face, my old friends took it for granted that I would end my days in an almshouse or even in a madhouse'. Indeed, Pestalozzi lived through a period of deep depression; with despairing heart and mind confused he roamed through fields and woods; even his wife had almost given him up; to himself his life seemed 'only nonsense and raving madness'.

Frau Pestalozzi, too, broke down physically and mentally under the burden of worry. She had heartily approved the aims of her husband and pluckily helped him in carrying them out. She had run the house, taught the girls spinning, and kept account of each child's earnings and purchases. But she could not keep up this orderliness for ever. As the years went on, the aristocratic lady no longer young found it increasingly difficult to endure 'spoilt young beggars' in her own home. Harassed by excessive demands, exhausted and disappointed, she fell ill, hovering for years on the brink of death; and when she at last recovered she had aged and greatly changed. She never regained her full strength, but she always bore her husband's restlessness with patient understanding. In all future ups and downs she showed unfailing loyalty and was ready to help financially whenever she could. It was her fortune, her inheritance, her jewellery which she gradually sank in Pestalozzi's enterprises as in a bottomless pit. She sacrificed everything for him. In moving words of devotion and gratitude Pestalozzi praised in her 'the purest and noblest heart' he had ever known. Throughout his life he was conscious of a deep sense of guilt, of having destroyed her hopes and her peace. Dedication to a higher purpose meant for both the sacrifice of personal happiness.

The greatest source of sorrow in the life of the Pestalozzis lay in the unfortunate development of their only son on whom they had set high hopes. Jean Jacques (born 13th August 1770), as he was significantly called, was an affectionate, good-natured child but physically and mentally weak, easily upset, without energy and strength. His upbringing was casual. During his first years Pestalozzi taught him intensively, keeping a *Diary on the Education of his three-year-old Son* which is the first record of his educational principles. But when the house was full of poor children he had no time to spare for his own son. He did not think this wrong; on the contrary, he felt it fitted in with his ideas of 'natural' education. He was undisturbed that Jacqueli, like Emile, could neither read nor write at the age of twelve. In compensation, he believed the emotional powers were developed all the better. It was in all probability, however, not the Rousseauesque upbringing but the lack of innate capacities that retarded the boy's development. His mother was more practical, and after bitter experiences she returned to the more conventional methods of education. She secretly taught her son reading and writing, and, above all, religion; but she, too, in the turmoil of the poor-school, did not have the time nor did she, reserved as she was, find it easy to create the intimate home atmosphere that would have given her child 'inner peace'.

Since Jacques did not seem to get on at home, Pestalozzi's friend Battier of Basle took him into his own family, sent him to a school in Mulhouse and later apprenticed him to his business. But there, too, he made no progress; he was lacking in application and attention; he gave no satisfaction. The biggest blow fell when the news came from Basle that the boy had been stricken with 'falling sickness'. It required an almost superhuman courage to retain faith in God's mercy when the unhappy father brought the broken youth back into his mother's arms.

Pestalozzi accused himself violently of having failed in his duty towards his son, of having entrusted him, in his blind belief in men, to the care of strangers who had let him go to ruin. The mother tormented herself with fruitless questionings whether perhaps her own 'pet failing' or her husband's 'main weakness' had been passed on to the son, or whether Pestalozzi's 'natural' methods of education had done him harm. But even with more normal conditions the outcome would doubtless have been the same. For Jacques' constitution was weak; his illness was probably an unfortunate inheritance from his father. Pestalozzi's excitability, on some occasions amounting to ecstasy, on others to frenzy, but always a mark of his genius, had in his son taken the pathological form of epilepsy.

At the time when there was illness and misery in the Neuhof and when for want of labour even the most essential crops could not be sown, there came help one day (about 1780) in the shape of a young servant Lisabeth Näf (1762–1836). She had heard of Pestalozzi's philanthropic enterprise and was anxious to offer her services to this good man. What she did for Pestalozzi earned her such a high reputation that even during her lifetime a legend grew up around her. It was said that she brought the neglected farm back into order, looked after the family, and generally behaved in such a sensible way that Pestalozzi came to rely on her advice in practical matters; also that her common sense impressed him so much that he took her as the model for the main character in his novel. Be that as it may, it is a fact that her untiring activity and faithful devotion soon made her the indispensable friend of the family, which she remained during her long and useful life. She was always called upon to help where help was needed; her great strength tempered by kindliness and her shrewd judgment of people and their affairs made Pestalozzi 'lay the burden of his life on the shoulders of this person'. For he considered her 'a very clever woman, though quite uneducated'. In later years he said to a young assistant: 'I should turn in my grave and be unable to rest in heaven if I were not sure that after my death Lisabeth was to be honoured more than myself, for without her I would have been dead long ago, and you, too, would not be what you are.'

Pestalozzi was unusually fortunate in receiving the help and devotion of good women. Is this merely to be ascribed to happy chance, or was it rather his own gift of drawing the best out of people that raised these women above the ordinary level? Another good friend, but this time one of noble extraction, was his neighbour the Countess of Hallwil (1758–1836). The unusual and sad experiences which had been her lot—a daring elopement as a very young girl, the sudden death of her husband, probably through poisoning by her stepmother, after only a few years of marriage, great responsibility for the family estate and, later, disappointment in her sons—had given this young dowager wisdom beyond her years. Though considerably younger than Pestalozzi and his wife she became their solace and support in many a difficult situation. In their frequent discussions of social problems she taught Pestalozzi something of the psychology of the upper classes. Even more important to him was her encouragement at the time of the collapse of his poor-school. When he could no longer bear to live in the Neuhof's empty rooms, he found peace in the ancient castle and relief in the company of a true friend. For she, as he later testified, was 'the only one' who did not lose faith in him, thereby restoring his faith in himself. The Countess of Hallwil was also Frau Pestalozzi's greatest friend. During the years to come when Pestalozzi lived away from the Neuhof, Anna stayed with her for many months on end. Pestalozzi found it impossible to express fully the gratitude he felt for the kindness and friendship she bestowed on his wife, which, he said, compensated her for much that she had lost through him and comforted her where he had made her sad.

During the long years of enforced retirement in the Neuhof Pestalozzi made the acquaintance of some interesting people in the neighbourhood. He exchanged views on psychology, philosophy, and politics with the young theologians who were tutors in county families; he discussed the education of the poor and questions of criminal law with the governors of the district. *Herr Pestalozzi's Letters to N.E.T. on the Education of Poor Country Children* is his reply to N. E. v. Tscharner's *Letters on Institutions for the Poor in the Country*; and *Arner's Report* is the outcome of suggestions received from D. v. Fellenberg. In associating with these high officials Pestalozzi was able to observe the practice of wise administrators, and he based the 'father of his people' in his popular novel on their example.

Pestalozzi became a member of the 'Helvetic Society' and went to meetings in Schinznach nearby. There he met the leading politicians of his country. On Tscharner's recommendation Pestalozzi's *Letters* were published in a well-known periodical, *The Ephemerides of Mankind*. This made him known to other writers and readers and was the beginning of his literary career.

The editor of the *Ephemerides*, the Basle town clerk Isaac Iselin (1728–82), whose *History of Mankind* Herder calls 'the preliminary' to his own *Ideas on the Philosophy of the History of Mankind*, soon became Pestalozzi's kind friend and active supporter. Up to his early death he showed a keen interest in Pestalozzi's ideas and sympathetic understanding of his disappointments. The encouragement he gave Pestalozzi to take up writing as a career was to have important consequences. He had recognized at once Pestalozzi's originality and advised him, also for financial reasons, to put to literary use his experience with the poor.

But Pestalozzi believed himself far too uneducated to be able to write. He confessed to having 'toyed with his pen' in his youth and to having published a few articles as propaganda for his institution, but claimed not to have read a book for thirteen years. 'I am happy when I hold a child in my arms, . . . but all I could say in writing would inevitably be far from perfect.' He did not wish to disgrace the *Ephemerides*. And yet he had to find bread and to clutch at every straw; so he became a writer from sheer necessity. He began to take part in literary competitions and with his usual enthusiasm soon became interested in this new craft. Henceforth he used it as a means of propagating his social and political ideas, since he was unable to carry them out in a more practical way.

The beginning was encouraging. To a prize-question from Basle: *Is it advisable to limit the luxury consumption of citizens of a small republic whose prosperity depends on trade?* Pestalozzi's answer was that within reason a certain amount of luxury is useful for an industrial State since it gives the people work and thus bread, and also promotes trade. Out of twenty-eight entries his essay was one of two sharing the first prize.

Another question for competition came from Mannheim:

What are the best practical means of putting an end to infanticide?
Pestalozzi took such an interest in the question that he went far
beyond the scope of the original problem and later published
his essay independently. Meanwhile he was making a thorough
study of the relations between the essential needs of man and the
morals of the people, between national customs and civil law,
and he acquired such valuable knowledge that he felt called
upon to spread 'truth and light' on these subjects.

Pestalozzi's writings in these years were still an odd mixture
of different forms and aims, and the work at his desk was being
done amid difficulties from within and obstacles from without.
He had as yet to find his literary style. He tried his hand at a
Moral Weekly; he wrote philosophical treatises; he even thought
of the theatre. He composed hymns to nature in the style of
A. v. Haller and wrote moral tales after the model of Mar-
montel. Caspar Füssli, the only one of his old friends remaining
loyal to him during the years of his humiliation, encouraged
him to continue with fiction, for a humorous sketch on *The
Transformation of the crooked, dirty, and unkempt City Watchmen into
straight, tidy, and polished ones* had revealed Pestalozzi's gift for
presenting realistic scenes. Now Pestalozzi was loath to write
for entertainment, but he overcame his reluctance; 'as I would
have dressed wigs at that time if that had enabled me to console
and support my wife and child'. He wrote, altered, rejected.
Meanwhile he was so poor that he could not even buy paper.
So he used up half-empty account-books, turning them upside
down and beginning at the end pages; and when he reached
Anna's entries he went on writing between the lines.

All this time Iselin gave his valuable advice and literary help.
He did not spare his criticism and even took the trouble of
purging Pestalozzi's manuscripts of faulty expressions and Swiss
idioms. For he found Pestalozzi's style sometimes obscure and
his descriptions often coarse. But Pestalozzi defended his bold-
ness in representing 'nature in the raw' with the plea that the
author's intention clearly vindicated his moral attitude. Besides, 'vice is before our eyes in real life, too'. Realistic writing,
he said, was the only possible choice for him. Indeed, his
style is a reflection of his character: his ideas rush from him,
whirl in ever-enlarging circles round a central point, impres-
sing first through their power of feeling before revealing the

full depth of their meaning. His writing is more emotional than intellectual.

He tried to work out a style that would make the deepest impression on the people. For in spite of his desperate poverty he would not submit to the taste of the time; he would not write for the educated reader. He intended to create a kind of 'people's catechism', 'using the limited concepts of the lowest classes, their language, and their mode of thought'. But its form should not be question and answer, the methods of school and church, but 'scenes, happenings, situations that warm the hearts of the peasants, lift up the spirit of the poor, and shed light for the lower classes on their most essential needs'. This demanded care and simplicity, knowledge of the people and human sympathy. Pestalozzi possessed these qualities. He had gained his understanding of the poor not by studying their psychology from the outside but by actually living with the simple people of his neighbourhood. The result of his insight was *Leonard and Gertrude. A Book for the People*.

Concurrently with this attempt to achieve great plainness of style Pestalozzi wrote down, mainly to clarify his own thought, similar ideas in quite a different style. This is his other early work, as fundamental as the novel for all his future thinking, 'a preface to all I am going to write', *The Evening Hour of a Hermit* (1780).

II 'THE EVENING HOUR'

From the time of the shattering experience of the poor-school Pestalozzi's mind had been occupied with the question 'What is man?' An educator intending to train children, a social reformer anxious to enlighten the people, a law-giver desiring to improve the State must be familiar with fundamental questions like this, even though he may not yet be able to give complete answers. Pestalozzi's theoretical inquiries are closely connected with his practical purpose; they are the philosophical justification of his political ends. 'You are my deepest need, and it is the desire of my heart to search for you, O aim and destiny of man.' This is the central problem of German philosophical thought in its classical period, the education of man to 'full humanity', the cultivation of the powers of every human being.

NEUHOF

Engraving by J. Aschmann after J. H. Schulthess, 1780

BURGDORF

Engraving by C. Wyss, about 1760

Only in so far as true humanity may be buried deep in the poor, may they need special help in order to bring it to light; though it may equally well be that 'the lowly and simple man' is sometimes closer to 'essential nature' than 'the erring rich'. Pestalozzi's theoretical question 'What is man?' soon turns into the practical one 'What does he need?' And he is as anxious to proclaim what he has discovered to be 'the truth' for furthering the education of the human race as to warn mankind of the evils which would befall them if they continued on 'the downward path to destruction'.

If *Leonard and Gertrude* (in its first two parts) is a realistic description of man as he is, the *Evening Hour* points to the goal of man as he could and should be. Its tone, therefore, is optimistic. Form and language are appropriate to the content; no balanced construction, no close-knit system, but exclamations, questions, aphorisms; it is in the rhapsodic style of the Storm and Stress period.

'On which path shall I find you, O truth, that can raise me to perfection?' Not through 'the thousandfold entanglements of doctrines and opinions' (Rationalism), nor through 'the diffuse mass of extensive knowledge' (Comenius), nor through 'the inert wastes of dark ignorance'; not, that is, on the path of reason but on that of feeling, along the 'course of nature'. Pestalozzi's conception of 'nature' is not unequivocal; it carries all the meanings which the eighteenth century has given to the word. It signifies the outer world as much as human nature, it is man's higher as well as his lower tendencies ('divine' and 'animal' nature); it is outside and inside, good and bad; there is sympathy between macrocosm and microcosm. On 'nature's' path, then, the seeker for truth has to go in order to know man and his world; and if he wishes to help mankind he must apply knowledge so acquired.

And to what goal does this path lead? What is the destiny of man? Pestalozzi's answer, 'the perfection of my nature', couched as it is in the Leibnizian terminology of the Carolinum, implies the successful nurturing of the powers given to man and happiness as his end. Yet Pestalozzi is not the exponent of a superficial eudaemonism. His ideal can be compared rather with that of the German classical writers when he says: 'The cultivation of the powers inherent in human nature towards

33

pure wisdom is the ultimate aim of education'; but he goes beyond them with his characteristic addition 'including that of the lowest man'. The key sentence of the *Evening Hour* explains what constitutes pure wisdom and indicates the nature of the truth which the hermit of the Neuhof believed he had discovered. It runs, 'Man must be brought to find inner peace.'

'The satisfaction of our nature's fundamental needs is the aim and the destiny of men.' Practical wisdom, not theoretical knowledge is what every man needs, whatever his station or calling. For although individual conditions vary, all men have the same basic desires and emotions; 'on the throne as in the cottage' love, gratitude, and obedience are the same. The 'truth', then, which Pestalozzi sets forth is 'The satisfaction of natural wants creates inner peace.' His interpretation exhibits his habitual integration of the physical with the psychical. The feeling of security in a well-ordered natural environment is, he says, the safest foundation and support of man's existence. Undisturbed rest in 'the wise order of nature' is 'source' as well as 'end' of the education of man; deviation from it is torment, failure, sin. What is this 'wise order' of nature?

Pestalozzi sees the natural relations of men as arranged in ever-widening circles. 'The circle of experience granted to every man in his particular situation is narrow; it begins close around him, first around himself and his nearest relations, then it extends from there; but in its extension it must always be related to the centre of strength and truth.' Man himself is 'the first object of creative nature', but he does not exist for himself alone; nature creates him 'also for external relations and through them'. 'The family relations of mankind are the first and most important natural relations.' A father's care brings 'order' into a house; the paternal home provides the foundation of a favourable development. (The important rôle of the mother will be emphasized in *Leonard and Gertrude*.) A healthy family life in its daily give and take develops unconsciously the child's capacities for love, confidence, gratitude, even before the notions of obligation and duty are understood. 'A son eating his father's bread and keeping warm at his hearth finds the blessing of his existence in fulfilling the duties of a child.' Out of the feelings of trust in and love for the members of the family grow the other moral qualities in relation to all men, and finally to God. Individual ethics widen to embrace eventually national morals. 'The power cultivated in a nearer relationship is always the source of man's wisdom and strength in more distant relationships.'

From the small circle of personal relationships man moves into the wider one of his occupation. Though it is necessary that each man be prepared for his individual calling, Pestalozzi emphasizes that the true significance of his occupation does not lie in itself but in its contribution to the perfection of the whole man and to his attainment of inner peace. Education for a particular occupation 'must always be subordinate to the universal aim of a general education'. This applies to all classes; for though there are vast differences between the needy and the rich, it is true in either case that if a man's essentially human qualities have not been cultivated, he lacks the foundation for his particular vocation, however great his outward success. 'Whoever deviates from this order of nature and gives undue importance to the education for a man's condition, occupation, position, or rank, leads mankind away from the enjoyment of natural blessings and into troubled waters.' When the rich flock on to 'glittering stages' in order to 'titillate their ambitions', we get the 'artificial splendour that satisfies times like ours'. The widespread loss of inner strength in members of the upper classes is then followed by the lowering of morale in the common people.

The largest outer circle surrounding man is the State. Here it is interesting to observe that Pestalozzi the Swiss is thinking in terms of a monarchic constitution. This may be an implied criticism of the government of his home town, or a sign of his personal disappointment at not having been understood by his own country. At the same time it reveals his impression of foreign constitutions and his hopes of finding the ideal conditions for the education of men in a patriarchal form of government. For a prince, he says, is in the first place a man, a child of his father. But as a ruling prince he is also the father of his nation, and this father-people relationship is the natural extension of an original close relationship. Trusting in the paternal spirit of their sovereign, the people expect from him 'the fulfilment of his duty, the bringing of his children to the blessings of full humanity'. For 'the higher' is father of 'the lower', so that he may bring them nearer to the fulfilment of their destinies. Princes who consider themselves children of God and the people their brethren are 'disposed towards performing the duties of their position'. In such a patriarchal State the obedience of the people, too, is a religious matter; it is likewise founded on their belief in God as the common father.

Also priests and judges are regarded as fathers and educators of the people; and thus ought to be the princes of the mind. Here follows the famous passage in which Pestalozzi reproaches Goethe 'that his course is not set according to nature'. 'O Goethe to you in lofty heights I look up from my lowly state, trembling and sighing. Your power resembles the oppression of great princes who sacrifice the well-being of millions of people for the splendour of the State.' Goethe is pictured as a sort of Louis XIV of the intellect because he does not use his high position for the purpose of educating the people. For, says Pestalozzi, 'poets are teachers'; 'they have the power to influence and to form'. And there is a faint suggestion that he believes himself to be a priest of God, a father of mankind, and that to win the confidence of the people is the ardent hope of his life.

The circles in which man moves also proceed inwards. 'The essential powers of mankind are not the gifts of art and chance; they lie fundamentally in men themselves.' It is his 'inner voice' (*sentiment intérieur*) that leads man straight to virtue and truth; a well-ordered existence in which this voice is obeyed is the necessary condition for the achievement of 'inner peace'. Peace is not complacency but security. The education of the individual as well as of mankind must, therefore, give this security and prevent deviation from this order. 'The just movement of man within his circle is the true measure of his virtue, and the true wisdom of government consists in the education of the nation for this just movement of every man in his circle.' If man departs from his natural position, the powers within him 'torment him with intense agony'; he is confused and lost, lonely and not 'well ordered'. His life is not blessed with 'inner peace'.

The centre of all these circles is God, 'God in my innermost being'. 'Man's closest relationship is with God.' Man finds peace and strength and wisdom in the belief that God is his father and he is God's child. The loss of his belief in this father-child relationship, in this divine ordering, entails the loss of his belief

36

in himself, disregard of 'our inner witness concerning right and wrong', and 'confusion of our fundamental principles'; it is, in short, 'sin'. Sin is the source as well as the consequence of unbelief. Thus the circles of our existence depend and act upon each other and are at once cause and effect of our human development. The bond that connects them all is love.

In a letter to Iselin (9th June 1779), 'the most important' that he had ever written to anyone, Pestalozzi shows how 'the general truths of the *Evening Hour* apply to political freedom and to the most precious part of the teachings of Jesus'. Here he emphasizes even more strongly than in the essay itself that personal virtue and social justice are based on love. It is the beginning and the end of all human relationships. Paternal and filial spirit in family and State, the feeling of being the child of God and the brother of all men, these are the foundations of political as well as of moral freedom. Therefore 'religion is education for the love of men', but the love of men is also the first stage of religion. 'The Man of God' who combined to perfection the love of God and the love of men, 'who by his suffering and his death restored to mankind the firm belief in being the children of God, he is the Saviour of the world, he is mediator between God and fallen mankind. . . . There you see the point of view, dear Iselin, from which I believe Jesus' teaching to be a necessity for mankind.'

Never before had Pestalozzi stated his belief so positively. He was to experience grave religious crises which almost shattered his faith in God and in men; but his original trust in the fatherhood of God and in the love of Christ was to withstand all ordeals. The belief of the young Pestalozzi, if still somewhat emotional, is fundamentally the same as that which the old man is to express in his *Swansong*, where it is supported by his philosophy and confirmed by experience. The *Evening Hour* is Pestalozzi's first but fundamental survey of man's destiny.

III 'LEONARD AND GERTRUDE' I/II

An unshaken belief in the original goodness of human nature pervades also the first parts of *Leonard and Gertrude* in spite of the scoundrels whom it portrays. Not 'nature', it proclaims, but circumstances are responsible when a man, and through him his whole set, goes down the hill. In order to prevent moral deterioration it is necessary to understand the circumstances which condition the evil and, if possible, to improve them. Pestalozzi always considers both, man and his environment, and the fact of their interaction. In a predominantly corrupt society, he says, man's inner nature is attacked by evil from outside; but if the good within him is strong enough it has the power to improve and enlighten ever-widening circles. This view explains the strong contrasts in *Leonard and Gertrude*; it is also the reason for Pestalozzi's suggestion that man's improvement must come from two sources—education, to strengthen the inner powers, and legislation, to improve conditions.

Pestalozzi's intention was, as already indicated, 'to make known to ordinary people some important truths in a way best suited to impress their hearts and their minds'. The purpose of *Leonard and Gertrude* was, therefore, not popular entertainment but the depiction of an ideal community through a graphic account of rotten conditions and a clear indication of means for their improvement. The further the book went, however, the more theoretical it became and the less Pestalozzi spoke to the poor. The small 'people's catechism' grew into a work of four volumes whose final chapters developed into a kind of memorandum for the Emperor elect of the Holy Roman Empire. Pestalozzi did not realize at the time that *Leonard and Gertrude* thus became the literary representation of the ideal educational enterprise which he had failed to establish in the Neuhof. For the story simply flowed from his pen, he 'did not know how'. Yet in spite of its lack of design *Leonard and Gertrude* is a single whole, and the interpreter must consider all four parts in order to understand Pestalozzi's unconscious intention. But only parts I and II can be called a novel, and only the first is 'a book for the people'.

Pestalozzi's method of approaching any task, even that of novel writing, was 'to copy nature'; so he tried to show in the first parts of his book 'what the people themselves feel, think, believe, say, and attempt'. Like Luther before him he observed the mother in the house and the man at the market in order to know what they said. He even went to the village inn to see at first hand what went on there. It is from these observations that he describes rural conditions, customs, and manners: the common grazing rights and the quarrels arising therefrom, the village tribunal with its public pillorying of the culprit, the school in the hands of a cobbler, the conditions of work and the social customs, the belief in the devil and other superstitions. In simple language he presents the daily round of a community in its alternation of work and rest, of sorrow and joy, as it really was at that time in that part of the world. Thus *Leonard and Gertrude I/II* became the first German novel based on village life.

Compared with the vivid description of rural conditions, the plot is of minor importance. It starts from the conflict arising between the bad old custom that inn-keeper and bailiff are one and the same person, and the new economic development of cotton spinning that has brought to the village money with which the peasants do not know how to deal. The man who as dishonest publican serves adulterated wine and makes a double reckoning against his customers, enjoys as magistrate unlimited power over his debtors and uses it for covering up his frauds and theirs. A network of lies and deceit, of bribery and blackmail surrounds the whole village; even its better elements are helpless to avoid entanglement. At this point, on the verge of despair, a simple young woman with great common sense goes to the lord of the manor to ask for help. Her husband, the village mason, who is engaged on the repair of the churchyard wall, cannot resist the bailiff's bad influence, for 'the church is so near the inn'. Gertrude's talk with the squire marks the beginning of a change. With the help of the pastor the young lord makes a thorough investigation into the state of the village, uncovers corruption and resolves on radical reforms. He finds the model for his improvements in the cottage home of the mason's wife.

Part I of *Leonard and Gertrude* describes the misery which rotten conditions and unscrupulous officials bring to a community; part II concerns the punishment of the villains and the causes of their moral degradation. The reforms proper are dealt with in parts III and IV; a better education of the children and a new attitude in the homes are shown to be the indispensable conditions for a good administration in the village and, beyond it, in the country. An ideal community is portrayed in the village of Bonnal. Good men and healthy conditions are indicated as the foundations of law and order and of peace and happiness. The implication is that given good will, it should be possible to realize the pattern anywhere in the world.

The actors in this story are the villagers seen in their various types. For the benefit of the simple reader extreme cases are chosen, and play and counter-play take place in the opposite camps of the good who are generally poor, and the bad who are mostly wealthy. The characters embody the idea of the book, the struggle of light against darkness; the bailiff and Gertrude represent the opposite poles of utterly depraved and ideal humanity. Around him flock the gang of morally debased but socially important villagers; she becomes the centre of a small but growing circle of enthusiastic reformers who gain increasing influence and are victorious in the end. Leonard does not play a significant part in the plot.

Bailiff Hummel is the gross example of a corrupt official who finds opportunity for personal lust and material gain in the wielding of power. He uses all available means to retain his position—false testimony, nocturnal raids, entertaining and bribing his accomplices. He is a hardened sinner; his philosophy is that everybody oppresses everybody else. He has gone too far to be reformed, but public exposure of his misdeeds destroys his influence. The important question is, what has made it possible for him to be so bad?

It is not Pestalozzi's opinion that wickedness is inevitable or that it is incurable; his point is that it should never be allowed to grow. At this time he still finds the causes of evil outside the human heart; neglect in childhood has brought misfortune upon the bailiff rather than guilt; from his life story 'it was as clear as daylight that he had to become what he has become'. And indolence on the part of authority gave him scope for his machinations; had there been 'order' in the manor, the village would not have deteriorated to such an extent, for the lower classes are dependent on the higher. How important to the community, therefore, are good government and sound education!

The cautionary effect of the bailiff's wickedness is increased by the tragi-comic description of his village gang. The sketching of the peasant types of Bonnal in all the shades of human weakness, the building up of grotesque scenes in their obstinate fight against the better elements, the rendering of disputes in the local dialect are all masterly. The representation of the good poor, on the other hand, is conventional and over-sentimental. Tears flow in plenty. The power of endurance attributed to them is often too great to be convincing. But the ideal character in the book, the contrast to all wrong and all evil, is Gertrude, 'the great mother'; she takes us 'out of the house of horror' into 'the cottage of humanity'.

'Thus God's sun runs its course from morning till evening. Your eyes do not see its steps and your ears do not hear its motion, yet at its setting you know that it will rise again, continuing to warm the earth until her fruits are ripe.' The reliability and steadfastness of this woman, her warm-heartedness and her kindness are such a matter of course that the author confesses to a lack of words for her praise. For what is it really that distinguishes Gertrude? 'In everything she does you would think that any other woman could do it just the same; if you watched her all day long you would not notice anything special.' Her importance does not lie in what she does but in what she is, and this is reflected in every one of her activities. 'You can taste in the soup she cooks and see in the sock she knits that husband and children have constantly been in her mind.' Pestalozzi believes it typical of woman to serve life and to live from a single centre. While man is occupied with the things of 'the farthest circles', her interests are directed towards 'the nearest circles', towards individuals and their needs. This concentration is due to her 'naturalness'. Pestalozzi sees a close connection between the function of woman in the life of the family and the nation, and the creative power of nature. Woman's nature, however, is also culture, it is of the greatest civilizing influence. With this observation Pestalozzi places Gertrude amongst the ideal women characters whom the German classical writers have created. Where Goethe uses the phrases 'beautiful soul' and 'the eternal feminine' to describe the essential qualities through which such women exercise their ennobling influence upon all around them, Pestalozzi adopts the expressions 'unity of powers', 'order', and 'inner peace'. Like them, Gertrude is a 'harmonious' being; but the difference is that Pestalozzi's ideal woman does not move in royal circles or stay in impressive mansions but lives and works in a poor village. Thus Pestalozzi has brought ideal humanity down to earth, and Gertrude's qualities affect the well-being of her community and that of the State from her 'humble cottage'. Moreover, she is not presented as the sweetheart of some man nor, in the first place, as the wife of her husband but as the mother of her children. As such she is the centre of the family.

From *Leonard and Gertrude* until his death Pestalozzi incessantly emphasized the rôle of the mother in the family and her great importance in education. He ascribed a boundless capacity for love, a ceaseless devotion to duty to her 'nature'; her service, her care, her sacrifices to her woman's instinct. He marvelled at the wonderful way in which the sensual in her turns into the sensitive, the tribal into the individual, how woman becomes mother not only of her children but of all living things. In the *Evening Hour* he had laid great stress on the 'paternal spirit' and 'paternal influence'; what moved him to place the education of man into the hands of woman? His experiences in the Neuhof had shown him a woman's (his wife's) great power of endurance. His own failure had made him think less of masculine ability. (The character of poor Leonard is perhaps the literary projection of his feeling of guilt.) The impact of Lisabeth's help had evoked and in turn was enhanced by the memories of Babeli's kind deeds. But mainly his own power of self-sacrificing love comparable to a mother's devotion, whose practical application was being denied him— all these factors contributed to the creation of the ideal of a loving mother which was to show erring mankind the way to salvation.

If Gertrude's character and her activities set the example for a new order, more influential people are necessary for its establishment. These are the squire and the pastor, later also the lieutenant.

Pastor Ernest is a conscientious shepherd of his flock as Pestalozzi's grandfather had been; he puts his duties towards human beings before those towards the church. Instead of dogma he preaches love, instead of the catechism he teaches morals. He is strongly opposed to 'mere words'; he attempts the moral improvement of the bailiff; he counters 'the stupidity of superstition' with 'the lessons of truth'. In all this he expresses Pestalozzi's own moral convictions at that time. In his spiritual attitude as well as in many personal traits Pastor Ernest has autobiographical significance. He, like the lieutenant in the later parts of the book, is the mouthpiece of Pestalozzi's intentions. Both these characters are therefore of predominantly theoretical importance and from the literary point of view tend to be dull.

The characterization of the squire Arner, an idealization of the governor N. E. v. Tscharner, is more lively. The young lord sets to work with zeal, showing a personal interest in the well-being of his people and understanding for their individual circumstances. As a judge, his main office, he tries to be humane; in the social position into which he was born he feels himself to be the father of his dependants.

Pestalozzi had already taken this patriarchal view of government in the *Evening Hour*. Impressed probably by what was happening in Prussia, he found 'the tone of the government in monarchies more paternal, nobler, and wiser' than in the Swiss republics. For that reason he had his fictitious land ruled by a prince. He did not share the revolutionary ideas of the young generation of his time, but was rather conservative in upholding the pattern of 'the good old times' and the responsibility of the sovereign to create order from above. He also left intact the division of society into 'estates'. Matters of justice, he says, must remain in the hands of the privileged classes. It is neither the common man's duty nor to his advantage to share in the responsibilities of his superiors; 'not all men can be fathers of the country'. Pestalozzi never entirely abandoned this view, the political counterpart to his conception of the organic order of life; but at the time of the French Revolution he modified it in conformity with his idea of personal freedom.

The squire appoints an honest bailiff and closes the inn. He considers it his main task to do something radically new 'with the poor people we call criminals'. 'Man's first duty', he declares at a village meeting, 'is to relieve the poverty of his fellow-men, so that everyone may obtain the necessities of life without anxiety and distress; and this first duty of all men is especially the first duty of those whom God has set above others to be their fathers.' His first practical innovation in the village is the parcelling out of the common grazing land. The influential villagers try with all their might to prevent it, but the reform party succeeds in the end. 'The people now recognized him as their father and were loud in their thanks.'

The new education has its starting-point in Gertrude's living-room. Here 'order' prevails. Everything has its proper place, every task has its definite time; the whole day runs according to plan. Even the children are not idle for one moment; they know no play, they have no leisure, for 'work is essential for country-folk'. From infancy they have to contribute to the family's livelihood; they must be trained for early independence. In Bonnal this means becoming expert in cotton spinning and weaving, for home industry is their 'individual condition'. But although the poor remain poor (this is their 'estate') they can and must be good men and women as others must be in their station. 'Bend your children to that yoke to which they must later submit, almost before they can distinguish right from left, and they will thank you until their dying day if you have led them to the good and shaped them for the conditions of poverty, even before they know why.' The education of the people consists, therefore, in 'directing their attention to near objects that will be of value to them in their individual conditions'.

While the children do practical work they receive their first theoretical instruction from their mother at home; in the living-room work and lessons go on at the same time. As they spin and sew Gertrude teaches her children to do sums. This she considers particularly important, because 'counting is the foundation of order in the head'. (Pestalozzi was later to make this conviction the starting-point of his teaching method.) The children also learn hymns and prayers and sing songs; for the few intellectual activities which cannot be carried out while working because they require the use of hands, e.g. writing, there is time enough on Saturday and Sunday evenings.

Work and learning, however, or education for their future calling or station, should be subordinated to education for manhood and womanhood. The poor man, indeed each man in his station, has only a limited range of activity, yet wherever he is placed he ought to be a whole man. There must be a balanced cultivation of all his capacities; otherwise his development will be diverted from its natural course with the result that he will become open to temptation and be a potential criminal. Along with the training of hand and of head there must be the education of the heart; the heart, too, must be 'in order' if men are to be happy. Mental and moral order are interdependent; order in the heart brings 'inner peace', inner peace creates contentment, independence, and freedom. Reversely, he who does not keep his house and his heart in order, 'who needs more and wants more than he can safely and easily get, who lives from day to day waiting for some lucky chance cannot help becoming a rogue and a very unhappy man'.

The moral and religious education given by Gertrude is similar to that given by the village pastor. Both educate through the example of their actions rather than by teaching and preaching. The traditional rites of Christianity are carefully observed, yet religion in *Leonard and Gertrude* finds its expression not so much in worship as in humanitarianism; it does not consist in emotionalism but in the love of God and of men, a love made manifest in deeds. When the poor share their bread with the still poorer, when neighbours help each other in illness and in need, when a dying woman forgives those who have wronged her, they act in the spirit of Christ. In this way Pestalozzi stresses the necessity of proving one's worth in this world. 'Religion does not call man away from earthly responsibilities but gives him strength to carry out every human duty until his last moment. Man is not made for religion but religion is made for man; it is not a thing apart that diverts him from his worldly business; it teaches and strengthens him to make good use of the world. The way to heaven lies in the fulfilment of duties on earth.'

The general tendency apparent in the novel, then, is the preference given to practice over theory, to the family over the school, to near objects in the home over remoter ones in the world. 'The important thing in a good upbringing is that a child should be well prepared for his own circle; he must learn to know and to do the things that will bring him bread to still his hunger and peace to content his heart.' Common sense is more important than book learning. This is best taught by father and mother. No schoolmaster can be to a child what his

45

parents ought to be. 'And so it is God's will that all men learn their most important lessons in their homes.'

Thus, says Pestalozzi in his *Swansong*, the description of 'living-room education' in *Leonard and Gertrude* contains in a nutshell what twenty or thirty years later, systematized and psychologically elaborated, he was to propound as 'elementary education'. 'Gertrude, as she appears in the book, is a child of nature in whom nature presents to perfection the essential results of an elementary education devoid of every single artificial device, and this in the specific form in which alone they can appear in the lower classes.' In keeping with Pestalozzi's original intention this social-political aspect of *Leonard and Gertrude* provides its main interest today; not the emotional appeal of the book as a novel, as in his own time.

IV DIDACTIC AND MORAL WRITINGS

Part I of *Leonard and Gertrude* came out in 1781 and was an immediate success. Enthusiastic reviews in literary journals introduced it to a wide circle of readers; odd chapters were inserted in almanacs; pirated editions appeared. 'The people' admittedly did not read the book, but educated men now regarded the lower classes in a new light. Pestalozzi's acquaintances began to revise their judgments about this failure turned famous overnight when they observed that a stream of visitors came to the Neuhof from all directions, and that his neighbour the governor had him taken to his castle in a coach to celebrate the success. (Pestalozzi made the footman sit by him inside.) These tokens of appreciation had a calming effect on Pestalozzi's mind; he mixed more with people again. To his surprise the Berne Economic Society presented him with a testimonial and a large gold medal; but he was so poor that he had to sell it. For the expected improvement in his financial circumstances did not come; no prospect of practical educational work opened up for him. Greatly discouraged, he translated the inscription of the medal 'civi optimo' with the words 'To the useless citizen for his useless book'.

Worse for Pestalozzi than the disappointment over the financial outcome was the realization that the favourable reception given to his book was based on a total misunderstanding of his true intention. *Leonard and Gertrude* was taken only as a novel without regard to its 'essential purpose', the revelation of the moral degradation of the country-folk in its cultural context. He himself was advised to press on day and night with novel writing for which he obviously had a gift, in order to earn 'a better mouthful of bread' for himself and his family, and he was reproached for not doing so. This 'maimed applause' roused his indignation. Even in his greatest need he could not bring himself to look for material reward. 'I wanted more, I wanted to influence through my work the state of my country's culture and to lay the foundation, through the talent which I was now admitted to possess, for better conditions for the poor than those I saw existing around me.' But the book made 'no real impression'; not one of the reforms which it implicitly recommended was given effect either with Pestalozzi's help or without it. He was not even consulted about so much as the setting up of a school.

In order to correct this misunderstanding Pestalozzi undertook to explain the ideas presented in *Leonard and Gertrude* in 'pictures' and 'scenes' in a 'less disguised' way. He began to re-write the book, turning the novel into a didactic manual for the use of parents. His object was to give definite instructions as to how the 'living-room education' was to be carried out. This was published the next year (1782) under the title *Christopher and Elsa, My second Book for the People*. It consists of a number of 'Evening Hours' in which Christopher, a peasant, reads aloud to his family chapters from *Leonard and Gertrude* which gives them the chance of discussing its content and of exchanging their own observations and experiences of life. In the long winter nights they talk about the right or wrong actions of the fictitious characters, comparing them with problems arising in their own similar circumstances. This literary device of venting his social and political opinions in the form of dialogue is from now on to be used quite often by Pestalozzi in order to make them more realistic and to drive them home to 'the people'. The characters in *Christopher and Elsa*, however, are from a realistic point of view too good to be true; these peasant people are themselves so ideal that they have nothing to learn from *Leonard and Gertrude*.

Christopher and Elsa has never been *A book for the People* as it set out to be. Since it has no story—assuming, as it does, the reader's acquaintance with *Leonard and Gertrude*—it lacks the pictorial qualities, the warmth of feeling, and the grim humour of its predecessor. It is tedious and, as Pestalozzi himself admits, written in a dry, sententious style. It was not read either by ordinary or by cultivated people. Also the modern critic finds it difficult to retain his interest in it, a difficulty which, in fact, Pestalozzi experienced himself in writing it: 'I found working on the first book compared to working on the second as much less difficult as is smoking tobacco compared to carrying stones.'

The idea of bringing out a Moral Weekly, that favourite form of public enlightenment in the eighteenth century, gave Pestalozzi no peace. First he had thought of taking over Iselin's *Ephemerides*. When this came to nothing he published during the years 1782–3 a paper of his own called *A Swiss Journal*. With the narrative sketches for *Leonard and Gertrude* in hand and a number of sociological essays in progress he had material enough almost to furnish its contents entirely alone. But the journal made little headway. Iselin who lived to read its first numbers reviewed it in the *Ephemerides* in restrained terms, objecting to some 'coarse expressions'. His disapproval discouraged Pestalozzi; he dropped the paper and did not even in later years include it in his *Collected Works*. Thus the *Swiss Journal* has remained almost unknown until recent times.

Yet it contains interesting enough articles. Some dramatic scenes as for example *Inside France* and *Kunigunde* which contrast the misery of the common people with the arrogance of the nobility are drawn so vividly that they made Iselin think Pestalozzi possessed a gift for the theatre. Their naturalistic style and revolutionary mood are astonishingly like those of the Storm and Stress plays. Both deal with the various forms of human vice—frivolity, greed, lust, conceit—and with temptation and crime. As in *Leonard and Gertrude* Pestalozzi shows that man surrenders to evil once he has lost his hold on moral principles. Pestalozzi had a remarkable insight into the human heart. In order to deepen it still further he occasionally visited the lunatic asylum. His short *Scene from the Mad-House* is a horribly impressive piece of psychological observation.

The most remarkable articles in the *Swiss Journal* are the essays on questions of economics, legislation, and education, subjects which Pestalozzi brought into close relation to each other. Their background is, as is the novel's, the changed economic situation which brings greater enjoyments but also increased dangers to the people. The solution of these new problems is found in a better education of the children.

At that time the 'peasants'—country-folk politically dependent—still formed the largest part of the population. In his patriarchal manner of thinking, known from the *Evening Hour* and from *Leonard and Gertrude*, Pestalozzi describes 'servitude' as 'I won't say the destiny but I must say the fate of mankind'. If servitude brings with it protection and safety, it is a comfort, because where man is being cared for, he serves willingly. On the side of those in authority and power, the care and protection of the people is their 'natural' duty. 'To serve faithfully and to tend conscientiously is, therefore, the mutual natural destiny of serving and ruling mankind.'

But, Pestalozzi argues, the servant no longer lives in this ancient state of nature. The rise of industry has altered the form of his dependence as much as that of his work; he has been 'thrown into an unnatural, unreasonable servitude', and his psychological, social, and moral security have all been shattered. The peasant and the craftsman of the olden times had to use their intelligence and honesty to plan and to finish a piece of work as a whole; but the monotonous manipulation of single parts required of the industrial worker produce in him thoughtlessness and carelessness, if not worse. When, moreover, he works in a shop instead of in his home, the bonds of family life are cut, too. This state of affairs has dangerous consequences for the individual as well as for the community. In the whole of Europe the old order has been 'turned upside down'. What, then, is to be done?

Pestalozzi's opinion is that this new development should on no account be reversed; a higher standard of living has its advantages. 'But in proportion to his increased earnings a man needs more education than in his previous condition. . . . Therefore even when utter misery is brought on a place by manufacture, I never judge it right to put an end to this method of earning but suggest rather that the people be enabled to get

49

the full benefit of their higher wages by educating them.' 'If one wants to make man happy one must guide and form not so much the things around him but rather himself.'

It is the duty of the upper classes, he goes on, to fit the lower classes for industry, i.e. to educate them for the responsibilities of a higher standard of living. For this, two things are important: the formative power of work and the steadying influence of the family. Children must be brought up in their own sphere, in the manner of their forefathers, so that order and happiness prevail in their own households. 'To live and be happy in his station and to be useful in his circle is the destiny of man and the aim of child education.' Therefore attention to the 'individual condition' of every child is an important educational rule, and a 'natural' upbringing by his parents is preferable to all book learning and education in schools.

Domestic stability will be upset when children are deliberately enticed from the station into which they are born and 'tempted to reach for a bread plate that lies higher than that of their father'. Domestic disorder is promoted most dangerously in high-schools and 'academic dens' and is therefore most prevalent amongst 'scholars, theologians, and advocates, in short amongst all those whose education entailed a preponderance of artificial guidance'. Even the upper classes must recognize that a contented heart is more important than an educated mind, for scholars spoil their achievements and artists obscure their works if they are unfit for the demands of daily life and inexperienced in the natural order of things.

Arner's Report on Criminal Justice is a forerunner of Pestalozzi's memoranda for the Austrian princes; it deals with the treatment of criminals. Ought prisoners to be provided with food and drink, with lodging and clothing in such a way that their imprisonment is no ordeal at all, or should they be punished with rod and rack and thrown into dark pits? Arner looks at the question from all sides and comes to the conclusion 'that the old brutal manner is most dangerous—and unnecessary—for punished, punishers, and all mankind alike'. The kind of punishment meted out by the State is dependent on the spirit of its government; a well-ordered State can afford to show mercy to its offenders. The degree of punishment should fit the gravity of the crime: hardened offenders must be dealt with

severely, but occasional wrongdoers may be treated with forbearance. The individual situation of the convicted person and
his local conditions ought to be taken into consideration; and
above all, it should never be forgotten 'that prisoners are human
beings, endowed with the same capacities, emotions, prejudices,
habits, and attachments as everybody else'; therefore they must
be approached like other human beings.

The main concern of the legislator must be directed towards
the criminal's moral restoration and his civil rehabilitation after
his release. For this purpose the building and the management
of the prison must be arranged in a more humane manner; the
prisoner must get adequate air, be allowed to work, be permitted to rest, and be rewarded for good behaviour. Ways
must be found to reach his heart in order to stir him and so to
prepare the way for his reform. Pestalozzi is convinced 'that no
punishment or revenge can reform a man if they are not
accompanied by kindness and love'. His demands are surprisingly modern, yet they have not been generally carried out
even to this day.

III *The Sociologist*
(1783–1793)

I 'LEGISLATION AND INFANTICIDE'

AT the same time as Pestalozzi was writing the *Evening Hour*, *Leonard and Gertrude*, and the *Swiss Journal*, he was also occupied with *Legislation and Infanticide* (written 1780, published 1783) which, as may be remembered, was prompted by the Mannheim prize-question. This sociological essay is based on the thorough investigation of actual criminal cases for which Pestalozzi had records sent to him from Zurich and Basle. But it is by no means written in a cool or objective manner. On the contrary, the author is carried away by his sympathy for tragic cases and becomes highly emotional. The work is a passionate cry for a humane spirit in legislation.

In those years many authors were concerned with the problems of infanticide and illegitimacy. Ever since Beccaria's *Dei delitti e delle pene* (1764) and Voltaire's remarks on it complaints had not ceased to be made that capital punishment was too severe a penalty for infanticide. John Howard's *The State of the Prisons in England and Wales* (1777) had dealt with the question of the treatment of women prisoners, while Jonas Hanway and Captain Coram had done much to improve the fate of parish children and bastard babes. The German Storm and Stress writers, including Goethe and Schiller, had taken the plight of the forsaken girl for the subject of their plays or poems.

Pestalozzi, for whom it was not enough to point out the misery but who urgently desired to alleviate it, realized at once that there was no satisfactory answer to the isolated question. For that reason he had withdrawn from the competition. His researches during the following years extended over the whole field of criminal justice and care of the prisoner, and he examined the connections between circumstances and crime, crime and punishment, punishment and education, education and national tradition, national tradition and morals. He felt compassion for the offenders not only because they lacked the material necessities of life; his belief in the original goodness of man was shocked at the perversion it had suffered in them. Convinced that it could not be completely extinguished even in the basest of them, he felt it necessary to restore the criminal to true humanity both by softening the obduracy which lay in him and by changing the circumstances which had prevented him from being good. The responsibility for social reform was laid upon the legislator.

For those unmarried young men and women who pursue 'higher aims', Pestalozzi argues, chastity is a moral obligation and a sure way to 'virtue'. But the common people, such as they are, cannot be expected to control their physical desires. Nature implants carnal appetites in every human being, and where marriage is difficult and laws are severe, there happen those abominations with which we are concerned. The State cannot prevent the satisfying of sexual passion; it can only punish those who act antisocially, who are in fact frequently the weak and the less guilty. If through its laws it forces them to be childless, it does violence to human nature; from the point of view of the State every childless woman virtually represents a form of infanticide. Its penalties arise from wrong premises. In order to prevent offence the State must see to it that as few people as possible remain unmarried and childless, and it must take care that inhumanity is not added to unchastity.

Every mother is attached to her child with the bond of her loving care; it is unnatural and inhuman for her to kill her own flesh and blood. Why does she do it? It requires little to make a poor girl lose her head; if she is forsaken and confused, over-wrought with pain and fear, she does in a moment of despair what immediately afterwards she regrets but cannot undo. It is not wickedness but weakness, not murderous intention but self-defence which lie behind her action. She must therefore not be punished by death but be treated humanely. If the causes of her plight were removed, its consequences could be prevented.

Two questions arise from the motives of the unfortunate girl: she wants to get rid of her child and to hide her disgrace. Would it prevent infanticide if she were helped to achieve these aims, and would society thereby gain or lose? Indeed, the State ought to take over the child and be father to orphans and educator to illegitimate children. But there must not be 'palatial orphanages' built in towns where the children would be 'systematically ruined'; they ought rather to be boarded out in the country with peasants or craftsmen from whom they could best learn the things which would give them 'bread and peace' later on. For (and here a familiar idea is introduced) 'the poor must be educated for poverty'. 'Ordinary people' are most suitable for this task, 'women who are seen surrounded by laughing, high-spirited children, and men who do their business simply and quietly, go to church regularly, and live in peace with their neighbours'.

Pestalozzi does not care for foundling and lying-in hospitals which, he thinks, do more to encourage irresponsibility than help society; with a fraction of their costs better results could be achieved. He suggests the institution of marriage guidance in the form of 'conscience counsellors' who should advise and help individual people in a spirit of fatherly love. It is, he admits, difficult to find the right people for this office; it demands understanding and tact, but it would with kindness and forbearance achieve more than the State with threats and punishment. The conscience counsellor would try to persuade the girl to name the father of her child and the young man to accept his responsibility. His good offices would be honorary and confidential, but his experiences should be communicated to other conscience counsellors under the seal of secrecy. In this way, through these counsellors, the State could bring unmarried fathers and mothers to perform their duties, and the bond between mother and child would not be broken. The parents should be encouraged to feel the wish both to keep their child and to be able to provide for it, for the child will be to them a source of moral improvement if they can love it without shame, but a source of degradation if its existence poisons their lives.

After having stated his views in general, Pestalozzi makes a number of detailed suggestions for future legislation, derived from the specific causes of infanticide. In the first place, laws ought to have a deterrent effect on the male sex, for often it is the seducer's deception that drives the expectant mother to despair. Laws should be for the wronged party the source of protection and justice, not of shame and disgrace, otherwise a woman may kill her child for fear of punishment. Country girls who are servants in town must be looked after, not led into temptation; unfortunate victims returning home must be forgiven and helped, not turned out and left to their fate. Circumstances at the time of confinement must be made tolerable; no employer, inn-keeper, or magistrate should be allowed to send a pregnant woman away if they do not wish to be regarded and punished 'as deliberate instigators of infanticide' themselves.

Since infanticide is the consequence of the passions and mistakes of many people rather than of one girl, it follows that it cannot be remedied by punishing this single deed in a chain of events. It can only be dealt with through laws 'which must be directed towards the first simple sources of immorality in men', and this in a positive rather than in a restrictive way. For it is evident that detailed attempts at improvement have no effect; men must be reached in their fundamental attitudes. 'The true and general remedy for infanticide lies in the earnest use of all those ways and means through which in all people, high and low alike, real goodness of heart and sincere enjoyment of everything beautiful, noble, and fine, and a genuine abhorrence for everything evil and digraceful can be achieved.'

'I imagine a sovereign whose legislation in general would conform with the fundamental needs of human nature, and I inquire into the course which he would adopt for taking action against the horrors of infanticide.' This legislator would know that the satisfaction of needs brings peace and content into the human heart, and he would bring his people to love God and their neighbours. The 'course of nature' (i.e. the means he would choose) would be for him 'the securing, ennobling, and limiting of the domestic circumstances of his people'.

A wise sovereign, says Pestalozzi, begins his work with the first stages of human development: he checks the sauciness of children by encouraging their obedience to their parents; he makes young folk earn their bread by the sweat of their brows so that they mature slowly. He knows that frank sexual instruction is the best preparation for the duties of married life and the most effective deterrent to licentiousness. He steers the high spirits of young men and the growing pride of young women towards honour and modesty and sees to it that they have an assured livelihood and get married early. All this suggests that 'enlightenment of all its peoples is an absolute necessity for the world'. This enlightenment must be brought about in such a way that it improves the moral standards and increases the domestic happiness of the people in proportion with their advancing intellectual achievements. He therefore finds: 'Everything that, directly or indirectly, contributes to the securing, putting in order, and retaining in order of the domestic happiness of man prevents, directly or indirectly, infanticide.' As to the execution of the mother who has killed her child, Pestalozzi concludes 'that the death penalty and all public forms of punishment are means ill fitted to check this crime'.

'What, then, should be done? I have no answer for people who still ask where the whole argument leads, just as I know no remedy against this crime for States who neither promote good morals through earnest attention to national education nor prevent the evil by restriction of corrupting civil laws ... I set my hopes on finding a king who is a friend of mankind and the father of his people; I set my hopes on his servant, the brother of his people; I set my hopes on the humblest man who has some influence in a corner of Europe and who is aware that the spirit of legislation and the power of government must be based on religion and justice, on humility and humanity, on love and on mercy, on truth and on virtue.'

II LOOKING FOR PRACTICAL WORK

The appeal for a philanthropist on the throne was a very personal one. 'I hope my essay on infanticide will prove that I am suited for a government post.' Pestalozzi did not write on social politics 'as a professor'; he was anxious to find a king who was father to his people and to be his servant, their brother, in order to influence legislation. His longing to be used actively was 'almost insuperable' and increased from year to year. He wished to do greater things than he had done so far because he was certain that he was able to do them. He offered his services in several quarters, not for his own sake but for that of humanity.

The only draft bill for which Pestalozzi's advice was sought in his home town dealt with a reform of the Consistory judging matrimonial matters. Lavater who had initiated it proposed some improvement of details and the removal of abuses, whereas Pestalozzi, as in *Legislation and Infanticide*, went back to the moral foundations. He again and again stresses the necessity of applying positive measures, the revival of sound old customs in domestic and occupational practice, the encouragement of everything good and useful, and wise government. But his suggestions were not permitted to get beyond the paper stage. Zurich made no use of the advice of her discerning citizen. Pestalozzi on his part lost faith in the recuperative power of the city-states. 'It is a humiliating thought, but true: any advance in good leadership of the people must proceed from the cabinets of monarchs; it certainly won't come from us; we are finished.' Switzerland was becoming too small for him.

The search for a monarch and for an opportunity for practical work abroad filled almost the whole decade preceding the French Revolution; the less successful it was the more desperate Pestalozzi became. Even immediately after the collapse of his home for the poor he had started to look around in Europe and had first thought of Berlin. There Frederick II had brought 'national enlightenment' to his country, and the newly annexed Prusso-Polish provinces seemed to offer suitable territory for popular education. After that he considered Vienna. He intended to publish a weekly journal there or to get in touch with the theatre. The Countess of Hallwil, a native of Vienna, probably introduced him to influential people. Soon he became more ambitious and made more serious attempts to go to Austria. The Habsburg Emperor was obviously the monarch envisaged in his dreams. Joseph II had just decreed the liberation of the peasants and was anxious to improve legislation and national culture. He was the most enlightened and most progressive monarch in Europe. No doubt he would be only too pleased to bring to his court a man with such extensive knowledge about education of the people. Pestalozzi tried to reach the Emperor's throne in various ways: he presented his experiences and his aims in the form of memoranda, sending them to high State and Court officials in order to rouse their interest; and he became a member of the Order of the Illuminati.

The Order of the Illuminati was one of the many secret societies of the eighteenth century whose purpose was to promote the welfare of the needy classes outside official administration. Its members included high and exalted personages. Pestalozzi's attention had been drawn to the Order by his friends in Basle; he now started a correspondence with its German representative, the Heidelberg Consistorial Councillor J. F. Mieg, and he joined it partly because he sympathized with its humanitarian aims and partly because he hoped that his influential fellow-members would pave the way for the implementation of his plans. But he did not succeed along this road. It was suggested to him that his ideas were 'not new, not attractive, not detailed enough for Vienna and Joseph's throne', and he was advised to make himself acquainted with the works of J. von Sonnenfels in which all his views had already been more clearly expressed. Pestalozzi found this criticism irrelevant. 'I don't think the question is, has somebody already written on this subject more clearly and in greater detail, but are there people who really do what the writing recommends, and who are able to do it?' He was annoyed, and he relieved his feelings at the expense of his innocent rival by introducing an intriguing Court official into *Leonard and Gertrude* part IV under the name of 'Helidor'.

Meantime, at home, he was busy enrolling members for the Order and founding a branch association 'For the Establishment of Domestic and Moral Happiness'; but this society had only a short and insignificant life after its breaking away from the main Order. Secret activities and high-born connections were alien to the protestant citizens of Switzerland, and in any event the general upset caused soon afterwards by the French Revolution rendered impracticable such private charitable endeavours.

The first Viennese statesman whom Pestalozzi approached was Count Zinzendorf. A correspondence with him extended over many years (1783–90) and raised high hopes in Pestalozzi; his disappointment was the greater when they came to nothing. Karl von Zinzendorf, a nephew of the founder of the Pietist

Community in Herrnhut, was an authority on finance at the Court of Vienna and later became a minister of State. He was interested in the social side of politics and contributed to Iselin's *Ephemerides*. There he read Pestalozzi's first articles; the governor von Fellenberg introduced Pestalozzi to him personally; and from that time Pestalozzi sent him the later parts of *Leonard and Gertrude* and memoranda specially written for him in the hope that he would recommend him to the Emperor. In his accompanying letters Pestalozzi gave him a more than plain hint as to what he expected of him: it was not only his personal wish to find a wider sphere of action in order not to have lived in vain; it was also important for the State that enlightened sovereigns should have wise ministers, and wise ministers experienced assistants to act as intermediaries between government and people. He himself, he hinted, had gathered considerable experience of this nature over the last twelve years. He was indeed 'bold enough to go into details to the point of impoliteness'. His memoranda contain suggestions for the better use of existing orphanages and workhouses and for the setting up of new industrial schools. Pestalozzi treated the same ideas at the same time more fully in the continuations and the new versions of *Leonard and Gertrude*.

In his letters to Zinzendorf towards the end of the seventeen-eighties a new tone is discernible. Worn down by his failure to communicate his ideas, he begins to lose faith in the higher motives of monarchs and now bases his hopes on the self-interest of man. If the upper classes will not help to improve the conditions of the poor from a sense of justice or from paternal benevolence, they will perhaps do so from personal interest. (*Leonard and Gertrude* part IV is also written in this vein.) He is convinced that better conditions for the lower classes would benefit the higher sections of society, 'that education of the people in economic matters will pay'. If no government action can be expected within the near future he suggests that 'Arner's legislation' should be initiated privately by individuals experienced in leadership who would thus serve their own interests at the same time; and he believes that the lesser nobility are best suited for the task of improving economic conditions in their own neighbourhoods. Their wise 'private enterprise' would also have political consequences, for it would strengthen the bonds between superiors and subjects which had progressively weakened during the last decade. If, however, the poorer nobility were not willing 'thus to demean themselves and to bury themselves in the country', experienced commoners should be entrusted with the enterprise. 'A man who can enable the common people to earn a good living, needs little himself and demands nothing.' Pestalozzi was such a man; and he wanted with all his heart to throw in his mite for the common weal.

The Count read Pestalozzi's writings with interest but saw the difficulties of their practical realization. He drew Pestalozzi's attention to the fact that the conditions of the Austrian country-folk in the various parts of the Empire were entirely different from those of the Swiss peasants with which he was familiar. He advised him to stick to the Neuhof, pointing out the delights of a life in rural solitude. It is doubtful whether he was very convincing in his recommendations to the Emperor; he had no belief in the monarch's genuine interest, and his own influence was not so great as Pestalozzi imagined. Besides, Joseph II died very early (1790), and with his successor Zinzendorf's counsel prevailed still less.

Leopold II, Joseph's brother, had already been in touch with Pestalozzi before his accession; Pestalozzi considered this connection to be highly promising. Like other enlightened monarchs of his time Leopold, as Grand Duke of Tuscany, had reorganized the legislation of his country, and Pestalozzi was ready to go to Florence in order to advise and help him. Through the Count of Hohenwart, formerly tutor to the imperial princes, later Archbishop of Vienna, he sent *Leonard and Gertrude* to the sovereign, a gift which was graciously received. A correspondence began; Pestalozzi was granted permission to address his writings to the Duke himself. In these letters his attempts to obtain a government post are even more urgent than in those to Zinzendorf. He offers his services in order 'to show in their true light, through careful and moderate practical experiments, the truths of *Leonard and Gertrude* which will continue to be opposed as long as they remain stuck on paper'; and he sent memoranda *On Civil Education*. He appeared to have every prospect of success; the prince 'showed quite extraordinary interest'. At last practical work seemed within reach. Pestalozzi was just going to submit a definite plan for an institution according with his ideas, when the Grand Duke acceded to the throne and the connection was broken off. Henceforth the Emperor was perforce engaged in higher politics, and fate soon intervened more decisively still: Leopold II died after a reign of only two years (1792). He had doubtless never seriously considered appointing Pestalozzi. 'Even in his last days', Pestalozzi wrote resignedly, 'he talked of me as of a good Abbé St. Pierre' (referring to the author of *Projet de paix européenne* (1713) which was regarded as utopian).

III ECONOMICS AND SOCIETY

In the 'eighties, while trying to acquire some influence upon the actual practice of government, Pestalozzi also studied the theory concerning the fundamental principles of legislation, and fragments remaining from this period indicate that he intended to write a book on the whole question. This was to strike 'a middle note between graphic portrayal and dry philosophy'; indeed, these notes lie between *Leonard and Gertrude* and his later work *My Inquiries*, in style as well as in content.

Pestalozzi now bases his social philosophy on the idea of 'property'. He distinguishes between 'natural property' or the things 'which my powers can obtain for the satisfaction of the needs of my existence' and 'positive property' or those goods 'which in generally accepted opinion are in my hands by right'. Originally the natural property of all men was equal, but this equality has been destroyed in the social state through the introduction of positive property. It is therefore the duty of man to re-establish a condition of as just a distribution of property as possible.

This leads to questions of rights and of security. 'A man's rights comprise everything that he can do without violating the positive property of his fellow man.' But he can use his rights wisely or foolishly. He acts wisely if he contributes to 'the perfection of the world', foolishly if he diminishes his own and other people's natural property. The right of property grants independence and freedom. Pestalozzi also derives the emotions of honour and respect from the concept of property, for property gives security, and security peace, while morality presupposes 'inner peace', and so morality itself is based on property. 'Is there, then, no pure moral or civil virtue and no true religion?', Pestalozzi asks himself and answers: 'Man is capable of considerable refinement and ennoblement, but he is human and arrives at morality and religion only along a human road.' (This almost materialistic conception of religion will be discussed later in connection with *Leonard and Gertrude* part IV.) The domain of law is limited in accordance with the eighteenth-century liberal conception of the duties of the State. 'The law of society is not moral, it is only a curb applied by power against the excesses of the animal' (in man). Legislation (the ultimate object of all these reflections) is therefore not 'a teacher of morality' but 'a guardian of morals through the spirit of order and restraint' which it establishes in the people through the protection of their property. Its aim is 'wisdom in the use of positive property' or, in other words, 'satisfaction of our natural needs, security, and increase in our enjoyments'.

The virtue most necessary for an orderly relationship of men in society is the power of restraint. No communal life is possible without 'limiting' the individual for the sake of the general. This limitation consists in the demand that everybody should find satisfaction 'in his place', in his station, and in his calling. Therefore his capacities must be educated for his 'individual condition'. The tradition of his narrow circle has evolved specific social, domestic, and occupational customs which facilitate the moral efforts of the individual. If he observes these customs and fits well into his circle, he enjoys peace and happiness. Here Pestalozzi returns to his favourite theme: 'Man's happiness is domestic peace and domestic contentment, and these are based on the limitation of his demands within the circle secured to him by society. It rests on the bringing-up of his children in his own footsteps, so that they may be certain of enjoying a living in the same corner of the earth; this is why the customs which set limits to behaviour in home, family, and occupation contribute to his happiness.'

The clarification of the concepts of rights and morality is only the preparation for examining those of wrongs and criminality. 'Positive property is the cause of all civil offence. The state of nature is without virtue and without vice. These only arise in connection with positive property. . . . Wisdom in the laws concerning positive property is the foundation of all preventive remedies for civil offences.' The wisdom of government consists, as has been said before, in making possible the satisfaction of the natural needs of the people; crimes are committed when this is not obtainable and must be achieved by illegal means. Satisfaction in itself is only natural and therefore no crime. But a violation of social order cannot be tolerated. It is a sign of a lack of self-restraint, a rebellion of the natural impulses against the yoke of society. Civil crimes are essentially 'nothing but the immediate consequences of human weakness', not wickedness. (Cf. *Legislation and Infanticide*.) Therefore one must distinguish between the legal and the moral aspect of crime, between retribution and prevention, between punishment and education.

Weakness is, however, no excuse; the law-giver must strongly oppose, i.e. punish, 'our anti-social egoism, this basic cause of the perversion of our natural impulses, or rather of our human nature itself'. But the purpose of penal legislation is, let it be remembered, 'only the safeguarding of the outer order of the State; it has nothing to do with the inner morality of man', because (here Pestalozzi adopts a Hobbesian point of view) the State itself owes its existence only to a convention based on power and fear. The penalties of the State are not directed against the inner failings of the criminal; 'they do not rest on the foundations of morality and true humanity but on the need of safeguarding property'. A wise government, therefore, is not based on fear and uses its power sparingly. It directs its attention not to retribution, but to prevention. The supreme aim of legislation is 'the establishment of domestic well-being through the securing of work and of bread for everybody in the country'. 'Assuring a livelihood for everyone is the main preventive of all crime.' 'A people who have their daily bread and decent clothes are glad to be honest.'

The practical proposals for preventing crime and encouraging morality are laid down in Pestalozzi's *Memoranda on Civil Education*, written for the Austrian princes. Whether these memoranda actually reached the monarchs is uncertain. Education for good citizenship, it is explained, must proceed along two lines: it must educate the people morally, and it must train their practical abilities for their particular occupations to make them useful members of the community. The nobility and the clergy are given the task of carrying out these proposals by virtue of their great influence with the people. The sovereign, the summit of the national pyramid, must bring them, too, to a sense of their social duties. They in turn will find satisfaction in their collaboration with the lower sections of society, for the inner and the outer security of all classes are inextricably connected. The 'happiness of the people' can in these times of change be achieved only by imbuing them with 'the spirit of industry'. 'Industry' (implying both application to work and skill in performing a specialized manufacture) must first be developed in children. The way to accomplish this is set forth in Pestalozzi's *Memorandum on the Relation between Vocational Training and Schools for the People*. This is, however, only a short summary of the ideas which are explained in greater detail in the second version of *Leonard and Gertrude*.

All this time Pestalozzi had been actively connected with the Swiss cotton industry. From his arrival in the Neuhof as a newly married man he had supported the home industry of his district by supplying material and employing child labour, and in his poor-school the children had been spinning and weaving. Even after its collapse his connection with home industry was never completely severed; but in the middle of the 'eighties he took it up again in the Neuhof itself. Although no children were now living with him, he had boys and girls of the neighbouring villages working there, especially in cotton-printing. He himself acted as middle-man between the home workers and cotton masters and as agent for a big material-printing works in the neighbouring village of Wildegg.

In 1785 the French Government issued a decree prohibiting the import of foreign cotton goods in order to protect its own East India trade. The Swiss cotton industry was very hard hit. Pestalozzi, who had expert knowledge and was skilled in writing, was commissioned to draft a petition for the repeal of the order. He was also asked to answer the questionnaire of the Bernese Council of Commerce as to how best to meet the difficulties which confronted the Swiss economy as a result of this prohibition. In the spirit of Adam Smith Pestalozzi recommends 'unlimited freedom of trade' which would benefit France and Switzerland alike; he speaks of 'absolute equality of rights' of big and small, town and rural, home and foreign enterprises. He considers all monopoly undertakings or State interference impracticable; good private concerns are, in his opinion, best left to fend for themselves. A government can further the economy of the country by enforcing law and order and by upholding tradition and custom. Here he returns again to the moral side of the matter. He points out that the economic rise of England, Holland, and Switzerland at the time of the Reformation was based on the secure foundation of their morals, their education, and their domestic order; and he advises the Churchmen of his time to direct their attention more towards the education of the people than towards their own philosophical enlightenment.

Since no attention had been paid to the views Pestalozzi had presented in theoretical form in *Christopher and Elsa*, he tried to make them more understandable in a narrative continuation of *Leonard and Gertrude*. This was written for 'cultivated circles', and part IV which deals with legislation is meant as a memorandum for Count Zinzendorf. The novelistic form is only a thin cloak in which Pestalozzi clothes his ideas on education, economics, and social reform; Arner, the 'father squire', with the help of the parson and the new teacher Glüphi, and also with the advice of an entrepreneur nicknamed 'Cotton Meyer', introduces to his domain a new system of labour and a new legislation. A new education is to lay the foundation for sound moral development. The school, as there has to be one, is to be modelled on Gertrude's 'living-room', and the village administration on the running of her home. The intention is 'nothing less than to bring the whole village into a new order'. After various difficulties have been overcome this aim is achieved. Bonnal becomes a model State on a small scale. Its moral and economic progress are made known to the duke; he comes and sees for himself, is impressed, and intends to introduce the same kind of reforms throughout the country. The 'circles' of living-room, work school, village administration, State government, all related to one another, have grown from one and the same centre into ever larger communities.

Glüphi, an ex-lieutenant with a wooden leg, is now the most influential character in the village. He takes over the part played so far by the pastor, to be the embodiment of the educational aims and therefore the literary image of Pestalozzi himself. He has not any special training but is filled with an unconquerable idealism and a love and understanding for children. His knowledge of men and his experience of life are greater than those of the pastor, which means that during the years since the beginning of the novel Pestalozzi himself had become more realistic and also more pessimistic. 'Love', he remarks, 'is no good for educating men except after or along with fear, for they must learn to root out thorns and thistles which no man likes doing nor does of his own accord, but only when he must and when he has been taught to do it.' The lieutenant has observed in Gertrude's 'living-room' how children may be taught from an early age. With her help he introduces the same 'order' into the school-room. He makes the children work (spin) and learn at the same time, relating the activities of their heads to those of their hands. To his surprise he finds the poor children more dexterous than he has expected, because need has developed their abilities early. He uses their natural capacities and makes 'vocational training precede teaching through mere words'. But he also puts 'clear ideas' into their heads by teaching them arithmetic which, like Gertrude, he esteems very highly. With the developing of their physical and mental faculties he combines the training of their manners, for he teaches them cleanliness, punctuality, and politeness. Everything in school has to go like clockwork. Thereby he wishes 'to lay in them the foundations of that equanimity and calmness which man can possess in all circumstances, if the difficulties of his future occupation have early become second nature to him'. In short, he teaches them quite differently from the way those people teach 'who can only talk big and do things on paper', for he believes nothing which could be helpful to them to be outside the scope of his task. He feels himself their father and spends almost every evening with them. 'Sometimes he carved wood with them, sometimes he made figures of wax, men and beasts, or houses and mills and ships.' 'If he lives, what he is doing will change the circumstances of the poor in Bonnal even more than the parcelling-out of the common and the rent-free acres which the squire promised them.'

It is Cotton Meyer, the squire's general adviser in economic matters, who recommends these innovations. He and his sister make manifest by their actions that entrepreneurs can procure work and bread for the people without exploiting them; they also show how, through careful training and regular employment, even the poorest spinners can learn to save and to attain some possessions of their own. After being made bailiff, Meyer makes before the assembled community the astonishing assertion that regular savings which would be comparatively easy to make would within twenty-five years produce a sum sufficient to pay off all dues and taxes lying on the land. Education for industry is, then, 'wisdom in earning and in spending money'.

The new legal order which Arner introduces in Bonnal consists in the starting of a village register from which property boundaries and alterations in these could be ascertained at any time, so as to prevent litigation; and in so-called 'account and property books' for every individual household. In this way Arner bases the prosperity of the people on the openness of their accounts, for he wishes them to believe in nothing but what can be 'counted, weighed, measured, and thereby proved'. Such importance did Pestalozzi, who could not keep accounts himself, attribute to 'the bright light of the one and one'! Next, the procedure of litigation is improved; but far rather should quarrels be avoided altogether. A positive legal order would help to prevent bribery, theft, sexual excesses and so on. The gallows are abolished. Arner's aim is 'to cure his people from the barbarism of their untamed lives or rather from the aberration of their natural human propensities'. His law-giving is crowned by a new order of divine service. This is to make religion a matter of the heart and not of the head and to bring the people out of superstition and fanaticism into 'the pure worship of God'. It is to guide man on the road to duty so 'that he wants to be what he has to be'. An effective means of making the people appreciate everything fine and good and of fostering their community feeling is to make the religious festivals real communal celebrations, as enjoyable as popular holidays.

But Pestalozzi's Bonnal is no Utopia in which improvements proceed unhindered. Before the reforms are carried out, great difficulties arise which jeopardize their success. (This check on progress may be explained by the change in Pestalozzi's own political and philosophical attitude, brought about by his deep personal disappointments and by the altered world situation.) The new ideas cause a conflict of opinion in Bonnal as well as at the ducal court. The intrigues of enemies (Sylvia and Helidor) bring Arner to the point of death. The literary importance of this incident is that it may now be seen how deep the roots of the new order have gone; whether the improvement of the people is entirely dependent on the continued existence of their kind 'father' or whether, whatever happens to the squire, things in the village will remain as they now are. The pastor says from the pulpit, 'Things seem to be arranged in the world as if men were not meant to be cared for by their fellow men. The whole of nature and the whole of history cry out to the human race that everybody should care for himself because nobody else cares for him, and the best one can do for man is to teach him how to do it.' This time, however, everything comes right in Bonnal, Arner recovers, and the patriarchal system is saved for the time being. The idea of self-help remains incidental in *Leonard and Gertrude*, but in the long run what Glüphi does bears richer fruit than Arner's legislation. Soon the idea of autonomy will play a decisive part in Pestalozzi's system of education.

Arner's recovery is speeded up by the arrival in Bonnal of a minister of State (such as Pestalozzi dreamed of) who on his return to the capital gives his sovereign a most favourable account of the village (just what in real life Count Zinzendorf had failed to do). He suggests the possibility of carrying out the reforms on a larger scale. The duke visits the village personally and speaks to the lieutenant 'who has waited for this opportunity for years'. It is certain: the government in its wider sphere is going to put the lieutenant's ideas into practice.

'The philosophy of my lieutenant and that of my book', i.e. Pestalozzi's own, is based on a different conception of 'nature' from the one he had had in earlier years. He is no longer convinced of the absolute goodness of the human being; he now distinguishes man 'as he is by nature'—wild, heedless, greedy— from man in society, which through restraint, order, and even coercion has made him 'something quite different' from what he was before. The task of the education of the people is to turn an 'uncivilized and debased rabble' into 'peaceful and contented human beings'. For this purpose education has 'to alter and to renew man within himself', but not by destroying his natural impulses but by satisfying his fundamental needs, thereby transforming, as Pestalozzi is to express it later, his lower nature into a higher one. Such a conception of education, he says, 'turns all the ideas of legislation actually put into practice in this enlightened century upside down'. The touchstone for the truth of the lieutenant's philosophy lies in the fact that in general as well as in details it is in agreement with the philosophy of the people, i.e. with the lifelong experiences of the most reliable peasants in Bonnal.

What Pestalozzi, through the pastor, has to say on religion is even more down to earth than his remarks in the first parts of *Leonard and Gertrude*. Religion helps man to overcome his sensual desires; it is closely linked with all aspects of his daily life. When the parson speaks of God and of eternity it seems as if he is speaking 'of father and mother, of hearth and home, in short of things which concern the people closely'. Religion consists mainly in morals; it does not exist for its own sake, nor for God's sake, but for man's sake. 'God is for man the God of men only through men.' Religious service is, therefore, the service of men; the worship of God and the love of men are interdependent. To lead a religious life means to 'walk in love', but love is no longer, as it was in the *Evening Hour*, a contented resting in God's hands; it demands vigour, activity as well as restraint, application and order. It consists 'not in sentiments and in words, but in the power of man to bear the burden of this earth, to alleviate want and to mitigate distress. The God of love has bound love to the order of this earth, and he whose worldly house is not in order is not in order for the love of God and the love of his neighbour.'

Pestalozzi had hardly finished *Leonard and Gertrude*, when he began to re-write the book all over again. He found it too long and thought this the reason for its poor success as a whole. Accordingly he cut the text almost by half, thereby making the structure more compact and the style more condensed; but the vivid qualities of the original were lost in the process. The second version is colourless and theoretical; its sub-title indicates its character: *An Attempt to simplify the Principles of Popular Education* (1790-2, in 3 parts).

The purpose of the book also necessitated a considerable change in content. It was now to be dedicated to Leopold II and to introduce Pestalozzi's ideas at the Court of Vienna. This self-recommendation to a monarch required that he should stress even more the patriarchal bias while pointing out at the same time the imminent dangers which threatened Europe's nobility, but which might still be averted by last-minute action such as he recommended. The main aspects in which the second version differs from the first are, from the political point of view, its enlightened despotism and, from the economic, its utilitarianism.

The idea of self-help of the people has vanished completely; on the contrary, Arner realizes more than ever that 'the belief that the people could be brought to order through liberty rather than through the interference of their superiors is a mere dream'. And in pointed reference to the slogans of the contemporary revolutionary movement in France he continues, 'It is a dream, a pernicious dream, which is now being proclaimed: "Man is free." Man is not free. The king is a slave and the citizen serves. . . . The nobility must be called to their duty, and then the natural order of things will be restored.' By a repeated use of the formula 'enlightenment from the throne' Pestalozzi hopes to call the aristocracy to a sense of their responsibility. Since his intention to impress a monarch is so obvious, the political utterances of Arner and of his friend, the minister of State, must not be taken as Pestalozzi's own. For there are also clear indications that as a Swiss republican he is fundamentally averse to this 'servility', and that he doubts whether the aristocracy will be able to fulfil their task.

But it is, at this time, his opinion that for the upper classes the most effective motive is self-interest. If they realized that better education of their subjects would permit them to be used to greater profit, they would support popular enlightenment for economic reasons. The 'first principle' of the book, underlying the entire reform, legislation as well as school education, is 'wisdom and strength in the acquiring, increasing, and retaining of property'. The welfare of States on a large scale, he thinks, is also based on the soundness of their economic system, just as, conversely, 'the general confusion of nations is nothing but a confusion of their economies'. Therefore the true remedy is 'the guidance of the people to economic wisdom'. Economic wisdom where States are concerned is the physiocratic doctrine of absolute freedom of trade; in the small spheres of private homes the happiness of individual households is to be attained through early vocational training.

Economic prosperity is, however, not an end in itself but only the condition for moral order. The 'first principle' is superseded by the 'higher purpose' of achieving the well-being of mankind through 'the union of their powers with their wills', i.e. their practical abilities and their moral efforts. To achieve such a union becomes the ultimate aim of Arner's legislation, based, as it is, on his conception of 'property' (implying, in its widest sense, civil and moral security). He therefore also introduces ecclesiastical legislation designed to connect 'religious wisdom in the individual' with 'wise governing in the State'. Since religion is for him (i.e. for Pestalozzi at this stage) not a matter of the transcendental but bound to the business of this earth, it has the task of guiding men towards a nobler existence; but this is possible only 'through the ties of social interaction'.

The chapters which Pestalozzi considered to be the most important of the book are those towards the end of the third part; they contain his detailed proposals about industrial schools for country children and correspond almost literally with his *Memorandum on the Combination of Vocational Training with Schools for the People* written for Count Zinzendorf. The industrial school follows the system which the lieutenant has introduced in his school-room; it, in its turn, has been taken from Gertrude's 'living-room'. The lieutenant (now called Glülphi) makes it the basis of his teaching that children are taught to earn their living from an early age. 'Spinning-wheels, weaving-looms, lace-bobbins were the first books he put into the children's hands.' He lays out a school garden, because the association of agriculture with industry, like that of the training of hand as well as head, is for him the only way to alleviate the misery of the poor and to achieve the happiness of the people. Through this 'spirit of industry' the children would be enabled not only to support themselves through their own work, at all times and at all places, but also to spread reliable industrial knowledge in their neighbourhood and so to raise the standard of living in village, county, and state and to put an end to the 'economic confusion' of the times.

Pestalozzi, the 'observer of human nature', is of the opinion 'that all public attempts to improve the conditions of the people must begin with such institutions for poor children and orphans'. It was his 'dream' to be allowed to set up such a people's school somewhere in the world, either under government auspices or as a private enterprise, 'in order to lead mankind in general to the pure enjoyment of their domestic circumstances. . . . Through the tiny spark of such orphanages or homes for the poor he tried to kindle the sacred fire in Europe which the continent needs so urgently, in order to show to societies, so seriously shaken in their foundations, the way to their salvation'.

IV   HEINRICH PESTALOZZI (I)

'There he stood,' runs Pestalozzi's fable *The Painter of Men*, 'surrounded by a crowd, and one man said, "So you have become a painter? You would have done better to mend our shoes." He answered, "I would have mended your shoes, I would have carried stones for you, I would have drawn water for you, I would have died for you, but you did not want my services, and in the enforced emptiness of my crushed existence there was nothing left for me to do but to learn how to paint." '

Pestalozzi had put all his heart into *Leonard and Gertrude*. The lieutenant's remark that he had in mind a man who could carry out the education of the people in wider spheres, was meant very personally. For ten years Pestalozzi had tried to persuade monarchs to be fathers of their nations and to bring happiness and a vision of truth to their peoples. '*Leonard and Gertrude*', he wrote, 'will be an eternal proof that I exhausted my powers in order to save aristocracy; but my efforts earned me nothing but ingratitude.' Leopold II would not listen; soon he died, and the thrones of Europe began to totter. In view of later developments it is perhaps fortunate that Pestalozzi did not succeed with the monarchs; they might have prejudiced his political outlook; and if he had, he would probably have run away from the imperial Court, just as he later cut short his few journeys abroad. The Swiss citizen 'got mad' at the sight of 'decadent courtiers'; they made him realize what a good republican he was and that he felt 'a thousand times more comfortable amongst the most rascally Birr peasants' than in the great world or in academic circles.

Any obsequiousness which he showed was only a means to an end. He wished to act, to become influential in the education of the people, and since he was not achieving it at home, he tried abroad. The fact that he did not succeed there either led to the worst crisis of his life. During the first few years after the collapse of his home for poor children he had kept up his morale by putting his great experience to literary use. But as time went on, aimlessly so he thought, and as he felt old age approaching (he was nearing fifty) without his having even begun the most important task of his life, he was seized with despair. His letters have a tired and resigned ring; his visitors describe his despondency and his cynicism; he himself in his relentless self-criticism tells years later in many reminiscences (having by then emerged victorious) of the severe mental and emotional disturbance he had suffered through the denial of his desire, his exclusion from the active forces of the time, and the annihilating judgment of his fellow-men.

His most fundamental characteristic, in his own judgment, an 'irresistible inclination to relieve the sufferings of men and to further their contentment and well-being', had grown into a veritable passion which he could neither restrain nor satisfy. Convinced of his abilities for his particular purpose, he strove 'solely and entirely to stop up the fount of misery' in which he saw the people around him sunk. In the pursuit of this goal he exercised tough endurance, great courage, and an ardent imagination. He pinned his hopes on every circumstance that seemed in the least auspicious; he placed his trust in every man who showed the smallest sign of interest.

But nobody believed in him. The judgment of the people that he was a failure and useless to the world remained unchanged 'like a rock' even in 'the splendour of glory' which the famous book had temporarily created around him. He was lacking indeed in the adroitness and worldly-wise efficiency by which other people so easily gained position and renown. 'The common run of men all knew well what they were doing; I only knew what I wished to do.' For the fulfilment of his wish he had neither the means himself nor the assistance of others. So he remained what he had been from his youth, 'everybody's fool'. He was always, in everything, alone like no one else, 'without friend, without prospect, without respect'.

Only in the field of writing was he acknowledged to have ability. He now had, everybody said, his 'weaving-loom' on which he could earn his living if he would only stick to it. If he worked on it diligently and had a piece ready every Michaelmas, all would be well. This general opinion made his situation worse. He did not like writing nor did it come easily to him, and yet he wrote in order to relieve his mind. He filled sheet after sheet to find in the end that his researches had only widened the gap between theory and practice and increased his incapacity for adapting himself to his circumstances. Writing could not take the place of the action in which he so urgently desired to engage.

He lived, according to his own report, as if 'stranded in a desert', and the consequences were disastrous. He lost all the graciousness and sweetness of his temper. The general misunderstanding and disbelief tore his heart, destroyed his peace, and shattered his trust in men, in himself, and in God. Like a 'broken reed' he drifted on the sea of life; the greatest gift he had possessed in earlier years, his belief in the divine in man, was in danger of being lost. He had little respect for human nature and he despised himself. He was ready to give up the struggle.

His friend Nicolovius reproached him for not being a Christian, saying that he reversed the text 'Seek ye first the Kingdom of God and all these things shall be added unto you.' The writer F. H. Jacobi told him that he found *Leonard and Gertrude* (second version) 'too materialistic'. In a remarkable letter to Nicolovius (October 1st, 1793) Pestalozzi explains his 'non-Christianity', justifying it from the experiences of his life. (It is interesting to note that Pestalozzi begins all his apologies and expositions, in letters as well as in books, with a survey of his personal development).

The failures of his enterprises, he writes, have caused in him a spiritual upheaval; they have turned him away from religion— to which he had been sensitive from youth—without, however, deciding him entirely against it. By making the 'partial truth'

74

of an economic doctrine his 'idol', he has lost 'the essential power which the true worship of God gives to the religious man'. But he has also seen that 'the mire of the world' in which he had sunk has its own order, and he has made it his urgent task 'to shed light upon the means by which man can find his way through it without sinking like myself'. He knows, of course, that this is only a limited, if useful, point of view, but neither he (at this time) nor the majority of men are able to go beyond this narrow circle.

He is well aware that there exists a 'higher truth' from which happier, wiser, and better men (like Nicolovius, for instance) derive great strength 'through making the consecration of their hearts the first business of their lives'. He has been led on a different road. 'The kind of truth to which I have devoted myself is not really the highest and noblest aim of the cultivation of man, it is only a good education for the fundamental needs of his earthly life. I cannot and must not conceal the fact that my truth is bound to the mire of the earth and therefore lies far below the angels' walk to which faith and love may raise mankind.' He admits to being without faith, but 'not because I hold faithlessness to be the truth, but because the sum total of my life's experiences have driven the blessed gift of faith to a large extent from my heart'.

As regards Christianity, he considers it to be 'the purest and noblest form of the doctrine that the spirit governs the flesh', and 'the only possible means for bringing human nature, in its essential quality, closer to its true destiny'. Yet he does not believe 'that the majority of men, because of their animal nature, are capable of becoming Christians' any more than they are capable of 'wearing earthly crowns'. And in his great modesty he includes himself in this majority.

Nicolovius, himself a sincere Christian, who drew this confession from Pestalozzi, reports after his first visit to the Neuhof that 'Pestalozzi is seeking for truth as earnestly as few people do', and that 'he is purified by the hell-fire of self-knowledge and filled with an apostolic spirit'. He was as little aware as Pestalozzi himself that this apology for his 'limited point of view' was already the beginning of the end of the 'idolizing' of an economic doctrine. The coming to terms with his experiences and the discussion with Nicolovius led him to the acceptance of a 'higher' point of view: the placing of 'inner ennoblement' or education of the whole human being above practical ability or vocational training. It cost Pestalozzi a hard struggle to reach this new 'truth', and he was able to realize it fully only when life had begun to treat him more gently. The depression of his spirits did not lift until the suppression of his true powers came to an end. It required a world revolution to restore Pestalozzi's mental balance and to direct his activity on to its proper course.

There was one thing, however, in this time of humiliation, that saved him from the last degree of despair: it was the inexhaustible power of his love. And so he did not go quite adrift; 'there was yet something higher in me'. When, in a mood of great despondency, he met a child in the street, lifted it up and looked into its eyes, he forgot heaven and earth. 'I should say I forgot the judgments of God and of men and experienced the bliss of human nature and its sacred innocence while losing, or finding, myself in the child on my knees. . . . So a deep feeling of love which was stronger than everything that troubled me, saved me from utter ruin.'

These years of suffering yielded, moreover, one profit: in his extremity Pestalozzi came to know the needs of the people as no happy man can know them. 'I suffered what the people suffer, and the people revealed themselves to me as they revealed themselves to nobody else. I learned to understand the people as nobody around me understood them.' This was what gave Pestalozzi the courage to be thankful for his misfortune.

Pestalozzi spent thirty years, half a lifetime, in the Neuhof in the greatest poverty. His inquiries into the essence of human nature and his flights of imagination concerning future schemes of education were carried out against the background of an unceasing financial struggle. The cotton works brought only poor returns; the farm was let during most of that time. But in spite of pressing needs Pestalozzi would not hear of selling his estate; he refused the offer of his friend Battier of Basle to take it over and pay him a life rent which would have enabled him to continue his writing without financial cares. He chose to remain in the place of his hopes and his disappointments, unwilling to give up his belief that he would one day be able to realize his 'dream', the poor-school, on his own ground. His wife supported him in this decision. They were both determined to retain the property, having in mind also the interest of their son. So the Neuhof always remained a home and a refuge for Pestalozzi and his family.

Limited means and depressed spirits did not help to improve his looks. His sufferings had left their mark on his face; the burden of his experiences had bent his back. His complete unconcern about tidy clothing and polite manners was a source of embarrassment to his friends. He liked to do his thinking as he roamed the fields in fair weather or foul. When he was encountered soaked to the skin, splashed with mud up to his knees, his stockings hanging down and his hair tousled, he was more than once taken for a tramp out to rob the mail and put into prison overnight without much ado; or he was taken for a beggar looking for alms and offered a penny. Such mistakes gave him the opportunity of getting to know from personal experience the almshouses of the cities or the charity of the rich. He treated these incidents as jokes, but they distressed his wife very greatly.

Of Anna Pestalozzi's life in the two decades before the turn of the century only a few particulars can be ascertained. She was often ill and lived therefore in seclusion for many years. Her religious conviction helped her to bear the disappointments and deprivations inflicted upon her. Her spiritual and social attitudes were quite different from those of her husband. She had no special liking for the poor. Her circle of friends included, besides the Countess of Hallwil, Zurich women who are well known in the history of letters, as wives of famous men or on their own merits: Barbara Schulthess-Wolff who preserved the original version of Goethe's *Wilhelm Meister*; Anna Magdalena Schweizer-Hess who kept an open house in which the Duke of Weimar and Goethe were visitors; Lotte Gessner, wife of Pestalozzi's publisher and daughter of Wieland; and many more who were all related in some way to each other. In these houses Anna and Pestalozzi himself were introduced to new literary publications and events. It is even possible that they became personally acquainted with Goethe. Nanette was a great reader, and she was always ready to copy Pestalozzi's untidy manuscripts in round hand. In this way she took part in his work; but the path of his destiny he had to travel alone.

Their son Jacques was, so visitors describe him, 'a quite in-significant man'. Pestalozzi had had his sickness treated by hypnosis and magnetism, the new cure which Cagliostro, a quack, was applying to people in the neighbourhood; but with-out success. Jacques was dull and irritable; he was periodically seized by terrible convulsions accompanied by delusions. In the intervals between these attacks he did small jobs and went on errands, but he was incapable of any mental exertion. When he was twenty-one and in rather better health, his parents allowed him to marry. Nobody seems to have questioned the wisdom of this step. His bride Anna Magdalena Frölich (1767–1814) was a lively and warm-hearted girl, known and attached to the Pestalozzi family from childhood. She loyally and unselfishly fulfilled her difficult task as Jacques' wife although she did not find much happiness. Of five children only the youngest, Gottlieb (1797–1863), survived. But she enjoyed the love and gratitude of the Pestalozzi parents who were devoted to her as if she were their own daughter.

After their marriage the young couple took over the farming of the Neuhof and later also the cotton works. But Jacques was always in financial difficulties; he was a grumbler and hard to please. His wife and Lisabeth, the faithful maid, ministered to him uncomplainingly, and his mother bore her sorrow with fortitude. Pestalozzi was greatly worried about the health of his son and felt responsible for his sufferings; he was also deeply disappointed in not having an heir to his idea. Once he had 'dreamed' of finding in Jacques his support and successor in his love for the people. But at the time when, as he thought, he was nearing the grave and when every hope had gone that he might himself impart his experiences to mankind, he had to realize that his only son would never be able to carry on his work. His heart was heavy when he watched other young men, once Jacqueli's play-fellows and now leaders of the patriotic move-ment. He felt drawn to them; and when he met young Nicolo-vius he cried out, 'Oh, if only you were my son! Then I should not be going out of the world so lonely.'

What attracted him so much to this young man was his fine character and his humaneness. Ludwig Nicolovius (1767–1839) was a disciple of Kant and a follower of the 'feeling philoso-phers' Hamann and F. H. Jacobi. He strove above all for 'the ennobling of his soul'; he always tried to rise above everything trivial. In 1791, when he met Pestalozzi, he was on his way to Italy with Count Friedrich Stolberg, the same who had accompanied Goethe to Switzerland in 1775. In him Pestalozzi at last found after long lonely years a man who understood and valued his philanthropic intentions. He was the first of his 'sons of a spiritual love', and there was not to be any disillusionment in their relationship. Although after only a few meetings they never saw each other again, they kept up their friendship by corresponding until Pestalozzi's death. Pestalozzi remembered Nicolovius' visit as 'one of the happiest'; Nicolovius, later Councillor of State under W. von Humboldt in the Prussian Ministry of Education, was instrumental in introducing the Pestalozzian method into Prussia's new teachers' training colleges and new elementary schools.

Nicolovius was the first representative of the German idealist movement whom Pestalozzi met. The second was Fichte.

Since the Neuhof had been taken over by their children, the parents lived away from it for months on end; Nanette in Hallwil, Pestalozzi in the neighbourhood of Zurich, if not further away. This gave him more leisure for uninterrupted reading and writing. Yes, also for reading; in spite of his assertion that he 'had not read a book for thirty years' he was now changing his method of working. He had begun not only to read books, but to copy out extracts and to write comments, 'a new career in my old age'. In order to broaden his knowledge of human nature and of political constitutions he studied problems of moral freedom and the natural impulses, of ruling and serving, of ecclesiastical and constitutional history. He read works, or reviews of works, by Shaftesbury, Rousseau, Voltaire, Hume, Mendelssohn, Kant, and Jacobi, contemporary writings and monthly periodicals, some in French and even in Latin. But his comments show clearly that he was no unprejudiced scholar; he was only interested in what was relevant to his purpose. Even his excerpts differ considerably from their original texts.

It was through personal contacts that Pestalozzi got into touch with contemporary philosophy without, however—any more than through his reading—being fundamentally influenced in his own way of thinking. In the winter of 1793–4 he took charge of the house of his cousin Dr. Johannes Hotze

(1734–1801) in Richterswil on Lake Zurich. This relative had always been a kind friend to Pestalozzi—it was he who had helped to make the Schulthess parents agree to the marriage between Nanette and Heinrich—although their ideas on politics and religion were at variance. Dr. Hotze belonged to the circle around Lavater and, though himself a countryman and therefore without civic rights, he defended the old régime. He was a well-known physician, and Zurich citizens and their foreign guests came to see him, sometimes as patients, sometimes as friends. Even the Duke of Weimar and Goethe were brought to his house by Lavater. In that winter, then, which Pestalozzi spent in Richterswil during Dr. Hotze's absence, his important meeting with the young Fichte took place.

Johann Gottlieb Fichte (1762–1814) had in the previous years taken up the Kantian philosophy with enthusiasm; it had made such a tremendous impression on him that he desired to communicate its 'beneficial effects' to others. In this particular year he was engaged in political research and had just published *A Contribution to the French Revolution*. Pestalozzi, too, was busily seeking to determine his own attitude to the latest political developments and to relate it to his views of human nature and social history; he was trying to lay his 'political foundations'. The discussions of the two thinkers dealt with these problems; and Pestalozzi was greatly surprised when Fichte told him that his 'intuitive method' had brought him very close to the conclusions of the Kantian philosophy. Fichte's views were 'of extreme importance' to Pestalozzi; they led him into a relationship with the contemporary philosophical movement and out of his paralysing isolation. On Fichte's advice he interrupted his work on a topical question *On the Political Atmosphere among the European Nations* to devote himself entirely to his 'philosophy of politics'. (The first work was later completed under the title *Yes or No*, the second was to be called *My Inquiries*.)

The question whether Fichte indoctrinated Pestalozzi with the Kantian philosophy and whether their meeting explains the change of outlook in the *Inquiries* as compared with *Leonard and Gertrude* III/IV on the one hand and with the *Evening Hour* on the other, is a moot point in the Pestalozzi literature. No doubt Fichte had 'illuminated' his mind and 'lifted up' his heart, as

Pestalozzi himself gratefully acknowledged; but after having experienced, and overcome, the impact of Rousseau, Pestalozzi never let himself be much influenced by any doctrine or any man. He was gratified to be compared with Kant; but whenever he felt other men's ideas encroach upon his own, he became wary. He was fond of asserting that modern philosophy was 'beyond his capacity'; he did not wish to go into 'cold definitions'. He saw a possibility of 'bringing philosophy nearer to the hearts of men through the stirring of emotions which are diametrically opposed to its usual principles', and he was more in agreement with the 'feeling philosophers' Herder, Jacobi, and Nicolovius than with such 'crystal-clear thinkers' as Kant and Fichte. He took from each what suited him, and for the rest his philosophy was original and unusual in the era of idealist systems. Only in recent times has it been adequately appreciated.

Meanwhile, Fichte in his turn was much impressed by Pestalozzi. Possible connections between his *Features of the Present Era* and Pestalozzi's *Epochs* have still to be investigated. In his *Addresses to the German Nation* he made Pestalozzi's system of education the nucleus of his scheme for national education, and in the ninth Address he introduced a beautiful memorial to Pestalozzi's personality and to his power of love, 'the life of his life'.

In the spring of the preceding year (1792) Pestalozzi had gone on the first long, indeed the longest, journey of his life. In matters connected with the will and estate of a deceased aunt, a well-to-do sister of his mother, he travelled to Leipzig and there stayed with his married sister, Frau Grosse, whom he had not seen for twenty years. His Swiss relatives had sent him as their representative, certainly not because he was the most knowledgeable man in monetary affairs they could have found, but probably because no fixed ties kept him in Zurich. He himself had hoped for years to realize his 'principal purpose' abroad; so he seized the opportunity of being able to look around in Germany and perhaps in Austria. There was even talk of a visit to Denmark. The negotiations concerning the inheritance were protracted and complicated; in the end he returned home before the business was settled, having agreed that his mother should make over her entire share to her daughter in Leipzig.

More important than his negotiation of this family business are his impressions of the social and political state of Germany; they were almost entirely unfavourable. 'They have weakened my vague desire for long journeys,' he writes in a most interesting letter; 'I now find nearly everything below my expectations and especially that of which I expected most.' So the question of his 'darling scheme' did not arise; the conditions in Germany were a great disappointment to him. The 'miserable quality' of the nobility and the 'knavery' of the citizens filled him with disgust; he found the scholars and the philosophers conceited and despicable. In these days of the French declaration of war on the ancient powers of Europe he detected an atmosphere of social fermentation everywhere, and he noticed the danger signs of an imminent struggle, of an era coming to an end.

Pestalozzi returned home at the beginning of the Wars of the Revolution. In Paris the Tuileries were stormed and the king dethroned. In Frankfurt the last Emperor of the Holy Roman Empire was being crowned while Austrian and German troops were already fighting with France. The cannonade of Valmy was the beginning of 'a new epoch in world history'; the allies had to withdraw, the Revolutionary forces had won their first battle with the *ancien régime*.

Switzerland was the close neighbour of France and bound to her by a centuries-old alliance. Would she be involved in the whirlpool of events? From his village Pestalozzi watched what was happening with sympathy. The declaration of the Rights of Man was something he had demanded for years. Would the new authorities establish the equality of the people when the monarchs had remained deaf to all remonstrances? Only slowly and not without many explanations and self-justifications Pestalozzi turned to the other side. But like all European enthusiasts for the new liberty he was soon repelled by the growing terrorism which obscured the original ideas. The Swiss guard were murdered, the Swiss regiments dissolved, innocent people executed without trial. Hope and despair alternated in rapid succession. Should he say Yes or No to the revolutionary movement?

In his neighbourhood rumours went round that he was in touch with the French, supporting their National Convention. This he denied. 'All my life I have striven for civil rights and popular enlightenment, but I have also always maintained as firmly as perhaps few other men, that these aims can be achieved best by preserving the social order and by introducing the various improvements gradually.' He still hoped that the idea of liberty would emerge purified from the fire of war, and he interpreted the excesses of the revolutionary power as a reaction against the 'mountain of guilt' which the French monarchy had accumulated.

Then he got confirmation that another rumour which had come to his notice was true: the National Assembly had made him an honorary citizen of France. His friend J. C. Schweizer, the banker, had probably proposed his name. The society of which he suddenly found himself a member included the most distinguished international personalities who had fought for liberty with word and deed: George Washington and Thomas Payne, Bentham and Wilberforce, Klopstock and Schiller. Pestalozzi was the more gratified by this great honour because his own country had so persistently ignored him. He now spoke up openly for France, called her his 'new fatherland', and was anxious to serve her in the field in which he possessed sound knowledge and experience: the education of the people.

For it was the education of the people with which he was solely concerned; the form of the government which carried it out was for him of minor importance. He used every political grouping in order to achieve his aim. Since the aristocrats had failed him, he approached the democrats; when they made him a citizen of their country he believed that he owed it to them to contribute what he could to their enlightenment. But his search was always for 'the foundations of truth which are independent of all external events and not stamped with any mark, either democratic or aristocratic'; and he was determined not to swerve a hair's breadth from his old conviction that 'the united effort of all good men to achieve the quiet wisdom which springs from domestic enjoyment is the sole foundation of true liberty'.

Now are renewed the humiliating attempts to find practical work, this time in France. The *Comité d'instruction publique* seems indeed to have taken an interest in Pestalozzi's plans. But this, too, came to nothing, and his hopes dropped to zero again.

IV   The Political Philosopher
(1793–1800)

PESTALOZZI had laid aside his essay *On the Political Atmosphere among European Nations* at a time when the Revolutionary powers were victorious, in order to avoid the impression that his sympathy with France 'countenanced the growing barbarism in the name of liberty'. When in 1793 the war situation—temporarily—changed in favour of the allies, he finished this work under the title *Yes or No*. In it he accuses and warns both political sides. Its main theme is that despotism of any kind is bound to ruin Europe and that hope of survival lies only in the voluntary yielding of governments to that 'which is reasonable in the demand of the people for liberty'.

Pestalozzi has lost his belief in enlightened despotism. He now even makes 'the courts' pretensions to absolute power' responsible for the people's unrest. In what he calls a 'psychological' survey of history he considers the political development of the European nations. He begins with the feudal period which in his eyes produced the almost ideal form of government, for in it everybody had his appointed rights; 'nobody was allowed everything, but everybody was allowed something'. The absolutism which followed it 'kicked the privileges of the lower classes out of existence' and so destroyed their social well-being. Yet the overweening pretensions of the mighty—which were, in fact, 'nothing but the violent demands of man's egoism in his natural state'—became in the social state more infectious than any physical disease. Their consequences were 'the claims of the plebeian to that which distinguishes the patrician, . . . the dan-

84

gerous misinterpretation of the natural liberty and equality of man'. At present, the survey ends, the new rulers of France are committing the same transgressions as the monarchs whom they are combating; they are thus destroying 'the right of and the necessity for revolution in the world' and losing the sympathies of all impartial men.

But Pestalozzi does not pretend to be impartial. He confesses to a bias in favour of the people, his intention being not to blame them for their mistakes but to find the causes of their unrest and the remedies for their failings.

Why, he asks, are the peoples drunk with liberty? What does man desire when he strives for freedom? Freedom, he answers, is not the right to do what is not prohibited by law but 'the cultivated power of the citizen to do what makes him happy as a citizen and to prevent what would make him unhappy as a citizen'; it is the right to the satisfaction of his fundamental needs. 'Man considers well-being his due. Only the unhappy and the unsatisfied look for freedom. Therefore, assure the well-being of the citizen, and you have stopped up the source of the liberty-mania.' Also it must be kept in mind that the liberty of the people depends in a high degree on their possession of the requisite physical power, the wielding of which in turn encourages that lack of restraint of human passions characteristic of them in their state of nature. For this reason it is essential that men should be led to control the violence of their natural passions and to confine them within proper limits. This the French leaders have failed to do and so have undone what was good in the Revolution.

The great question concerning liberty, he goes on, is, how can social security be safeguarded against all forms of despotism, be it monarchy, city council, National Convention or any other? Pestalozzi advises the French legislators to promote the return of the people to their traditional moral standards: domestic virtue, honesty, moderation, and dignity. 'Do not imagine yourselves free, make yourselves free! It all depends on what you are yourselves!' Only 'vigilance in the preservation of the pure emotions attendant upon a religious attitude in the people' can lead to the self-restraint on which all civil liberty must be based. A disruption of social and religious bonds would lead to a rapid and complete decline of Europe.

Pestalozzi also appeals to the old European powers to beware, before it is too late, of the wave of rebellion spreading over the whole continent. It is impossible, he says, to save Europe from the ruin which her present tensions and her growing exhaustion threaten to bring on her, without improving the knowledge of the people, without a quickening of their power of self-help, and without establishing a just system of representation. Therefore it behoves the old powers to restore the spirit of the ancient German Constitution, but in accordance with the needs of the present time, 'for the protection of the peoples and for the safeguarding of a social state satisfactory to human nature'.

Freedom, then, is the ability to govern oneself. Independence requires moderation and the control of egoistic physical appetites. Again Pestalozzi brings the discussion of topical political questions back to general moral principles. His remedy—'a balance between the powers of the people and the powers of the government'—is not very revolutionary. But the outspoken language in which he attacked the excesses of despotism—by which, however, he meant just as much 'the egoism of our nature' as the failings of certain rulers—made the publication of his essay at that time impossible. It circulated only in a number of handwritten copies among his personal friends.

But a pamphlet by Pestalozzi was distributed in France in which he makes propaganda, in the interests of his new 'fatherland', for the use of the potato (hitherto only an animal food) for human consumption, in order to save bread. He recommends the composition of a national song and the introduction of a national festival in praise of the potato and suggests calling it 'the plant of security' or 'the plant of independence'. In another leaflet he advocates a 'moral sansculottism' which should give away voluntarily what the political sansculottism seizes by force. That the individual's demands for property and rights be subordinated to the claims of true freedom and love for the people—this is Pestalozzi's moral answer to the political problems of his time.

Pestalozzi was still hoping against hope that the Revolution would be confined to France and that Europe would take over its ideas voluntarily. But the success of the French armies and their approach to the Swiss frontier stirred the oppressed within that country, and Pestalozzi turned his attention to events in his immediate neighbourhood.

The country people in the Lake Zurich district, although politically, socially, and economically dependent on the city, had through diligence and efficiency worked their way up in the cotton and weaving industries, and they now demanded political rights corresponding to their economic achievements. But they met with strong opposition. The city government not only refused to concede certain legal rights but even imposed penalties on the country people for demanding them.

During the months which Pestalozzi had spent in Richterswil he had come to know the mood of the country population. He openly defended their claims which he considered justified, and set forth his views in several pamphlets. In these he advocates a reform of the Zurich Constitution since it no longer met present conditions, and the immediate liberalization of manufacture and trade. Civil rights, the granting of political equality to the dependent population, should be introduced gradually. He urged both sides, town and country, to come to an agreement in order to avoid the use of force, and he offered his services as an intermediary. But the city government remained obstinate, and the oppressed people became desperate. Pestalozzi on his part made himself more unpopular than ever in Zurich by his plea for the people, and despite his efforts the political issue was to be decided by violent action and interference from without, what he had hoped to avert.

Until the time of the Swiss Revolution Pestalozzi lived in Fluntern on the outskirts of Zurich where he put his political theories into practice by lending his name to the weaving-works of a relative, a non-citizen. So there was a firm of 'Heinrich Pestalozzi' registered in the city roll, and Pestalozzi actually took part in the selling of silk cloth, for he had expert knowledge and trade connections from the time of his cotton business.

Since his meeting with Fichte Pestalozzi had continued his inquiries into the physical, social, and moral aspects of human development. They were to lay the foundations of his political belief and to provide his 'philosophy of government'. The book resulting from them is the most difficult and most abstract work

Pestalozzi ever wrote; it cost him immense labour. Alongside it ran, as in earlier years *Leonard and Gertrude* had run alongside the *Evening Hour*, a series of stories and 'pictures' illustrating the same ideas in narrative form. He called them *Illustrations to my ABC-Book or to the Principles of my Thinking* (1797), later simply *Fables*. (At various times of his life Pestalozzi called different works of his, containing fundamental ideas, 'my ABC-book', here his *Inquiries*, earlier *Leonard and Gertrude*, and later his *Elementary Schoolbooks*.)

He had written a considerable number of fables during more than a decade (1780–90); the French Revolution and its dangerous repercussions on Switzerland then gave them political point. They are, therefore, unequal in content and also in literary value; generally speaking the earlier ones are better than the later. As in his previous writings, Pestalozzi uses in his own way a favourite literary form of popular enlightenment; he does not seem to be influenced by well-known collections of fables like Gellert's or Lessing's.

All Pestalozzi's fables contain a distinct moral which is always the same and is usually expressed in a negative way: it points to the harm done to man's spiritual nature by his animal nature, if it gains the upper hand, or by transitory events in 'time' to the unchanging values of 'eternity'. Many of them are animal fables. Pestalozzi describes an animal State with only two classes of society, those who devour others and those who are devoured by others. The first have absolute power because they are the stronger; they rule according to principles laid down 'in their mouth'. This is *The Animals' Idea of Justice*:

'The lion said, "If I have had the meal which is my due, I am the most generous beast under the sun. Only the word 'rights' must not be mentioned to me. My teeth gnash when I hear this word."

'The fox said, "Everywhere in the world there must be duties and rights. If anybody thinks that he has any rights due to him from the lion, he should come to consult me."

'The dog said, "Crawling before the mighty and barking at the weak is a certain means of obtaining one's rights."

'The ape said, "Only fools rely on what is their due. Long arms are a certain right, and long fingers a great convenience."

'The elephant listened with disgust to what the lion, the fox, the dog, and the ape said about rights. For he in his great strength was unassuming and good-natured.'

There is no middle class in the animal State which alone would be able to mediate between the mighty and the weak. For it is no solution, and the world would not be bettered by reversing the animal order and turning the oppressed into the oppressors. If all animals became apes emulating lions, crying 'We all want to rule', there would be nothing but rebellion, war, and general ruin.

'The spirit of our time'—the danger of shaking the foundations of the domestic well-being of the lower classes—is the theme also of fables taking objects of the vegetable kingdom as examples. A fungus springing up on a dung-heap in one night and disappearing in the next is a mere nothing compared to the plants of the earth which take years to grow. Worms gnawing slowly cause greater harm than sudden thunderbolts. In order to cure an evil it has to be attacked at its roots, as is told in the fable of *The little ailing Tree*:

'His father had planted it. It grew up with him; he loved it like a sister and looked after it, as he looked after his rabbits and his lambs.

'But the little tree fell ill; its leaves withered. The child wept as he tore the withered leaves from its branches. One day the little ailing tree bent its top towards the child and said, "The wrong lies at my roots; if you helped there, my leaves would grow again."

'The child dug under the tree and found a nest of mice among its roots.'

Pestalozzi believed that he knew the remedy for the sickness of his time; but he nearly despaired of its ever being applied. He created his fables during a time of profound pessimism while he observed the dangerous consequences of the French Revolution; he drew man in his animal state since it seemed to him that everyone was seeking his own ends. In great concern he wrote *Where is this going to end*? 'A man's ancestor relied on his sword; his grandfather on his fist; his father on his tongue; himself on his quill. What is his son to rely on? There is nothing left for him but the straw of the shipwrecked.'

However, he says, man must not forget that the world is not the same for him as for animals. Human freedom is not like animal freedom—mere feeding without restraint. If man's rights are violated they can be restored by wisdom and love. However various men's opinions may be, the course of the world is always the same, and the laws of nature unchangeable. Even suffering and misfortune have their positive side, as is exemplified in the fable of *The bowed and downtrodden Man*:

'Fields on either side jeered at a downtrodden path. This annoyed a bowed and lonely man who was walking along the path. He said to the fields, "The path has been trodden down for your sakes." "However much you may defend it," replied the fields, "a downtrodden path is dead and barren earth." These words moved the man's heart. A tear fell from his eyes on the dust of the path where he walked. Suddenly a cloud rose from the spot on which the tear had fallen, and the downtrodden path said to the weeping man, "My dust, if watered, dissolves and improves the fields which are ignorant of my sufferings and which jeer at me." This comforted the weeping man. He looked towards heaven and said, "My dust, too, will dissolve and improve fields which are ignorant of my sufferings and which jeer at me." '

II 'MY INQUIRIES'

Since the time of writing the *Evening Hour* Pestalozzi's mind had been occupied with the question 'What is man?', the fundamental question of all his philosophical speculation. He had treated it at different times in different ways, pedagogically or politically, optimistically or pessimistically, according to his varying experiences. In the seventeen-eighties he had asked, 'What is man's natural right and what his natural happiness? Are the advantages of his social state a substitute for the loss of his natural rights?' His answers at that time were still couched in the terms of the *Evening Hour*. Man's happiness is brought about by the satisfaction of his natural needs. Since he has lost his natural rights, they must be replaced by social ones, if his basic needs are to be satisfied. Satisfaction and happiness are the basis of morality. Man can become a contented and therefore a moral being in the social state if it provides for the satisfaction of his needs. The essence of the social state is, however, the imposition of restrictions. If these are voluntarily accepted (as in the social contract) they are the foundation of virtue.

Morality in the social sense is thus seen to be bound up with self-restraint. Or in other words: Man is virtuous only when he is content; he is content only when his individual needs are satisfied; they can be satisfied only when he restricts them. 'Consequently restriction of our desires is the source of virtue.' 'The progress of mankind from the natural to the moral state depends on the cultivated power of self-restraint.' It follows from these arguments that in the 'eighties Pestalozzi regarded the social state with its self-imposed restrictions as a distinct advance upon the state of nature.

In the following years, however, he began to doubt whether the progress which mankind had made in the social state was really so great, and the results of his further inquiries appeared to him 'not at all pleasant'. Partly from personal disappointment, partly because of the changing political situation, he took an increasingly gloomy view of the benefits of society. The first drafts of his work *My Inquiries* are proof of his laborious attempts to come to terms with such conflicting ideas as might and right, individual and society, necessity and freedom. In these fragments the borderline between the natural and the social state becomes fluid; the latter is distinguished from the former only by its function of safeguarding property. Morality appears no longer as based on satisfaction which is voluntarily restricted, but is first thought to be 'the balance of my self-interest and my benevolence', and later 'the preponderance of my benevolence'.

Pestalozzi's next step is the recognition that morality has its origin neither in natural nor in social virtues, but that it springs from free will. In order to avoid a sharp division between the various human states he connects his new conception of free will with his former idea of the 'individual condition', though he raises it above all social implications. In the final stage of his inquiry morality becomes something entirely independent, a third state.

My Inquiries into the Course of Nature in the Development of Mankind (1797) is a highly individual book and extremely difficult to understand. Based as it is on close observation and experience of human nature with its paradoxes, it is full of contradictions. Its value lies therefore not in the rigour of its logic but in the penetration of its insight into the human heart. Although Pestalozzi had worked through a great deal of material in preparation

for it, he yet claims 'not to have any knowledge of the philosophy either of previous or of present days'. 'Man is my only
book; on him and on experience of him my philosophy is based'.
His inquiries can, he says, take no other course than that 'which
nature has taken in my own development'; they can neither
seek nor find anything but 'the truth that lies in myself'. He is
convinced, however, that this individual truth will touch men's
hearts more closely and throw a brighter light on their essential
problems than would mere theorizing, for his own knowledge
has been gained by the observing and the suffering of evil, and
these experiences are the same for all men.

In spite of Pestalozzi's refusal to admit any dependence on the
century's 'enlightenment', correspondences cannot be denied
both with contemporary and earlier philosophers. He freely
uses the terminology of Rousseau's, Locke's, and Hobbes' political philosophies, interspersing it with that of Shaftesbury's
'moral sense' theory. He also introduces certain concepts relating to free will and duty from the Kantian ethics made known
to him by Fichte, while the religious attitude he expresses owes
something to Nicolovius and F. H. Jacobi. Here and there Soc-
ratic and Platonic touches appear, and in some of his views regarding the contradictions in human nature he comes very close
to Pascal. But whatever ideas he may have borrowed from other
thinkers, he uses them in his own way and blends them with his
own conception of the natural order of life.

In this way an edifice of thought has been erected which em-
braces all his earlier conclusions; every stage is based upon the
previous one. Not only is each 'state' dependent on the other;
every single concept is looked at from two sides, from above and
from below as it were. Pestalozzi's way of thinking in concentric
circles has now, so to speak, turned upwards into the third
dimension, like a spiral.

The title of the book is not very appropriate to its content, for
it gives only a slight account of the 'development' of mankind as
compared with, say, contemporary German works like Iselin's
History of the Human Race or Herder's *Ideas on a Philosophy of History*. It is rather a theory of the essential quality of man, based on
an empirical study which strikes the reader as surprisingly modern. The original title was, in fact, to be *My Book on Man*.

The *Inquiries* start from the contradictions which seem to be inherent in human nature, and the question is asked, 'What am I and what is mankind?' (Note the first person singular in which the whole essay is written.) The work is composed in three parts. I. The foundation of my inquiries; II. The essential results of my book; III. My new point of view in agreement with that of the first part. In the beginning of part I Pestalozzi gives a short summary which serves as an exposition of his foundations. 'Man, through the helplessness of his animal state, is driven to develop judgment. His judgment leads him to acquisition; acquisition to property; property to the social state.' These concepts are primarily regarded as having constructive significance, for the original object of man's achievements is the satisfaction of his simplest needs. But very soon they overstep their primitive purpose. Before man can apply his abilities to a positive end, before he has properly cultivated them, he has misused them. The self-concern which had initiated their development has turned into self-interest, and so his selfish nature has corrupted his achievements. Thus, for example, property is no longer the foundation of social security (as Pestalozzi believed at an earlier period when he took a more optimistic view of human nature) but rather a 'Pandora's box from which all the evils of the world come forth'.

As a means of checking this misuse, man has conceived the idea of a social contract. The social state, thus created, has the function of securing him the right to acquire what he, as a physical being, needs for his well-being, and of protecting him from suffering what may disturb his well-being. 'The social state leads him to power and honours, power and honours to subjection and domination.' In the discussion of the term 'power' Pestalozzi's pessimistic view of society becomes evident and it is clear that these inquiries have been caused by his concern about the meaning of wrong-doing and undeserved suffering. For, he says, social rights fulfil no more than natural rights their task of establishing a true state of justice; they only serve to make life in society possible at all. What, in fact, prevails in the social state is not right, but might, domination of the strong over the weak, power of the man in possession over the dispossessed. Power would be permissible if the man who wields it recognized the claims of his fellow-men (as was the case in the patriarchal state). But power in itself is lawless. It corrupts the strong who use it and disappoints the weak who trust in it. From above as from below, then, 'the influence of man's selfish nature' destroys the positive purpose of the social state, which therefore constitutes no real advance upon the natural state. 'Social law is not at all moral law but a mere modification of the animal law.'

The paragraph on 'liberty' which follows deals with the problems that have become urgent through the French Revolution. 'All these conditions [power, honours, subjection, domination] necessitate a state of law. The state of law calls for civil liberty. A lack of civil liberty leads to tyranny and slavery, i.e. to a state in which men live socially together yet without laws to control and improve them.' The state of law is, then, distinguished from a mere social state, civil liberty becoming the substitute for the lost natural liberty. Man, it is argued, has a tendency towards independence. In the freedom of the natural state he makes use of it by exercising his physical power. In the social state there is (or there should be) civil liberty that guarantees his personal independence. Where civil liberty is violated, tyranny reigns. The people deprived of their liberty become slaves. There are two ways, both equally terrible, in which they may react against this: they may either be cowed and degenerate or exert all their physical power and rebel.

And this has happened. The corruption of power has roused the feelings of self-preservation in the people. But in trying to save themselves they, too, have sunk back into barbarism, and in our 'ageing continent' there now reigns sansculottism. In dismal colours Pestalozzi paints 'the picture of man as it is before my eyes' and the picture of the States of Europe disintegrating through their 'animal corruption'. Human feelings are outraged, force displaces law, governments ignore justice. The powerful treat the weak with contempt, the middle classes are reviled, the upholders of truth threatened. Is there, then, no truth and right? How has man become like this, and must he remain like this? Or is there something better in him (here Pestalozzi quotes Goethe's poem 'Man should be noble, helpful, and good') which 'distinguishes him from all other beings whom we know'?

'I follow the course of nature in another direction,' continues the before-mentioned summary, 'and find within me a quality of benevolence which makes use of my social acquisitions, my honours, my possessions, and my power in order to ennoble myself. If this quality is absent the advantages of my social state will debase me.' Having so far considered these concepts from the point of view of self-interest, Pestalozzi now treats them under the heading of 'benevolence'. This, too, he holds to be an original tendency of man's animal nature (just as Shaftesbury includes it among the 'natural affections'); its motive is the desire for a peaceful life. Benevolence is to be found where physical satisfaction can be obtained easily. Where it requires exertion, benevolence soon disappears. (But this, Pestalozzi remarks, is a good thing, for man advances only through the overcoming of difficulties.) Thus, a peaceful life is the aim of social as well as of physical existence, and the art of good government consists in regaining that lost natural peace.

Even love springs from instinctive benevolence; even the most powerful despot prefers to enjoy his spoils without harming the weak. But this is still not real love. Love can be called so only when it is united with fidelity, when it comprises self-denial and recognition of the independence of the other person. Also religion derives from this natural inclination towards peaceful conduct; all mythological conceptions and religious hopes show this longing for peace. But although Pestalozzi traces the origin of religious forms from man's animal nature, he believes that the true essence of religion is 'as divine as the true essence of human nature'. Just as man is endowed with a nobler kind of love so he is capable of making a greater effort in order to let the spirit govern the flesh; he possesses a power 'which attacks my animal nature and raises my hand in an inexplicable struggle against myself'. (Here Pestalozzi has already gone beyond the problems of part I, anticipating the findings of part II; he is so full of his new discovery that he is incapable of tracing it step by step.) Man can use this power in different ways, for doing what he likes or for doing what he ought. In the first case it leads him to injustice and sin, in the latter he tries to act according to his better judgment, thus 'ennobling' himself.

Although it is true, Pestalozzi concludes, that man 'cannot be made human in other than animal ways', it is equally true that he cannot become truly human as long as he remains in his animal state. If he did not conceive of a state of being beyond the grave he would not care very much for truth and for right. His striving for these ideals is proof of a nobler quality, of the 'divine' in him. It is the sign of 'the divine spark in my nature and of my power to try, condemn, and absolve myself'.

The second part is introduced by the important sentence, 'I soon saw that circumstances make man; but I also saw that man makes circumstances; he possesses the ability to direct them according to his will.' The first words repeat the old idea of the importance of the individual condition of life, familiar from *Leonard and Gertrude;* those following express the new 'master-truth' which the *Inquiries* elaborate; both conceptions exist side by side. Pestalozzi now sets forth to disentangle this 'mixture of chance and freedom'. He finds that man has advanced only through his struggle against circumstances, by exertion and labour. On the other hand, man's feeling, thinking, and acting spring from his animal nature. The question is whether he is content to remain in his animal condition, or whether, in spite of the exertion it requires, he wishes to raise himself above the level of instinct in a search for truth and for right. If he does not, he remains an animal being, debased, 'in disorder'. If he seeks for truth and right, he finds them. 'He is free by his will, and by his will he is slave.' The solution of the apparent contradiction in human nature lies in 'the different views of truth and of right of which my nature is capable', i.e. in the different standpoints which man can take towards the demands of life; and Pesta-lozzi now arrives at the 'most essential' point of his book, namely that truth and right (the higher values of life) appear differ-ent to man if he approaches them through his instinct, or through his social aspirations, or in the light of the best and nob-lest part of himself. He can, therefore, perceive an animal truth, a social truth, and a moral truth, and so 'I am within myself a threefold being, an animal, a social, and a moral being.' Hence the question 'What am I?' must be answered from three dif-ferent points of view.

Pestalozzi now considers these three different states of human nature one by one, not as independent conditions, but in their mutual relationship, each as seen from the other two, all as co-existent levels of the personality.

The state of nature in human beings (in the meaning which

Rousseau attributed to it) is the highest degree of animal inno-cence. In it there prevails pure benevolence. But another con-dition is also called the state of nature (e.g. by Hobbes) in which man, already corrupt, follows his selfish desires; this is barbar-ism. Does, then, a state of unspoilt nature exist at all? Pesta-lozzi's answer is that it exists only for a moment, at the birth of a child. The further man grows up, the less can he rely on the soundness of his instinct and the more does the corruption of his nature progress. Yet he retains the idea of his original innocence, and this image of pure benevolence becomes the ideal of per-fection which he is striving to achieve. It is the foundation of the moral state. But it can never be the foundation of the social state. For the fundamental social idea, justice (so Pestalozzi ar-gues) has been evolved from the experience of injustice (social inequality) and is on an altogether different plane from the idea of individual morality. Social virtues do not protect man from the consequences of animal selfishness. In the social state, as in the state of nature, man tends to do wrong so that wrong may not be done to him. If, however, his experience of doing and of suffering wrong is united with his feeling of benevo-lence and with his striving for self-perfection, then he attains the moral state. 'Only in the moral state, through my own free will, am I capable of suffering wrong rather than doing wrong. As an animal being, I become obdurate and corrupt through the suffering of injustice; as a moral being, I become gentle and wise through the knowledge and the experience of injustice.'

The social state comes into being through the imposing of restrictions on the natural state. This controlling activity oper-ates only when it is necessary, i.e. when man has become cor-rupt, when he has lost and forgotten his original innocence and benevolence. In the social state, man acts essentially in the same way as in the corrupt state of nature, the only difference being that he now has to gain the means for his animal satisfaction through labour and exertion. He does this for the most part without regard to his fellow-men. Thus, the social state is a con-tinuation of the war of all against all which begins in the animal state and only alters its form in the social state. This is the reason why lawless power prevails in the world. The justifica-tion of this power rests *de facto* on the domination of the strong over the weak and on the rulers' ascribing to their subjects the same preponderance of 'animal nature' which characterizes themselves.

True social justice, however, is based on the recognition of man's independence as an individual and on the belief in his better self. It can exist only when his animal desires are restrained. This is possible only by 'mutilating' his animal nature. The important point is whether this mutilation is imposed on him by force from without (even wisely, as in the patriarchal state), or effected freely by himself from within.

For even granted that man had been restrained successfully by social means, the question still is whether this has made him a better man. Is social law and order the highest form of his existence? Does he find contentment as a citizen and inner peace through social justice? Even if he attained everything possible in his station and his occupation, even if he were 'a free citizen' in the full meaning of the word, the social state does not make him content, it does not satisfy his higher needs. It has destroyed the innocence of his natural tendencies without having substituted for it other virtues. The gap which it has created demands to be filled. It is here that the moral side of man's nature links up with the social side. If man imposes the necessary restrictions on his animal nature by his own free will in recognition of his moral duty, then a true state of justice will be established. In this case his moral effort revives and unites with his forgotten original benevolence to raise him from the state of corruption to a state of true humanity.

The moral state is something quite unique and in no way the result of any other state; it is entirely the achievement of the individual. 'I possess a power within myself to regard all things of this world independently of my animal desires and of my social circumstances.' This power has its origin in man's discovery that he can become a moral being if he decides 'to make what he ought to do the principle of what he wills to do'. The animal state is devoid of morality, and also the social state can exist without it; people can live socially together, observing law and order without possessing what Pestalozzi calls morality. For, he says, morality 'is not social in its essence'; it is wholly the concern of the individual. 'No man can feel for me "I am", and no one can feel for me "I am a moral being".'

Up to this point Pestalozzi has considered morality as independent, thus coming very near to Kant's conception of the autonomy of the will. But soon the organic aspect of his thinking is evident again. Physical satisfaction, social justice, and finally morality, he says, seem to bear the same relationship to each other as childhood, adolescence, and maturity. (Here a certain development in time from one state towards the other is to be noticed.) Man must work his way through the dreams of his childhood pleasures (under the sway of the senses) and through the subjugation of his apprenticeship years (under the burden of social pressure) to his destiny of being master of his life, to freedom, independence, and the acceptance of moral law. Without his experience of deception and compulsion he would lack the impulse to make the effort of overcoming them and would never reach this mastery. The effects of these states of ignorance and of the absence of rights remain with him all his life, but his conscious recognition of the treachery and corruption which exist in the world contribute to his moral improvement.

There is, in fact, no pure morality possible on earth. Such an idea is contrary to the constitution of man's nature in which the animal, the social, and the moral powers exist not separated from each other but in close inter-relationship. Purity would bring man back to the point from which he started, to innocence and to ignorance of the evils, the vices, and the dangers of the world. It is mid-way between animal innocence and pure morality that living man exists, unable to remain in the one or to rise to the other. Only in the struggles and experiences of this intermediate state can he attain that morality which includes and ennobles his whole nature and his relationships (an almost existentialist conclusion).

Pestalozzi is now in a position to link his new 'master truth' with his old conception of man's condition and near relationships (familiar from the *Evening Hour*). 'My morality is, in fact, nothing but the ways and means by which I apply my pure will to raise myself above the lower states of my existence—or, in plain language, to do right—in measure with the particular degree of my knowledge and the particular state of my circumstances.' That is to say that man as a father or as a son, as a superior or as a dependant, should try to the best of his ability to act not in his own interest but in the interests of those to whom he owes care, protection, gratitude, or obedience. The nearer the moral object is to him as an individual in his particular condition, the stronger is his motive for fulfilling his duty. The more remote tasks and obligations are, and the greater the number of people participating in them, the less powerful, or even negative, are the incentives to perform them.

'The physical presence of moral objects' provides, therefore, the 'sensory inducement' to a moral attitude; its consequence is the union of self-interest with benevolence. But this alone does not make man a moral being; he becomes one only through the exertion of his free will. On the other hand, Pestalozzi argues, a duty imposed merely by reason and principles (the rigorous Kantian command of the moral law) cannot affect him so powerfully as near objects touching his heart. The abstract idea of personal or political obligations does not stimulate his moral activity to the same extent as does the tear of an infant or the need of his country. A policy based on social and political class-distinctions such as rulers and subjects, aristocrats and democrats, instead of on human relationships between individuals or groups of men, makes it increasingly difficult to lead mankind through the social state to their destinies as moral beings.

'The essence of my book', then, consists in the findings that man cannot remain in the simple state of his animal nature; that he has created circumstances which have changed the world into which he was born, so that he has to act in accordance with these changed circumstances as well as with his correspondingly changed self; but that he also has a power within himself to rise above these circumstances if he chooses to use it. Man is, therefore, a threefold being. 'As the work of nature' he is determined by her laws like the ox in the field and the goat on the rock, unable to change a hair on his head even in a thousand years. 'As the work of the world' (of society) he is a drop falling from the top of the Alps into a stream, drifting along the rivers finally to end in the sea of death. But 'as the work of myself' no wave washes man from his rock, and no extent of time extinguishes the trace of his work. These three different states of being are the consequences of the three different perspectives possible for man. As the work of nature he follows his animal inclination. As the work of society he feels bound to do what the social contract obliges him to do. As the work of himself he is independent of selfish desires and of social obligations; he feels free as well as in duty bound to do what, at the same time, has an ennobling effect on himself and a beneficial one on his fellow-men.

The consequences of these findings ('the conclusions of my most fundamental thought') are of immense importance for the true guidance of men. Education and legislation must follow 'the course of nature'. They must recognize man as an animal being and arrange their institutions in accordance with his organic relationships in order to preserve his natural feelings; they must make it possible for him as a social being to live in society unhurt and unharmed; but most of all they must, through strengthening his power of self-determination, educate him to be a moral being, able 'to restore himself from his corruption'.

Part III shows the conformity of these essential principles with the simple statements of part I. In laborious repetitions (which we here try to avoid) Pestalozzi considers the previously mentioned concepts (judgment, acquisition, property, right, power, liberty, etc.) from the three different points of view, 'as works of nature', 'as works of society', 'as the work of myself'. He takes his standpoint, as it were, on a middle plane (where, of course, man has to live) and looks from there upwards and downwards. He finds that if man uses his social achievements 'as works of nature' (i.e. of corrupt nature), his self-interest exceeds his benevolence by far. This is the state of affairs which was before his eyes when he painted the picture of man and the disintegration of the European states in such dismal colours (in part I). If he employs them 'as works of society', he will submit to the social order for the sake of conformity and through pressure from without. But if he uses them as 'the work of myself', i.e. as a moral being, then he will respect law and justice by his own free choice. Then he will use property, right, even power positively; tyranny and rebellion will disappear, and liberty be established.

Although the general trend of the book is clearly towards the 'third state', Pestalozzi does not tarry in the rarefied atmosphere of self-abnegation, knowing as he does that man as a human being cannot achieve pure morality. His repeated use of the phrase 'But in this world . . .' indicates the necessity of applying his 'master-truth' to the exigencies of life as it actually is. This becomes particularly evident in the paragraph entitled 'love'. The power of love, like any other faculty, achievement, or quality, can be exercised in one of three ways, as instinctive affection, from social obligation, or from moral decision. It was, however, Pestalozzi's personal experience which had caused him such great sorrow that neither innocent benevolence nor pure self-denial is an effective attitude in this life. 'Without social power benevolence is a paltry matter to the world, an embarrassment to the man who gives it as well as to those to whom it is directed.' This observation, which is taken up again at the end of the book in a mood of sad resignation, is only one of many examples for the fact that the idealist was obliged to make concessions to the realities of life, and that therefore his book does not head straightforward towards its goal but for ever turns back towards the 'actual conditions'.

Also religion is considered from three points of view. As 'the work of [corrupt] nature' it is error and superstition; as 'the work of society' it is traditional cult and communal worship, the outward form of an inner sentiment. 'True religion ['the work of myself'] is, like morality, entirely the concern of the individual.' It has, like morality, an ennobling influence on man; it is, in fact, 'a matter of morality'. 'Christianity is wholly morality, therefore entirely the concern of individual man.' Consequently states or nations can have no true religion, no Christianity.

The *Inquiries* culminate in the discussion of 'truth and right' whose sole source is found in man's free will. As the product of nature or of society man does not have the will to establish truth and right. These become possible only 'if I as an individual apart from my social relations feel able and destined actually to bring into my nature a feeling for right which is not in me by [physical] nature, but which I believe I can bring into my nature by my own free will'. Through his own moral intention man can raise himself above his animal and his social state and thus help to establish truth and right in the world.

The final conclusion of the book is that man is capable of solving the contradictions inherent in his nature and of mitigating their consequences in society only if he realizes that the demands of his senses impede any improvement, and if he therefore 'gives judgment against them in spite of himself and in spite of his social relations'. Or in other words: 'The establishment of the well-being and of the rights of man is essentially dependent on the subordination of myself as an animal and a social being under myself as a moral being.' This individual and ethical solution is, through its application to all men, also the general and political one; it finds its expression in Pestalozzi's desire 'to retain a sensitivity to truth and right in man in the midst of the corrupt social state and in spite of it, and to restore, as far as possible, his original peacefulness and benevolence'.

It appears then, that the *Inquiries* express more positively than any other book of Pestalozzi the predominance of self-determination over circumstances, the importance of free will, in short, the contemporary idealist way of thinking. This has been explained by the Fichtean influence. Yet this work, like its predecessors, retains Pestalozzi's conception of the natural relationships, and the new idealist philosophy is, as it were, superimposed on his old view of life as organically ordered. It is exactly this attempt to reconcile incompatibles which distinguishes Pestalozzi's philosophy from the systems of Kant and Fichte. For whereas they refuse to allow the natural impulses to play any part in man's moral existence, his ideal is a harmony of the achievement of man's moral effort with the restoration of his original 'animal innocence', a balance of the satisfaction of his physical and the fulfilment of his moral nature.

Thus his work, dealing as it does with the contradictions in human nature is, as mentioned already, not entirely free of contradictions itself; they have their origin in himself. In the years in which Pestalozzi wrote this book he was tossed about between hope and despair. He believed in truth and right, yet he says, 'How rarely are they to be found in the world!' He had faith in man as he could be if he so willed, yet he suffered grave disappointment in man as he actually is. He almost lost his belief in himself, because men did not believe in him. The last words of his book are a kind of obituary on himself, as on someone who died prematurely, like an unripe fruit falling from a tree; but as it fell it whispered 'Even in my death I shall nourish its roots.'

The *Inquiries* are without doubt the most searching of Pestalozzi's writings; they are the philosophical foundation of all his later educational work. He had set out to seek his philosophy of politics, but he found that just social conditions are dependent on the moral attitude of individual man. So he came from politics to ethics, and, since he could not be content with abstract theory, proceeded from ethics to education. The new view of education which he was to develop is distinguished from his previous one by the great emphasis laid on the encouragement of man's self-activity as compared with the improvement of his circumstances. This means that education is to be pursued by developing man's own powers (from within) rather than by the manipulation of the environment (from without), and that national culture is to be brought about by the efforts of men as individuals rather than by the achievements of the group. He worked out those views in laborious studies during the following years and arrived at definite methodological and didactical principles.

Although the *Inquiries* contain the key to his teaching method, the response to his book at the time of its publication was like that to all his doings; his contemporaries did not understand it. Pestalozzi relates how a well-known man genuinely fond of him said to him with Swiss candour, 'Pestalozzi, you now see yourself, don't you, that when you wrote the book you did not quite know what you were driving at.' Only Herder who himself had an intuitive way of thinking gave it a sympathetic review (*Erfurter Gelehrte Anzeigen*, 1797), pointing out minor faults so that the author should avoid similar ones in future, but detecting in the work as a whole 'the birth of the German philosophical genius'. Pestalozzi felt so encouraged by this appreciation that he asked Herder's permission to send him the second part of his *Inquiries* on which he was working, for his advice before publication. For the general criticism that his philosophy was unintelligible made him rethink his fundamental principles. How much of this continuation to the *Inquiries* was ever accomplished cannot now be ascertained; it certainly was not finished.

The few fragments which remain and which have been edited in our time under the title *On Barbarism and Culture* give only a slight idea of what Pestalozzi had intended the whole work to be. Their subject is again the problem of suffering and doing wrong, now extended to the wide field of culture and its corruption. He searches for the 'psychological' reasons for their existence and for the 'psychological' means of their removal. (What exactly Pestalozzi means by the term 'psychological' will be dealt with later in its appropriate context.) The tone is on the whole more optimistic than in the *Inquiries*, and although the starting-point is the same, the results go further in the direction of a more active 'art' of educating man.

The argument is as follows: Human nature has lost its original innocence. Obviously it is destined to lose it, so that it may develop through 'need'. Property and power are 'barbaric' means of development in the social state; they do not fulfil the demands of a true order of justice. Only freedom in a state of justice can create 'culture', and the true means for achieving culture are those which by the exercise of free will (effort) bring about the moral state. Effort is a means to perfecting human nature. It enables man to make the world different from what it would be without it. Its opposite, indolence, is an obstacle to self-perfection and a source of barbarism. A good society rests on the 'individual effort' of all its members.

Now a new line of thought begins. This effort must be 'psychologically organized', otherwise it would have dangerous consequences. Man would either take reward and success (the results of his effort) as his right and become presumptuous, in which case his achievement would lead to obduracy and to 'those evils of social power from which we suffer' (barbarism); or if his achievements fail to receive recognition and even bring misfortune upon his head, they would have an oppressive effect; in this case they would lead to demoralization and finally to rebellion. The means to prevent these social evils consist therefore in the 'art' (a new term, now used frequently) of guiding man's effort towards his moral improvement and towards mitigating men's sufferings, and so to restore the state of benevolence which nature without man's effort no longer provides.

From this point start all the lines of thought which Pestalozzi is to follow in the years to come: his social thinking, concerned with the fight against injustice; his political, discussing the problem of the best form of government and, in particular, of a new constitution for Switzerland; his psychological and educational work dealing with new means for developing the faculties of man. He is to be specially concerned with the last, the 'art' of cultivating human powers in such a way that there should be agreement ('harmony') between their end (the well-being of men) and their origin (human nature).

Another fragment of a work probably written in 1799, which on its recent publication has been given the title *Language as the Foundation of Culture*, forms the bridge between the philosophical *Inquiries* and their continuation on the one hand and, on the other, Pestalozzi's first psychological and didactical essays leading to his 'method'. Its principal statement is: 'Social man is an artificial being,' i.e. no longer as nature has created him; and in his artificial existence he must, through education, be brought to the point where he is able at least to satisfy his fundamental needs as easily and generally as he would have been able to do in the freedom of his natural state. (Pestalozzi's use of the term 'art' in its complex meaning will also be discussed in its proper place, i.e. in the chapter on *How Gertrude teaches her Children*.)

Practical attempts to provide such a type of education, says Pestalozzi, are likely to go wrong in one of two ways: either they do not do enough for the social education of man, in which case his animal inclinations are left too free; or they do too much, in which case he becomes obdurate, and his animal tendencies only change their outward appearance, having been transformed from the state of 'nature' into that of 'art'. The attempt by a new education to improve social well-being must therefore be based on a foundation which avoids both these pitfalls. 'Where should we seek for this foundation but within ourselves and in the better powers of our nature?'

This foundation, the argument goes on, is however only a foundation; and if a building were to be erected on it without, or contrary to, the rules of 'art', it would collapse in the same way as if there had been no foundation at all. The rules of 'art' must, therefore, be designed to help man acquire knowledge and skill, so that he may live content in human society, or in Pestalozzi's own words, 'that he may therein act in accordance with his better judgment and be able truly to effect his own ennoblement.'

The knowledge to which man must be brought consists in his becoming aware of 'the truth of all things'. What is truth? 'What truth is for higher beings we do not know; for man, truth is what he can express in words. Language is the evidence of the ways of perceiving the nature of all things, which man has himself created. It is the artificial reproduction of impressions which nature has made on his mind.' Therefore, teach man how to use language correctly, make him articulate!

In this unexpected conclusion Pestalozzi has arrived at the point from which his 'method' starts. He is to define his new idea of language in *How Gertrude teaches her Children*, while he will treat the sociological questions in his *Epochs* on the basis of the results of his method.

III   THE HELVETIAN REPUBLIC

The first Coalition War ended with the victory of Revolutionary France over the allied powers of Europe. Bonaparte's star was rising; his brilliant successes in Italy were a constant threat to Switzerland. In the spring of 1798 the French, in spite of previous assurances to the contrary, marched into the neighbouring country on their way towards Central Europe, and during the next few years some of the clashes and conflicts of the second Coalition War took place on Swiss soil.

Since the fall of the Bastille the Confederates had watched the danger of revolution approaching their own cantons. After the French invasion the Zurich country-folk took advantage of the threat to the city government by renewing their claims for political rights. What the oppressive rulers had for so long refused to grant out of arrogance and shortsightedness, they were now forced to concede under external pressure; they at last accepted the principle of freedom and equality of all subjects. But the time for limited concessions proved to be too late; France insisted on the total abolition of the aristocratic confederacy and demanded the introduction of a democratic and unitary constitution on the model of the Cisalpine and the Ligurian Republics. In April 1798 'The One and Indivisible Helvetian Republic' was proclaimed.

In the beginning of that year Pestalozzi, while staying again by the lake-side, had tried to persuade the country-folk to show moderation in their demands, and the citizens to make concessions, in order to avoid bloodshed. Because of his close connections with both parties he played an important rôle as political mediator. After the barriers between town and country had fallen he called upon both sides to establish the new order with dignity and good will. The most urgent task now was to put an end to the general insecurity and to form a lawful government. He expressed the hope that the Helvetian patriots would succeed in keeping French influence out of their internal affairs.

Pestalozzi had not wished for the Revolution; but once it had come he meant to be true to its principles because they were those for which he had fought all his life—abolition of social privileges, equality of all citizens, and freedom of trade, with taxation reforms to follow. So he did not regret the collapse of the old Confederacy and looked forward to the building of a more modern State. He accepted the Helvetian Republic unreservedly.

On his return to the Aargau, which was now independent of Berne, he became involved in the public enthusiasm which followed the Revolution. In Brugg a tree of liberty had been erected; the populace danced around it in ecstasy, almost in frenzy, and Pestalozzi received and gave the kiss of brotherhood. But he soon sobered down. He thought of the ideas of the Revolution for which the political upheaval had only prepared the way, and of his own task for which the time had now come. He could not bear to see his country revolutionized without the immediate introduction of measures for the moral and political education of the people. He hastened to Aarau, the seat of the Helvetian government, and 'convinced that the country urgently needs a considerable improvement in education and schools for the lowest sections of the people', he offered his services. This application for a practical position is very different from all his previous ones; it is short, confident, the offer of an experienced citizen addressed to equal compatriots. It was as good as certain what the reply would be. He was accepted.

It was at this moment that a decisive turn for the better took place in Pestalozzi's life; it produced a soaring of his spirits and gave a tremendous impetus to his work. All his previous activities now seemed to have been only a preparation. The political change raised at once both his personal prestige and his professional prospects. For the new policy took a direction which he himself had followed all along, and it lay in the hands of men who were his intimate friends. Amongst the Ministers of State were compatriots of his college years; A. Rengger, the Minister of the Interior, was the son of his neighbour the pastor in Gebens-dorf. The most important of all was P. A. Stapfer of Brugg (1766–1840), previously Professor of Philosophy and Divinity in Berne, now Minister of Education. His ambition was to prove to the world 'that our Revolution is of pure benefit to mankind'; therefore he set out at once to improve the standard of national education. Although he remained in office for only two years he has won fame by the fact that he took Pestalozzi into the service of the State. He thus gave him the chance of putting his ideas of popular education into practice. 'The men of the Helvetian Republic', Pestalozzi wrote later, 'did me more good than any man had ever done; they restored to me my own self.' Thus the Revolution marks the beginning of the practical realization of Pestalozzi's 'great dream'.

The new government had been established; the task now was to bring the new citizens to the understanding and use of their new rights. Partly by order of the Directory, partly of his own accord, Pestalozzi wrote a number of pamphlets in which he asked the people to support the government and the government to consider the people. He addressed his appeals especially to the Roman Catholic population of the central Swiss cantons who opposed the unitary Constitution. In order to win them over for democracy Stapfer suggested the publication of a journal in which the new ideas and the new laws should be explained in plain language. He offered the editorship to the author of *Leonard and Gertrude*. This was Pestalozzi's first official commission, and he was very grateful for it. *The Helvetian Journal for the People* had a certain success in its initial stages, but it appeared for only a few months, and Pestalozzi was its editor for only six weeks.

For he had meanwhile turned his attention to the problem with which the survival of the Helvetian Union was intimately bound up, the question of the tithe. Immediately after the proclamation of the Republic the personal bondage of the feudal peasants (villenage, corvée) had been abolished; a difference of opinion now arose about the handling of their material dues (ground taxes and the tithe). The tithe had originally been a church levy, but after the Reformation it had come into the hands of private landowners and into the purse of the State who used it for the maintenance of schools, hospitals, and poor-houses. It was drawn mainly from the peasants of the country districts, while tradesmen, citizens, and the aristocracy went scot-free. The question now was whether this centuries-old unjust tax should be abolished by waiving or by redemption, and the answer was dependent on another question, how the money for social welfare institutions should be provided.

Pestalozzi advocated abolition by waiving because the burden had far too long been carried by the poorest section of the community. The first principle of a just government, he says in his first pamphlet *On the Tithe*, is equal taxation of all citizens. If every man enjoys the same rights, he will be ready to make the same sacrifices.

As a result, the tithe was indeed abolished unconditionally; but with this action the old sources of State income ceased to flow before new ones had been found, and the government got into extreme financial difficulties. In a second pamphlet on the tithe Pestalozzi therefore came to a most characteristic conclusion. For a new system of taxation he now proposes not 'equal' but 'just' burdens; each citizen ought to be taxed according to his financial capacity; in modern terms, progressively. With regard to the tithe he repeats his previous opinion that the way in which it had been levied during the last centuries was a shameful injustice, and he defends the rights of the feudal peasants. But since the country was in need, and since he had little faith in the generosity of the rich, he appeals to the poor peasants to forgo their legal rights at this moment. For through the Revolution oppressed serfs have been turned into free citizens, capable of free decisions in the interests of all. 'Good, poor, faithful feudal peasants! For hundreds of years you have supported the country by your unjust suffering; support it today voluntarily by your generosity. Citizens! The country is in danger. Save it or let it perish; it is in your hands!'

Pestalozzi's suggestion was, of course, impracticable. In order to solve the financial troubles the feudal dues were re-introduced, with the option, certainly, of redeeming them; but redemption payments over and above other taxes would have been an intolerable burden for the poor peasants. They therefore lost confidence in the new State and ceased to support it. For lack of a satisfactory financial policy the Helvetian Union was unable to survive.

IV STANS

Another of Stapfer's plans designed to promote the enlightenment of the nation was for the foundation of a teachers' training college, the principalship of which he offered to Pestalozzi. He refused however. For him the time had now come to put into actual practice those ideas which had failed to be realized in the Neuhof and had been expressed only on paper in *Leonard and Gertrude*. He wished to tackle educational reform where public education began—in the schools. 'I want to be a schoolmaster', he said. He submitted to the Ministry a memorandum with proposals for an industrial school, similar to that addressed to Count Zinzendorf and to the content of the last part of *Leonard and Gertrude* (second version) but with a democratic bias. On Stapfer's recommendation the Directory agreed to give such a school their financial support. It was to be situated in the Aargau.

While these discussions and arrangements were going on there was news of terrible bloodshed in the canton of Unterwalden. The Roman Catholic population had been incited by their priests to oppose the democratic Constitution and were ruthlessly punished by the French with slaughter and devastation. Hundreds of people were killed, and children lost their parents and their homes. The Swiss government soon took steps to repair the damage which had been done in their name. They used the Pestalozzian plan already approved and decided to open a poor-school in Stans, Unterwalden. In this institution homeless children were to be brought up 'to earn their living themselves by gaining the independence necessary for their moral welfare and in keeping with their dignity as human beings'. Citizen Pestalozzi was given the task of running it. This offer was the first proof that his lifelong attempts to acquire some influence on the education of the poor had at last found the approval of the government. He was overjoyed and delighted to accept. 'I was so anxious to be able to realize the great dream of my life', he wrote, 'that I would have started work in the highest Alps almost without fire and water, if only to have a chance to begin.' A few days after the decision, on December 7th, 1798, he arrived in Stans. It was the beginning of a new life for him.

The difficulties which he encountered were immense. Pestalozzi was fifty-three years old; a short time before he had called himself a tired old man on the brink of death. His wife, like all his friends, was convinced that at his age he was attempting the impossible, and implored him to desist. But he would not listen; he was impatient to prove his worth. 'I am undertaking one of the greatest tasks of our time. If you have a husband who deserves all the contempt and rejection meted out to him, there is no hope for us; but if I have been misjudged and am worth what I myself believe, you will soon have help and support from me. I am no longer what I was in the olden days, and this enterprise is as different from the previous one as my wrinkles are from the smooth face I had of yore.'

The conditions in Unterwalden were anything but inviting. The general opposition against the Directory was stronger and the secret alliance with Austria, the enemy of the Revolution, closer than had been assumed. The officials of the canton as well as those of the Capuchin convent in whose outbuildings the poor-school was to be housed were unfavourably disposed towards the scheme. The population, whose stubbornness obstructed even actions highly beneficial to themselves, remained hostile to Pestalozzi in whom they saw only a protestant and the representative of a hated government. The reconstruction of the buildings was protracted and not even finished by the time of the opening in January 1799. Mortar dust everywhere, bad weather all the time, kitchen, rooms, beds, none of them ready —that was the situation when the first children arrived. The one thing that was not lacking was—money! The government did not spare it. And Pestalozzi brought a heart filled with love and the determination to restore human dignity to the neglected children of Stans.

The children, fifty to begin with but soon increasing to seventy or eighty, were at first incredibly rough and demoralized. In his famous *Letter about my time in Stans* (1799) Pestalozzi gives a vivid description of their appearance then and of their subsequent development. 'Many came with scabies of long standing so that they could hardly walk, many with open sores on their heads, many in rags crawling with vermin, many so thin that one could count all their bones, sallow, stupefied, with fear in their eyes and wrinkles of distrust and anxiety on their brows; some were bold and arrogant, habitual beggars, liars and cheats; others were crushed by their misery, meek but suspicious, frightened and glum. Lazy indolence, lack of practice in the use of faculties and skills were general. Out of ten children hardly one knew the ABC.' But 'trusting in the powers of human nature which God has given even to the poorest and most neglected children', Pestalozzi began his work. He was convinced that great need stimulated the better faculties which, he was sure, lay deep within them, but were stifled by adverse circumstances. He was determined to improve these in order to make their inner powers 'shine in a bright light'.

On this task Pestalozzi entered alone except for a house-keeper, without assistants either for the teaching of the children or for the supervision of their work or for their personal care, and this not because of a lack of funds but of set purpose. For the first thing he was trying to create was an atmosphere of home life in which the children could develop naturally, and in order not to endanger this aim through adverse influences he himself had to be everything to them—father and teacher, master and servant, even mother and sick-nurse. He was of the opinion that the characteristics of a home had to be emulated in institutional upbringing, that 'the spirit of the living-room' was the basis of a good education, and that parental love was the first demand on a good educator. For that reason he refused all 'artificial' means of teaching, making use only of surrounding nature, the daily happenings, and the children's spontaneous activity. He was opposed most of all to mere words, 'those dangerous signs of good and evil'; he preferred to let things speak for themselves and to let circumstances awake the emotions and faculties of the children. There was nobody, he said, who could have helped him on these lines and who would not have considered such a task beneath him.

In spite or because of these difficulties and this lack of help, within a short time a spirit of love pervaded the house. Pestalozzi was with the children day and night; everything happening to them came from him. He shared their joys and their fears, their food and their sleep, their work and their prayers. 'They were not in the world, they were not in Stans, they were with me, and I was with them. I had nothing, I had no house, no friends, no servants, I had only them.' It was the most intimate human relationship, the most perfect fulfilment of his wishes.

The power of his love could not fail to affect even the most insensitive hearts. 'Before the spring sun had melted the snow on our mountains, one would not have recognized my children.' About seventy young beggars formerly so unruly now lived with each other like brothers and sisters, in peace and harmony, with a consideration and affection for one another such as are often wanting in smaller households.

Pestalozzi did not teach the children morals but made them do things; he demanded self-restraint and quiet and laid down certain restrictions necessitated by their large numbers. He did not hesitate to box their ears when they deserved it, nor did they mind being punished; their mutual confidence was such that it could not be shattered by occasional differences. Thus simply, quietly, and lovingly he set in their hearts 'the seeds of a disposition benevolent and responsive to truth and right'.

The children's occupation consisted in working for their own immediate needs, although the programme point of making the house self-supporting was not fulfilled. The main object of their upbringing was to awaken in them the will to work, to encourage in them steadfastness and the desire for an independent and honourable adult life. 'The prospect of not always having to remain miserable, of living one day with acquired knowledge and skill amongst their fellow-men and women, of becoming useful to them and of enjoying their respect'—this prospect brought out in them an inner power which surpassed all expectations.

When the difficulties of the initial period had been overcome, when the house was repaired and winter over, the result of Pestalozzi's devotion seemed astonishing. The pastor and the first administrative officer of Stans unanimously reported to the Directory: 'All is well in the Poor-School. Father Pestalozzi is up to the neck in work day and night.' 'One would hardly believe one's eyes and ears how much he has achieved in so short a time.' Pestalozzi himself felt freed from the depression that had weighed him down for many years; he was blissfully happy and extremely thankful to have found the fulfilment of his 'dream' and salvation for himself. 'Everything is going well', he writes to the Countess of Hallwil with whom his wife was staying; 'I am wiping out the disgrace of my life; the virtue of my youth is being restored.' For years, he continues, he had lived like a man sunk shoulder-deep in the mire, unable to move although wishing to go on an urgent journey; he would have liked 'to spit in every man's face'. But this was now past; his life was again like the life of every other man, and he was glad to be reconciled with fate and mankind. 'All my vitality is now concentrated in a small circle which in all its aspects is bliss to me.' He lived 'as in a fairyland'. Until his dying day he counted the few, laborious, exhausting weeks in Stans amongst the happiest days of his life.

However, the daily routine did not always remain on the heights of human happiness. On the contrary, if considerable results were achieved, they did not lie on the surface, whereas grave defects were obvious. It could not be otherwise. The task which Pestalozzi had undertaken was bound to overtax the powers of one man singlehanded. Later he himself could hardly understand how he had done it. The sad thing was that it was not the essentials of education but trivial, incidental matters which consumed his strength. A missing hearth plate endangered the moral aim of his work! And he was always having to cope with the opposition of parents and guardians; like those of the Neuhof days they believed they were doing Pestalozzi a favour by leaving their children with him. 'Many of them asked the Capuchins and other people whether I could not find anything else to do that I was so keen on keeping their children.' They made the children home-sick so that they ran away. Others arrived in their stead; it soon was 'like a dovecote'. Many came only to get clean clothes. Yet on the whole the children showed more sense than the parents and were ashamed of their bad behaviour.

It was hardly surprising, then, that Pestalozzi had no time for keeping detailed accounts. Therefore even well-meaning observers began to have misgivings about the lack of organization, the absence of a definite plan, and Pestalozzi's obsessive insistence on doing everything himself. The school was, after all, a public institution, and the honour of the government was at stake.

The lack of a definite plan in his teaching was by no means due to carelessness but to Pestalozzi's considered intention. He had originally planned to combine schooling with manufacture in order to make the institution self-supporting; but this could not be done. It did not worry him. He now looked upon the enterprise as the first experiment in a new kind of education for the poor; he learned with the children and through them. He taught them the rudiments of reading and writing in quite a new way, which took as its point of departure their faculties and their circumstances. He was more concerned with the developing of their inner powers than with obtaining spectacular results in learning regarded as 'mere words'; so he attempted 'to make training in attentiveness, in carefulness, and of a reliable memory precede that of the artificial powers of reasoning and of judgment'. In the same way he looked on industrial work 'more from the point of view of training the physical abilities for working and earning than from that of gaining an immediate profit'. His method was not to follow any established doctrine but to make use of the existing circumstances; not to put fixed notions into the heads of the children but to awaken their latent faculties. He later called this procedure 'the result of a simple psychological idea which I conceived intuitively'. This 'simple psychological idea' led to a revolutionary attitude in the field of education; it turned the traditional method of teaching upside down. The pre-Pestalozzian way started from the object; Pestalozzi started from the child—he humanized education.

At that time Pestalozzi was not yet aware of the importance of his views; and much less did his superiors realize what was happening in the poor-school of Stans. The local officials were uneasy about the obvious lack of order; the State ministers who would have been more understanding had more urgent worries. And so any pretext sufficed to bring the experiment to an abrupt end. The second Coalition War had gone in favour of the old powers; the passive resistance of the people of Unterwalden turned into active threats. The Helvetian government had to be careful. When in the beginning of June Austrian troops approached from one side and French troops from the other, the local Commissar requisitioned the school building for hospital purposes, partly from panic, partly from a desire to seize this opportunity for getting rid of a nuisance. (The house was never used for the specified purpose.) Children with relatives were sent back to them; those who could not find homes remained with the Capuchins. Pestalozzi left Stans the very next day (9th June 1799). He had kept his poor-school for five months.

Only one who has understood the extreme happiness of these 'blessed days' can imagine the great sorrow which Pestalozzi felt at his departure from Stans. He was, he said, like a shipwrecked man who had at last seen land and was once again thrown back into the fathomless sea. The old story of his inefficiency was brought up again. The general opinion was that 'it is foolish to think that because a man had written something sensible in his thirties, he is capable of doing something sensible in his fifties'. Exhausted to the point of numbness and with shattered nerves he would stagger in the streets as if out of his mind, looking so ill that strangers were distressed at the sight of him. He spat up blood, and his life was in danger.

Friends took him to Gurnigel near Berne, at an altitude of some 4,000 feet, to give him a rest and a chance to recuperate. It was the first time in his life that he had been in the heights of the Alps. He looked down upon the beauty of his country, 'the majesty of her mountains, the silver gleam of her lakes round which are sprinkled homesteads and villages, the splendour of her woods, the riches of her meadows, the green banks of her rivers'. All this was spread before his eyes and yet was lost upon him in his constant thought of the misery of the poor, the undeserved suffering of mankind. He remembered times past when foreigners came to Switzerland in order to seek out men like Bodmer and Breitinger; he knew that in his own days they came only in search of mountains, valleys, and waters. He felt how low the country had sunk and how urgently she required to be restored to her old glory. Although he was distressed about her present state he was yet confident of the latent powers of her people, and this conviction comforted his heart. 'I shall not cease to my dying day to bring to light as far as I can that which lies hidden in their hearts.' 'With the same old will and the same old purpose' he came down from Gurnigel, seeking nothing but to take up his work where he had left it, 'in any corner whatsoever'.

'After this test', he said to friends in Berne, 'I don't despair of anything.' He had gained decisive experience which ought not to be lost to the world. The time in Stans had thus seen the dawning of his practical activity as well as of the particular qualities of his teaching method. It confined his general idea within a particular purpose; as he puts it himself, it 'curbed his unbridled intentions'. If it had been the desire of his youth to be a politician, it was the decision of his mature years to restrict the sphere of his work to the education of children, to start at the bottom of the ladder and to approach his goal step by step. It was to be the experience of his old age that he would never reach the goal, that even in the limited field of education he would remain in the first stages, that he would only be able to point the way which others would have to travel.

There was another benefit which the time in Stans conferred on him. The living among young people restored his confidence in men and in himself. He regained his belief in the divine spark in human nature—'the virtue of my youth'—never to lose it again. It was the love of children that re-created his real self.

V The Methodologist
(1800–1805)

T HIS time it did not take long to find a place where Pestalozzi
could continue his experiments, for he was willing to put up
with the meanest hedge-school. Again it was Stapfer who
arranged for him to be allowed to teach in Burgdorf. Stapfer's
secretary J. R. Fischer had already been sent to that town some
time earlier in order to organize the teachers' training college
whose principalship Pestalozzi had refused. The combined
efforts of the two men were to start the Helvetian Republic's
programme for educating the nation.

The small town of Burgdorf in the valley of the river Emme
lies picturesquely on the slopes of a hill crowned by an ancient
castle. Pestalozzi himself had no connections there but he was
introduced by Stapfer to influential citizens who proved to be
very helpful. Besides, the seat of government was now not far
away in Berne, and its members gave him valuable support.

At the end of July 1799 Pestalozzi started work in the poorest
school in Burgdorf provided for children whose parents were
not full citizens. He was to assist the schoolmaster in teaching
seventy-three boys and girls. The conditions he found there
were typical of popular education everywhere at that time.
The schoolmaster was a cobbler. Most teachers in elementary
schools were employed in some sedentary craft; they had to
earn their living by the skill of their hands because their only
fees were the few pence and contributions in kind which the
children paid irregularly. They were often rough or pitiable
creatures, uneducated and little respected; no intelligent

citizen's or farmer's son would have dreamt of becoming a schoolmaster, unless for idealistic reasons. Many of them could not spell properly themselves. They kept school in their own houses while cobbling or sewing; wife and children, sometimes also neighbours and friends, not to speak of domestic animals, would often be present. The teaching consisted in making one round of the room in the morning and one in the afternoon to hear the children individually; for each child learnt his own lesson set by his parents: spelling and a little reading; writing and arithmetic only in exceptional cases. The main object of learning was to know by heart the catechism and parts of the Testament and the Psalter. The children repeated aloud to themselves so that a terrific din was created. When at times it seemed to die down, the schoolmaster would shout, 'Boys and girls, why are you not learning your lessons?' Also it was taken for granted that the children should attend school only when there was no more urgent work to be done at home or in the fields.

Pestalozzi made his children keep quiet and taught them all together; he addressed his questions to all of them and made them answer in rhythm. He made them spell out words orally before they were shown them in print. He would begin with the shortest words with only one consonant and one vowel, then go on to words of three or more letters. Similarly in writing and arithmetic he would spend a long time on the simplest combinations of letters and numbers before advancing to the next stage. Most important of all, he refused to let them learn anything by heart which they did not thoroughly understand. In this way he would talk to them from morning till evening without wearying.

His colleague regarded these strange ways with distrust, for Pestalozzi's results were very different from his. Soon the rumour spread in the town that the catechism was in danger. The parents met together and decided that they did not care to have the new method practised on their children; the citizens should try it out on their own.

Thereupon Pestalozzi's friends managed to get him into a small dame-school. Here, as Pestalozzi himself describes, there was an atmosphere of pedantry and the pretence of responsibility, but he bore this 'yoke' for fear of being thrown out again. From morning till night he 'crowed' his ABC to a comparatively small number of citizens' children, for he was anxious to continue the experiments broken off in Stans, experiments in 'psychologizing' education. From his birth, he argued, a child learns through sense impressions; nature teaches him. In the same way the teaching given by man should be 'nothing else but the art of assisting nature's game for achieving her own development'. The course of instruction as well as the material objects which are to be its instruments should correspond with the developmental order of the child's faculties. At every stage the child should not be denied anything already within his capabilities, nor be burdened and confused by anything outside his present mental scope; teaching should thus be 'psychological'. And, most important of all, knowledge should first be acquired through sense impressions; only afterwards may it be expressed in words.

When Pestalozzi had taught according to these principles for eight months in the lowest town school, a public examination was held before the Burgdorf school board. Their report was very favourable and showed great understanding. It points not only to the remarkable progress of the children of this school but also to the suitability of the new teaching method for the simplest domestic conditions; it gives public recognition to Pestalozzi for 'having already bestowed lasting benefits on the youth and the educational institutions of the country'. This recommendation led to Pestalozzi's promotion to the Second Boys' School where he became the only teacher of about sixty children between the ages of eight and twelve.

It might seem that Pestalozzi had turned within a few months from his life's purpose of educating the poor to an interest in evolving a new elementary teaching method. Yet even when he began to teach in Burgdorf he did not give up hope of starting in the Neuhof the industrial school originally conceived. He would have liked at that time to add to his property the neighbouring estate and castle of Brunegg which was up for auction, but he had not the means. The longing to set up a poor-school remained with him all his life. Sometimes this yearning was submerged by the urgent tasks of the moment, but it always revived until at last it found fulfilment. The following years are devoted to finding a way of educating children which could be used even in the poorest industrial school. It must be clearly emphasized here that Pestalozzi looked upon the work in middle-class institutions on which he now embarked, and the public approval he won there, only as a means to an end. For the new teaching method which gained success after success and made him known all over Europe was not in itself the work which was his life's aspiration. At the height of his fame he was furthest from his goal, just as in his humblest days in Stans he had come nearest to reaching it.

When Pestalozzi had arrived in Burgdorf he had been given rooms in the ancient castle on the hill. J. R. Fischer (1772–1800) also stayed there; he was Government Inspector of the Burgdorf schools and in this respect Pestalozzi's superior, although in age he could have been his son. Fischer also thought it his duty to further popular education; he, too, was a philanthropist. On his initiative a number of poor children were evacuated from the war-devastated canton of Appenzell in eastern Switzerland and taken into well-to-do Burgdorf families. A young man called Krüsi who accompanied them was to be trained as a teacher in the future college. He was the third man to find lodging in the castle.

Fischer observed Pestalozzi's new method with interest; his is the first account of it in existence. (Pestalozzi later inserted it in his own work *How Gertrude teaches her Children*.) Pestalozzi admired Fischer likewise; but since Fischer had his own ideas, Pestalozzi found himself rather hindered than helped by his presence. It is therefore not likely that the fruitful collaboration which the government expected of these two men would have resulted from their living together. Before this could be put to the test, however, Fischer left Burgdorf for unknown reasons without having established his *Ecole normale*, and shortly afterwards died from typhus. Pestalozzi took over the responsibility for the education of the Appenzell children and acquired in their tutor his first assistant.

He now applied for the use of the whole castle, previously allocated to Fischer's scheme. With the granting of this he gained at last freedom of action within a school of his own. Some boys of the Second Town School, others from Burgdorf whose parents were interested in Pestalozzi's experiments, along with the Appenzell children formed the nucleus of the new institution.

The Helvetian Government let Pestalozzi have Burgdorf castle rent-free, with wood for heating purposes and gardening land; they also paid him a salary and were willing to support his assistants. They subsidized the publication of school books which he produced in the following years and protected them against piracy at a time without copyright. Because of these advantages, his plan to open a poor-school in the Neuhof was dropped for the time being.

Things now seemed to be going well. With the help of Stapfer, though not of the government, a 'Society of the Friends of Education' was founded in support of Pestalozzi's enterprise. To make his ideas known to its members Pestalozzi wrote a short report called *The Method* (1800) which begins with the words, 'I seek to psychologize human education.' At the same time he worked on a more elaborate account of his method, later to become famous under the title *How Gertrude teaches her Children*. He published elementary school books and tables of words and figures which had been drawn up to illustrate his theories. He devoted his nights to these writings and to an increasing correspondence, while his days were given up to teaching ever-growing numbers and to devising and trying out new ways of instruction. His task absorbed him completely; he was at once exhilarated and exhausted. A year after his severe illness his chest was again affected and his life again endangered.

It was indeed very fortunate that Krüsi was able to come to the rescue. Up to that time Pestalozzi had obstinately refused to accept any help whatsoever; now he was sure enough of his method to be willing to train an assistant. He could not have wished for a better one. Hermann Krüsi (1775–1844) was intelligent but unassuming, willing to learn, and warm-hearted. He was young but had experience of life; as a message boy and farm labourer he had come to know his country and its people, but he had also become aware of his lack of education. In order to learn more, he had taken the post of schoolmaster in his native village at the age of eighteen, and when the opportunity arose to receive training as a teacher he came to Burgdorf with the Appenzell children. After Fischer's death he found in Pestalozzi what he had sought. He became his disciple and was for almost two decades his most faithful assistant. He kept

Pestalozzi's writings in order and helped him to work out the school books. He remained modest and quiet, was loved by the children, and because of his tact and understanding was later chosen to teach the girls.

Shortly after Krüsi had joined Pestalozzi he arranged for his friends Tobler and Buss from Basle to come and help in the new venture. J. G. Tobler (1769–1843), also from Appenzell, had had almost no education as a boy, but had saved enough money as a manufacturing hand to begin a divinity course in Basle. He continued this study while being tutor in a private house. After having taught for several years with the help of the best-known educational manuals of the day, he still felt he was not accomplishing enough; so when he received the invitation to join Pestalozzi, of whom he had already heard, he accepted at once. He stayed with him for several years. His special interest was in child psychology.

The account which J. Ch. Buss (1776–1855) gives of his youth has been incorporated by Pestalozzi in *How Gertrude*. He was the brilliant son of a servitor in the Tübingen Foundation (the famous theological college), had gone through grammar school with distinction and mixed with the students as an equal. There was no doubt in his mind that he would go up to the Academy of Arts and Sciences where Schiller had been a student a few years earlier. But just at that time a new regulation excluded young men of the lower classes, and this frustration of his cherished hopes made Buss discontented and rebellious. Reluctantly he took up the book-binding trade, and in his wanderings he came to Basle. A sentence from Pestalozzi's writings which he chanced to read touched his heart: that it was the object of his method 'to enable man to help himself, since nobody else will and can help him'. He went to Burgdorf, taught art and mathematics, and regained the youthful high spirits which he had temporarily lost.

'So our team', recalls Krüsi in the memoirs of his life, 'consisted of four queerly assorted members: a novel writer, a divinity student, a book-binder, and a village schoolmaster, each in his way inadequate and unprepared, yet with warm heart and good will. Whoever saw the four at that time, . . . could not be blamed for expecting little from their activities and the results thereof. Yet we succeeded. Beyond the expectation of all who knew us and far beyond our own, the institution won confidence and respect.'

In the autumn of 1800 an educational institute was formally opened in Burgdorf castle for children of parents able to pay a definite though modest school fee. The intention was to combine with it a teachers' training course of approximately three months. A school for poor children was to be run separately. The 'Society of the Friends of Education' opened a subscription in its aid, but the contributions were disappointing. So without much worry or hesitation Pestalozzi admitted non-paying children to the main institute. It was to be a long time yet before his beloved poor-school came into being; nor could a properly organized teachers' training college be established. But the school for middle-class children flourished. The sons of Burgdorf citizens came as day boys, and those of government officials from Berne lived in as boarders. Before long there was not enough room to accommodate them all; the old castle buildings had to be converted into more suitable dormitories and class-rooms. Within a few months the household consisted of ninety people and soon passed the hundred mark; of roughly seventy pupils—boys only, between five and ten years of age—twelve were poor. The original three assistants were joined by others. Visitors who had come to observe the method stayed on and took part in the teaching. Women helpers looked after the domestic requirements and the physical needs of the children. Thanks to their devotion and efficiency the house was clean and tidy, the food sustaining though plain, and the children fit and well.

From the time of getting up at half-past five in the morning till going to bed at nine o'clock in the evening, the boys were kept constantly busy, for it was Pestalozzi's conviction that occupation prevented the forming of bad habits. Their day began with prayers, separate for the two denominations, and included more than eight hours of instruction in four periods, interrupted only by a short break before meals and a half-hour's play time after them. (No more mention is made of domestic work; there were now servants.) Yet the children showed no signs of fatigue; on the contrary they enjoyed their lessons, for these did not consist of a mass of incomprehensible matter to be learned mechanically but were designed to satisfy their natural urge for mental activity.

The aim of the teaching was to develop the children's own powers and faculties rather than to impart facts; to show not so much what as how to learn. The important thing was not the end result but the process of learning; therefore the teaching in Burgdorf modestly claimed to attempt nothing but 'to lay the foundation to elementary knowledge' (roughly to be described as the three R's). This was done in an entirely novel way. Spelling and reading were practised with the help of movable letters which could be put together and taken apart as often and as variably as required. For the learning of sums and of fractions pebbles and beans were used, or apples and cakes would actually or in the imagination be cut into pieces. Only after the arithmetical processes were thoroughly understood with the help of visual and tactual aids, did dots and finally figures come into use. Similarly, writing began with the drawing of rising and falling strokes and of open and closed curves. The children were thus enabled to draw without instruments straight lines and faultless circles, and to develop a good hand and an accurate eye. The most startling innovation was the use of slates and slate pencils instead of paper and pens; these permitted repeated corrections and improvement of the scripts to the point of perfection. For all these lessons the children were divided into groups according to ability and not to age. The quick pace of their progress and the soundness of their knowledge compared to the attainments of traditional teaching methods were described as astonishing.

Oral work was given to the whole group together, and any child knowing the answer called it out, so that a lively but friendly competition of voices filled the room. The urge of the young for physical exercise was met in their gymnastics and singing lessons. The boys marched, played, or sang in a big hall or in the courtyard; in summer they bathed in the river. At least two teachers were constantly with them to share their meals and their games. In this way they won their love and their confidence and found little need to give punishments. All visitors remarked on the happy relationship between teachers and pupils and the ease and cheerfulness of the children.

Pestalozzi himself was no longer engaged in teaching; he

lacked the patience required for carrying out in detail the work of his genius, once established. Perhaps it was one of the reasons for the success of this institute that he left the daily routine in the hands of his less brilliant but more practical assistants. His main concern was to work out the principles of the new teaching method and to guide the large community on the model of a family. He looked upon all its members as his children, and they all called him 'Father'. He was the centre of the house, its heart and soul. In order to keep in close touch with them all, he always conducted evening prayers himself. This was the one daily occasion on which the whole community came together. There he would speak of the day's happenings, basing general observations on small incidents. He would make the children take part, discussing with them their mistakes and encouraging their good intentions. If the foundations of knowledge were laid during the day, he planted the seeds of love in the evening. The unforgettable impressions received in these gatherings have been recorded by many teachers and pupils.

When the institute had been in existence for about eighteen months Pestalozzi invited the Notability of Berne to hold an inspection. They sent two distinguished experts to observe the teaching on several occasions, and some weeks later published a report in the name of one of them, J. S. Ith, president of the council for education. It gives a highly favourable account of the work being done in Burgdorf. It points out the striking difference between the deadly boredom in ordinary infant schools and the lively activity in the Pestalozzian institute and suggests as its reason Pestalozzi's principle of using and developing the children's own faculties. 'Everything the child learns is acquired by his own observation, by his own experience.' It calls this way of teaching 'essentially new and therefore a real discovery' and considers it a duty 'to commend this method because of its intrinsic excellence, to further it, and to desire its general use as one of the most important benefits to mankind, especially to their more numerous and more neglected sections'. It expresses the hope that the Helvetian Government will give this institute their special protection.

The immediate consequence of this recommendation was the government's promise of continuing financial aid. The Pestalozzian method was made, so to speak, the official way of instruction; a fixed number of young men were to be trained in it at the nation's expense. Various cantons were asked to send selected candidates to Burgdorf, but they did not readily do so, partly because of the opposition of other educationists, partly because of their own varying school policies. (The centralized Helvetian Government had meanwhile been defeated.) So once more the proposed teachers' training course did not materialize. If nevertheless many young men were trained in the Pestalozzian method it was in a more casual way, not under a formal organization. The most gifted pupils grew up to be teachers, and interested people came from outside, took part in the life of the institute, and on going home introduced 'the method' in their part of the world.

Ith's report made a particularly great impression abroad. It was reviewed in leading German periodicals, and the general opinion was that it gave a clearer idea of Pestalozzi's method than his own work *How Gertrude* published at the same time. It was this report more than anything else that made Pestalozzi's name known all over Europe.

All his life Pestalozzi suffered from a persistent feeling of guilt towards his family for having neglected his first duties as a husband and as a father. None the less he would never have contemplated leaving off his experiments for his family's sake. On the contrary, he repeatedly appealed to his wife to give up her 'constant doubts' and to be confident of an improvement in their circumstances. 'Don't lose hope, or rather try to gain more every day', he wrote. 'Considering the extent of my undertaking, it is not possible that it should succeed quickly, but succeed it will and must; everybody is convinced of that.' Just at the time when the difficulties in Burgdorf seemed to have been overcome, Pestalozzi's only son died in the Neuhof (1801). During his last years his epileptic fits, followed by paralysis and amnesia, had so reduced his vitality that there could be nothing left for him but a wretched existence or a merciful death. At the age of thirty-one poor Jacques was released from his sufferings. The unhappy parents came from Hallwil and Burgdorf to meet at the graveside; they had long since buried their hopes for their son's recovery.

When she was freed from her burden, Pestalozzi's daughter-in-law went with him to Burgdorf to take over the housekeeping in the institute, which she managed cheerfully and courageously in the face of considerable difficulties. Like 'a good angel' she cared for all in sickness and in health because she had, as Pestalozzi says of her, 'an unequalled mother's heart and was, where love, loyalty, care, kindliness, devotion, and sense of duty were concerned, specially made for looking after children'. She remained with him until she entered into a second marriage with the much respected, well-to-do Laurenz Custer which brought her the happiness she had lacked during the difficult years with Jacques Pestalozzi.

In thinking of his wife Pestalozzi was obsessed by the fear of losing her or of dying himself before having repaid all her sacrifices and given her the peace she deserved at the end of her life. The older he grew the more he longed for her presence; and when the worst of the builders' work was over he invited her to stay with him at Burgdorf. 'Now as never before I would give all the world's honours for a quiet room all four walls of which are paid for, and where I can see you all together, laughing. When I behold this I shall cry, "It is finished".' It was a happy day when after many years of involuntary separation Anna Pestalozzi, with Gottlieb her grandson and Lisabeth the faithful servant, moved into Burgdorf castle (November 1802).

Frau Pestalozzi was at that time in her middle sixties and ailing, but still of impressive appearance. Traces of her former beauty shone through the expression of suffering on her face. Although she did not take an active part in the daily work of the institute, her presence had a beneficial and steadying effect. Her social graces soon made her quarters the favourite meeting-place of the house. Friends and visitors were received there, and Pestalozzi found at her fireside the longed-for peace after the turmoil of the day. She in her turn had grown wise with age; with gentle patience she knew how to calm his passionate outbursts, and she bore his eccentricities 'with more than ordinary generosity'. It was a great satisfaction to her to see his immense efforts rewarded at last. So all the sacrifices had not been in vain! She was thankful that her own sorrowful life had been blessed in the end. When she was taken seriously ill, she was ready to die. But when contrary to expectation she re-covered, circumstances in Burgdorf had so changed that she had to leave her husband once more. The old couple did not then realize that it was to be several years before they could live together again.

The assistants who gathered around Pestalozzi were dear to his heart as if they were his own sons. He now sought helpers as eagerly as he had formerly refused to have any. The realization of his own shortcomings and his constant fear of dying before his work was done gave him no peace; he longed to ensure that it would go on after his death. His gratitude for their help was excessive. 'I am what I am through you, and what my work will be will be through you', he said. While it must be acknowledged that the working out in detail and the application of his method was done, and could only be done, with the help of his assistants, it must also be said that they contributed little to the essential principles; and when their suggestions went beyond the limits of their particular fields they were apt to obscure Pestalozzi's original intentions, as will be seen later.

The young men were deeply attached to and influenced by Pestalozzi. Inspired by his example, they were ready for any sacrifice in his cause which had become their own. Their work in the institute was hard and by no means remunerative. The living together of such diverse characters in such close quarters led to frequent difficulties. But Pestalozzi's fine mind and loving heart created such a generous atmosphere that most of them stayed with him for years, and when they left they spread abroad his spirit.

The most important assistant was Johannes Niederer (1779–1843), born like Krüsi in a poor home in Appenzell. A young man with bright blue eyes, red hair, and a high, stubborn brow, he was very intelligent, ambitious, and headstrong, and well trained in philosophy and divinity. He had given up a good church living to take charge of a neglected village in order to make it 'a place of wisdom and virtue'. When he came to know Pestalozzi, he found him 'perhaps the most noteworthy complement to Rousseau'; his growing fame attracted him irresistibly. From 1800 he wrote him enthusiastic letters, and for several years Pestalozzi pleaded with Niederer to join him. At last he gave up his parsonage (Pestalozzi helped him in the settling of financial obligations) to become Protestant minister and teacher of scripture in the Burgdorf institute. He came equipped with all the weapons of Fichte's and Schelling's philosophies which he immediately brought into action in a campaign of propaganda and apologetics for the Pestalozzian method.

A very different character was Johannes von Muralt (1780–1850), frank, cheerful, and disinterested. He came of an old Zurich family, was well mannered, cultured, and widely travelled. In Paris he moved in the same circles as the brothers Schlegel and Mme de Staël. The latter asked him to be tutor to her sons in her house at Coppet. At the same time he met Pestalozzi who invited him to become a master in Burgdorf. He decided in favour of Pestalozzi and was for many years his loyal assistant, a good friend to his colleagues, and a much loved teacher to the children.

There were assistants whose names are no longer of interest. Others grew up from among the pupils, e.g. Johannes Ramsauer, the most gifted of the Appenzell evacuees, and later Joseph Schmid (1787–1850) from Vorarlberg in Austria. Soon after the opening of the institute Schmid, then a fifteen-years-old rough peasant lad, had walked in, full of the natural unspoilt vigour which Pestalozzi so admired. He had a strong will, an inflexible spirit, and a great mathematical gift which quickly brought him to the top rank of assistants. He was remarkably successful as a teacher of mathematics, and his ambition was to give the Pestalozzian method a mathematical foundation. Pestalozzi was extremely proud of this prodigy and completely lost his heart to Schmid.

Besides the regular teachers there were a number of student-teachers sent by their governments, and visitors arrived on their own initiative to study the method. For in the meantime Pestalozzi's institute had become known very extensively through the publication of Ith's report, the reviews of *How Gertrude*, and the circulation of his exercise books. His educational discovery was discussed in widely read periodicals by writers such as Wieland, Herbart, and Friedrich Schlegel; they considered it to be among the most important innovations of the new century. Pestalozzi himself approached, publicly and privately, influential people in Switzerland and abroad, asking their support for his enterprise by means of subscription to his exercise books. The consequence of this publicity was a stream of visitors from all the four corners of Europe, in greater numbers and of greater significance than those to the Neuhof many years before, after the appearance of *Leonard and Gertrude*.

'Thousands' came, according to report; old folk and young, experts and laymen, males and females. There was hardly a day when the castle was not full of strangers 'from every imaginable country', for Pestalozzi's method had been heard of 'from Petersburg to Naples'. Some visitors looked upon it as sensational; others stayed weeks or even months to study it seriously. Some acclaimed it enthusiastically, others were sceptical; others again made a point of examining it without prejudice. There exist many reports by these observers giving detailed descriptions of what they saw. The opinions expressed differ in content and value, but all are agreed in admiration for a work dedicated to humanity. The writings of these visitors introduced the Pestalozzian method far and wide.

A few examples can be given. In Frankfurt, then a free imperial city, a considerable number of educated families became interested in the new way of teaching, and a local centre was set up in the form of an experimental school with which Friedrich Fröbel was soon to be connected. In North Germany the free city of Bremen was among the first to introduce the Pestalozzian method. Prussia was at that time planning to improve elementary education and teachers' training in the provinces newly annexed in the partition of Poland, and sent an educationist to Pestalozzi to investigate the suitability of his method for their purpose. At the same time a private schoolmaster from Prussia, J. E. Plamann, came to Burgdorf and on his return to Berlin opened an institute on Pestalozzian lines in which Otto von Bismarck received his elementary schooling. The first government which officially sent students to Burgdorf to be trained as teachers was the Danish. After a stay of several months two young Danes started an experimental school in Copenhagen; but it did not survive more than a few years.

So Pestalozzi had become the head of a famous modern school! It would have been ungrateful not to be pleased by this achievement which was in such marked contrast to his previous experience. The great number of free places in the institute involved constant financial worries, it is true, and these were increased after the fall of the Helvetian Government; but the success of the method seemed to have been established firmly enough to withstand all political disturbances. Pestalozzi rejoiced especially in the family spirit of the community whose 'father' he was. He felt that such a happy situation could hardly be surpassed. In this respect, the time in Burgdorf was certainly his most successful. Only much later, under the impact of bitter disappointments, does he blame himself for having during those years 'paid homage to the world's honours' and betrayed his true self, instead of pursuing his goal and serving the poor.

11 'HOW GERTRUDE TEACHES HER CHILDREN'

The opinion held on a book by contemporary readers is often very different from the judgment passed on it by posterity. While Pestalozzi's *Inquiries* remained almost unknown from the time of their publication to the end of the nineteenth century but have been increasingly appreciated ever since, the opposite is true of *How Gertrude teaches her Children* (1801). The fame enjoyed by Pestalozzi in his lifetime was founded on it. For it proclaimed something entirely new in the field of popular education, the principle of self-activity in acquiring and using knowledge in its first stages. It was a further development of the 'master-truth' stressed in the *Inquiries* that every decision of the will is 'the work of myself'. If this was Pestalozzi's postulate for the realm of morals, he now made a similar assertion for the field of the intellect. 'Everything I am, everything I will, and everything I ought to do has its origin within myself. Should not, then, my knowledge also have its origin within myself?' The application of this conception to learning and teaching brought about a Copernican revolution in the method of school instruction.

Yet although his findings have been accepted widely the book in which they were first stated is now hardly ever read, and this for various reasons. It is extremely difficult, because Pestalozzi wrote down his ideas while he was still struggling with them and before they took their ultimate shape. Although he believed himself to be sure of his principles, he admitted that he had not yet completed his theory. Obviously he intended to create a system of education consisting of three equal parts, intellectual, physical, and moral, but in *How Gertrude* he goes into much greater detail for the first than for the other two. Thus the book is not evenly balanced and creates the impression that intellectual education is the most important of the three, a view which Pestalozzi did not hold. Also, since Pestalozzi was untrained in scientific accuracy, he uses his terms loosely and ambiguously. Having established his principles in one part of his system, he extends them for the sake of symmetry to others where they do not fit. Moreover, the practical application of his principles and numerous examples of instruction procedures take up a disproportionately large part of the book; they are extremely boring and dry, if not actually mistaken. Worst of all, Pestalozzi keeps vacillating between two different points of view, the idealist conception of the self-activity of the human mind and his old conception of life as organically ordered. Both run side by side throughout the book without being fully reconciled.

What adds further to the difficulty is that Pestalozzi stands on the shoulders of other thinkers without being aware of it. His arguments and terminology are reminiscent sometimes of the empiricist theories of Locke and Hume, sometimes of the rationalist doctrines of Leibniz and Kant. But they are always blended with his own philosophy of life and his new conception of self-activity.

However complicated the presentation may be, *How Gertrude* contains important principles for a new method of teaching. Although many of its special applications are out-dated, its general theory is still of interest. Twenty years after the first publication Pestalozzi himself considered this book as 'partly refuted by time yet valuable in its record of how the method came into being'. Almost a century and a half later it is still worth the effort of study, not only as a biographical document but because of its tremendous influence on the practice of school teaching.

The book consists of fourteen letters to H. Gessner, Pestalozzi's publisher, the same to whom the *Letter from Stans* had been addressed. (Pestalozzi liked to write in the first person singular and to speak to a particular friend; this made the discussion more real.) Gessner, without Pestalozzi's knowledge, chose the title in the hope of repeating the success of *Leonard and Gertrude*; it does not fit the content at all. The sub-title, Pestalozzi's original suggestion, *An Attempt to help Mothers to teach their own Children* is equally misleading; the book is far too difficult to fulfil this purpose. Its arrangement in letters is not conducive to detecting a clear line of thought. A determined effort to trace one would produce perhaps the following: A historical-biographical introduction describes how Pestalozzi came to develop the method and how his assistants came to work with him (letters 1–3). The greatest number of letters (nos. 4–11) deal with intellectual education (the first part of the system); one letter only (no. 12) concerns physical education, and the last two (nos. 13 and 14) moral and religious education. Letters 4–11 contain the general principles of the method as well as their application to school subjects. The general principles stated here for intellectual education are later made to apply also to physical and moral education. The practice of school teaching, again, is divided into three parts, the teaching of language, of form, and of number (letters 7 and 8). But, as has been said before, the arrangement of these ideas is not very 'methodical'. All too often the train of thought is interrupted by expressions of emotion. It is therefore necessary to adopt a more systematic order of presentation than Pestalozzi's own in an attempt to make his theory of education more easily understandable.

If at the outset the question is asked what made Pestalozzi try to establish a new method of teaching, the answer is that he had been observing people in their education, their occupations, and their social relationships, and had found their thinking superficial, their work inefficient, and their community life corrupt. He believed the prevalent ignorance, poverty, and revolution to be the consequences of these defects. He detected their root cause in the fact that education had so far been directed to man's lower nature rather than to the inner powers of his better nature, to the masses rather than to the individual. For culture, as he had said earlier, can be achieved only by in-dividual effort; therefore education must consist in the raising of every single man if all men are to be 'ennobled' and the general standard of culture improved. This, he thinks, can be brought about only through the strengthening and developing of all the powers and faculties possessed by the individual. The neglect of this idea had made traditional education ineffective, even harmful. Pestalozzi blamed the schools for this failure, holding them responsible for the state of barbarism in which the people lived, and he considered it of the utmost importance that 'Europe's school evils' should be remedied, not by half-hearted measures, but by a radical change. 'The public school cart throughout Europe must not only be driven better, it must be turned round and put on quite a new road.'

This new road is the course of nature. 'I wish to wrest education from the outworn order of doddering old teaching hacks as well as from the new-fangled order of cheap, artificial teaching tricks, and entrust it to the eternal powers of nature herself, to the light which God has kindled and kept alive in the hearts of fathers and mothers, to the interest of parents who desire that their children grow up in favour with God and with men.' In order to grasp Pestalozzi's full meaning it is necessary, first and foremost, to investigate his use of the term 'nature' and of its opposite, 'art'.

The term 'nature' is used by Pestalozzi with many shades of meaning. (See also part IV chapter 2, *My Inquiries*, and part II chapter 2, *The Evening Hour*, above.) It stands for the nature of the external universe or physical nature, and for human nature, but mostly for the latter since Pestalozzi was always concerned with man. Nature, physical or human, is in his view 'unalterable and eternal'; there is no possibility of development in the modern sense of the word. Pestalozzi speaks of a 'mechanism of nature', meaning the ordered arrangement or the laws of nature (the Newtonian concept). Later, under the influence of Niederer who was acquainted with Schelling's philosophy, he changed the word 'mechanism' into 'organism'. These laws (this is important) are the same for external nature and for human nature, for man was created in accordance with nature, and his powers and faculties are, within limits, in conformity with the forces of nature. When Pestalozzi claims to establish 'a psychological method of instruction' he means to say that he is trying to find a way of teaching which shall be in agreement with discoverable laws of human nature. 'Psychological' is thus for human nature the equivalent of 'natural' for external. Since nature is one, it follows that there can also be only one true method of education, the 'natural' or 'psychological' method. This will be in accordance with universal nature, will lead man back to his own better nature, and will bring out his full humanity.

But, as has been indicated in the *Inquiries*, human nature has its two sides, a higher, 'divine' nature and a lower, animal nature. Pestalozzi's belief in the higher nature had, it is true, grown much firmer since the time of the *Inquiries* through his reassuring experience with the children in Stans. 'Man is good and desires what is good,' he says in *How Gertrude*; 'if he is evil, it is because the way along which he meant to follow good is blocked for him.' Yet he knows that it is not only circumstances which have made it impossible for man to be good. Man himself tends to 'deviate from the course of nature'. If he is left to himself (to 'blind' nature), the evil in him grows rampant. In order to prevent this and to strengthen his higher powers, nature must be 'lent a hand'. The assistance of nature is what Pestalozzi calls 'art'.

'Art' (in opposition to nature) is for the teacher a conscious acting according to principles, and for the pupil his methodically cultivated powers. (Pestalozzi introduces an unfortunate confusion by using the term 'art' also to denote 'craft' or manual 'skill' as opposed to mental accomplishments.) It is the aim of art to bring 'order' into nature. Thus it assists nature, but if its assistance is to be effective it must also follow 'the course of nature'. Hence art imitates nature and attempts to restore the original goodness of nature by helping it to follow its own course more easily.

Education, then, is the art of bringing to life and fortifying the good which is inherent in every human being; it consists in guiding the child towards the best realization of himself and of the things of the world. It does not impose anything alien upon him but draws out what lies in him, either latent or obstructed; it takes as its starting-point the child himself. It cultivates his own powers and encourages his independence. Thus the educator acts, as Socrates has said, more as a midwife than as a begetter of men. He merely prepares the way which the pupil must travel himself.

Given these premises it becomes necessary to discover the laws according to which the human mind works, if appropriate principles for educating the intellect are to be formulated. Pestalozzi postulates a fundamental power of the human mind

underlying all mental activity and making possible all knowledge. He calls it 'Anschauung'.

'Anschauung' is the most difficult of all Pestalozzian terms,
even in his own language, because he uses it in so many different
ways. In English the various meanings will have to be rendered
by a number of different terms which, it is hoped, will help to
make the Pestalozzian concept as clear as is possible. Pestalozzi
applies the term to every aspect (or phase) of the mental operations which he considers relevant to the formation of ideas, or
concepts. Thus it may mean sense-impression, observation,
contemplation, perception, apperception, or intuition, as the
transition is made from relatively receptive and unconscious
processes to full mental awareness and activity. The Leibnizian
theory of perception (and apperception) seems to lie behind
much of Pestalozzi's epistemology although he does not share
Leibniz's view that all perceptions are innate. He thinks rather
that these have two sides, content and form. The content which
is composed of a chaos of sense impressions from external
objects is given to the human mind. The form is imposed on
this sensory manifold by the ordering mind. Objects have to be
observed or contemplated; impressions from them come through
the senses; the objects are perceived by the mind.

So far the mind has been considered as predominantly passive.
The next more active side of 'Anschauung', the higher degree of
perception (apperception), is that fundamental faculty which
makes perceptions conscious and enables the understanding of
objects through the forms of thought. It is here that the Kantian
influence becomes most apparent. In this context Pestalozzi himself uses the expression 'intuition' or sometimes even 'imagination'. By this he envisages an active power of the human mind
which spontaneously brings into play the logical principles. From
this he concludes that all knowledge is 'the work of myself'.

Though this fundamental power ('Anschauung' in its most
active and conscious aspect) is potential in every human being,
it may not be developed at all; it may still be at a low unconscious
level. It must therefore not be 'left to itself' but be 'turned into
an art', i.e. it must be cultivated, educated, made conscious, if
man is to be enabled to reach the highest possible degree of
knowledge. 'Simple' sense impressions giving the lowest unconscious form of perception, runs Pestalozzi's argument in his

own terminology, produce only 'obscure impressions' which at a more advanced stage may develop into more 'definite impressions'. Through 'art' or making conscious the mental process, definite impressions can be turned into 'clear images' which in turn can be raised to 'distinct notions'. 'Definite', 'clear', and 'distinct' are used for ascending degrees of clearness. Or to put it differently, through education the child can be led from the stage of receiving obscure, chaotic sense impressions to a recognition of particular objects ('clear images') and thence to the general significance of these ('distinct notions'). In short, his power of 'Anschauung' must be raised from the lowest (unconscious) to its highest (conscious) level.

Although the process of intellectual education goes, as it were, upwards from the purely sensory to the clearly conscious, it must also be remembered that the converse is equally important and that the foundations must always be kept sound. The first demand on education of the intellect is, therefore, 'to make Anschauung [sense-impression, observation, perception, intuition] the foundation of instruction'. For knowledge is reliable only if all previous stages are contained in its final result, or in other words, distinct concepts are true only if they are grounded on sense impressions.

Truth is, of course, the highest aim of intellectual activity. With Pestalozzi, it is closely bound up not only with sense-perception but—to anticipate further conclusions—it is also given a moral value since its achievement demands effort and perseverance. In this way sensory, intellectual, and moral education are all related. Further, since moral education is also founded upon truth, and truth upon sense-impression, the fundamental power in moral education will also be 'Anschauung', as will be shown later.

On this basis, then, specific principles have to be formulated for guiding the child's education which must (to repeat) be in accordance with 'psychological' laws, i.e. with the laws of human nature.

External nature is homogeneous and consistent, and human nature, too, is a unified whole; a balance exists between man's body, soul, and mind. Therefore all his powers and faculties must be cultivated equally so that this balance may be maintained, or restored if it has been disturbed. The unity of man's nature requires a 'harmonious education', and the system of a harmonious education must also be well balanced; all its principles must be in agreement not only with nature but with each other. It is, however, a special quality of his method, says Pestalozzi, that any one of its parts has the effect of cultivating all human powers, because each part is complete in itself and comprises all others.

There is continuity in nature. 'She does not leap, nor does she permit any gaps.' She completes each phase before she moves on to the next, and having entered the second phase she completes it like the first. In the same way, teaching should advance very slowly, proceeding by small steps from simple to more complicated stages, attempting the more difficult only after having brought the easier to perfection. In this continuous progression secure foundations are of particular importance.

These principles are also applied to the objects of instruction, requiring that the essential should always precede the inessential and that near objects should always be preferred to more distant ones. Pestalozzi tries to combine the two latter demands by asserting that 'the essence of things' is nearer to children than their changing attributes, and that because of its proximity the essence makes a deeper impression on them and is therefore easier to understand. These complicated arguments which are inconsistent with parts of his earlier reasoning stem from his desperate struggle to bring all his principles into agreement with each other.

The most important and the essentially new principle for his time is that of spontaneity or self-activity. It demands that all knowledge should 'have its origin in the child himself', or in different words, that the fruits of perception should 'bear the mark of freedom and independence'. It implies that the child should not be given ready-made answers but should arrive at solutions himself and that, in order to enable him to do this, his own powers of perceiving, judging, and reasoning should be cultivated, his self-activity encouraged.

The aim of the new method is to educate the whole child. Intellectual education is only one part of a wider plan; besides being valuable in itself it has important moral and practical implications. By grounding his knowledge securely and helping him to master it completely at each particular stage of his development, it is claimed that the method produces in the child an awareness of being able to do what he wishes to do. This gives him a feeling of satisfaction and of confidence in himself which is the foundation of a happy and useful life. The contentment and inner peace thus won lead him to be loving and helpful and guide him towards his goal of regaining his original benevolence. Hence Pestalozzi asserts that the method 'promotes good and prevents evil because it is in agreement with nature'.

When Pestalozzi attempted to apply his 'psychological' principles to actual instruction in school he found that the traditional subjects of reading, writing, and arithmetic could not be regarded as the starting-points of learning, for their instruments of understanding, e.g. word, line, and number are formed by man's mind in order to make the world intelligible (in order 'to raise perceptions into concepts'). He therefore demanded that these instruments of understanding should be developed in the child before he was taught the traditional subjects. The school curriculum, he said, should be concerned not with the transmission of the products of learning but with the active process of search, not with dead letter work but with sensory intuition, not with parrot-like repetition but with rational thought. In short, instruction must be reduced to 'the elements'. What does this mean?

'The elements' is another term which Pestalozzi uses with various meanings. They may represent the simple in the sense of easy (opposite: difficult) or in the sense of irreducible, indivisible units (opposite: complicated); again, they may indicate the earliest stage (opposite: advanced) or the natural essence of things (opposite: artificial). They are not objects or qualities of objects but mental acts by which man constructs for himself an ordered and intelligible world.

Pestalozzi describes how one day, when his notion of going back to the elements was still vague, there flashed through his mind the idea that the elements which he sought were form, number, and language. These three—and only these, for the mind apprehends all things through them—were the instruments of turning perceptions into knowledge. The laws governing their functioning must be found, graded, and related with each other, so that with their help the child may be guided 'from obscure impressions to distinct concepts.' If this could be done, the art of instruction would be made to correspond to the nature of mental operations.

Form and number are categories of thought; they are the foundations of the mathematical sciences. The first stage of geometry or, as Pestalozzi calls it, the alphabet of form consists in reducing the confused mass of actually existing forms to a limited number of regular forms, the better to comprehend them. Such regular forms are, for example, the straight line and the square which provide an elementary groundwork to which the plane dimensions of any object may be related. (Pestalozzi does not consider a third dimension. Fröbel with his better knowledge of mathematics suggests the cube as the first of his 'gifts'.) The next stage is the verification of the observed spatial relations; it is done by measuring. Measuring requires a high degree of accuracy; it leads eventually to 'distinct concepts'. From the measuring of geometrical forms the child proceeds to their imitation by drawing; and only after drawing does he go on to writing. For written letters are to be taken as lines having definite relation to the square. Thus Pestalozzi argues that the traditional school subject, writing, has to be preceded by more elementary activities.

Number is 'the element' of arithmetic, or rather of its simplest form, counting. Counting is adding one unit to another, and all four arithmetical operations are, in fact, only abbreviated versions thereof. Once a unit has been adopted, it has to be maintained throughout the same operation. In arithmetic, as in geometry, the square is the basic pattern; it lends itself to be added to, or to be multiplied, or divided, as required. In this way the science of number is supported by the science of form and given the necessary foundation in sensory experience, so that its abstract operations may not become mere functions of memory. The teaching of arithmetic must therefore begin with the use of real objects and proceed via substitute objects (fingers, pebbles, dots) to abstract numbers. The aim of teaching 'elementary' arithmetic is 'to raise the child's natural power of reasoning into an art'. In going back to the elements, says Pestalozzi, children learn to do their sums more accurately; 'but besides learning sums they learn how to think, and even their sums they learn by thinking'. The influence of this new elementary method on school teaching was tremendous.

If the first instruction in the mathematical sciences is facilitated by the reduction of their subject matter to 'elements', the early stages of teaching the arts meet with great difficulties. And so Pestalozzi's experiments with language are less successful. Although he starts from a reasonable view of the significance of language (which reminds the reader of Herder's discourse *On the Origin of Language*) his attempts to apply it are regrettably mistaken. With regard to its significance, he had already suggested in the continuation of the *Inquiries* that language is the foundation of culture; he had called it 'the artificial reproduction of all natural experience'. Repeating this definition in almost the same words in *How Gertrude*, he now makes language the foundation also of individual education. For, he explains, whereas all other sources of knowledge, even the sciences of form and of number, are one-sided and scrappy in their findings, language transmits 'the general result of mankind's mental development'. Endowed with these advantages language is seen to fulfil the first demand of a 'psychological' method of instruction, namely to correspond both to the original form of the objects themselves and to the original form of human comprehension.

The difficulties begin when Pestalozzi tries to reduce language to the elements, or conversely to arrange the teaching of the mother tongue in successive stages. He suggests the teaching of sounds as a method of training the speech organs, and the teaching of words to enable the recognizing of single objects, both of which processes should precede the teaching of language proper as the means whereby man must be led to describe accurately the world and his own experiences. He invented exercises which are highly mechanical and in no way superior to the 'parrot-like jabbering' which he so despised in traditional teaching. For example, he devised a series of sound exercises composed of vowels plus consonants (ab, ad, af; bab, gab, stab) forgetting that these syllables are mostly without meaning; and he worked out long lists of word exercises which supply the child with the names of objects, but not with language. His mistake was to apply educational principles excellent in themselves to a subject for which they are unsuitable (e.g. the law of continuity: the series of words starts with the letter A and continues uninterruptedly to the letter Z). He later realized his mistakes himself, deeming the vast amount of language exercises he had worked out over the years no longer worth the printer's ink.

But at the time of their first invention large editions of various *Exercise Books* were published in order to aid mothers and teachers in their teaching of young children. There exists an *ABC of Measurement* and an *ABC of Form* whose details were compiled by Pestalozzi's assistants but whose fundamental introductions he himself wrote. An *ABC of Language* in the form Pestalozzi had in his mind never appeared; the *Manual for Mothers* containing the word-exercises mentioned above is the work of Krüsi following Pestalozzi's instructions. All these books are extremely dry and dull and by no means convey the spirit of the Pestalozzian method which, according to all reports, pervaded his own institutes—whether in spite or because of these exercises is difficult to say. These books and the misapplication of principles valuable in themselves are responsible for the fact that 'the Pestalozzian method' was for a long time regarded as a special teaching technique and not, what it was meant to be, as mediating a new spirit in education which should guide the child to think and act rationally and independently.

Pestalozzi's hopes for the efficacy of his method went far beyond intellectual or even educational aims and were over-optimistic. Convinced as he was that only individual activity leads to general culture and that the swallowing of uncomprehended information by the mass of the people was responsible for the prevailing barbarism, he was of the opinion that in the method's fundamental principle 'Anschauung' (the active power of the human mind) he had found the solution even to the political problems of his time. He ventures to assert 'that the defects of instruction in Europe or rather the artificial inversion of all natural principles has brought the continent to the state in which it now is; and that there is no remedy for social, moral, and religious revolutions either past or future but to turn away from the superficiality, incompleteness, and humbug of our popular instruction and to recognize that intuition ['Anschauung'] is absolutely the foundation of all knowledge'.

Pestalozzi dealt with intellectual education in such disproportionately great detail because he thought that the corrupt state of popular school instruction needed his particular attention. It does not follow that he attributed minor importance to physical and moral education, but he had to tackle first things first. The further he developed his method the more stress he laid on the other branches of education. One year after the publication of *How Gertrude*, in the *Report prepared for my Friends in Paris* (1802), he specifically states that intellectual education must be subordinated to moral education. But in *How Gertrude* the training of practical skill and the cultivating of the will are treated cursorily. In spite of their brevity, the last chapters of the book dealing with these questions are important. The present study in its concern with the development of Pestalozzi's thinking must therefore take them into consideration at this point while leaving a fuller account of their subject matter to a later and more appropriate stage. Some repetition will thus unfortunately be inevitable.

'Physical education' means with Pestalozzi the training of skills, bodily, practical, and vocational. Because of the individual's place in society such physical education is the necessary complement to intellectual education. Knowledge without skill, he says, would be 'the most terrible gift which a hostile genius ever made to the age'. Knowing and doing must be connected in such a way that if the one ceased the other would cease with it. Therefore a child's powers of doing must be developed in the same way as his powers of thinking; physical education must be carried out on the same principles as intellectual education.

Physical education, too, must be turned into an art, i.e. it must not be left to chance (to 'blind nature') but must proceed according to rules and in a definite order so that it may bring mankind to the full height of physical capacity of performance, and finally, of happiness. An ABC of physical exercises must be found according to which children advance continuously from simple to more complicated activities. Physical education, too, must begin with the elements; all practical skill must be based on the most elementary body movements (Pestalozzi mentions striking, carrying, throwing, pushing, pulling, turning, etc.) after the mastery of which the more difficult manipulations of a future occupation may be approached. Thus the procedure is analogous to that laid down for intellectual education. The central power (corresponding to the 'Anschauung' of intellectual education) is here called 'physical attitude'; and just as knowledge was developed from obscure images to clear images and from these to distinct concepts, so practical abilities should proceed from general bodily control to particular skills and thence 'to a grasp of the principles underlying them'.

The theoretical approach to a practical question in order to achieve a parallel to the method of intellectual education appears forced. What Pestalozzi really means to say is that the skill demanded of man in his condition of life (he thinks, of course, in the first place of the poor factory worker) should not be a mere knack but be built upon sound foundations and methodically developed; that a man should know how and why he is acting as he does, and that through early training his labours should be made easy for him and thus be transformed from a burden into a freely accepted task. The last two points provide the link between physical and intellectual and moral education; work should be done intelligently and willingly. The principle of true balance is further implied in the statement that the aim of physical education, namely vocational efficiency, is only a stepping-stone to a further aim, 'social virtue'. Again this is dependent on a man's individual condition. He should be trained in those skills which are nearest and most essential to him in his particular station, but he should be trained in such a way that in exercising them all his faculties are brought into balanced play and that he acts as a whole human being. He must be educated to be not only a skilled labourer, or an artisan, or a scholar, but a satisfactory husband to his wife, father to his son, citizen of his country. He must be able in his particular place in the community to be self-reliant and to help others. This demand, says Pestalozzi, is possible of fulfilment, for the same laws which prepare the way to knowledge facilitate social virtue.

The application of these laws to the practical education of poor children for industry and their relation to education as a whole are the subject of later writings.

The third part of Pestalozzi's system, also treated rather briefly in *How Gertrude* but including the most essential points of later relevant works, is concerned with the foundations on which the child's moral and religious education must be built. In this context Pestalozzi does not speak of 'elements' but of 'seeds' from which man's moral being 'grows'. The use of these words indicates that the organic conception (the principle of continuity) predominates. Pestalozzi tries to combine it however with the idea of spontaneity and self-activity.

The question asked—and finally answered—in the last two chapters of *How Gertrude* runs, 'How is religious feeling connected with the principles laid down as governing the general development of man?' Here, too, Pestalozzi follows the 'psychological' way asking the further question, 'How does the idea of God develop in my soul?' He answers: 'The feelings of love, trust, gratitude, and the readiness to obey must be developed in me before I can apply them to God. I must love men, trust men, thank men, and obey men before I can aspire to love, trust, thank, and obey God.' And how does man come to love, to trust, and to obey his fellow-men? Pestalozzi finds that these feelings have their origin in the relationship which exists between mother and child.

The mother is driven by 'the force of her physical instinct' to tend her child, to feed and to nurse him. The child, thus cared for, is satisfied and happy; the seed of love grows in him. The mother protects him from danger and comforts him in trouble; the child develops trust and gratitude. Soon these feelings are extended to other people in his environment. He loves and trusts people whom his mother loves and trusts; the seed of brotherly love is sown in him. Even obedience, a feeling for right or wrong, a sense of duty and a growing conscience (at a later phase the results of a conscious act of will) are first developed through feeling while still 'on his mother's knee', in a passive acceptance of her resistance to his more violent desires. Thus, Pestalozzi concludes, the satisfaction which the mother gives to the child's physical needs awakes his moral feelings; these grow 'naturally' from his organic relationship.

But when the child's own powers grow stronger, when he begins to sever the close relationship with his mother, then the time has come for a more active education. The moral sense had its origin in instinct; its further development must be a matter of art. For when the child enters 'the world', there is the danger that his instinct will weaken and that he will lose his love, trust, and gratitude. If at this crucial point his moral powers cannot stand up to the desires of his physical nature, then 'the world becomes his mother, the world becomes his

God'. Therefore education must now be 'snatched from blind nature', the laws of morality must be set against instinct in order to maintain, or to restore, the child's capacity for love. This acting against nature would not be necessary if the world were still 'God's original creation', innocent and uncorrupted. But it is this no longer; it is 'a world full of war and self-interest, full of paradoxes, force, arrogance, lies, and deception'. If the child were exposed to the corruption of the world without higher values to oppose its influence, self-interest would be the sole motive of his actions. In order to forestall such an outcome, his feelings must be subordinated to his conviction, his desires to his benevolence, and his benevolence to his free will. This can be accomplished, for a power of deliberate effort, an original benevolence and a striving for moral perfection are inherent in his higher self.

However lofty the aim, it is important that the natural origin of the moral sense should not be overlooked and that moral education should always be based on love. For the rest, moral education follows the same laws as have been laid down for intellectual and physical education. Continuity in moral development is achieved if the animal nature is subordinated to the moral powers at each stage only as that stage is completed. Thus the child's early education should not be a matter of the head but of the senses and of the heart; and his further instruction should proceed slowly from cultivation of the emotions to exercise of judgment, so that it may long remain a matter of the heart, a matter for the mother, before it becomes a matter of reason, a matter for the teacher. Through a continuous series of 'artificial means' the influence of the mother's love should be made to endure until the child is old enough to do right from his own conviction by a free decision of will.

The moral development of the child is, as has been said before, the basis of his religious education, since the feelings formerly directed to men are later transferred to God. During his infancy his mother took the place of God; in the next stage of his development God takes the place of his mother. He loves, trusts, and thanks God as his father or his mother. Trusting in God as he trusted in his mother, the child now 'does right to please God, as he has so far done right to please his mother'.

The 'art' which the mother has to use in the course of the

child's further education consists in introducing the world to him not as a place of corruption, but as God's original creation. As she teaches him to recognize and to name natural objects (here is the connection of religious with intellectual education) she points out that God has made them. The child's pleasure and joy in the beauty of nature bring about in him a love for and gratitude to the creator. When she helps him to calculate and to measure, to draw a straight line or to pronounce a difficult word, she says, 'Try to do it perfectly, as our Father in heaven has done his work perfectly.' Thus the child learns to know God in his perfection 'in trying himself to reach perfection'.

But man is not in this world for his own sake alone (here the concern turns from the individual to the community, as in the *Inquiries*); man reaches 'inner perfection' only through the perfecting of his brothers, i.e. by helping them in their strivings for perfection, or by brotherly love. Brotherly love (charity) was developed in the child out of his love for his mother. To help his fellow-men, especially those in distress, to please his mother or God (which amounts to the same thing) becomes a part of man's nature; it is the consequence of the divine in him. The mother made God known to the child in her demands of him, and he found God in his obedience to her. Love and duty thus become one and the same to man. The more he loves God, the more he forgets himself, the more divine does his own nature become.

In this circular form of argument (first used in the *Evening Hour*) Pestalozzi has, as he claims, 'united the worship of God with human nature'. In *How Gertrude* religion remains, as it was before, a humanistic form of religion; there is no indication of a transcendental God or of a historical revelation. It is also an emotional experience. 'God is the God of my heart', says Pestalozzi, 'the God of my brain is a chimera.' (This is directed against the Deism of the Enlightenment.) The aim of religious education is the realization of the divine in human nature, of the eternal that exists 'in myself'.

All this shows what firm faith Pestalozzi now had in the potentialities of the human heart. Although he knew it well in its darker aspects, he yet goes henceforth on his untrodden path 'as if it were a well-paved Roman road'. In his later writings he is to distinguish even more clearly between the divine essence and the earthly manifestation of human nature, taking each as the complement of the other. He organizes education with man's higher potentialities in mind, but at the same time he does not lose sight of present facts. He connects the ideal with the actual. For if human nature were as good as God created it, there would be no need for education, nor for a new method; but if on the other hand man did not have a divine spark in him, education would not be possible.

III NATIONAL EDUCATION

The two lines of thought along which Pestalozzi carried out his observations on the development of man, the sociological and the educational, recur together in his essay *Pestalozzi to his Age*, commonly called *Epochs* (1802/3). It remained unfinished and has become known only in our day. Even in its fragmentary state—it is not very far from completion—it is of great interest not only as the hitherto missing link between Pestalozzi's two fields of inquiry but also for the solution it gives to the 'apparent contradictions' in human nature with which the *Inquiries* had been concerned. The remedy it suggests against the decline of culture, though out-dated in its particular form, is still of value in its essential principle.

The *Epochs* contain an outline of the 'development' of mankind which, in spite of the title, was abandoned in the earlier *Inquiries into the Development of Mankind* in favour of a more systematic study of man. Only traces of a historical approach can be detected in that work; it would appear, therefore, that these earlier attempts were temporarily abandoned to be taken up later and made into a separate work. They are, however, now treated in a new way, for a more optimistic view of 'nature' is apparent. While the *Inquiries* stated that self-interest is essentially part of man's dual nature and has as its consequence the misuse of property and of power, the *Epochs* attribute the corruption of the age to man's departure from the true course of nature and hold the essence of nature to be good and its restoration possible. While the *Inquiries* express despair at the evils of the world, the *Epochs* wrest the hope of salvation from the idea of intuition ('Anschauung').

Pestalozzi divides the history of the development of mankind into five epochs. In each the self-interest of man's animal nature advances to bring about ever-increasing corruption. He does not say when these epochs are supposed to be placed historically, only that he himself has experienced the corruption of the fourth, and so we may deduce that we are at the end of the fifth. Pestalozzi's essay can be compared with Fichte's *Fundamental Traits of the Present Age* (1803/4), but in Fichte's work the fourth and the fifth epochs are in the future, and his ideal of national education is as characteristically different from the Pestalozzian as is that of his later *Addresses to the German Nation* (State control) from that of *How Gertrude* (family education). Pestalozzi's epochs differ from each other mainly in their being nearer to or further from 'intuition'.

In the raw, uncivilized state of the first epoch the powers and faculties of man are activated by the instinctive and lively intuition of his artless nature. Man is brutal and relatively unintelligent yet guileless and benevolent. He recognizes the things of his environment only as particular objects and possesses only particular skills. His resistance to unfavourable circumstances is weak, and he easily falls into barbarism.

In the second epoch man's intuition enables him to grasp general truths. His faculties have now created definite forms of civilization, religious cults, civil law, and social and occupational divisions of society. But he uses these first products of his self-activity not for the 'ennobling' of his nature but for its corruption. The temper of this epoch is cruel and ungenerous, if strong and adventurous. It is the age of heroes, magicians, and seers.

Human activity in the third epoch has become dependent on the products of cultivated 'art'. It is no longer based on intuition and has therefore lost its sound foundation. As man's social accomplishments increase, so does the corruption of his nature; but while this corruption has in earlier epochs been the result of chance, it now is the result of 'art' (i.e. man's own deliberate creation). It is organized by the church, the State, the institutes of learning. Knowledge becomes abstract, emotions are debased to words, particular skills are developed to the detriment of general ability. The mark of this (the historical) age is 'an increasing weakening of the first foundations of the knowing, willing, and doing of good'.

In the fourth epoch the hardening of the emotions and the deterioration of man's original powers reach extremes. The favourites of fortune deem no means too low for the defence of their might which they consider their right. Their corruption infects the less privileged classes of society; these begin to rebel against the wrongs committed by the more fortunate orders (pre-revolutionary period).

The consciousness of a situation past endurance which was expressed only in 'views' in the fourth epoch now produces 'deeds' in the fifth. But since the people's striving for independence arises from their confused passions, it cannot lead to true liberty. The feature of this (the revolutionary) period is brutality. So we have come full circle and are again in a state of barbarism which differs from that of raw, uncivilized people only in 'that their barbarism is based on strength, while ours arises from weakness'.

Here we stand, says Pestalozzi, faced with the necessity of making a radical decision. Either we give up seeing the significance of culture in truth and in right and accept force as the foundation of the social order, or we realize that the course of our development from the first to the last epoch has not brought us to the desired goal and that we must return to purer principles and start again from the beginning. The only good, the almost incomprehensible hope offered by this era of destruction lies in the possibility that in the midst of corruption man may yet be able to use the achievements of previous epochs for the ennobling of his inner self. After thousands of years of vain efforts to find wisdom and peace in the world, efforts which have cost him unspeakable suffering, man must at last be brought 'to look for the foundations of truth and of goodness within himself'.

What, then, is to be done? It is the destiny of man, says Pestalozzi, not to be led by instinct alone but 'to raise himself by an effort of will and by means which have their origin in the essence of his true nature and not in its state of corruption'. Here he distinguishes clearly between the original goodness of human nature and its age-long debasement. 'The essence of my nature, the eternal spirit in man, ever makes judgment according to the truth of nature and desires the good,' he says; but man as he is, as he has become in time through ignorance and incompetence, does not know himself and does not act in conformity with his better self. 'Yet man need not remain as he is; to seek perfection is not his instinct but his duty, and as such it is not chance or a dream but the reward of his earnest effort; it is the prize of his will, the prize of his virtue.' With these words the conflict which seemed to be inherent in human nature is settled and the apparent contradiction of the *Inquiries* resolved.

'It is the will for the good that our age lacks.' Therefore, the means of remedying the evils of our time must in the first place be an active fostering of the will for the good.

For the purpose of moral or religious education (here treated unmistakably as identical) it is important to safeguard the child in his earliest years against fear and insecurity, the experiencing of which may give a wrong direction to his emotional development. His morality and his worship of God must be developed from his feelings of love for and trust in his father and his mother, and he must learn to have faith that God will be to him what his father and his mother can no longer be. Organized religion, the church, too, must always take care that its spiritual essence shines through its outward forms. In the same way, Pestalozzi demands of civic and of intellectual organizations that they administer law, justice, and education not with an eye to mere outward appearance, but according to the inmost essence of each. The inmost essence of these forms of culture is what Pestalozzi calls their 'truth'. The recognition of truth, he declares, comes from intuition. Thus, truth is the aim of development, and intuition, the most elementary power of the human mind, its basis. Only through going back to this fundamental principle which accords with the essence of human nature will it be possible to raise man to a state where he can recognize 'truth and right in the spirit and in truth, as sacred and inviolable, with authority replacing that of his father and mother'. For it is not the intention of our Father that man should perish through the corruption of his instinct but rather that he 'be brought to recognize his true nature and be led towards perfection, even as our Father which is in heaven is perfect'. This is the religious justification of Pestalozzi's method of education and of its basic principle, intuition.

All founders of religion and all law-givers, he goes on, tried to organize their ecclesiastical and civic institutions with a view to this final perfection. But they erred in the means they chose because in practice they confused the state of human nature as it is, its corruption, with its original and at the same time potential state, its true essence. Only the Saviour of the world based his work upon the pure essence of human nature in the face of the general corruption of his time. He alone succeeded in bringing back the father-child relationship between God and man and a feeling of brotherhood among his disciples. Similarly for his own time which he judges extreme in its social corruption, Pestalozzi bases the ennobling of man 'on the belief, still existing amongst the people, in the relationship of man to God as of children to their father', or in other words, on the example of Jesus who made this relationship the foundation of his work.

Here the essay *To his Age* breaks off. From a short fragment belonging to it and published by Niederer after Pestalozzi's death it becomes still clearer that Pestalozzi meant to model his method closely on the teaching of Christ. The phrases used for the one are equally valid for the other. 'The Saviour was the first who tried to raise our race to liberty and personal independence. His whole system of teaching is nothing but an attempt to reconcile the knowledge, the will, and the skill of our race with each other and with everything that exists.' 'He has, like no one else, brought to light the means for meeting our moral, social, and intellectual corruption.' He has created 'a system of means' which, setting out from a general and elementary starting-point, proceeds continuously and harmoniously to the 'psychological' fulfilment of their final end, inner perfection. In short, the Saviour was the first to base the education of mankind on the belief in the dignity of man and the saving power of his better self.

Pestalozzi's faith has now found its final form and expression. It is the belief in eternal goodness which realizes its supreme embodiment in Christ. He thus makes the imitation of Christ the guiding rule of his life; and being convinced that all men should do likewise, he makes 'the love of God and men' the basic principle cf general education.

The political situation in Switzerland during the first years of the nineteenth century was unstable and confused. The Helvetian Republic had not fulfilled the hopes it had raised.

The patriots were disillusioned, the peasants disappointed, the aristocrats embittered. The French were masters in the country. The State coffers were empty, war devastated the land, and the discontented rose against their political opponents whom they held responsible for all the misery. In consequence the government changed hands from the revolutionaries to the more moderate republicans, and soon the Helvetian Republic had to give way altogether to the pressure of the conservative aristocrats. But since both political sides, republicans and conservatives, were still of almost equal strength and could not come to an agreement about the form of government, France interfered as before and imposed a constitution on Switzerland which suited her own ends.

The principal points at issue between the different Swiss parties were two: the problem of State finance which had been ruined by the abolition of the tithe, and that of a new form of popular representation which had become acute through the proclamation of liberty and equality. The friends of the people feared that the democratic achievements of the Revolution would be lost if the government came into the hands of reactionaries.

Again Pestalozzi took part in the political strife of the day. In contrast to previous occasions his opinion was considered, for he was now a famous man. It was, however, valued differently in the different camps. The enemies of the Helvetian Republic spread the rumour that he was responsible for the French being in the country and threatened to kill him at the first opportunity. The friends of democracy elected him to be one of a deputation who were to bring their views on legislation to the ear of Napoleon Bonaparte himself. For the First Consul had called a consultative assembly to Paris to discuss the question of a Swiss constitution. As representative of his native canton of Zurich and of some parishes in the Emmental Pestalozzi went to Paris in November 1802, only a few days after his wife and grandson had arrived in Burgdorf. But Napoleon did not consult the deputation in the matter because he knew that most of them were in favour of a central government. It was in his interest to keep Switzerland divided, weak, and dependent, and so he decreed the adoption of a federalist constitution. The so-called Mediation Act of 1803 restored the independence of the

nineteen cantons and thereby the domination of the aristocratic conservatives. The hopes of the centralist party were
crushed.

Pestalozzi was very active in Paris. As a public representative
he drew up several memoranda *On Legislation for Helvetia* and
On a Constitution for the Canton of Zurich; as a private citizen he
engaged in propaganda for his teaching method. In his political
pamphlets he asserts that the function of legislation is to create
a sound financial order, a just administration, and a public
system of general education. With regard to the first he demands
progressive taxation as he had already done in his second
pamphlet *On the Tithe;* as for the second he claims unconditional
recognition of the liberty and equality of all citizens. The
crowning achievement of Helvetian legislation should be the
introduction of popular education in its three parts, viz.
elementary education (the harmonious cultivating of all
powers and faculties of man), vocational training (the combination of the spirit of industry with the requirements of
agriculture), and moral education (the ennobling of the individual and his education for the brotherhood of men). In order
to make education the irrevocable possession of the nation, this
last demand is to be expressly provided for in the Constitution.
Pestalozzi's proposals are summarized in the sentence, 'May
we succeed in securing national education for Helvetia by law.'

In his efforts to make his method known in Paris Pestalozzi
hoped to promote popular education both in Switzerland and in
France. He thought that his French citizenship should facilitate
a French edition of his writings. A subscription to his *Exercise
Books* was to bring the foundation of a poor-school nearer its
realization. In all these activities he was generously supported
by friends old and new. His former patron Stapfer, Helvetian
Ambassador in Paris, was the centre of a circle of people
interested in popular education. Politicians like Lezay,
Roederer, and Laharpe did their best to spread knowledge of
'the method'. Young men like Horstig and Muralt came to
lectures and discussions in Stapfer's house. But the attempt to
interest the First Consul in national education failed. To a
request for an audience for Pestalozzi Bonaparte is reported to
have said that he could not let himself be involved in the teaching of the ABC. And with his refusal of the centralist party's

constitutional demands Pestalozzi's proposals for democratic legislation were also doomed.

Since Pestalozzi realized the fruitlessness of his mission and felt irresistibly drawn back to Burgdorf, he left France without having set eyes on the First Consul. Of Paris he had seen nothing; he might just as well have been in Moscow. He walked through the streets as if blindfolded and was capable of looking for hours for a house which was under his very nose. But he had made friends and won a valuable assistant in Johannes von Muralt whom he had captured from the famous Mme de Staël.

Pestalozzi did not raise his voice for years on questions of politics because censorship was re-introduced in the country. Also, through the fall of the Helvetian Republic his educational work was seriously endangered; the State subsidy ceased and the enemies of his method came into the open. So he kept quiet in political matters and worked exclusively for the stabilization of his educational enterprise.

The opposition to the Pestalozzian method had various explanations. In some instances it was simply due to envy of Pestalozzi's success and renown, in others to the anxiety of religious and political orthodoxy to preserve traditional practices. In 1803 a feud began between Pestalozzi and Pastor J. R. Steinmüller of Gais, Canton Appenzell, a former friend of Niederer's. Steinmüller had himself organized a teachers' training course, and jealousy of Pestalozzi's success moved him to wage a vindictive campaign. He spread abroad his view that Pestalozzi's method was mere play-work designed to save the children the effort of thinking and was entirely unsuited to the rural schools of Switzerland. He also spoke offensively about Pestalozzi's private life and his personality. Yet he had seen the Burgdorf institute only once for three-quarters of an hour. Niederer refuted his charges in the *St. Gallen Weekly*; this is the first example of Niederer's fierce apologetics for the elementary method. Pestalozzi's own replies have a more conciliatory tone. He invited his opponent to his house to study the matter more thoroughly, being convinced that he would then become 'a lover of truth' and take part in its dissemination. The victim of attack was forgiving, but the aggressor would not relent.

In Germany the schools of the so-called Philanthropists had

been flourishing for several decades. Their aim was to educate children for a useful and happy life, and they tried to achieve this by using realistic teaching methods. Teachers such as Campe, Olivier, Salzmann, and Gutsmuths were widely known and esteemed. They themselves were convinced that they had uttered the last word on education. Their main objection to the Pestalozzian method was that there was nothing in it which they had not said just as well, if not better. If Pestalozzi had only read some of their books he would have gained valuable knowledge. The Philanthropists had indeed modernized school teaching considerably in turning from theological studies to natural science, but they confined their instruction to children of the middle classes and were mainly concerned with intellectual education.

Other German critics again found Pestalozzi's method too intellectual. Wilhelm von Humboldt thought it 'a terrible idea' to make mathematics the main foundation of popular education and regretted that the imagination was given too little scope. Goethe missed in it a feeling for tradition in science and art; he also disliked the dealing with 'mere figures and forms' and disapproved of the conceit which the education of the individual and the encouraging of self-activity were in his view bound to create. He knew of course only the striking features or the 'fireworks' of the method; but his aristocratic outlook was diametrically opposed to Pestalozzi's democratic ideals. (Pestalozzi for his part retained his early opinion of Goethe, 'the prince of the mind', which he had expressed long before in the *Evening Hour*.)

The most serious opposition came from conservative circles in his own country which were closely connected with the orthodox branch of the church; it was directed against Pestalozzi's idea of religion. The opponents on this score included people so diverse as the simple peasants in Pestalozzi's neighbourhood and the president of the Bernese government. The former accused him of having abjured God; the latter arrived in Burgdorf one day at the head of a deputation formed to examine the method for its religious soundness. The result was a statement by the Bernese Council of Churches that Pestalozzi's institute 'lacked proper Christian instruction'.

Pestalozzi's belief in the divine spark in man, the fatherhood of God, and the love of Christ, and again, his slight esteem for the activities of the church were certainly unorthodox; yet he was anxious to maintain the traditional forms of worship in his institute and had made arrangements for the separate religious education of the two denominations. He was convinced that his own idea of religion was truly Christian, and this was also the opinion of all who really knew him. He took the accusation seriously, however, since it could only too easily become a dangerous weapon in the hands of his enemies. He therefore not only set out to prove the falsity of this particular accusation but to revise his method generally, lest moral and religious education had so far been treated too cursorily. He had already realized himself that this vitally important part of his method required further consideration.

Niederer's reply to the Council of Churches upholds the Christian content of the Pestalozzian method with passionate eloquence and shows that its psychological principles cultivate the mind and heart of children more effectively than the often empty forms of the church.

Pestalozzi's feelings about these controversies vacillated between a longing to die and a desire to fight. He was often depressed by the ill will of his enemies and frustrated in his activity; but at other times he was all the more stimulated to carry out his work against all 'Pharisees and Sadducees'. During the following years he made it his main task to rewrite *How Gertrude* which he had found inadequate soon after its publication, and to develop his method on broader lines.

After the fall of the Helvetian government there was no central administration in Switzerland; the decisive power was now with the individual cantons. Burgdorf belonged to Berne. The Pestalozzian institute lost not only its State subsidy but also its national importance. The roof over Pestalozzi's head threatened to fall just when he had hoped to be at the end of his troubles. For the castle of Burgdorf was allocated as an official residence for the chief magistrate, and Pestalozzi was asked to leave. The loss of the house and a change of locality were bound to disturb the life of the institute and break up personal connections; so Pestalozzi sent urgent requests to the government in Berne to reverse their decision. He indicated their moral

obligation to continue the support granted by their predecessors and pointed out that the aims pursued in the castle
justified generosity. But the aristocratic ministers were not
interested in popular education, nor were they favourably disposed towards Pestalozzi himself for his Helvetian politics.
Being aware, however, that the institute was being watched
from abroad, they were careful not to go too far and offered
Pestalozzi other accommodation, the vacant mansion of the
Order of St. John in Münchenbuchsee.

As soon as it became known that Pestalozzi was to leave
Burgdorf a number of invitations reached him from various
European countries and from other parts of Switzerland. The
Grisons as well as the newly created canton of Vaud expressed
their desire to have his institute in their territory. The Universities of Dorpat and of Vilna asked him to come to Russia
as adviser on a programme of schools. (The liberal Czar
Alexander I had become interested in popular education
through his former tutor Laharpe who had met Pestalozzi in
Paris.) As in previous years, Pestalozzi seriously considered
going abroad. But he soon gave up the idea, not only because of
his age but also because he was now more interested in completing his system of education than in founding new institutes.
The canton of Vaud, on the other hand, presented several
advantages. It had been a mainstay of the Central Government;
former Helvetian ministers lived there; a considerable number
of his pupils came from that district. The political atmosphere
there was more favourable to his purpose than that of Berne.
However, a disadvantage was the fact that the language spoken
in Vaud was French. Before deciding, Pestalozzi went to see the
castle in Yverdon offered to him, and to consult with the government in Lausanne. And since the House of St. John was only to
be let to him on a yearly basis, he accepted the castle of Yverdon
as well as that of Münchenbuchsee.

It seems strange that Pestalozzi who disliked organizing
burdened himself with two new enterprises at the same time.
Or was there some prophetic wisdom in his decision? The
parting from Burgdorf was sad indeed. Some five years before
Pestalozzi and Krüsi had started there to teach a small number
of children. At the end of June 1804 the people vacating the
castle numbered over one hundred. Some of the boys with the

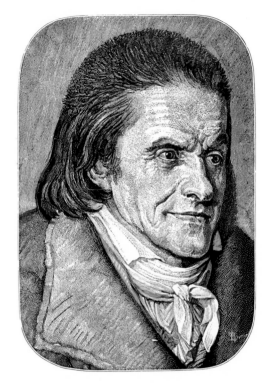

PESTALOZZI

Chalk drawing by F. M. Diogg
about 1804

YVERDON

Engraving by F. Hegi after S. Rösel, about 1810

masters Buss and Barraud went to Yverdon; the main body of
the institute was transferred to Münchenbuchsee.

Only a quarter of an hour's walk from Buchsee was Hofwyl,
an experimental farm turned into an educational organization
arranged in different sections according to the social classes of
the children. It was run by Philipp Emanuel von Fellenberg,
another well-known Swiss educationist who had adopted and
successfully applied many of Pestalozzi's principles. (Goethe
later took this institute as the model for the 'Pedagogical
Province' in his *Wilhelm Meister*.) Fellenberg was the son of the
governor who used to be Pestalozzi's neighbour in his Neuhof
days; he was a highly educated, energetic young man and an
excellent organizer. In his institute there was discipline, order,
and financial success. Pestalozzi on the other hand found the
detail of business a tiresome burden; he often complained that
it kept him from developing his method. So it was natural that
his assistants came to suggest a combination of the two institutes.
Since his childhood Fellenberg had been known and loved by
Pestalozzi (he had been a playfellow of Jacqueli's); he pursued
similar educational aims. If he took over the business part of
Münchenbuchsee, which would be easy for him, Pestalozzi
would be free for his educational research—an ideal arrangement. The institutes were to keep their individual characters;
Fellenberg did not wish to profit from his management. The
respective rights and obligations were carefully drawn up in a
contract and accepted by both parties.

No sooner had Pestalozzi signed the agreement than he regretted it. He thought he had acted in the interests of all, yet
the handing over of authority 'rent his heart'. He felt that he
had lost his independence. It was not long before the two
principals had their first difference of opinion. In order to avoid
unpleasantness Pestalozzi went with Krüsi to Yverdon, leaving
the institute of Buchsee in the hands of Muralt and Tobler.
(Niederer was seriously ill during the following months and did
not play an important part in the ensuing events.) Since the
segregation of social classes was one of the points at issue Pestalozzi took the poorer children to Yverdon so that only the more
well-to-do remained in the care of Fellenberg.

The teachers who stayed behind in Münchenbuchsee were
not happy there. Fellenberg's strict régime was too great a

contrast to the easy-going community life they had experienced in Burgdorf. Whilst there they had known only kindness and friendship, whereas now they were held to obedience and duty. The children, too, felt the lack of love; they became silent and said only yes or no. The different conceptions of education were bound to lead to disputes, and on several occasions when Fellenberg's authoritarian decisions offended the Pestalozzians, there were violent clashes.

Pestalozzi tried again and again to make peace or to let matters slide. He suggested to Fellenberg to have more faith in others and not to overburden himself. 'Use less force! Laugh more and enjoy yourself and have confidence in the outcome of our work!' For himself, all he wanted was peace to continue his research. But a new conflict arose over the renewal of the contract. As a consequence Fellenberg offered his resignation, but Pestalozzi refused to accept it. Fellenberg then proposed to hand over the management to a committee of teachers. But they would not dream of excluding Pestalozzi's influence. On the contrary, the ties of the Pestalozzian community were so strong that they longed to rejoin their old friends. Pestalozzi left the decision entirely to them. And just as they had been the instigators of the connection with Fellenberg, so they now put an end to the episode of Münchenbuchsee. In all his sorrow over the quarrel Pestalozzi felt deeply gratified by the unwavering loyalty of all his staff. He 'would not exchange the hearts of these men for all the treasures of the world'. After a year of trial and error 'Father Pestalozzi' and his 'sons' were reunited in Yverdon.

It was by no means Fellenberg alone who was to be blamed for the failure. There is little doubt that the right which he upheld so rigorously was mostly on his side. He had done all in his power to save Pestalozzi's institute in a difficult financial situation. But his adherence to convention where Pestalozzi was utterly spontaneous, his stress on class distinctions in contrast to Pestalozzi's conviction of men's equality, his disciplinarianism as opposed to Pestalozzi's belief in freedom for the children, all these spelled attitudes so different as to be irreconcilable. Pestalozzi himself describes the situation in innumerable comparisons. 'You live in the present as in your spiritual home, working with all the power of your earthly condition and your social status upon and through the world as it really is, in order to make it what you wish it to become. . . . We seek happiness for men in their own nature and faculties, independently of their station, their honours, their worldly power, and their fortune.' 'He [Fellenberg] has riches and honours. May he achieve what riches and honours can achieve. We seek for something which riches and honours cannot and will not achieve. Need is our portion, poverty our instrument, and our great aim the doing away with all the disturbances wrought by riches and honours in what is necessary for the peace of mankind.'

He often compares his gathering years and growing weakness with Fellenberg's 'heroic power' and 'royal demeanour'. Yet he knows very well where his own strength lies: in the art of awakening the inborn powers of men, of respecting and fostering their independence. He indeed looks down upon 'riches and honours', believing that true wealth can only be found within human nature itself. It is this, the inner peace of man, which alone he considers worth the struggle.

IV HEINRICH PESTALOZZI (2)

During the years when a long stream of visitors was pouring into Pestalozzi's institute a large number of reports were written on the method and its creator. Most of them agree in essential points. Many begin with a sketch of Pestalozzi's personality and describe the shock which the visitor experienced on seeing the famous educator for the first time; his looks were so much against him. There he was, a little old man in untidy clothes, with a pock-marked face and unkempt hair, addressing his guest with a flow of words accompanied by wild gesticulations, unless his hands were engaged in getting hold of his victim's coat buttons, thus drawing him nearer and nearer. What he said could hardly be made out for he spoke in his native Zurich dialect. But when the initial surprise had been overcome his visitors fell completely under his spell. The expression of his large black eyes, the kindness in his sensitive mouth, and the firm clasp of his hands made them forget his neglected appearance.

They found Pestalozzi perpetually astir; a sense of urgency seemed to drive him on. With unequal steps, bent forward, oblivious of things around him, he would roam from place to place as if in pursuit of some fugitive thought. He was always stumbling or falling but did not care in the least. Though originally delicate, his strong will and great sense of duty enabled him to get through a tremendous amount of work. Day and night were the same to him where his cause was concerned. When the burden of his work became too heavy he stimulated his weary nerves with black coffee and kirsch. In the small hours of the night he would often get up from his bed to write down by lamp-light what had come to his mind in his dreams.

He was rich in imagination and lively in perception, but the expression of his ideas caused him great difficulty. He wrote laboriously, revising and correcting his works endlessly. However clear a thought was in his head, his rendering of it in words made it complicated and heavy. From the time that he had assistants at his disposal he used to dictate his essays and letters, go over them several times and have them copied again and again. As he dictated he liked to lie on his bed fully clothed, murmuring into his beard while chewing the tip of his neck cloth. Or he would leave the formulation of his ideas altogether to his assistants. For in the field of theory as well as in practice he was better equipped for starting than finishing. When a new experiment seemed to succeed he lost interest and let others continue. This earned him the reputation of being an erratic worker; yet he held steadily to a single aim, pursued it all his life, and carried it out against formidable odds.

He made himself out more lacking in education and qualifications than he really was because he set little store by the knowledge and the accomplishments of his time. In formulating and applying his educational ideas he relied solely on his own observations and those of his assistants who worked on his principles. This rugged independence was one of the reasons of the strong impact he made upon people. But it was also a source of danger to the survival of his institute, for this had become dependent entirely on his person. If the defects of his qualities were ever to gain dominance, catastrophe was bound to follow. For he would no more readily submit to, than exercise, control.

He was much more a man of feeling than of intellect, and his mood changed readily. When he believed his enterprise to be flourishing, his eyes would sparkle; when it appeared to fail, he would look like death. In his approach to people he was full of trust and without reserve; he took everybody to be as honest and as benevolent as he was himself. This had the effect of drawing out the best in good people, but less scrupulous persons could easily deceive him. His disappointment used then to be as vehement as had been his former enthusiasm. His emotions were easily roused; his love was strong, and in anger he could say harsh words. But he would never wound anyone deliberately; he always excused the wrong-doer and took the blame on himself. When his temper had got the better of him he would go to the other later and apologize. He forgot quickly and lived mainly in the present. Thus he was flung from the height of bliss to the depth of despair or from wrath to forgiveness in rapid succession.

Some observers therefore speak of inconsistencies in his character. Yet he was consistent in an intensity which pervaded his every activity but manifested itself variously. Sometimes, for instance, he would shut himself off from all society in order to concentrate wholly on his research. But generally he loved to be among people, was fond of play and of games and full of laughter. His talk was witty and he enjoyed a joke over the coffee-cups. His sense of humour was evident in his speech as it is in his writings; it provided an outlet for his bitter experiences and reconciled his companions to living with him—not always an easy matter!

Visitors from abroad often remarked on what a great patriot he was, and that he could only be understood fully as a citizen of Switzerland. His close contact with nature and deep roots in his native soil, his democratic attitude and love of independence, his own brand of idealism tempered with realism were so different from the qualities of his contemporaries in Germany that he could never have belonged to that country. On the other hand, his eccentricity was so opposed to the conventionality of his fellow-citizens that it might be held to be explicable as a trait inherited from his Italian Renaissance ancestors.

A remarkable characteristic of Pestalozzi was his ability to divine the inner needs of people, though he was usually blind to the externals of behaviour. A countless number of anecdotes have been told about his charity. When a child ran to him he would lift it up and kiss it. He would shake hands with a notorious criminal who frequently escaped from jail whenever he met him on his way to a closer confinement, give him a thaler and say a few comforting words. ('If you had been taken care of when you were a child', he used to add, 'you would not now be where you are.') When he met a beggar on the road he would give him all he had. Once, when his pockets were empty, he took off his silver buckles and arrived in town in shoes tied with straw. Another time, he rushed into the house of a friend and asked for the thalers he needed to hand to a woman giving birth to a child in a barn. He forgot, of course, to repay the loan, for his left hand did not know what his right hand had done.

It goes without saying that his family and his assistants gave up all they had for him, and equally that he accepted their sacrifices. His wife and his daughter-in-law put their dowries and legacies into his enterprises without ever seeing a penny of them again. Lisabeth gave a lifetime of service for very small pay. An increasing number of gifted young men chose poor living conditions and uncertain prospects to be allowed to work at his side and for his idea. His secretary would be roused from his sleep in the middle of the night when the master needed his help. Sacrifices and hard work were necessary for the end in view and were offered and accepted unquestioningly.

Pestalozzi's most outstanding feature was his utter devotion to the well-being of men. He believed in the divine spark in every human being, but in himself it shone with a brighter than usual light. His goodness and benevolence rose to the highest form of Christian charity. The more was demanded of him, the more he was able to give and the happier he became. His self-denial was by ordinary standards excessive, yet to him it was the natural expression of an irresistible urge. He surrendered himself completely and never expected gratitude. Even his enemies had to admit that he was utterly disinterested.

His love of man became such a passion that it overruled all other considerations. It prevented reasonable argument and the clear knowledge of men; it made him blind and partial and subjected him to sad disappointments. It directed the course of his wife's life into paths unsuitable for her, and was the source of great suffering. It drove him mercilessly to dare all and risk peace and security for the sake of the needy and the poor. It had such a force that it overran all obstacles. It was this love of man which, as Fichte says of him, gave 'life to his life'.

Pestalozzi was aware of the apparent contradictions in his character. He tried to account for them to himself and to others and to find the link which he believed to exist between the particular quality of his work and his particular disposition. Thus many of his writings are directed to self-clarification and begin with a review of his own development, though an intended history of his life was never completed. These auto-biographical sketches are full of self-accusation and self-justification, frequently displayed in a grim humour.

It is the contrast between his lack of ability in practical matters and his sensing of a call to a definite mission which more than anything else is the theme of his self-explanations. 'When I read his books,' he writes of himself, 'I think he is almost a Brother Claus' [Niclaus von der Flüe, a Swiss monk of the fifteenth century for whom Pestalozzi had a great admiration]. 'When I see him with my eyes I feel he is a poor devil; and when I hear people talk of him I believe he is trying to empty the sea with a spoon.' More than once he quotes Lavater, his old friend now dead, who knew only too well his carelessness but also his abilities. 'I would not trust him to look after my henhouse,' he had said; 'but if I were king I would make him my first counsellor.' 'Lavater was right,' Pestalozzi admits, 'I can't do a thing. All I undertook was beyond my powers. A reasonable person would never have touched it.' And yet he had come so far. How had it been done? 'There was nothing in my favour but a firm determination, an irrevocable decision —I will do it; a conviction not to be shattered by any experience—I can do it; an irrepressible, urgent feeling—I ought to do it.'

He looked upon his failings and peculiarities with careless contempt or with deep concern, according to his mood of the moment. He was often seized with a feeling of guilt that he was not prepared more or of a cooler temperament and so better fitted to serve his country. He compared his incompetence, untidiness, and carelessness with the worldly-wise efficiency of 'ordinary people', holding himself inferior to any trained man. At such times he was ready to throw the burden of his business matters on to broader shoulders; but when he had done this he felt 'like a poor mouse who had run into the mouth of a rattle-snake of its own accord'. It was therefore from bitter experience that he came to the conclusion that in spite of his failings he would reach his goal in his own way and in no other; and at heart he was convinced that his weakness was at the same time his strength. For, as he said (with an eye on Fellenberg), his place was not in the bright sunshine but in the dark shadow; his lot was not to reap but to sow; and the fruit of his seeds hung 'on a blade of straw' and not 'on a proud palm tree'.

Since the question of financial profit or loss was of no consequence to him he could look at things in greater detachment than anybody 'who looks at the world through business or professional glasses'. Ordinary people, he said, acted according to the notion 'that nothing under the sun was absolutely true or absolutely right, but that all truth and all right had to be understood in such a way that one could always get away unscathed in the end'. He was completely sincere and did not fear to stand up for truth and right even at the risk of bringing misfortune upon his head.

He was firmly convinced that the endeavour to realize truth and right was the most urgent task of his time and that its accomplishment was his personal duty. When he considered the qualifications of others for this task he had no doubt that he himself was the most adequately equipped. For during the long years which he had lived in the depth of misery he had learned to know wretchedness and the sources of poverty 'as nobody else knew them'. But when he measured his competence against his ideal it was all too clear how far the former fell short. Then he was stricken by fear that the inadequacy of his abilities might prevent the success of his work, and he could not bear the idea that his enterprise might be obstructed or even ruined through his personal defects. When he had experienced failure after failure he often asked himself, 'Why can I not stop?' But he clung to every straw and would not give up.

And so he steered his course in the only way possible for him. His task cost him immense sacrifices but he was happy to make them. 'To strive for the well-being of all man is in my nature,' he writes; 'I should say it is in me by instinct.' 'My whole work is the work of my heart.' The good which he could do in this way sprang from this centre of his powers. It was this which gave unity to his character.

Looking at the requirements of his work he had the feeling that no man on earth was less well prepared than himself; it demanded practical efficiency, a calm head, mathematical ability, philosophical knowledge, command of language and of business affairs. 'I had none of these and yet I have won through. The secret is love; it has a divine power if it is true and fears not the cross.'

Pestalozzi was the more thankful for his success because of the contrast between the extent of his achievement and the insignificance of the means at his disposal. When he compared the present state with the failures of earlier years 'the cup of his joy was full to overflowing'. He took the happiness now experienced to be the reward for previous despair. 'One must have been very wretched, not to deserve happiness but to be able to catch it as it flies past.' He acknowledged the fact that the thorny path of his life had been necessary. 'My work has succeeded because my life was so hard.' Having triumphed over fate he was now able to claim to have reached results which no expert could dispute, results 'whose certainty equals their importance and of which I can say, they are beyond every reasonable doubt'.

'Yes, my friend, it is achieved; I see my work prospering.' The restlessness of his heart was now stilled. 'Quite new views fill me with calm. My belief in mankind is restored.' Thus he writes to Nicolovius ten years after that confession written from the Neuhof when he feared to sink in 'the mire of the world'. And to Stapfer who had helped 'to cast the seeds into doubtful soil' he writes, 'We thought we had sowed a grain, but we have planted a tree whose branches will spread over the earth, calling under its shadow all peoples without exception.'

Yet it is not pride but humility that shines through his happiness, for he accepted his success not as his due but as a gift, and he regarded himself not as its creator but as a tool used by a greater hand. 'It is not my work; it is God's work. Mine was the love with which I searched for what I did not know, mine the faith with which I hoped for what I did not see. I praise the Father in heaven whose strength was made perfect in weakness, and human nature appears to me in a praiseworthy light, since I now know from experience that it is given to man to unite all his powers in love for the service of his fellow-men.' A new relationship to God speaks from his letters and addresses. He uses the name of God more freely than before, for faith in his wise guidance had returned. He 'feels safe in the arms of his Father', and his strength came from this feeling of security.

An incident belonging to this period deeply affected Pestalozzi and confirmed the belief in God which he had re-won. As he walked one dark night (November 1804) from Lausanne to Yverdon, he was knocked down and trampled by horses drawing a wagon. With great presence of mind he jerked himself clear before the wheels could catch him. His clothes were torn but he was unhurt, and he felt as if reborn. 'I asked myself, was it I who did this? I answered with certainty, no, not I but God did this. And since God did this for me I have been a different man. Before, I thought I would have to die like Moses before having set foot in my Canaan. I don't think this any longer. I shall live and God will work through me. He who has saved me will also save what is infinitely more valuable. I now do not desire anything. I do not desire any institute, seminary, place, or man; I only desire what God desires, and that will come of itself.'

This was one of those moments of renewal which occurred from time to time in Pestalozzi's life. It initiated a period of intensive literary activity. His writings during the following months produced the capital on which he was to live for many years. His work went better than it had done for twenty years. Neither black coffee nor *bouillon à la reine* was necessary to refresh his mind. Serene and filled with creative power he devoted his time to developing his method. The 'dream' of his life had become a reality; what had been his desire to start was now his duty to complete. Along with his restored belief went an ever-increasing use of biblical language: 'as the hart panteth after the waterbrooks', so his soul 'was athirst to fulfil this duty'. He was resolved to satisfy this thirst until his dying day.

All his life Pestalozzi had been preoccupied with the idea of imminent death. Now it had lost its terror. He had begun his work; others would continue it. He had found 'the sons of a spiritual love'; they would propagate the seeds of his mind. It gladdened him to see those who would reap the harvest. 'Like the fowls of the air and the lilies in the field' he took no thought for the morrow but lived for the day. 'The fulfilment of the future is made certain by the completion of the present. I know no greater wisdom than holding on in the present with all the power at my disposal.' He felt that he would die in peace if to his last hour he did not concern himself about anything but 'the true and faithful carrying out of the thing nearest and closest at hand at every single moment'.

VI The Educationist
(1805–1815)

I MORAL AND RELIGIOUS EDUCATION

THE 'irrefutable' foundations of a system of education had been laid. Now Pestalozzi set himself to working it out in detail. During the ten years from 1805 to 1815 important essays on the method were written, and even the works of later years are based on the findings of this period. Especially the year 1805/6 was, within his four walls, the most peaceful he had experienced, his mood the most serene, and the results of his research the most fruitful. Away from the bustle of the institute he lived with Krüsi in a small attic of Yverdon castle, devoting his energies almost entirely to writing.

His studies during these years pursued the science of education in three directions: further research into the general principles of the method, development of the means of instruction, and organization of educational institutes. The last consisted mainly in efforts to stabilize the existing institute in Yverdon as the economic and experimental basis for any further enterprise, but also in the never-forgotten desire of his heart to found a poor-school with a training-course for elementary teachers. An account of this, his darling plan, will be given in the next chapter dealing with his ideas on vocational training and the education of the poor. The development of teaching aids was to a large extent the task of the assistants and belongs, therefore, to the history of the Yverdon institute and the spreading abroad of the method. We are here concerned with Pestalozzi's work on moral and religious education which he treated in form as only one side of general education but regarded in fact as identical with its basic principles.

Pestalozzi's intention was to base moral and religious education on the same laws as govern intellectual education. But the working out met with difficulties. Moral education did not so easily lend itself to confinement within a method as intellectual education, nor did Pestalozzi's way of ambivalent thinking which is especially prominent in this particular field. He vacillated between the ideas of an elementary and a balanced education, between an organic and a dualistic approach, a realistic and an idealistic point of view. His hope was doubtless, as has been said before, to combine them all and to establish a system of natural education but—this must be admitted straight away—he did not possess the constructive power to complete and expound it in one representative work.

External circumstances had also an adverse effect on Pestalozzi's writing. The political and economic situation, which had been comparatively favourable during the first year of his stay in Yverdon, deteriorated during the time of growing French hegemony in Europe. Pestalozzi had to give his mind again to affairs of the institute; his essays then in hand were left unfinished and thus failed to fulfil their purpose of making known the real meaning of his method. The foundation of a 'Swiss Society for Education', with the help of whose members he hoped to raise the standard of popular education, also failed to have the expected success because of the unstable political circumstances. Even his own periodicals, the *Journal of Education* (published by Gräff, Leipzig, 1807) and the *Weekly Notes on the Education of Man* (published by the Pestalozzian Institute, Yverdon, 1807–11), started for the same purpose and run by Niederer with great energy, did in the long run more harm than good.

Almost all the works of that most fertile period remained, therefore, either completely unknown during Pestalozzi's lifetime and right up into the twentieth century (e.g. *Mind and Heart*) or were published only in extracts (e.g. *Views and Experiences*). This is one of the reasons for the warped judgment of his method that prevailed for more than a hundred years. Not until work was begun on the Critical Edition of Pestalozzi's complete writings (1927 ff., still in progress) have these become available in their original form, thus providing the material for a new and truer understanding of his intentions.

The immediate cause for a further development of the method was, as will be remembered, the need to refute the criticisms of opponents that the method was predominantly intellectual, that it neglected moral education, and that it was contrary to the Christian faith. In *Mind and Heart in my Method* (1805) Pestalozzi explains why he had not dealt with moral education in the first place. In matters of the heart, he says, men have not strayed from the path of nature to the same extent as in matters of the head. The divine spark, love, is for ever present in the human heart; it only lacks direction and aid to become effective. One way of helping it is through the training of the mind, for through intellectual education the moral powers of effort, self-control, and independent decision are cultivated as well. As for moral education as a separate study, it is difficult to formulate laws and to establish results. If morality is put into words, there is always the danger of achieving its opposite, mere prattle and sheer hypocrisy. All the same, Pestalozzi expresses surprise that people could so mistake his true intention—to restore innocence and benevolence. Intellectual education alone is not enough to achieve this aim. Especially in times of cultural corruption it is necessary to strengthen those positive powers which have their origin in the hearts of individuals. These are based on the power of love. For this reason, elementary education of the heart must take precedence over that of the head, not, admittedly, as a matter of method, but as one of importance. ('Elementary education' is now the term substituted for 'the method'.)

A main principle of the elementary education of the heart is that it is independent in content but corresponds in form with the laws of the elementary education of the mind. This cannot be otherwise, says Pestalozzi; since human nature is a single whole, the 'natural' education of mind and heart must be the education of that whole. Like intellectual education, moral education should begin from an elementary starting-point, proceed continuously without leaps or gaps, and approach completion by easy stages. It should not impose anything alien on the child but draw out what is in him. All his faculties should be developed equally, yet through the cultivation of one all the others will be strengthened. Not a widening of his range of experience but its limiting to near objects is desirable. Through constant practice his capacities must be turned into abilities; they must be 'made habitual' (a new term). Habits must become acts of will, mechanical skill conscious self-activity. And just as elementary education of the mind does not consist in instruction on thinking but in the cultivation of the capacity to think, so elementary moral education is not a matter of talking about religion and virtue but of awakening moral feelings and of their translation into good actions. This can be done in practice by developing moral education out of those first relationships which nature has given the child in his immediate environment.

The basic power of intellectual education is intuition ('Anschauung'). In the *Report for his Friends in Paris* Pestalozzi had attempted, for the sake of symmetry, to base moral education also on a so-called 'innere Anschauung'. Now he drops this difficult term in favour of a simpler one. It is love which he makes the foundation of morality. Up to this point, love had been one among other moral elements. Now he calls it the original power, the beginning, centre, and end of human development, the most fundamental emotion, the divine spark. Since moral education concerns the centre of the human being it is at the same time the centre of education as a whole, and from this it follows that its basic principle is also that of the other branches of education; or in other words, without love intellectual education, too, is ineffective.

Before the content of elementary moral education is discussed, another approach of Pestalozzi's must be considered by which he tries to combine moral and intellectual education, and at the end of which he again arrives at the pre-eminence of love. The connecting link now is, surprisingly, language. In a (fragmentary) essay *On the Significance of Hearing* (1803/4) Pestalozzi continues the train of thought begun in *Language as the Foundation of Culture*. In the earlier essay he had found in language the means for arriving at truth. Now he calls it 'the gift which makes man truly human'. For through language man is enabled to communicate his feelings and to establish personal relationships. Language is the means through which he expresses his love.

The first voice that reaches the child in his cradle is that of his mother. She talks to him whenever she tends him; when she nurses, feeds, and dresses him, she speaks to him about everything she does, not however like a dry schoolmaster but in the tones of love. This emotional association of the voice of his mother with the objects of the world explains why this early teaching makes such a lasting impression on the child. He learns to know the world in an atmosphere of love. The mother is the mediator between child and nature; through language and 'Anschauung' (intuition) she leads the child to truth, and through his association of her loved person with his environment, to universal love.

This is what distinguishes the human mother from the animal. If she contented herself with using only what nature and circumstances provide, she would remain the nurse of the child's body such as other mammals are. But she is the mother of a higher being, and it is her duty to promote the development of his sense impressions into moral feelings. The transition from the animal way of life to the human is brought about through intuition, language, and love. 'Life or death depends on the combination or separation of these three elements in the child's education.'

The importance of the mother and of the first impressions made by his environment on the child's moral education is expressed most beautifully in Pestalozzi's *New Letters to Gessner*, a re-casting of *How Gertrude* which unfortunately never received the finishing touch. (It was published in 1807 in the *Journal* as part of the *Views and Experiences* but is really an independent work.) The construction in widening circles is reminiscent of the *Evening Hour*, the ideas on the relationship between mother and child of *How Gertrude*. The content, then, is not really new, but presented for once so clearly and impressively that these letters deserve a short mention.

Their subject is the final aim of the elementary method, a balanced education of all human powers. If at a graveside people were to say: 'This was a man such as all should be; he could be relied on, head, heart, and hand', this would be the best which could be said of anybody. They would not say this of a partially developed man. Only one who had matured equally in mind, heart, and body deserves such praise. How had he come to achieve this balance? Pestalozzi gives the answer to his inquiries at the outset. Such a man's father and mother

PESTALOZZI AND HIS GRANDSON

Oil painting by F. G. A. Schöner

1805

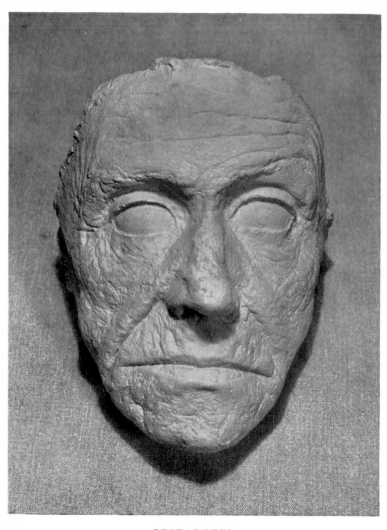

PESTALOZZI

Terracotta mask by J. M. Christen
about 1809

had encouraged the growth of all his faculties; society and his country had given him scope for his activities; and by believing in God and doing good he had raised himself above his lower nature so that it was easy for him to do and be what he ought (letter 3).

The educator wishing to bring a child to this end must, there-fore, ask the following questions: What has nature provided within man, and what in his environment, that can be used for his well-balanced education? (Pestalozzi omits, at this point, to put the further question—which, however, he answers later —what the educator has to add to these provisions of nature.)

The child possesses the powers of feeling, thinking, and acting. They all start from a common centre that guides, strengthens, and limits them. This centre is love. It is the foundation of all other moral feelings, just as it sets man's mind working which, again, is the motive power of all his activity. In order to guide the child towards becoming the man that he should be, 'a noble being, meeting the claims of his condition and circum-stances, and happy within himself', there is 'no other way than to bring his activity into agreement with his love' (letter 4).

Just as man himself is organized towards love, so his environ-ment has been ordered by God to serve as a means for his moral education. His nearest relationship is with his father and mother who are connected in a thousand ways with his personal development. Even if a child has no parents in a moral, in-tellectual, or physical sense, these have to be replaced by others so that the paternal and maternal spirit may not be denied to his upbringing. For only through this spirit is a child treated as an individual; it alone gives satisfaction to his personal wants and provides the feeling of security he needs if he is to become a 'noble' human being.

It is in the home, more than anywhere else, that the best conditions exist for a well-balanced education. Watching his mother's daily work has a beneficial influence on the child's moral development; his father's example stimulates his in-tellectual and physical powers. These are the truly 'elementary' means of developing all the child's faculties in a natural way and of making his skills habitual. For the child lives in these conditions from morning till night; his family's work, joys, and sorrows provide the first impressions on which all further experiences can be built. The love he receives calls forth his own love; it awakes his other moral faculties. Even the checking by his parents of his faults and misdeeds does not jeopardize this love; on the contrary, it strengthens his better powers in the struggle against his animal nature. In a home where 'love and action are in agreement' the success of education cannot fail; 'the child must—he cannot do otherwise—become good'.

Of course, this sort of education requires parents to whom the world is nothing and their child everything, who, 'be it on the throne or in humble cottages', are able to use for their child all that is good, and to keep out all that is bad. What is really necessary to make men better are fathers and mothers 'who have the will and power to be to their children what they ought to be'. Pestalozzi knows, of course, well enough that 'the woman of the world' and 'the man of our time' are tempted by a thousand pleasures to neglect their child. Yet his faith in 'the good mother' is unconquerable. He calls her 'the salt of the earth' and believes her to be, in her position, God's representative on earth. On her heart he bases his hopes for a revival of the true spirit of the home and for a regeneration of the culture of the people (letter 5).

The next circle around the child comprises the other people in his environment; he becomes conscious of being the brother of his brothers, the neighbour of his neighbours, a member of his community, an inhabitant of his village, etc. In the child's earliest stages of extreme helplessness he comes to know these people as helpers in his weakness. But with the growth of his own faculties he comes to recognize them as individuals independent of what they are to him. By degrees he learns to know 'the whole crowd as they really are'. He realizes that even his mother is not there for his sake alone. The more his powers grow, the stronger becomes his desire to take part in the daily life of the community and to widen the scope of his activities. Having in his earliest childhood experienced the love of his parents he will now act with the same love in this circle of a larger family whose father is God. His love of men and sense of brotherhood, thus developed, will not by any means be a passive emotion but will require effort, knowledge, and skill. The active practice of love demands an ever higher degree of development of all man's powers.

Beyond the circle of people in the child's environment comes that of nature, of everything animate and inanimate. Here, too, the child develops from a mere capacity for sense impressions and an unconscious feeling of satisfaction to a recognition of objects as existing independently of himself. He enjoys animals and plants, their life and beauty; he also learns to know hardship and struggle, evil and death. He observes animals in their cruel game with each other, yet this experience need not kill his love. On the contrary it awakes his compassion; he thinks, 'Man must not be like these animals', and he rushes to halt the horror and to heal the wounds (letters 6 and 7).

The last letter (no. 8) deals with the conflict that exists between man's good intentions and his imperfect performance. However certain it is, says Pestalozzi, that a child has the capacity for love, it is equally evident that its growth is impeded by his selfishness. His parents, too, all men, the whole of nature are filled with animal desires which oppose their better tendencies. This apparent contradiction can be overcome in education only by guiding the child 'to the inner sanctuary of his being', by fostering his better self which alone is the foundation of his moral growth.

'The saving counterpoise' against the weakness of human nature is found by the mother in her idea of truth and love, in her belief in God. The more deeply she feels that alone she is incompetent to guide her child on the way to a nobler existence, the more urgently does she look for help from the source of love and power. In it, in her belief in God, she finds comfort and security against the imperfections of the world; it is 'the necessary supplement' to those means which nature provides for her child's education. The child for his part, seeing his mother's belief in God, will develop similar feelings for his Father in heaven; and through this first recognition of a divine being all his other emotions will be refined and purified.

It is interesting to note how similarly and yet how differently Pestalozzi traces the origin of religion in the mother and in the child. The former struggles against her animal desires and rises for the sake of her child to a belief in the God of love. The latter comes to trust in God as his Father through his love for his mother. Again Pestalozzi decides neither for a dualistic nor for a psychological interpretation of religion but blends both in one uniting view.

If *How Gertrude* deals mainly with intellectual education, the *New Letters to Gessner* with moral education, and *Mind and Heart* with the formal agreement of the two, the *Views and Experiences* (1807) were to bring about a synthesis of the different sides of education and to show that it is this harmony which mainly characterizes an education 'according to nature'. Pestalozzi struggled hard thus to complete his educational theory, but he did not finish this work either. A more systematic mind than his would have been required for the uniting of subjects, views, and intentions as diverse as those contained in this work. As it is, it vacillates between the setting up of an ideal and the belief in the possibility of achieving it on the one hand, and the recognition of an imperfect reality and of the obstacles to a practical realization on the other. He put too much into it; the book was to serve at once too many purposes. So it became polemic and apologetic and missed its main object, the presentation, in a straightforward way, of elementary education as a whole.

There exist more drafts and versions of the *Views and Experiences* than of any other book of Pestalozzi's; they were published for the first time as recently as 1957. As far as can be seen from the original version, the work falls into three main parts. First there is a review of Pestalozzi's youth and the early history of his enterprise (this is the part that was published in the *Journal* of 1807). It draws a parallel between his own bitter experiences—which, in his view, have turned out to be a benefit —and 'the blessing of need', the formative value of everyday experiences in the education of the poor. There follows a discussion of the means of education. It describes the essential character of natural education and its 'very core', moral and religious education, stressing the preponderance of the 'eternal', unchangeable qualities of human nature over the accidental differences of individual conditions, and claiming therefore the validity of the method for the education of all men. This part, however, also deals with the question in how far the Yverdon institute is suited to carry out these ideas, and develops into a defence of the institute in reply to criticisms made after an inspection by a commission of the canton of Vaud. And finally, Pestalozzi frames a proposal for the organization of educational institutes which, though based on one and the same method of education for all, should, in their specific forms, be different according to conditions and circumstances. This part ends with an exhortation to philanthropists to help in the establishing of poor-schools and the training of schoolmasters required for them.

The work contains—often in paragraphs which digress from their main theme—valuable remarks on a balanced education 'according to nature', on the power of goodness, on the divine in nature, and on the Christian character of the method. It is these points which deserve special consideration rather than the often diffuse argument of the book.

An education according to nature, Pestalozzi explains, consists in bringing into coherence all the means of education which must affect the child as a whole. Since the method has been derived from the unity of nature it must react similarly on the unity of the human being. The child's separate faculties can and must be cultivated, it is true; but only through a balanced cultivation of all his powers does he realize his destiny of attaining full humanity. Such a harmony of education is a reflection of the harmony of creation whose originator is God.

Just as God is the creator of the world, so the divine spark in man, his love, is the origin of all his activity. Love is the great power which governs his emotional life; his intellectual and physical faculties, too, cannot be set in motion without it. This proves, says Pestalozzi, that moral and religious education is the very centre of a general education. Since, however, the child must also be prepared for his vocation and his place in society, the other sides of education must be co-ordinated with moral education.

The place where a well-balanced education can be carried out most satisfactorily is the home. Therefore an education according to nature starts in the family. No school, no teacher however good, can do for the child what is essentially the task of good parents. Where institutions are unavoidable they must be imbued with a family spirit so that the child may not lack the love of a father and a mother. For it is not 'corporations' but individuals that have an educative influence, and this influence should be directed not on an impersonal group but on each individual child.

The essential character of such an education remains always the same, just as human nature is for ever unalterable. Its basic principles are therefore valid for all men in all circumstances. But its particular application must take different forms in different conditions, since society has given men positions of inequality. So the education of 'the rich' will be different from that of the poor although both must conform to the laws of human nature. If man is to be helped on his way towards a nobler existence this must be done on the basis of powers and faculties common to all; yet the particular circumstances of nations, classes, and individuals must not be overlooked. (Note the to and fro between the general and the particular, the constant and the changing.)

If education succeeds in cultivating equally all the powers of the human being, its success seems assured. A man thus harmoniously educated will develop a feeling of dignity; he will cease to think of himself as a mere physical being and to use his powers for worldly purposes only. He will, instead, begin to see himself as a moral being and use his attainments for higher purposes.

'But the world . . .!' And so Pestalozzi goes round and round in circles. Man is capable of a nobler conception; the world obstructs this; he must be helped to achieve it; yet nothing alien ought to be imposed on him; his better self must be strengthened; for in him is the divine spark etc. etc.

In the end it is always Pestalozzi's belief in the good that conquers all doubts. 'Trust firmly in the self-consistency of the good and in its power to fortify all other good with which it comes into contact', is his advice to the educator. 'On such a basis man is powerful among his fellows, if only he so desires.' If man looks for the good with confidence and endeavour, he will certainly find it. But he must concentrate on the good which he is pursuing and not make the mistake of attacking error and meanness. Acting as if there were no evil in the world, he must go straight towards his goal, 'fearless and powerful through truth and through love, yet with forbearance and mercy'. His fight against stupidity and selfishness should consist in 'meeting the bad with pure goodness'. The good must be developed to such a degree that, if it comes into conflict with the bad, it will be strong enough to resist and not be overwhelmed. Yet the educator must be patient and unselfish and must leave the ripening of the good to the laws of nature and the freedom of man, just as the farmer has to leave the growth of the seed to the laws of the seasons. If only the good prevails in the end, he should be content, whether it has come to pass through his efforts or through another's.

There is yet another consolation: If the evil in the world reaches an unbearable degree, such a state of affairs gives rise to 'a quiet yet powerful impulse in man to restore himself from his corruption'. Nature herself has given him the power of self-restoration. If she has worked for thousands of years 'to wrench man out of his animal state', and if he has as yet not attained a state of morality, truth, and right, then 'it is surely not our nature but our will that is to be blamed that we stand where we do'.

For nature is of God. 'According to nature' means, so Pestalozzi explains, 'according to the will of the creator of nature, according to God's will.' Since God has created man according to his will, he must be developed according to the laws inherent in his nature and brought to that destiny which God has intended in his creation. Education according to nature is, therefore, the bringing of man nearer to perfection, the guiding him towards 'becoming, as far as is possible, the image of God'. Helping him to recognize the divine spark within him is the same as strengthening his feeling of dignity as a human being. Human dignity, then, is both the aim and the starting-point of education, which only its potential existence makes possible. If man can be brought to this nobler view of himself, he will regard other men, too, as higher beings, as children of God, as his brothers. Then even 'the world as it is' will become another, a new world to him. Even its lowest beings will then be taken as manifestations of God's will, and this view will again stimulate his moral and religious activity.

Through his conception of divinity in nature and his belief in the good, Pestalozzi is able to find an explanation for the existence of evil in the world. Even if the experiences of 'time' cloud the effect of 'the eternal' in human nature, in the end 'the good which God does' prevails, and the bad which man does proves to have been its tool. 'The power of nature increases through the resistance of nature.' This can be called the theodicy of the method of education according to nature.

Pestalozzi also shows that this form of education is in agreement with Christian teachings. Jesus Christ came into the world 'not to destroy the eternal laws of nature which so obviously are the will of his Father, but to fulfil them'. In his time, as in Pestalozzi's own, corruption had reached a high degree, but he did not found his doctrine on the institutions of the world, but on 'the power of the divine within human nature'. (Here the *Views and Experiences* continue the thoughts expressed in the *Epochs*.) He rejected the means of organized civilization and made religious decision the concern of the individual person, regarding every man as a child of God. His fight against error and force was 'the contest between the claims of moral freedom and those of the senses', between divine and animal nature. 'He laid the foundations of morality in the worship of God and the love of men.' In propounding this view, he did not teach men in mere words and doctrines but inspired them through the example of his life. He was—Pestalozzi quotes an expression of Lavater's—'the ideal of human nature personified'. From this it follows 'that pure Christianity is essentially the elementary doctrine of morality'.

Christianity, then, is the fight against the demands of the senses, the elevation of the spirit over the flesh. (Cf. Pestalozzi's letter to Iselin in connection with his *Evening Hour*.) The same is true of education according to nature; its aim is to curtail the demands of man's animal nature and to guide his spiritual nature to its divine destiny. 'In the spirit of Jesus Christ elementary education teaches the child to strive for the highest and best of which his nature is capable.' And if human achievement may be compared with divine, it may be said of it, 'He who follows this doctrine will know that it is of God'. The agreement of the elementary method with the teachings of Jesus is thus established; it is 'one and the same thing'.

When Pestalozzi had reached this point in his theory of education he thought he might be allowed to claim in all humility that the idea of a 'natural education' was no longer a dream but a fact.

II PRACTICAL EDUCATION

The third part of Pestalozzi's system, practical education, which he comprehensively calls 'physical education', has still to be considered. It comprises the training of the body (physical education proper), the preparation for a manual occupation, and indeed all education applying 'art' in the meaning of skill and practical efficiency. Under this head comes also the education of the poor, for the development of their working capacities is, of course, an important factor in their general education. Pestalozzi's writings dealing with practical education are based on the results of his previous investigations. Again he stresses the point that human nature—and consequently education according to nature—is 'in the true meaning of the word triune', that strengthening the faculties of the body and training for an occupation must be an integral part of the education of man as a whole, and that moral and intellectual considerations must play a part even in physical education.

That the principles of physical development are in agreement with those of intellectual and moral development is the theme of a short essay *On the Training of the Body: An Introduction to Elementary Gymnastics* (1807). The human body, it argues, requires 'art' for its development as do the mind and the heart, for only through art does it reach its highest form, good health, strength, and an upright bearing. The last is the outward sign of inner dignity; it distinguishes man from the beast. This belief, says Pestalozzi, is generally accepted, at least in the upper classes. Yet the physical exercises practised by them—riding, dancing, fencing—produce only particular skills without relation to the whole of human nature; they strengthen the body without regard to the mind and the heart. The poor child, however, does not enjoy even a partial training of his body; his health is actually damaged in school where he must sit still, contrary to his natural impulse for movement, and also at home where a cramped position in front of the loom may deform his body for life. It is clear, then, that the physical education of the people must be greatly improved.

In physical as in the other branches of education it is not the performance but the performer which is of first importance. The aim of elementary gymnastics is not a high achievement in jumping, running, wood-cutting or any other physical skill as such but the strengthening of the child's powers to use his hands and his feet for all necessary purposes in all possible circumstances.

As for procedure, elementary gymnastics only have to make use of what nature herself provides. There is, first, the child's urge for activity. He seizes everything, plays with anything, is never still. There is also the child's immediate environment. For nature, having planted the impulse to move and to be active in the child, has given his mother the corresponding desire to satisfy this urge and has thus created in his family circle favourable conditions for his development. As with his mind and heart, so with his body; the elementary means of education start from the relationship between mother and child and are developed and determined by the conditions of his environment.

The earliest training of the body is so simple that it can hardly be called an art. Every mother knows and practises it. At first, she stands her child on a table, then on a chair, then on the floor; she first holds him by his hand, then only by a finger; finally he can stand by himself. The father goes further; he makes the boy throw a ball, jump over a box, climb a tree, etc. These practices of the father and mother do not lend bias to the training of the child's body; although they are entirely instinctive they are well balanced and continuous and help the child to achieve a general facility of movement.

This 'natural domestic gymnastics', says Pestalozzi, is the necessary foundation for an 'art' of elementary gymnastics which proceeds according to the laws of the child's physical development. It is also in agreement with the laws of his moral and intellectual development. In an 'elementary' training of his body the child's attention is directed on himself and the things around him; through his play and his games the range of his experience is widened; he is thus made aware of what gives pleasure and what pain. His emotions, too, are involved in these exercises because they originate from his father and mother. Thus the elementary training of his body enables him to act in the spirit of love. He can run messages for his mother, lend a hand to his father, look after his younger brothers and sisters. His physical skill is thus being used for moral ends.

The 'art' of gymnastics proper begins at the point where the mother's influence diminishes. In accordance with the principles of intellectual and of moral education elementary gymnastics is described as 'a series of exercises for every part of the body arranged in a continuous order and designed to comprise the whole range of articulated movements which the child will eventually have to perform'. The detailed exercises worked out by Pestalozzi's assistants are not considered here. But it must be said of them generally that the analytical reduction of all the child's physical activities to muscle movements for the sake of building them up again methodically represents a similar mistake to that made earlier in reducing language to sounds; the activities of movement or speech become bereft of meaning. The synthetic procedure is much more relevant, namely Pestalozzi's demand that the functions of the body be brought into harmony with the activities of the mind and of the heart, a harmony which, he thinks, had originally existed in the uncorrupted state of nature.

If practised in this way, Pestalozzi concludes, elementary gymnastics is another means of general education. In relation to the body it assists man in the independent use of his physical faculties; in relation to the mind it makes him aware of his physical powers and their best possible use; in relation to his morals it enables him to make the spirit govern the flesh. Thus it exercises all his powers and faculties and makes him fit to fulfil the tasks which await him in his particular circumstances.

It may be noted that in the Yverdon institute the connection between physical training, intellectual education, and moral attitude was always maintained. But those of Pestalozzi's followers who took up the analytical side of physical training tended to regard bodily efficiency as an end in itself, to the detriment of general education. School and military exercises were thus too often reduced to mere mechanical drill. Only much later, under the influence of Ling in Sweden, were gymnastics again regarded as part of a liberal education of man as a whole.

The application of the principles of elementary education to vocational training and the preparation for citizenship served the double purpose of completing the system and of helping the poor. For however much Pestalozzi stressed the point that the method was valid for all classes of society, his particular interest was in the humblest; and moving with the times he was now concerned with the education of the factory worker employed in small manufactories still using hand-looms, not yet steam-driven machines, as opposed to the peasant supplementing his earnings by home industry who had engaged his interest earlier. He was convinced that the means of education suitable for the industrial worker could only be worked out in poor-schools, and also that an adequate education of the future workers in poor-schools would be a means to alleviate the evils of industry.

Pestalozzi's ideas about vocational training (or, as he calls it, 'elementary education for art') can be considered under three heads: the principles of vocational training in agreement with those of the other branches of education; his views on industry, its dangers and the means of overcoming them; and finally his ideas on the education of the poor and his attempts to carry them out in the first decade of the nineteenth century. His observations on these points can be found in the various Memoranda which he drew up for the governments of Aargau, Vaud, and Neuchâtel, in short articles which appeared in the *Weekly Notes*, and in the relevant parts of *Views and Experiences*. All these were written during the years 1805–7 but, with the few exceptions mentioned above, remained unpublished at that time.

Vocational training as such, Pestalozzi expounds, consists in the development of all physical faculties, starting with elementary gymnastics and leading in a continuous series of exercises to a facility in the most complicated movements which industry demands. Since there are 'male and female industries', the training of boys must be different from that of girls; the former, preparing for warping, weaving, dyeing (Pestalozzi was, of course, thinking in terms of cotton manufacture), must above all strengthen the arms; the latter, leading to sewing, knitting, lace-making, should aim at a greater dexterity of the hands and fingers. The kind as well as the order of exercises thus vary according to the particular demands of different industries. Every stage, however high or low, must be completed and brought to perfection with regard to knowledge, effort, and experience before the next may be begun. Understanding, diligence, and application are required to make skill perfect and habitual.

The essential point of 'elementary' vocational training is, of course, that it must be in agreement with intellectual and moral education. It was, Pestalozzi thought, the engagement in his craft of the whole man that had in former generations created a satisfactory domestic background, a feeling of personal security, and social and political stability. The agreement of skill with knowledge and good will, or in other words, the close connection of economics with education and morals is, consequently, the aim of a 'really elementary' vocational training. (It will be remembered that Pestalozzi had expressed similar ideas a quarter of a century earlier in his *Swiss Journal*.) Vocational training as practised usually neglects many human faculties; it turns man into a 'living machine'. But 'elementary education for industry does not keep man in the solitary confinement of a particular trade but gives him the entire freedom of his truly cultivated powers'. It satisfies his mind and his heart and aims at 'the various forms of human perfection'. It is, therefore, 'the true means of humanizing industry'.

Yet the necessity for differences of application according to the differences of social status is stressed here more than in any other field of education; Pestalozzi's old conception of the individual condition of life breaks through again. Vocational training, like moral and intellectual education, starts, of course, in the home. Early observation of the activities of the two parents, and later the constant opportunity for active participation in the work necessary to maintain the family, are the preconditions of a practical preparation for life. The basic pattern of the domestic situation is, he says, the same for all men. But, he continues, the use made of it must vary according to the social station and the particular circumstances of the individual or the group. Practical education of 'the rich' must be different from that of the poor, vocational training of the town child different from that of the country child, of the agricultural worker from that of the factory worker; in short, it must be in agreement with man's actual condition.

If man learns to meet the requirements of his occupation in a 'really elementary' way, he will gain 'physical independence' of exterior circumstances, of other people, and of his own animal impulses. He will be able to perform all sorts of work, not only specific manipulations; he will acquire a desire to work rather than a wish to receive alms; he will achieve 'a higher view of life' and not run a selfish race after money. This more educated conception of life will in its turn have a beneficial effect even on his occupational earnings. Elementary vocational training, then, brings about a higher standard of living for the individual and also better social conditions for all. For through success in his trade as the result of his general education the individual will be able to fulfil his responsibilities as a citizen and thus further the welfare of his community and his country.

During the years of French hegemony in Europe Swiss industry encountered great difficulties through the exigencies of war and the consequences of Napoleon's Continental System. At first the trade blockade with Great Britain had, through eliminating a formidable competitor, brought about an unexpected boom; but lack of raw material (cotton) and export restrictions on finished goods soon resulted in a depression, for Napoleon's system was mainly devised to protect French industry. The Swiss economic situation was grave. In his estimation of it Pestalozzi does not, however, regard the repercussions of world politics as a sufficient reason for the deterioration of Swiss trade. As always, he traces social and economic distress from interior causes. In his *Views on Industry, Education, and Politics* (published 1822 but written 1807 as part of a long memorandum on poor-schools) he sees the real danger of industry in the moral depravation of the factory worker, caused by the monotonous and mechanical kind of work he is forced to do, in the fact that he is losing his dignity as a human being. In former times, Pestalozzi declares, the 'essential means' of economic stability (the powers inherent 'in human nature itself') had been effective. Believing as he does that they remain for ever the same, he argues that in these powers must lie the remedy for the present predicament. What is necessary to restore a healthy economic state is, therefore, first, to discover and, second, to apply these 'essential means'.

It is a universal principle, Pestalozzi goes on, that necessity leads to effort and effort to invention of the means to maintain and improve living standards. The more inventive a people are, the more prosperous they become; the sounder their morals, the better use they make of their gains. The men who founded industry in Switzerland possessed a high degree of general culture, i.e. an earnest sense of religion, honesty, and efficiency, combined with a true attachment to family, home, and country. These qualities led them to industry, thrift, and economic stability.

The present decline springs not so much from an unfavourable international situation as from 'a weakening of the essential qualities' which had once been the foundation of industry; and this weakening has taken place because circumstances have become too easy so that people no longer exert themselves. Need is changing into glut, and this does not fail to have its effect on man's animal nature. It debases his faculties of invention and retention to a dead repetition of a mechanical skill. The prevalent heedlessness and moral enervation can doubtless continue to procure the necessities of life for some time; but since these are the results of a sham prosperity without sound foundations they cannot withstand for long serious assaults from without.

Not only the pattern of labour, but also the relationship between masters and workers has changed. The rich have become more pretentious and the poor more careless than of old. Both are divorced from the soil; their earnings consist in money which they spend only to increase their pleasures. The master manufacturer no longer regards his workers as human beings and fellow-men but as means to greater riches, and the factory hand likewise thinks only in terms of maximum individual gain. The degradation of the working population is the consequence of a lack of responsibility in the upper classes; the source of both is the abandoning of the simple life and of the will to exert themselves. The decline of the inner powers entails the disappearance of the means of prosperity. Industry, then, founders not on political blockades but on 'the rock of selfishness' in man's behaviour.

What is happening to individuals and business houses is repeated on a larger scale in cities and states. The government of earlier times was a patriarchal superior power concerned with the welfare of its dependants. The present rulers are an impersonal administration without human interest or understanding of a living community. If a sense of responsibility and personal reliability disappears from public affairs, the well-being of a country declines in the same way as that of private enterprises.

The means to restore social prosperity exist 'within ourselves' (the old formula of the *Inquiries*). Recovery is possible only if both economy and administration are based on the sound moral and domestic qualities of the private individual. 'Only the good which is still within us can lead us to the better which we lack.'

Up to this point Pestalozzi's argument has been familiar and repetitive; now he introduces a new concept: he contrasts the individual with 'the mass'. To the latter he attributes the degradation of morals and the decline of civilization.

'The art of our civilization', he says, 'builds its institutions more on the needs of men in the mass than on their requirements as individuals.' This is a dangerous development. For the preponderance of mass demands suppresses all the better powers of human nature, so that with the progressive ruining of civilization a correct assessment of the indispensable needs of the people becomes ever more difficult. The dispossessed man as well as the State who is responsible for him are confused about their respective demands and obligations.

The more 'artificial' the social state becomes, the larger is the number of people without property; for property, once regarded as the lawful means of increasing and securing profit generally, has through the artificiality of its development deprived the mass of the people of, rather than provided them with, its enjoyment. (Cf. Pestalozzi's observations on property in the seventeen-eighties.) This overwhelming majority of men without property have no other means by which to sustain and improve their living standards than their physical and intellectual faculties, their capacity for work.

But this capacity remains ineffective if it is not educated to satisfy man's essential needs. Only through a general education will the poor man be enabled to regain in the social state the equivalent of his lost share in the free produce of the earth. A claim to the cultivating of all his powers and faculties is therefore his social right; it is the counterpart of the rich man's claim to the securing of his property. To recognize this claim is a public duty; it is 'an important corner-stone in the artificial organization of the social state', and together with the sanctity of property constitutes the basis of civilization.

The right of the working classes to education, he goes on, exists not only for their own sakes but also for that of the property-owning class and that of the State; for a disregard of this right has a demoralizing effect on all and leads to a pre-dominance of 'the physical force of the mass' over the just claims of the individual. (Cf. Pestalozzi's later work *To the Innocence*.) Civilized nations have always understood these implications and tried to let all people benefit from education.

The Christian religion, as the Mosaic law before it, goes even further in the recognition of this right. It regards property as a sacred trust to be used in the service of love. A true Christian, therefore, believes it his duty to help the man without property whom providence has placed beside him, 'especially with regard to the education of the powers and faculties which God has given to all men, irrespective of their social position, in order to enable them to help themselves'. As a Christian, he regards such an assistance as a service to God and an implementation of the teachings of Christ; as a citizen he considers it a realization of the true meaning of community life.

This Christian spirit, Pestalozzi admits, is almost entirely lacking in modern times. Yet, he says, we must not despair of ennobling mankind and improving the lot of the poor. We must connect our means to these ends with the qualities of truth and goodness which are still alive in the people. Therefore it is important to find out exactly what is really true and good if we are to avoid the error of assisting the prevalent sham civilization and supporting the unjust claims of the mass, an error which would lead to catastrophe. Only the education of the better qualities of the individual can effectively avert the dangers which threaten industry in particular and civilization in general.

These are Pestalozzi's *Views on Industry* and *On Education*; those *on Politics* are not given in the fragment as so far available. But they can be deduced from what had been said before. And in a postscript to the publication of this fragment (in his *Collected Works*, 1822) Pestalozzi makes his ideas on politics quite clear. He believes that the nations can be brought back to the satis-factory state of previous generations—which, he thinks, was such 'a blessing to the man without property'—'not through ex-terior means of constitutional changes but only through the edu-cation of the individual in every social class to all that is good, noble, and beautiful'. He expresses the same opinion in private letters, namely that good legislation must begin with cultivating the moral, intellectual, and practical faculties of every single man in the land, even the lowest. The cure of the evils, then (this is very different from the views of his youth), has to come not from above but from below, not from outside but from within.

How the education of the poor child for industry is to be carried out in practice is laid down in the second parts of Pestalozzi's memoranda on poor-schools.

The essential qualities of human nature, so Pestalozzi never tired of repeating over and over again, are universal and unchangeable. All men must first and foremost be regarded as human beings endowed with the same powers and faculties, the same rights and claims. In every man there is the divine spark. What distinguishes men from each other is not their innate qualities but their social conditions; these are not created by nature but have developed in time. The differences must be taken into account in education since man lives in society, even though the needs of the essential, and therefore universal, elements of his nature remain the primary consideration.

The most important difference dividing men in society is, according to Pestalozzi, that between poverty and wealth. Both have their advantages and disadvantages; for his own part Pestalozzi inclines to regard 'riches and honours' as a source of danger rather than as a means of ennobling man. Poverty, on the other hand, which 'has since the days of Jesus Christ been called sacred' is an incentive which makes man exert all his powers. 'Necessity is the mother of invention. It stimulates the senses, sets the limbs in motion, and what is more, it stirs the heart and evokes the noblest feelings in human nature.' This advantage inherent in their very circumstances must be used in the education of the poor.

In Pestalozzi's time some special pleading was still required to convince people that the poor ought to receive education, a privilege hitherto granted only to the well-to-do. He argues that it is not permissible either to leave everything to nature or to be blind to the social disadvantages of poverty. There must, he says, be a distinction between 'the inner qualities which God has given to the poor and the external circumstances which the world has created for them', and it must be realized 'that poverty and depravity are not necessarily inseparable evils'. It is therefore necessary to find out what the poor man requires 'as a higher being', and to base the education of the poor in the first place on the unchangeable character of his human nature before dealing with the accidental attributes of his social condition.

Having emphatically stated his main point that the principles of an education according to nature are the same for all men, Pestalozzi is now concerned with their different applications in different circumstances. For, he says, even the best education can benefit man only if 'it appears in the form and the frame in which alone each particular class of society can recognize truth and right'. Just as an educational enterprise for the upper classes which disregards the claims of riches and honours would not meet with their approval, so a scheme for the education of the poor, if it is to have any prospect of success, must not infringe the time-honoured customs of this class nor replace its wonted satisfactions by new and less acceptable ones.

Elementary education of the poor ought, however, by no means to encourage 'fantastic dreams' of abolishing class distinctions; it is far removed from the idea of 'helping the lowest peasant to get silk stockings, velvet clothes, and a clergyman's hat'. It does not set out to teach the poor child a multitude of skills although it intends to save him from the one-sidedness of the traditional school instruction and mechanical factory work. It is not a crumb dropped from the rich man's table but a right which is his on the grounds of his human nature. It intends, in fact, to educate the poor child in such a way that he will, though remaining poor, be able to lead a life both useful and satisfying, of dignity and human worth.

A good education of the poor must use all the advantages of his condition to make him alert, hardworking, and constantly busy. In this way he will be taught to help himself and others and to carry the burden of his life as if it were no burden but a habit, 'his second nature', as it were. The road to this sort of life is not strewn with roses, Pestalozzi admits; but when the poor man arrives at a state in which he has conquered necessity not only by habit but by a conscious act of will, then 'he may be called a human being in the fullest sense of the word'.

The education of the poor can follow the course of nature all the more easily in that the poor have remained closer to nature than the rich. The latter, Pestalozzi thinks, have lost a great deal of that dignity which originally distinguished human nature; but 'need of itself retains much of it in the poor'. The elementary method is, therefore, in a true sense the method for the poor, for it does not attempt to produce geniuses but hopes to bring peace and contentment into the hearts of thousands by giving them the means of creating and extending their life's satisfactions through their own exertions, in their actual conditions, within the limits of their individual capacities.

An institution which is really suited to prepare poor children for the life awaiting them must imitate their future conditions in its organization. The first demand on such an institution is that it must be wholly unpretentious. Instruction should as far as possible be given 'during work' (i.e. industrial work, cf. *Leonard and Gertrude*); the occupation of the children must be continuous and appropriate to the requirements of the particular circumstances. But most important of all (and this is a true Pestalozzian demand), the atmosphere of the house must be that of a family. The parental spirit, although not existing 'by nature' in such an 'artificial' organization, must be consciously created by the head. Love and sympathy, those most effective means of developing human powers, must not be denied to a child growing up in an institution if he is not to suffer serious deprivation; for they are the foundations of true humanity.

The people best equipped to educate the children of the poor are not to be looked for in the upper classes but within their own class. 'Nobody will or can truly and effectively help the poor in their circumstances but the nobler among themselves.' Poor young men, superior in mind and in heart, must be found and made familiar with the principles of the Pestalozzian method. The training of elementary schoolmasters is therefore indispensible for the establishing of schools for the people. The first poor-schools which Pestalozzi had in mind were to be training schools for young men who would be taught to run further poor-schools (schools for the people) themselves. Teachers' training and popular education were thus interdependent.

These are the views which Pestalozzi laid down in his memoranda on the education of the poor. Endeavours to put them into practice re-appear at various stages of his life. After the departure from Burgdorf, at the time of his growing fame in Yverdon, yet another attempt was made to re-establish a poor-school. For the teaching of middle-class children did not satisfy Pestalozzi. 'What I have here is not what I want,' he wrote, 'I sought a poor-school and I am still seeking it. This alone is the desire of my heart.' In former years, he goes on, he had thought to find the natural means of education through practice in a poor-school. 'Now the course of my life has led me to seek the realization of a poor-school through the organized means of a natural method of education.'

Seeing that the castle of Wildenstein near his Neuhof in the Aargau stood vacant, he applied to the cantonal government for permission to use it for the planned institution. Financial support was to come from three sides: from 'generous philanthropists', from the canton of Aargau, and from his own middle-class school in Yverdon. (This financial help together with gain of practical experience in the new teaching method was for Pestalozzi the main justification of its existence.) A committee was formed to administer subscriptions expected to come from patrons all over the world. Some enthusiasts actively promoted the scheme, especially in Germany, but the money received was not enough to bring it into operation. Other reasons contributed to prevent the plan from being carried out at that time. The year 1807 was unfavourable for an enterprise not directly concerned with the cause of the war, the Aargau government had no great confidence in Pestalozzi's business abilities, and his own school in Yverdon was growing so rapidly that it required all his energies. So the realization of his dream had to wait for yet another decade.

III   ELEMENTARY EDUCATION

The great work *On the Idea of Elementary Education*, based on a paper which Pestalozzi read to the 'Society of Swiss Friends of Education' in Lenzburg (1809), tries to present what the *Views and Experiences* attempted but failed to achieve, a comprehensive survey of the Pestalozzian method of education as far as it was completed at that time. Yet this work cannot, any more than the previous one, be taken as the representative account of Pestalozzi's educational thought, for in its present form it is not entirely his own; it clearly shows signs of Niederer's editorial help. Niederer's alterations cannot, it is true, be pointed out in detail since Pestalozzi's original version is no longer available for comparison, but the Pestalozzi expert recognizes certain differences in style and construction. Before these are indicated here a word must be said about Niederer's assistance in general.

Pestalozzi was wont to complain of the difficulties he had in controlling 'the wild flow' of his ideas, in giving his thought a definite form. It was, therefore, an act of friendship on Niederer's part to come to the rescue with his philosophical training and to help Pestalozzi in his obvious struggle. His advice had already been given on the publication of the *Views and Experiences*, not, it may be said, to its advantage. Now he edited, with Pestalozzi's full consent, the Lenzburg address for the *Weekly Notes*, the Yverdon educational journal, giving it a philosophical foundation and a firm construction and extending its length to a full-scale book.

Niederer was well-informed and quite up-to-date with the philosophy of his time. He was familiar with the ideas of Fichte and Schelling, and he made it his business to link the Pestalozzian method of education with these idealist systems. It was his aim 'to raise education from its base position' and 'to give it the rank and the dignity of an independent science and art'. Moreover, Fichte in Berlin had made Pestalozzian education the starting-point of a national regeneration. Should not, then, a restoration of culture come, first and foremost, from the place of its origin?

The grand design (this must be made quite clear) was based entirely on Pestalozzi's own wishes and hopes. Pestalozzi was, at first, extremely grateful for Niederer's help. He needed men, he said, who could 'prepare in a digestible form what was brewing in his cauldron'; and in any case he considered the working out of the method to be not his personal business but one for the whole community. Even later, when their opinions had already begun to differ, Pestalozzi still thought Niederer 'irreplaceable for giving the method a philosophic foundation'. But his gratitude diminished when Niederer set himself up as the official methodologist of Yverdon and believed himself to be a better interpreter of the Pestalozzian doctrine than its founder. 'I no longer understand myself,' Pestalozzi remarked, as yet in jest; 'if you want to know what I think, you must ask Dr. Niederer.' They pursued very different aims: Pestalozzi the improvement of popular education which he hoped to achieve in a practical manner, Niederer 'the idea of elementary education', a theoretical conception to be elaborated philosophically. The latter's attitude, so alien to Pestalozzi's way of thinking, and his growing ambition which made him go too far in imposing his own personality, caused Pestalozzi to resent and, finally, to resist Niederer's influence. In assessing, some years later, Niederer's assistance in the working out of the method, Pestalozzi called it 'presumptuous and immature', although at the time when it was given he had unhesitatingly accepted it.

The difference in the intellectual outlook of these two men, manifest for the first time in the work to be discussed, is of great importance because it not only affected this particular book but was to be the cause of the unhappy events leading to the decline of the institute and casting a shadow over the last years of Pestalozzi's life.

But in spite of Niederer's interference with the text it must be remembered that the ideas expressed in the work are unquestionably Pestalozzi's own, for Niederer was himself a convinced apostle of Pestalozzi's doctrine. It is not the content but the form which he altered, whether for better or worse. Pestalozzi later included *The Idea of Elementary Education* in his *Collected Works* saying in the preface to this new edition (1821) that although Niederer's influence was clearly noticeable in the work, 'the irrefutable truth of the main idea is still to be considered valid'.

The occasion on which the Lenzburg Address was originally made was, as will be remembered, a meeting of the 'Society of Swiss Friends of Education'. From the tone of the published version it is clear that Pestalozzi wished to refute before these 'noblest and best men of the nation' the objections which had been raised against the method, and to point out the difficulties under which the Yverdon institute had to work. He was particularly anxious to deny the charge that the method was anti-religious, and to prove its agreement with Christian doctrine. He asked his audience to give the matter their careful consideration so as to arrive at a true understanding of what had already been achieved, and a just estimate of what had yet to be done.

The book deals with all aspects of elementary education in so far as they were already worked out and brings them under one main principle, the unity of human nature. It is not necessary, however, to recapitulate ideas which have already been discussed at the points where they first arose. Only new developments will be indicated and a few examples of Niederer's influence given.

Niederer's style is most clearly discernible in the characterization of 'the essence' of the method and in the terminology used. To begin with, the change-over from the expression 'the method' to 'elementary education' and even to 'the idea of elementary education' is probably due to his learned advice. The essence of elementary education is now stated to be 'organic-genetic' as opposed to 'historic-genetic'; or in other words, it is derived not empirically but by deduction from the main characteristics of human nature. (This is the point around which the disagreements arose.) Elementary education is 'positive' (evokes the powers), 'individual' (starts from 'the I' of the child—cf. Fichte), 'universal' (valid for all men), and it 'reconciles all contradictions'. It is possible 'because nature herself lays down its principles', and it exists 'because it has always been and will always be'.

The procedure of elementary education is explained here more clearly than in any earlier writing. 'Because of the peculiar properties of human nature as manifest in real life' (the division of man's faculties under three categories: will, intelligence, and practical ability) elementary education must be divided into moral, mental, and physical education. But the training of each single faculty must be directed with due regard to its relation to the others; it must activate all powers and faculties and thus affect the whole personality. The aim is to promote the unity of human nature by making habitual a balanced use of man's powers. This aim can be achieved through educational measures arranged in a 'psychological' order.

The question is whether the psychologically arranged measures as so far designed are adequate for their purpose. There follows a description of particular principles in which those of intellectual education are treated comparatively briefly because they were already available to the public elsewhere. It is worthwhile noting, however, that in a short survey of other educational systems those of Comenius, Basedow, and even Rousseau are repudiated, while the ideas of Herder, Hamann, and Novalis are approved; an indication that the emotional is preferred to the rational. It is also interesting that Greek education is not discussed here under the heading of intellectual education but later in connection with moral education, for 'the Greek's idea of culture was founded upon the development of a man's powers through free and independent living, not upon the expansion of his knowledge'.

The task of moral education—'which as an expression of domestic life is really in itself the whole of elementary education' —is 'to raise to the level of reason' (i.e. to make rational and moral) the mother's instinctive activities concerning her child. (Note the shifting of emphasis from the person to be educated to the educating person, an indication that education should be carried back to an earlier stage.) Raising man's actions generally from a physical to a spiritual level is what is called Christian. For this reason it is said that 'elementary education is not any man's new discovery; it already exists within the Christian doctrine'; elementary moral education is in agreement with the Christian faith. The agreement of intellectual education with Christianity is alleged in the assertion that there is no difference between learning and living, that every mental effort is a moral effort and thus religious and Christian.

Education in 'art' is treated in a new way here in so far as the term 'art' is now for the first time used in an aesthetic sense. Education in art, then, consists in 'awakening the child's sensibility to everything beautiful'. (Pestalozzi himself had never spoken of beauty before.) Now there is mention of an 'intellectual' or 'intuitively developed' education in art (in the sense of Kant's and Schiller's aesthetics), which precedes a 'mechanical' or 'practically realized' education in art. The former leads to education in music and fine art, the latter to crafts and industry. With regard to the child's preparation for his future occupation and social station *The Idea of Elementary Education* emphasizes (in the same way as Pestalozzi's other works) the predominance of general education over particular training, and of strengthening the powers to act over attaining efficiency in a special department of 'art'. For, it is insisted, specialization without integration dehumanizes man, demoralizes the masses, and thus ruins the peoples of Europe.

The Pestalozzian method which seeks to secure this integration is declared necessary not only for the individual person but for 'all mankind'. In answer to criticisms the question is asked, 'Is it really desirable to strengthen the powers of the people?' and the answer given, 'We believe in the universal goodness of all God's gifts; we believe [note the plural] that the cultivating of these gifts should not be left to arbitrary choice but be the central aim of responsible persons.' To accept this responsibility is, therefore, not only a matter of education and politics, but of religion.

The aims of the existing institute in Yverdon and the obstacles in its way are explained in a paradoxical manner. It is admitted that an 'artificial' community can never be the same as a natural one. But since family life 'as it really is' by no means corresponds to family life as it should be, schools are necessary as preparatory institutions for a new spirit of home life. They are artificial, it is true; but wise art is sometimes preferable to corrupt nature. (Pestalozzi had often argued the other way round, but the institute had to be defended.) The spirit in which institutes are to be run must, of course, be that of a good family, reflecting 'a conception of life as a whole', and this spirit must pervade not only the general atmosphere but the teaching of every individual subject. 'Elementary education thus recognizes the principle that all instruction should consist in making use of the child's actual life; it recognizes the truth which has perhaps never been recognized before, that it is life itself which educates.' This idea of the educative value of life was, indeed, quite new at that time; it is expressed in the Lenzburg address for the first time and is to be Pestalozzi's educational maxim in his old age.

At the end of the address Pestalozzi—the true Pestalozzi—once more takes his audience 'into nature's workshop', to join him in a study of 'the child's psychological development under the care of his mother'. It is at this point that, for the first time in Pestalozzi's writings, developmental psychology in a modern sense appears. Pestalozzi distinguishes four stages in the child's life: (1) the development of his feelings (love and confidence) through the physical satisfaction provided by his mother; the extension of these feelings beyond his mother, and the naming of the things which give him pleasure (infancy); (2) the development of his consciousness, the recognition of persons and things in his environment, still under the protection of his mother (childhood); (3) his growing independence of her through his increasing powers and knowledge; his joining the community of persons and making use of the objects of his world (boyhood); (4) the widening of his range of action, his urge 'to know, master, and possess the world' without the help of his mother, the knowledge of evil (adolescence).

As to the last period, in which moral decisions are taken, Pestalozzi makes the following comment: the young person can achieve a sound moral attitude only if at this crucial stage of his developing moral independence he has found security through belief in God just as he had formerly found it in his mother's loving care. The transition from the one to the other must be continuous, without disruption or upset. It is the most important task of elementary moral education to maintain such a continuity.

The school which a child thus brought up enters must in all three branches of education build on the experiences which he has already gained at home. It must slowly but steadily 'turn a life of nature into a life of art' (wherein art must follow the course of nature). Does it, in fact, do so, Pestalozzi asks, and his answer is: The existing schools are just as unfitted for this task as 'the mothers of our times' are for theirs. Both must be helped. 'If school education is to follow the course of nature, this must first be restored in the homes.' Thus, in a circular argument (well known since its first occurrence in the *Evening Hour*) home and school education are shown to be interdependent (like the training of teachers and the education of the people mentioned above), and it is precisely this all-embracing purpose which is identified as the essence of elementary education. As long as education has not reached this goal, its attempts cannot be called a method but are only 'experimental approaches'. In fact, says Pestalozzi, the word 'method' has been used by his followers far too soon, and applied by his enemies too narrowly to the technique of instruction. 'What can truly be called by this name is the entire domain of the idea of natural education.' This, if ever achieved, will be no new discovery but an old fact re-established, 'because it unfolds the good which was already there'. It should not really be called 'the Pestalozzian method';

it exists in its own right. It is the psychological counterpart to organic nature.

The older Pestalozzi grew the more modest he became. He was fully aware of the imperfections of his achievements. 'Not everything has succeeded; little has been accomplished.' That is the reason why he keeps asking 'noble-minded people' to give his ideas serious consideration and to carry them on after his death. For he wished nothing more than that others should add something better to what he had only begun.

As long as he lived, however, he could not rest. When the Lenzburg address was before him in print and Niederer's influence observable 'in every line', he at once began to write yet another comprehensive account of his ideas which he believed to be more truly his own, and of which he wrote to Nicolovius that it would probably be his 'best and principal work on natural education.' In it, he is said to have treated of 'human nature, and man's conditions and circumstances, and the idea of natural education in the spirit of the *Inquiries*, but much more intuitively and practically'. Pestalozzi had great hopes for the success of this work. In the summer of 1812 more than half of it is said to have been completed. At the same time, during a severe illness, Pestalozzi dictated to Krüsi his memoirs on 'the course and the fate of his institutions and the obstacles which made the path of his life so thorny and troublesome'. The title of this work was to be *The Ailing Pestalozzi to the Healthy Public*. It also had already reached considerable proportions.

But both works remained unfinished. The disturbances and difficulties then arising in the institute did not permit the quiet necessary for their completion. The manuscripts were put aside. It is, however, to be assumed that Pestalozzi took them up again many years later and incorporated them in his *Swansong*. This, then, must, according to his own judgment, be regarded as his 'best and principal work'.

In connection with Pestalozzi's observations on the child's psychological development made at the end of the Lenzburg address, another work dealing with the same subject may be mentioned here although it was not written until several years later (1818–19); namely Pestalozzi's *Letters on Early Education addressed to J. P. Greaves*. (The original German version is lost;

the letters are available only in their English translation.) They show Pestalozzi's ideas on the relationship between mother and child in their most developed and, at the same time, most concise form. Here Pestalozzi makes education begin at the earliest possible stage, declaring the most important period in the child's development to be that from birth to the end of his first year.

He concedes that both the infant's reaction to his mother's care and the mother's response to the infant's needs are instinctive, that they are expressions of their animal nature. The important thing is that they should not remain animal but become human, i.e. that the child's higher faculties should derive from the satisfaction of his primary needs, and that the mother's instinctive love should become conscious. If Pestalozzi had, until now, stressed the importance of the transition from boyhood to adolescence, from the child's being protected by his mother to his independence, he now emphasizes that of changing from the animal (instinctive) to the human (rational) state which marks the beginning of the conscious relationship between mother and child.

For, as he had said before, all evil arises from man's selfish nature, and so his moral nature, his ability to sacrifice his own well-being for that of others, must be developed as early as possible. Good can be brought about only through good; love and not fear develops the heart. A mother's love, then, is the most formative influence in a child's development. Her love, however, must not be indulgent and weak, but wise and firm; she must resist the child's selfishness and teach even the infant to overcome his animal desires.

The mother's fitness to educate her child depends on her will and ability to educate herself. These *Letters to Greaves* contain Pestalozzi's first observations on the education of woman to be an educator. The conventional idea of woman, he says, is that in her feeling predominates. This he admits to be true, but nevertheless finds it false to conclude that acquiring knowledge and bringing reason to bear on her feelings must necessarily destroy her sensitivity. The main thing in a woman's education should be to establish a balance between the faculties of mind and heart, so that all her cultivated powers form an integrated whole. If this is achieved, her acquired knowledge will enhance rather than endanger the harmony of her soul.

THE EDUCATIONIST

IV YVERDON

When the institute had been transferred to Yverdon and built
up again from the remnants of the past, Pestalozzi had not meant
it to remain there permanently. Apart from the fact that he was
always hoping to establish a poor-school on his own ground in
the Aargau, he would have preferred to stay in a German-
speaking part of the country, for neither he nor his principal
teachers had a perfect command of the French language. Yet
the institute established itself quickly in Yverdon and within a
few years had gained great importance and world renown, an
outcome due rather to blind circumstance than to deliberate
intent.

The castle of Yverdon, a former stronghold of the Dukes of
Savoy built on a Roman site, was in Pestalozzi's time in the
hands of the municipality. They had it repaired and fitted with
every convenience, and placed it rent-free at Pestalozzi's disposal
for as long as he lived. It contained many large halls suitable
for assembly and classrooms, spacious dormitories, and wide
passages, and it was furnished simply but adequately. A large
courtyard, broad avenues, and a nearby meadow were ideal
playgrounds. The lake of Neuchâtel was only half a mile away.

The number of residents—pupils, teachers, servants, and
Pestalozzi's family—rose within a year or two to 250; besides
Swiss, Germans, and French, they included Italians, Spaniards,
and Russians, even Americans. To these were added day pupils
from Yverdon, boarders of branch institutes opened in the town,
and later also girls from a newly founded girls' school. All ages
were represented, and although the majority of boys came from
middle-class homes, a fair percentage of poor children were carried by the fee-paying pupils. The idea was that family circumstances, social background, and even intellectual distinction
should make no difference in their treatment; all children were
regarded as equal. A natural way of life, with plenty of exercise
in fresh air, nourishing food and bodily care—'order and regu-
larity, exertion without overstraining, alternation between lessons and games and between one subject of learning and another'
—this was the programme set and probably carried out during
the first years at Yverdon. It ensured the children's health and
happiness.

As in Burgdorf, so in Yverdon the children's tasks were firmly prescribed, for Pestalozzi could not bear to see inactivity. They had ten lessons daily, the first starting at six o'clock in the morning before they had washed or tidied their hair. But the lessons were a pleasure to them, including as they did nature observation, woodwork, gymnastics, and various games. Wednesday and Sunday afternoons were given over to long walks. In summer the boys went bathing, in winter skating and tobogganing; and often the young Sons of Switzerland could be seen marching, fencing, and shooting in the nearby meadow.

The fundamental educational principle was, as might be expected, the encouragement of the child's natural gifts and powers. 'We try to use the subjects of learning which we teach more as instruments to train the intellect than as a means of expanding knowledge', is the key sentence in a *Report to Parents and the General Public* published in 1807. Since, however, the parents demanded for their money that their children should acquire some positive knowledge and since, moreover, the majority of pupils were older than the children of Burgdorf had been, it was inevitable that specific school subjects should be taken up. So, besides 'elementary education', geography, history, and the natural sciences were taught, and mathematics became of particular importance. Music, physical training, handwork, and religious instruction were added to the curriculum, and later also the classics. The basic principle in the teaching of all subjects was, of course, 'Anschauung' (here: observation). The children were not given the products of learning but were guided to find them for themselves. They were taught to use their own eyes and hands and minds. Exercises in language and arithmetic were in the first instance related to objects and circumstances in their environment before being applied to literature and pure mathematics, and geographical understanding was first aroused on walks and through making models before maps were used. Because of the considerable number of French-speaking children, all lessons were given in both languages, and the different grades of each subject were taught at the same time of the day so that the children could pass from one stage to another according to their abilities and progress.

The lessons were given by specialists who had worked out their subject in accordance with the Pestalozzian principles. Thus a number of men started their careers in Yverdon who later became well-known methodologists in various fields. Karl Ritter of Frankfurt laid the foundations for the modern teaching of geography. Young men from Zurich, Hans Georg Nägeli and Michael T. Pfeiffer, created a new 'natural' method of singing. Pestalozzi himself undertook a methodological treatment of Latin grammar! Most effective of all was the work of Joseph Schmid who had a genius for mathematics. His teaching of this subject won general admiration and was mainly responsible for the institute's educational success. Yverdon thus became in the years that followed a centre of modern instruction for middle-class children. The more methodically the individual subjects were taught, the better were the results achieved; but the greater the institute's teaching success and worldly renown, the further it moved from Pestalozzi's real intention.

Yverdon became more and more the concern of the teachers. Pestalozzi, it is true, was the institute's heart and soul, but administration and instruction were almost entirely left to his assistants. He was too much occupied with his general ideas to be troubled with the carrying out of details. But he would appear at any time and at any place and at once make his influence felt. He would look into a classroom for two or three minutes, make the subtlest psychological observations, and afterwards give valuable advice to the teacher. The livelier the class and the brighter the pupils' eyes, the better pleased he was. 'If he saw little activity in the classroom, or even the teacher seated, or with a book in his hand, he would say nothing and leave the room quickly, shutting the door noisily behind him.' He gave his assistants great freedom to make their experiments and encouraged their independence to such a degree that it endangered his own position. For only as long as a spirit of love reigned among them could this freedom be used to advantage. As soon as the teachers began to presume, the edifice built on trust was bound to collapse.

In many letters and addresses remarks can be found which express Pestalozzi's gratitude to his assistants for the important part they played in building up his enterprise. It was their faithfulness, he says, which often saved it from ruin and which, he hoped, would carry it on after his death. 'O Niederer, greatest of my sons,' runs a eulogy in one of his *Addresses to my House*, 'you are my support; my House rests in your heart. Your eyes strike a lightning which is to its benefit, though it is often a danger to my own weak eyes. Krüsi, you represent the spirit of the House in its beginnings, the spirit of sacred love. My soul is attached to you. I would not recognize my House and would fear for its existence if your united support should ever fail.' There were also Muralt and especially Schmid, Pestalozzi's 'Benjamin' whom he loved more than all his other 'sons' and whom he called 'my delight, my joy, and my pride, the darling child of my heart'.

On the occasion of Pestalozzi's sixty-second birthday Schmid proudly presented a manuscript on the principles of mathematical teaching; in the following year it came out under the title *The Elements of Form and Number* (1809). This was the first work on the teaching method of a particular school subject to be published; moreover it was written by a pupil who only a few years earlier had come to the institute as 'a raw child of nature'. Pestalozzi was overjoyed with the book. It was a brilliant achievement. Schmid's talent and energy were indeed extraordinary, but his success made him conceited and arrogant.

Pestalozzi preferred to select his assistants from among his own pupils and liked them to be poor. He thus could be sure that they were 'unpretentious' and untouched by previous 'corrupt influences'. They were made to help with the teaching when still very young; simultaneous teaching and learning of all its members was indeed one of the institute's main features. Pestalozzi demanded a tremendous amount of work from his helpers, as he did from himself. They had to be completely dedicated to the cause, and for years they gave their services from a willing heart. Not only did they teach from eight to ten periods a day, but they were also occupied with the children outside lessons, for Pestalozzi made no difference between teaching and educating. The unmarried teachers—and during the first years of Yverdon all the men were unmarried—had their meals with the boys, their beds in the dormitories, and did their work in the classrooms. The principal masters had the additional task of supervising a particular group of children of various ages, each being a sort of house-father to a small family for whose personal well-being he was responsible. Preparations, corrections, and research were done at night when the children were asleep, the time at which, be it remembered, Pestalozzi himself dictated his works to one of his helpers.

Thrice weekly after supper staff meetings were held in which the children's progress, the teachers' own work, the development of the method, and problems of organization were discussed. These often went on until late in the night because they created passionate controversies. Pestalozzi himself seldom attended the meetings but made each master inform him of his experiences, just as he saw each boy at least once a week after having received a report from his special tutor.

In dealing with the children Pestalozzi had an unusual tact which they at once felt and valued. Whenever he approached them their faces lit up, for he had always a kind word for each. They, like the masters, called him 'Father Pestalozzi'. When at one time Schmid issued an order that they should say 'Herr Pestalozzi' and take off their hats to him, they thought this ridiculous, and Pestalozzi insisted in having the order dropped. He had a habit of putting his thumb on a child's brow and pushing his head back a little to be able to read his eyes. Often he did this without saying a word, which only increased the impression. Difficult boys he would take up to his room, talk their concerns over with them, advise them on how to get rid of their faults, promise his help and discretion, and usually succeed in awaking in them the desire to improve. Some would be with him thus night after night, and when they came up, he would take them in his arms and ask, 'Have you anything to tell me?'

The effect of Pestalozzi's personality on masters and pupils was, as Niederer says, 'truly moral and almost religious'. To the former he was 'the spirit of the method personified', to the latter 'the inspirer of their moral attitude'. In their attachment to him and in the spirit of love emanating from him lay the secret of the institute's unity. Pestalozzi was the living example of his theory that the educator must act in the spirit of a father and strive to awake a sense of brotherhood among his pupils. He expected his assistants also to base their authority on love rather than on fear. If penalties were unavoidable they should consist in admonishment and deprivation, not in corporal punishment. Nor did he believe in marks of distinction, orders, and prizes such as were commonly given in other schools. The reports issued in Yverdon did not contain marks and placings but remarks on the boys' progress and observations on their behaviour. The reward of their efforts was considered to lie in their achievement.

Visitors to Yverdon observed the children's contented looks and intelligent expressions and concluded that they must all have very good brains. But the reason for their contentment was that they were neither strained nor repressed but given tasks which were in accordance with their capacities. 'If it were customary in all schools to cut the children's noses off and there were one school in which noses were left on, visitors would probably be just as amazed about the children's natural looks', was Pestalozzi's comment. The Yverdon children looked intelligent because their education was 'natural', and they were happy because there was friendship and confidence between masters and pupils. During the first and best years of its existence a true family spirit pervaded the House, and more than by any public recommendation was Pestalozzi gratified by a word from a simple peasant: 'This is not an institute, it is a household.'

The occasions on which the whole House came together and which were designed to foster the community spirit were the weekly assemblies, religious services, and social festivities. Daily morning and evening prayers were held by those Protestant and Catholic masters who were ministers of their church. The weekly address on Saturday evenings was always given by Pestalozzi himself. He then surveyed what had been done during the week, using the everyday happenings as starting-points for comments on the broader issues of life. Or he dealt with religious principles, relating them to the children's own experiences. He spoke on the futility of knowledge without love but also on the uselessness of love without knowledge. His aim was to evoke a religious spirit in the children and to make the desire for a good life 'habitual' in them.

New Year's Day especially was made a festival of reflection, resolve, and new beginning. The large halls were decorated, a choir would sing specially composed part-songs, presents were exchanged, and richer fare provided. The highlight of the day was Pestalozzi's address. It would give an account of past achievements and state the aims and requirements of future developments. These *Addresses to my House* are the most immediate expressions available of Pestalozzi's relationship to his assistants and pupils, and also to his work. They reflect most vividly both the changing and the lasting emotions of this passionately loving man who struggled and strove so tirelessly. They are testimonies of his self-searching, his humility, and his fear of failure as well as of his sense of mission, his dedication, and his faith. They made a deep impression on the audience of his day and do not fail to affect as strongly the present-day reader.

The first day of a new year, he would say, is the beginning of a new life. Just as life is renewed, we must renew ourselves. This basic idea recurs in all the addresses. Certain other themes are also often repeated: the contrast between time and eternity, the blessing of suffering, and the life in the spirit; the aim of education as the awakening of the divine in man; the call for truth and right; the request to members and friends of the House not to break the bond of unity; but also the confession of guilt for all that was wrong or inadequate. All addresses culminate in the praise of love and in thanks to God for having brought the House so far.

Yet each address has a particular tone. That of 1808 was given under the shadow of previous tensions among the staff. In tones of profound gloom Pestalozzi blames himself for having failed in his work; he can only hope, he says, that his successors will do better than he after his death. He had a coffin with a skull on it placed in the hall beside him, and pointing to it he cried, 'I am no longer able to help. I am not yet purified. I have not been worthy of my work. I shall go, but you will remain. Be better than I have been, so that God may complete this work through you.' When in the following year the House was still going on, even flourishing, in spite of all difficulties, he was able to say, 'God has saved it. He has saved it through all my errors. It is God's work.' He knew that the responsibility for the community's well-being was entirely his own, that the harmony of the House depended on the power of his paternal spirit. 'O God,' he prayed, 'maintain in me the only power which you have given me, maintain my love in me.'

Pestalozzi would speak to the whole House, but he would also address the various groups separately, the smallest children, the younger and older boys, the students and principal teachers, his friends and relatives, each by their names. He would advise them individually on how to live wisely in the following year. He tells his assistants that it is more important to cultivate their pupils' hearts and minds than to transmit knowledge, and that it is better to be gentle than severe. 'Become perfect in love. Don't attribute more value to the ability to instruct than is its due in the framework of education as a whole.' To the pupil teachers he recommends a sense of brotherhood towards the children under their care, for only through brotherly love can the educator attain that paternal spirit which his position demands of him. The finest words in the New Year's address of 1809 are directed to the children: 'God's nature which is in you is held sacred in this House. We do not hem it in; we try to develop it. Nor do we impose on you our own natures. It is far from our intention to make of you men such as we are. It is equally far from our intention to make of you such men as are the majority of men in our time. Under our guidance you should become men such as your natures—the divine and sacred in your nature—require you to be.'

The means of educating children to become good and true men—this is the main subject of Pestalozzi's *Addresses to my House*—is love. It is a great mistake, he says, to believe that he is seeking to educate through the partial activity of training the intellect, through a new method of teaching. 'No, I seek to educate through the universality of love.' For 'love does not rule but forms, and that is more'. Such a love must, of course, not be blind and passive but active and understanding. Its aim is to call forth a similar active love in response.

If New Year's Day was celebrated in a serious fashion, birthdays and anniversaries gave opportunities for merry-making. For Pestalozzi had the Swiss fondness for large festivities, for singing and dancing and eating and drinking, if possible in the open air. His birthday was made the occasion for confirming the unity of the House and bringing together again those members who might have fallen out temporarily. Dramatic and musical performances took place in the great hall which was gaily decorated. At the end there was a collection among the well-to-do pupils for the poor of Yverdon parish, and a particularly good meal concluded the day. A number of reports exist on Pestalozzi's fortieth wedding anniversary which show that it must have made a lasting impression on the participants' minds. After the more solemn part of the celebrations in which speeches were made and songs sung a dinner was given for three hundred persons. Then there was dancing. Father Pestalozzi and his dignified lady led in an old-fashioned measure. On another occasion the whole House sailed gaily along Lake Neuchâtel to Grandson. Pestalozzi had hired a boat and bought up the entire harvest of a vineyard to give his children pleasure. He himself was always the merriest and got tremendous satisfaction from seeing his large family happy.

The Pestalozzian community consisted not only of the people living together in Yverdon castle. There were individuals and groups staying in the town but taking part in the life of the institute during the day. There were friends living abroad but belonging in spirit to the community. Strangers who came to have a look were admitted to social functions, to lessons, and even to staff meetings; they thus became 'Friends of the Method'. The institute's doors were open to anyone; visitors of all sorts entered, and left to spread the method in their homelands.

In the first place, there was the friendly relationship with the town. The municipality of Yverdon supported Pestalozzi's enterprise to a larger extent than had that of Burgdorf, not only because Pestalozzi had come to Yverdon on their express invitation, as a famous man and not as an unknown hedge-schoolmaster, but also because the political atmosphere in the canton of Vaud was more congenial to his ideas than that in Berne. The Yverdon citizens whose sons went to school in the castle as day boys were on amicable terms with Pestalozzi and his assistants. The de Guimps family in particular proved very helpful as advisers and mediators between town and castle, especially later in times of difficulty.

Then there was the setting up of an institute for girls. It had always been Pestalozzi's particular desire to give mothers, present and future, the means towards fulfilling their educational duties. In the Neuhof and Stans homes for poor children boys and girls had been educated together as in a real family. But since the Yverdon institute had become predominantly middle-class, admission had to be restricted to boys. When the demand for an education of girls (also of the middle classes) became ever more urgent, a separate house was opened in the town (May

1806). Krüsi was in charge; his sister Elisabeth and a friend of hers took over the teaching, and Frau Custer, Pestalozzi's daughter-in-law, did the house-keeping.

It is surprising and yet in a way understandable that the curriculum for the girls' school was hardly different from that for the boys'; only woodwork was replaced by more feminine kinds of handwork. The girls took part in all the social activities going on in the castle. Before long a number of them and their mistresses became engaged to masters, a fact which was commented on by certain prudes. During the first years of its existence the girls' house was run none too efficiently as an annex to the boys' institute; but in 1809 it was given a properly trained headmistress who now developed it from the small beginnings into a flourishing institute for the higher education of girls.

Rosette Kasthofer (1779–1857) was an active and efficient woman with a clear and independent mind. She had come to know the Pestalozzian method when on a visit in Münchenbuchsee some years earlier and had thoroughly studied it under the guidance of Muralt. On this occasion she fell in love with the attractive young man, but an engagement was shunned by him. A mutual esteem soon grew up between Rosette Kasthofer and Pestalozzi. He offered her a post in the girls' school because he saw in her 'a female Niederer'. But for a long time she did not consider herself well enough prepared. When she finally accepted she brought order into the haphazard establishment. In 1813 it was made over to her as her own.

The children's parents were another important factor in the educational community. Pestalozzi invited them to take an active part in the life of the institute, for he was aware that they had a vital interest in its development, having entrusted it with their most precious possessions, their sons. Between those parents who lived abroad and the institute a regular correspondence was kept up (copy books covering many years and containing hundreds of letters going out from Yverdon are still in existence). Pestalozzi or his assistants not only gave detailed accounts of the respective sons' progress but also of the institute's educational problems in general. He gratefully accepted suggestions and criticisms and also economic advice from the business men among the fathers. Some, for example, tried to persuade him to raise his fees because they thought that otherwise the institute could hardly survive. And not infrequently they gave loans or donations in times of financial crisis.

The friendly relationship which existed between Pestalozzi and a number of well-known Frankfurt families is only one example of many. The connection had been established by G. A. Gruner who had been in Burgdorf and published a book on Pestalozzi and his method. Impressed by it, the de Bary, Lejeune, and Bethmann-Hollweg families sent their sons to Yverdon. It was as a tutor to the latter that Karl Ritter, the geographer, came to Pestalozzi. Karoline von Wolzogen, Schiller's sister-in-law, brought her son personally and studied the method herself. J. J. Willemer the banker had his son Abraham educated in Yverdon; he went to see him there together with Marianne Jung, his future second wife, Goethe's Suleika. Frau von Holzhausen's sons spent two years in Yverdon. The children of these well-to-do families were accompanied by their own private tutors. These men became of considerable importance both for the development of the institute and that of the science of education. One of them was Mieg, another was Fröbel.

Johann Elias Mieg (1770–1842), himself a theologian, came from a Heidelberg family of churchmen, a member of which had once introduced Pestalozzi to the order of the Illuminati. During the four years of his stay in Yverdon Mieg was not only the trusted agent of the Frankfurt families' wishes and interests but also one of the most valuable members of Pestalozzi's staff, using, as he did, his intellectual abilities and business experience to the advantage of the institute as a whole. He was teacher, administrator, and accountant all in one. His rectitude and impartiality won him the friendship of the most diverse members of the community. Pestalozzi entrusted him with the entire management of the House. It was thanks to Mieg's soundness and efficiency that as long as he was there the institute was run economically, a thing which never happened before or afterwards. When in later years financial difficulties increased to breaking point, everybody believed that if only Mieg could come back all would be well again.

Friedrich Fröbel (1782–1852), on the other hand, was a solitary figure among so many intelligent young men. He was still suffering from the after-effects of an unhappy childhood but resolved to turn his own sad experience to general advantage by providing for other children a happier upbringing and a better education than he had had himself. He was greatly struck with Pestalozzi's ideas on education and sent literature on the new method and memoranda of his own to his brother, a pastor in Thuringia, and to the reigning Princess of his homeland Schwarzburg-Rudolstadt, urging them to have the method introduced in their country. His own theory of education is fundamentally influenced by Pestalozzi's ideas, but he soon began to dissociate himself in his theory as well as personally by stressing the differences rather than the similarities of their respective systems. Fröbel's philosophy of education is speculative and deductive, tracing the development of man 'as from the absolute', while Pestalozzi the realist, in Fröbel's opinion, 'takes man as he appears on earth'.

Very important for the introduction of the Pestalozzian method in foreign countries were the student teachers, the largest group of whom came from Prussia. Training young men for the task of popular education was, of course, one of Pestalozzi's main desires. Almost within a year of having begun his work in Yverdon he had asked the Vaudois government for an inspection of his institute in the hope of having intelligent young men sent to be trained for the task of teaching according to his method in the rural schools of the canton. The commission who examined the institute acknowledged the results achieved but thought that the method was not yet sufficiently tested for general adoption. Pestalozzi had been very disappointed but was all the more anxious to develop his method.

Some years later (1808) the longed-for official recognition came from the government of Prussia. The collapse of that country brought about by the Napoleonic wars necessitated an entire reorganization of the State, and this was to be based on a new education of the people. Pestalozzi was among the spiritual leaders approached for guidance. Fichte in his *Addresses to the German Nation* advocated the self-activity on which the Pestalozzian method of instruction was founded as the starting-point of a new national education. Freiherr vom Stein in his *Political Testament* recommended the reanimation of the German spirit through 'a method based on man's inner nature'. The advice to send young Prussians to Yverdon to be trained there as the new teachers of the nation came from Nicolovius. He now held a high government post which enabled him to put into action those

ideas 'whose light had been kindled in him' during the unforgettable encounter with Pestalozzi many years before. Teachers'
training colleges and elementary schools for the whole nation
were planned, and the method to be adopted was to be the
Pestalozzian.

The first Prussian student teachers stayed in Yverdon for three
years. They were teaching and learning at the same time and
received some theoretical instruction on the principles of the
method from Niederer, but it cannot be said that they followed a
well-organized course. They were, however, thoroughly imbued
with Pestalozzi's ideas, and they for their part contributed a
good deal to the work of the institute. On going home they
spread the new spirit of education in their country, first as teachers, later as elementary school headmasters and training college
principals. Of all the countries interested in Pestalozzi's method
it was Prussia which made the greatest effort to understand its
true significance and to put it into practice; and in many cases
it was through its realization in Prussia that the Pestalozzian
method became known overseas.

As the years went on Yverdon became, in Niederer's words,
'the centre of Europe's educational culture'. Visitors came from
many different countries and were of very various types: ministers of State from Prussia, the Crown Prince of Bavaria, the
Countess Brunszvik from Hungary, a poor journeyman mason
interested in teaching, or an unknown man of whom Pestalozzi
knew no more than that he was 'someone who sought his advice'.
It must be admitted that Pestalozzi was particularly anxious to
please reigning princes paying him a visit, and this may seem
strangely incompatible with his democratic views. But the reason
was that he hoped of every travelling monarch, 'This one is sure
to set up schools and to free his serfs.' In order to further the
realization of this hope he spent a great deal of time and effort
in explaining his ideas to these people; but, he said, if through
his explanations even one child received a better education, his
trouble was well worth while.

The establishment of Pestalozzian schools in various European countries was the work of men and women who had been
teachers in Yverdon and either returned to their native lands or
emigrated to foreign parts. Among the first were J. de l'Aspée,
the above mentioned journeyman mason of Wiesbaden in Hesse,

and Betty Gleim of Bremen. Swiss teachers like J. von Muralt, W. Egger, and G. F. Hofmann introduced the method in places as far apart as Petersburg, Budapest, and Naples. Very promising, but temporary, was the development in Spain where Don Manuel Godoy, 'the Prince of Peace', had a military academy run according to Pestalozzi's principles. Holland and Sweden were also actively interested. Pestalozzi's connections with England were not established until after the lifting of the Continental Blockade which, while it lasted, impeded cultural communication. Pestalozzian schools in the United States of America were established through the combined efforts of W. Maclure and J. Neef. It is surprising that the method did not win more active approval in France, but the reasons are clear: Napoleon was not interested in popular education, and later, during the reign of the Bourbons, Pestalozzi's ideas were rejected as revolutionary. This opinion, to anticipate future developments, became increasingly general during the Restoration period and was responsible for the closing down of many a Pestalozzian school in various parts of Europe.

The Pestalozzian institute in Yverdon reached its peak of prosperity in 1809. Pestalozzi ventured to say that his method 'has been put to the test of eight difficult years and has not been found wanting'. He was happy and grateful that his ideas were finally realized, that they were accepted abroad, and that their future development seemed secure. Later, however, in *The Story of my Life* he considers these years of worldly success as a 'sham fortune' and an 'aberration' from his real course. And even during the time of growing fame the difficulties arising from the living together of people so diverse and of such strong personalities were beginning to disturb the happy community life.

Schmid, as will be remembered, had worked out a scientific method of teaching mathematics by which he achieved brilliant results. Pestalozzi now expected something similar from Niederer in his subject. But Niederer was increasingly neglecting his work in the institute. He could not, he said, waste his time on the 'material needs' of everyday life; his duty was the propagation of 'the idea of elementary education'. This irresponsibility arising from intellectual pride was a source of grave concern to Pestalozzi.

219

The plan to base the renewal of Switzerland after the upheaval caused by the Napoleonic Wars on a nation-wide education, such as was being introduced in Prussia, and to make Yverdon its centre, prompted Pestalozzi to apply to the Federal Government for an inspection of his institute. This was the last attempt of the old man to gain official recognition in his own country. Niederer encouraged the idea, Schmid disapproved of it. Pestalozzi hoped for a repetition of the favourable consequences of Ith's report in 1802. But the report given this time by the government's main expert, Father G. Girard, was harmful to Pestalozzi's ends rather than helpful. It acknowledged the good results achieved in the teaching of mathematics, refuted the charge of irreligion, and attributed existing defects to the institute's unusual development. It was by no means unappreciative, but like the earlier report given by the Vaudois Commission it answered in the negative the main question, whether the method should be generally introduced in the country.

The verdict caused great consternation amongst the staff. Pestalozzi was of the opinion that the experts' visit of five days had been too short to give them a true impression; and being unable to ask for another visit he tried to undo what had been done. It was in vain. The report was published and led to the decline of the institute. The masters tried, each in his own way, to remedy existing defects. In pursuing their different courses their paths crossed, and sharp disputes arose, especially between Niederer and Schmid. The latter was ruder than ever, even to Pestalozzi. Pestalozzi tried with tact and understanding to hold the discrepant parties together, but the assistants disregarded his efforts to keep the peace. Their open quarrels were, in fact, only the final flare-up of a long, smouldering antagonism fundamentally due to the struggle for the first place in the institute and at Pestalozzi's side. Matters came to a head because of the rivalry between the two men over a girl, a certain Luise Segesser. Niederer was preferred, and in the summer of 1810 Schmid left Pestalozzi's house in a fury. Some teachers who were on his side (Fröbel amongst them) had gone earlier. A short time after his departure Schmid published a book *Experiences and Views on Education, Institutes, and Schools* (1810) in which he openly attacked Pestalozzi's institute and his practice of education.

The happy bond of brotherly love was broken. Pestalozzi was

greatly troubled; he felt he had lost in Schmid his right hand and had no strength left to continue his work. The rot, once begun, continued to spread. In the same summer Muralt, Hofmann, and Mieg resigned their posts, tactfully, it is true, and for legitimate reasons; but the simultaneous departure of so many good teachers had an adverse effect on the institute. It made a bad impression on the parents, and the number of pupils which had already diminished owing to the hazards of war dropped even more, while the financial difficulties increased. From now on Pestalozzi was never again to experience a time free of worry and anxiety. And Niederer, the victor in this fraternal strife, spent all his time and energy in a most unfortunate literary feud.

The government report had served Pestalozzi's opponents as a pretext for open attacks. The conservative Bernese Professor of Constitutional Law, K. L. von Haller (known for his main work *Restoration of the Political Sciences* which gave the name to the subsequent period in European history, the Restoration period), turned a review of the report on the Yverdon institute into a political diatribe accusing Pestalozzi of revolutionary, even anarchistic motives (*Göttingen Literary Intelligencer*, 1811). Canon J. H. Bremi wrote in the same vein in the Zurich *Friday News* (1811). Pestalozzi was very much hurt that such a malicious assault should come out of his native city. Niederer, then, as the spokesman for the whole institute, set out with heavy artillery to destroy Pestalozzi's enemies once and for all. In two large volumes of philosophical argument, *Pestalozzi's Educational Enterprise in Relation to Contemporary Civilization* (1812/13), he explained and vindicated Pestalozzi's ideas. Pestalozzi himself was persuaded to contribute a short *Declaration*, for he felt obliged to support Niederer. Probably because no publisher could be found for such an unpromising production a printing press and a bookseller's shop were set up in the institute for the distribution of this and other polemic matter, without any technical or commercial knowledge and without Pestalozzi's approval. The result was that over the next few years masses of waste paper kept accumulating, and the end was financial ruin.

It appears that Pestalozzi had lost control altogether. The word went round that 'he was quite unable to govern'. Here is seen the negative side of Pestalozzi's respect for his assistants' individuality and his encouragement of their independence. They were now proving to be unworthy of such freedom. Each thought he knew better than the master what should be done and was abler than he to administer the House. Thus there were many leaders or—which comes to the same—none, for Niederer, too, was inefficient. Pestalozzi's ideas which had been stated so impressively in works and prospectuses and put into practice so eagerly in the first years of the institute's existence were no longer carried out satisfactorily. The children's parents and other observers noticed a regrettable fall in the standard of education in Yverdon.

Pestalozzi tried to close his eyes to the decline. 'I am keeping calm. The reduction in the number of pupils does no harm to the essentials of my aim, on the contrary. Everything will be all right.' But sometimes there is a note of weariness in his utterances. 'When I pass a wagon which is drawn by an old horse I feel inclined to send away the driver and to release the horse, so that it may run free in the fields. I then think of myself and long for a few hours' rest. . . . But I must stay on.'

A number of unhappy events demanded of the old man persistent fortitude. In the spring of 1812 he fell seriously ill, having damaged his inner ear by his own carelessness. For several months his life was in danger, and only much later did he admit how excruciating the pains had been. In the face of death he wished to give an account of what he had intended to do and what he had in fact achieved, and began to dictate his autobiography (*The Ailing Pestalozzi to the Healthy Public*, 1812). But when he received the first indication that he might live, he said, 'I would not have liked to die. My ideas are not yet understood. I have still a great deal to make clear.'

Then there was the danger of losing the castle of Yverdon. The Allied Military Command required the town's largest buildings to be turned into hospitals, and what was worse, the population knew that a typhus epidemic was raging amongst the troops. The Cantonal Government sent a deputation of petitioners to Allied Headquarters in Basle, and without being specially invited Pestalozzi joined them. They were almost ashamed of their unkempt companion, yet it was he who succeeded in having the order revoked. He was granted an audience of Czar Alexander I and talked to him about the necessity of popular education with such enthusiasm—while speaking he came closer and closer to the monarch and was even on the point of getting hold of his coat button—that the Czar embraced him cordially, granted his immediate request, and promised to do all he could to further his enterprise. The sad aftermath of the stationing of troops in the vicinity (they were finally billeted in the nearby village of Grandson) was the death of Pestalozzi's daughter-in-law Anna Magdalena Custer. During a short holiday in that resort she caught the infection and died within a few days.

Meanwhile the institute's financial situation became ever more precarious; the debts now amounted to 20,000 francs. One means of procuring money would have been the publication of Pestalozzi's complete works, for they were in great demand and out of print. Negotiations with Cotta, the famous Stuttgart firm, proceeded favourably but were not brought to a conclusion because there was no one in Yverdon who could conduct business matters efficiently.

Everyone's hopes were set on Mieg; he was to bring order into the muddle. He returned for only a short time, and the relief he effected was only temporary. For the causes of the decline were other than economic. The institute's success depended entirely on Pestalozzi's personality, and this could not be changed. He was neither capable of administering the House himself nor willing to hand over the responsibility to anyone else. The situation which had prevailed in Münchenbuchsee was now being repeated in Yverdon. Yet it had another equally significant side. As long as Pestalozzi was master, peace and friendship reigned in the House; when he lost control, outward order might return, but the spirit of love was dead.

Frau Pestalozzi had once more come into money. Again she gave the larger part of it to satisfy the most pressing creditors. On the urgent request of her friends she had the rest of her capital and the Neuhof taken out of Pestalozzi's control and secured by deed for Gottlieb, her grandson. Pestalozzi felt hurt by this action although he had to admit that it was a wise one. Shortly afterwards the self-appointed managers of the institute suggested, as a means of saving, that Pestalozzi should remove his family because Frau Pestalozzi had her own separate table and Lisabeth gave the children too large pieces of bread. Pestalozzi was loath to be parted from his wife and upset about the injustice done to Lisabeth. Yet he agreed to the harshest measures

223

and was ready for any personal sacrifice if thereby his House could be saved.

But it was not saved even though Niederer tried to play the 'dictator'. To the astonishment of all came the news of the engagement between Niederer and Rosette Kasthofer, the head-mistress of the girls' school. This connection enhanced his pres-tige. From his position of strength he conceived the idea of recalling the efficient Schmid. A desire for reconciliation was also felt by the other. Schmid had withdrawn his insults and promised to control his temper; Niederer was willing to try once more to combine his philosophical knowledge with Schmid's practical ability for the good of the institute. Pestalozzi was overjoyed.

Schmid at once took the reins into his strong hands. He paid the rest of the debts out of his own savings. He dismissed some staff, reduced the salaries of the rest and increased their teach-ing hours. His colleagues admitted the necessity of these measures but felt hurt by the harshness of his procedure. Pestalozzi who had resisted Niederer's influence let Schmid have his own way and was even grateful for what he did; so much was he impressed by his organizing ability. When things were a little easier again it was found possible to bring back Pestalozzi's family. At the end of her life Frau Pestalozzi was gratified to see, as she thought, her husband's work saved.

The year 1815 passed in peace and harmony. But in the middle of December Frau Pestalozzi died at the age of 77. Her life had not been such as she had hoped and deserved. It had been a life of deprivation and sacrifice: a life by the side of a genius who inspires but exhausts the people around him. She had been the first to recognize Pestalozzi's noble spirit and the only person never to fail him. She had approved of his enter-prise and supported it as best she could, but it had cost her her personal peace and happiness. Yet she died in the firm belief that God had guided all for the good, and that he would protect her husband's House even in the future. She was buried in the Yverdon castle grounds between two old chestnut trees, at a place where she had often liked to sit, and was mourned by the institute and town alike.

Pestalozzi's grief took the form of passionate self-reproach for having given her such a sorrowful life; yet his anguish was relieved by the certainty of her forgiveness and the hope of their reunion. Thus he dwelt less on the loss he now experienced than on the abundance of what he had possessed, and he rose to a state of acceptance 'which turns even the days of greatest suffering into sacred days of inner ennoblement'. In his New Year's address of 1816 he was able to call the past year 'a year of blessing and of salvation'.

It was the last year of internal peace. However little Frau Pestalozzi had interfered in the institute's affairs, her gentle presence had had a calming effect. Pestalozzi's request to his assistants (in his New Year's address) not to betray her belief in the institute's salvation was in vain. Immediately after her funeral the quarrels amongst the staff flared up to such a degree that they led to the institute's destruction.

Yet throughout these years of ups and downs, while a great number of pupils and teachers were making demands on him, an endless stream of visitors pouring into the institute, internal disagreements endangering its peace, and financial difficulties and hostile attacks threatening its existence—throughout all these disturbances Pestalozzi went on building the edifice of his method. And in the last year, the stormiest of all, he wrote his great political work *To the Innocence, the Earnestness, and the Generosity of my Age and my Country*.

VII   The Social Reformer
(1815–1827)

I 'TO THE INNOCENCE'

THE political changes during the years 1813–15, the fight against and the victory over Napoleon, could not but affect the fortunes of Switzerland. On their march towards France the Allied armies invaded the Federation, thus violating her neutrality. (It was in connection with these troop movements that Pestalozzi, in his audience with Czar Alexander I, saved Yverdon from billeting.) Napoleon's downfall enabled Switzerland to throw off the enforced Mediation Act and to draw up a Constitution of her own choosing. But on this question the political parties within the country disagreed again, as in 1803. The conservatives, whose stronghold was Berne, wished to retain a federalist system with the main power vested in the cantons, while their opponents, under the leadership of Zurich, tried to re-establish the pre-Napoleonic (Helvetian) order, i.e. a centralized government. It took the country's representatives more than a year to work out the general form and particular details of their new Constitution.

At this decisive stage in Swiss history Pestalozzi spoke again on politics. He had refrained from doing so during the time of his country's dependence on the French Empire. But now he felt compelled to give good counsel, for, said he, in his long life he had seen the coming and going of many a constitution and so could with confidence advise on the best and most humane way of governing the country.

He still believes that a centralized government is preferable to a federalist and better suited to restore the spirit of the 'good old

226

times'. But his main concern is not with the outward form of the new Constitution. As in his earlier writings on legislation he points out that it is the mental and moral attitude of the legislators which is most important because it creates the conditions for the liberty or bondage of the people. His work *To the Innocence* is then, strictly speaking, not a political treatise but the outcome of all his previous inquiries on educational, social, and cultural questions, the summing-up of his ideas on the right way of guiding men.

Thus its trains of thought are familiar from earlier works; the writing is repetitive and, for the sake of emphasis, it goes round and round in circles. Because of its great length the book demands considerable patience from the reader. Yet in the end the main ideas emerge more clearly than in other Pestalozzian works. They are, in fact, so significant and topical that a reading of the book should be strongly recommended—if only it were not written in such a forbidding style.

The difficulty of establishing a truly liberal constitution, Pestalozzi argues, arises from 'the corruption of our time'. The contemporary political situation is one of confusion and darkness. Hence, while 'the ordinary man of our time' would resort to force for the solution of political difficulties, Pestalozzi advises the legislators to seek 'light'. 'Knowledge of the evils which lie in ourselves and act against ourselves—that is what we need.' Responsible leaders of their country must first of all have a clear and true idea of 'the spirit of the time', for it is precisely this spirit which is threatening mankind, this 'corruption of civilization' in which 'man sails on, driven by the current of worldly impulses, without suspecting the existence of whirlpools into which he finally falls'. Thrice within a short time the type of political corruption has changed: the lack of moral independence at the end of the *ancien régime* first turned into Revolution and sansculottism and then into 'a refined art of tyranny which came near to exterminating the human race' (the Napoleonic régime). The present breathing space of greater legal security seems to indicate that these 'vicious attacks of brute force' have subsided. But this impression is wrong. Force still presents a threat to mankind. For the various maladies of the times all spring from the same source; and although their symptoms may for the time being have disappeared, their poisonous cause lies still unpurged 'within ourselves'. It would be dangerous to disregard the deep-rooted reason for the prevailing corruption. Men might easily lose their hard-won sense of right and their conception of peaceful co-existence if they were left to pursue their downward path. 'We have been warned as mankind has seldom been warned before.' If the European nations are to be preserved from anarchy and a repetition on an even larger scale of their previous experiences, there is only one way left to save them: 'Let us become better men, so that we can be better citizens and can again have States in the true meaning of the word.' In order to reach this goal it is urgently necessary to know the origin of all political errors and to search for the remedies, and so to save future generations, indeed the whole human race, from a collapse of civilization.

The source of all the world's evil, as Pestalozzi had said before, is man's selfishness. In a nation, it leads to 'sansculottism', in a government, to tyranny. Both these forms of 'barbarism' are the expression of the same impulse which belongs to man's animal nature. But barbarism's polar opposite, namely 'culture', also derives from a human power, from that in man which counteracts his selfishness and enables him to become a moral being. If the lower impulses of society are to be overcome and its higher potentialities realized, their common origin within human nature must be recognized. In interpreting man's dual nature Pestalozzi employs categories similar to those used in the *Inquiries*, but now he applies them to groups of society and the contemporary political situation rather than to the individual.

He now speaks of only two 'states' opposing each other in man: the animal and the human. (The intermediate state—the social—was even formerly described as being only a more civilized form of the animal state and is therefore now taken as being included in the latter.) Man's achievements on the lower level of existence are called 'civilization', his higher forms of attainment, the results of a 'truly human' effort, are what constitutes 'culture'. (A distinction between 'civilization' and 'culture' was first made by Kant in his *Ideas on a Universal History with a View to World Citizenship*, 1784.) Culture is 'entirely the creation of the individual', never that of 'the crowd'. The great danger of the times as seen by Pestalozzi is the increasing influence of people in the mass, the preponderance of the 'collective existence' over the 'individual existence'. (These are the terms now used in place of 'animal state' and 'human state'.) 'The mass', consisting as it does of physical beings, exhibits all the characteristics pertaining to animal nature: selfishness, cruelty, force. Therefore it can produce only civilization; it is outside those relationships between individuals which form the basis of culture.

Man's animal nature, Pestalozzi declares, finds the satisfaction of its physical needs more easily by combined than by individual effort. The urge towards a collective existence is therefore motivated by the desire for life's enjoyments. Admittedly, man's selfish appetites are restricted by the social order; but it only regulates his behaviour, it does not affect his motives. A man who is 'merely civilized' acts, at best, according to social laws, but not to moral law. At worst, his animal tendencies are even encouraged by society. For the more people are massed together, the less there remains of personal responsibility. Acts of inhumanity which the individual would detest are committed unhesitatingly by a crowd.

'The wrongs of the Revolution [and of the subsequent Dictatorship] did not fall upon an innocent continent like sin upon Paradise.' The terror of the preceding decades was not merely the product of evil governments, it was also the consequence of the people's moral degradation. For in the mass they have lost the power of independent moral decision. They follow the impulses of their lower nature without thought or feeling and commit acts of brutality unworthy of human beings. They have neither conscience nor shame. Thus man in his collective existence has brought upon himself the existing corruption by acting in this modern world as primitive man did in the wilderness. But there is this difference between them: modern man is no longer like primitive man in a state of innocence. He ought to know better and yet he goes wrong in his inclinations and intentions. The responsibility for the prevailing barbarism must, then, be entirely his own.

Man's individual existence, on the other hand, is based on those qualities and faculties which distinguish him from all other living beings. It enables him to rise above his physical appetites and 'to turn civilization into culture'. His relationships on this higher level—for man cannot exist alone—are those small yet ever enlarging circles: the family, the occupational group, the

229

local community. With them lies the responsibility for education, religion, and all forms of social welfare, and they all have their origin in the home. These conditions 'in which man has, as it were, been placed by God' provide, Pestalozzi repeats, 'the only means to the ennobling of man and the only basis of a true national culture'.

The most important organization of the collective existence is the State. Pestalozzi's evaluation of the contemporary State is decidedly negative; it is sharply opposed to his high regard for natural relationships. The modern State, he says, retains man's taste for physical power because self-interest is its main feature. Its aim is security, not ennoblement. In a conflict between individual and society it is bound to support the collective against the individual existence. State legislation is concerned with law and order in their outward forms; it has no influence on man's inmost intentions. No government, not even the best, provides a sufficient safeguard against the preponderance of collective over individual demands. No political constitution takes account of man as a higher being.

The collective existence in its most concentrated form is seen in the Head of the State. Bonaparte (as Pestalozzi calls him with deliberate contempt) is the terrible example of one who has pushed the demands of the collective existence to the utmost limits, thus exposing the full extent of their evil. The essential characteristic of his disastrous career is, according to Pestalozzi, that he destroyed the independence of the individual by interfering with his organic relationships. Bonaparte delivered education, religion, and social welfare into the hands of brute force; he regarded 'even the child in his mother's womb' as the property of the State; in fact, he extended the claim of the State to all spheres of life. Thus he ruined the foundations of culture. He made himself the representative of power and became 'the scourge of the world, the symbol of man's self-glorification in its ugliest form'. His power and his influence were greater than those of any previous monarch. That he was able to gain and retain them was 'a masterpiece of man's greatest art in its greatest corruption'.

How can this immense achievement be explained? Pestalozzi suggests that Bonaparte appealed to men's weakness. He roused their animal nature and employed their temerity, greed, and lust for power with complete disregard of their dignity, liberty, and rights. He turned them into the slaves of his will and used them like puppets for his own purposes. His war against humanity had a dreadful success. Yet there was also a good side to its horror. It showed the world how terrible the social state can be if it is considered only as a state of collective and not of individual existence. It revealed how easily men can be convinced that selfish action is their social right. Bonaparte 'enlightened' mankind about the nature of sovereignty; he carried the State's omnipotence to extremes and thereby demonstrated more clearly than had been done for centuries that 'a government must protect the God-given rights of the individual not only legally but also psychologically'.

This predominance of the collective over the individual existence affects all from the Head of the State downwards right to the mass of the people. Ministers of State who in times of liberty were fathers of the people have become bureaucrats and believe that the government exists for their sakes, not for the people's. Craftsmen who used to be proud of their skill now chase after money and pleasure to the detriment of their work. Even the home is losing its original influence, for 'the man of our time' looks on education as a business affair, and 'the woman of the world' no longer knows how to be a mother. This decline in domestic life prepares the ground for the corrupt civilization, and we have 'the world as it is today'. Observation of men and women arrived at this pass justifies the saying 'The people are bad'. Indeed they are bad, Pestalozzi agrees; but he adds, they are no worse than their rulers. If they are badly governed they cannot be expected to be good. If people are despised, their better powers are smothered, not evoked.

Yet Pestalozzi's hope never fails. True governmental and civic spirit is not, he believes, entirely dead; it has only been suppressed by corrupt civilization. Efforts to revive it must be directed not to the outward symptoms of the disease but to the root cause of the condition. The depraved masses must be raised to a higher level of existence by an appeal to their minds and their hearts. Since they have lost the power of self-help they must be assisted through the application of 'art'. In short, they must be educated. As was to be expected, Pestalozzi's 'only remedy' against corrupt civilization is the education of every individual in every nation. 'There is no other hope left for saving the morally, mentally, and socially degraded continent but through educating its people to true humanity.'

Where can the prototype of education be found if not in the home, in the activities of the mother, in so far as these are distinguished from those of other female animals which are not human? The positive part of the *Innocence* includes a eulogy of the early relationship between mother and child and of the influence of family life as the source of culture. Since these themes have been treated before when they first occurred in *How Gertrude* and the *New Letters to Gessner* they must not be repeated here. But a few words are permissible to complete the account of this latest work and to bring Pestalozzi's ideas up to date.

The impression may prevail, he says, that what a mother does for her child is prompted by her instinct. But this is not so; on the contrary, her actions are as different from the instinctive actions of female animals 'as Heaven is from earth'. And in this difference lies the secret of human education and culture. A young animal develops quickly and independently, almost without the aid of his mother. But a human child needs sustained help and care, and these are given him from the hour of his birth by his mother with complete unselfishness. It is this moral attitude that turns her female animal instinct into a human mother's love. Pestalozzi calls this loving care her 'fidelity'.

The mother's fidelity awakens the child's emotions. As before, Pestalozzi derives the child's higher faculties from his response, at first instinctive and later conscious, to his mother's love. The main point he wishes to stress is that there should be no rupture between the child's 'animal' and his 'human' stage, that education should ensure a continuous development from the lower to the higher level. Such a slow, gradual, and secure growth of the individual is the great advantage of home education and the basis for a healthy development of nations. It is, in Pestalozzi's opinion, the main condition for their survival. 'The delivery of our continent from the evils from which it suffers is possible only through such natural individual care'; and this, again, can only be given if 'the purity, strength, and dignity of home life are restored'.

For a home which is merely a place of living together is not such a centre of education. 'Only unselfishness has formative power.' Only men and women of inner dignity can create an inspiring home atmosphere. On the other hand, man can make a good home only if the State makes it possible for him to retain his human dignity. History shows, Pestalozzi says, that great national cultures have always grown out of individual culture. The well-being of Venice and Holland arose from the high standards of individuals. England's Habeas Corpus Act, which safeguards the personal freedom of her citizens, laid the foundation of her greatness. Switzerland, his own country, gained renown through the wise and honourable management of her domestic affairs. The nations' true power and greatness are thus dependent on the cultures which their individual citizens create. These cultures in their turn must be protected by the constitutions.

Pestalozzi deplores that European culture at the time of his writing was not what he wished it to be, that it was shaken even to the point of collapse. Yet in his unconquerable optimism he believes that as long as man has the will to raise the level of his behaviour there is hope for his survival. With this will to self-improvement the evils of corrupt civilization would disappear. Men would become free again and regard other men as human beings. Kings would be more humane and ministers more understanding. Craftsmen would work better and the poor advance in self-help. Most important, women would know again how to be mothers. For their assistance, a book should be compiled containing the most elementary principles presented in the simplest form (one of Pestalozzi's favourite ideas). Family homes and elementary schools should thus become places where children are educated for the lives they are actually going to live. In short, education should be made a science and an art.

Pestalozzi believed that the moment at which he wrote (1815) was decisive for the creation of a new culture based on individual effort. (It was indeed his earnest belief that any particular moment 'in which we live' is decisive for such an effort.) His country had just been freed from political tyranny; she ought now to be made truly free through the education of her citizens. The State cannot do this as a State, but through its constitution it can and must restore the spirit of liberty which alone makes possible an 'individual existence'.

At the end of his book Pestalozzi seems almost to contradict the previous arguments by expressing the opinion that a citizen would find the desired freedom and independence more readily in a monarchy than in a republic. (Cf. however his earlier utterances on this point, especially in *Leonard and Gertrude*.) He hoped great things from the 'Holy Alliance' of the three European monarchs who had promised to make 'paternal spirit' the guiding rule of their government. He even intended to dedicate his work to Czar Alexander I of Russia who at that time was greatly admired in Switzerland.

But as has been said before, it is not the particular form of constitution but the attitude of the citizens which mainly concerns him. The domestic virtues of industry and reliability which he considers essential for combating corrupt civilization are, he believed, still alive in the middle class, 'the core of the nation'. 'We are ourselves the State.' Therefore he does not direct his advice to 'the State' as an abstract institution but 'to the Earnestness, the Innocence, and the Generosity' of responsible men in his fatherland and in Europe, and he asks their support for educating the people. For, he says, political unity at home and even the most desirable outcome of the Swiss constitutional struggle are only matters of the 'collective existence'. True liberty and the resulting harmony among citizens and nations can only be achieved on the basis of the individual's self-determination. The liberty of every individual and every nation is the necessary condition for the well-being of all mankind.

The remedy which Pestalozzi suggests in the *Innocence* is essentially the same which he had already set forth in the *Epochs* and recommended to the Helvetian Government (1802). Differences in detail may be accounted for by the different stages he had reached in his educational theory at the time of writing these works. At the previous stage it was intellectual education with its main element 'Anschauung' which he believed to be the panacea for the corrupt civilization. With the development of his system, moral education and especially the rôle attributed in it to the mother became ever more important. In this development lies also the difference between the *Innocence* and the *Inquiries*. In the earlier work the will 'to ennoble myself' was shown as the fight of man's higher against his lower nature; the aim was the suppression of man's animal nature; the underlying philosophy was unambiguously dualistic. Now an uninterrupted, continuous development is traced from natural instinct to moral perfection (as in the earliest works of all, the *Evening Hour* and *Leonard and Gertrude*). Even so a certain antinomy remains in the *Innocence*, but its tone is less pessimistic than that of the *Inquiries*, though equally realistic. The shift, then, is more one of emphasis than of substance.

The viewpoint and the content (but not the style) of the *Innocence* are astonishingly modern. If a few names and historical references were replaced by others of topical significance, the book could be taken as *A Word in Season* (its sub-title) to the twentieth century. The exposure of the dangers to civilization by a growing mass-influence with its consequent lowering of mental and moral standards; the identification of a state of insecurity and fear bringing with it the desire for the aggressive use of force; the suggested remedy—education of the individual for personal independence and inner security and thereby for respect for freedom and confidence in humanity—all these may offer even today a valid diagnosis of and therapeutic for the ills of our civilization. In Pestalozzi's time his advice remained unheeded. The *Innocence* made no impression, either on his country's legislation or on the nation's moral attitude. The Federal Act of 1814 re-affirmed a conservative decentralized government in Switzerland, and the Congress of Vienna established the Metternich system in Europe.

II FULFILMENT AND FAILURE

The death of 'Mother Pestalozzi' had removed the one person whose mere presence was wont to pacify the contending parties. That their ageing 'Father' deserved similar consideration never occurred to the egotistic young men. Schmid had brought order into the institute, but also a domineering tone which was all too different from the previous friendly atmosphere. Niederer deplored the 'Corporal's spirit' and the falling standard; he feared that the institute was developing into a 'profitable boarding-school' instead of being the starting-point of a new education. Further conflicts arose between those fundamentally different men. Each complained about the other to Pestalozzi and in the last resort blamed him for the existing confusion.

It was not Niederer, however, but the German student-teachers who brought matters to a head. They openly revolted against Schmid's authoritarian régime, and in the spring of 1816 sixteen masters resigned their posts. Among them was Krüsi, Pestalozzi's oldest assistant. His leaving shows that the situation must have become unbearable, for he cannot have taken the decision lightly. He had been with Pestalozzi for sixteen years. From now on he devoted himself entirely to a boys' school in Yverdon which he had begun as a boarding-house some years earlier at the time of his marriage and settling in the town. He was never to be reconciled with his formerly beloved 'Father'.

Niederer accused Pestalozzi of betraying his higher purpose by allowing the institute to be run in an unworthy way, and of being untrue to himself. He expressed doubts of his paternal love and reproached him for being partial to Schmid because he submitted to his demands. It was around Schmid that all the arguments turned. Most of Pestalozzi's staff was agreed in disliking him. Only Pestalozzi himself clung to him in the belief that he was the man who could save the House. Yet he loved his other 'sons' and could not bear the thought of losing them. Again and again he implored the quarrelling parties to make peace. But the rift between Schmid and Niederer had become too wide to be bridged. One of them had to go. On Whitsunday 1817, after having conducted a communion service, Niederer announced from the pulpit of the castle chapel his breach with Pestalozzi. Soon afterwards he raised financial claims in connection with the girls' school which his wife had taken over. This led to a Court action over a period of seven years which was finally settled by the award of a trifling sum in Pestalozzi's favour. All this destroyed the father-son relationship, rent Pestalozzi's heart, and ruined his institute.

When Niederer announced his departure, Pestalozzi rose in anger to reply, but controlled himself saying that he was not going to desecrate the church further. When Niederer's letter stating his claims arrived, Pestalozzi was seized with such rage, even frenzy, that he was in danger of losing his reason. He was taken to Bulet in the Jura mountains where, as previously in Gurnigel, he quickly recovered from the first effects of the shock. But a depression and a disinclination to return to Yverdon remained with him for a considerable time.

What can have been the reason for Niederer's cruel behaviour? It was probably an expression of grief at the loss of his life's purpose. For he was no longer the indispensable mainstay of the method. Pestalozzi had shaken off his influence. Returning as he did in his old age to the conception of the organic relations, Pestalozzi had given up certain tenets of idealist philosophy which Niederer had introduced into his theory. Also, realizing the threat, under Niederer's management, to the institute's financial success which was essential as the economic prop to the prospective poor-school, Pestalozzi had turned for help to Schmid whose strength lay in efficient organization and who did not interfere with his theories. Niederer on his part had always looked upon elementary education as the concern of philosophy. When he saw, as he believed, Pestalozzi descending from the realm of ideas to that of reality he thought it his duty to stop him and even to oppose him. Thus from defender he turned accuser, losing at the same time all feeling for personal relationship.

Pestalozzi loved Niederer and would never have parted with him of his own accord, but Niederer's attacks against 'his Schmid' stiffened his resistance. As often in his life, he made the mistake of blindly trusting one who knew how to handle him to the detriment of others more downright. Thus he overestimated Schmid's abilities and even his attachment to himself at the expense of his older friends. As always, he accepted the greater share of the blame himself and was willing to forget and forgive. He was ready for any sacrifice except the abandonment of Schmid.

Naturally all this harmed the institute severely. Since so many masters had gone, about one hundred boys were left almost without tuition. Senior pupils had to be entrusted with some of the teaching. They took advantage of the situation and demanded recognition as teachers. (One symbol of this status was having coffee with Pestalozzi after the mid-day meal.) Pestalozzi tells how they suddenly banded together 'like insurgent English factory workers' in order to get their 'rights'.

From a wish to help in this emergency a well-meaning friend, M. A. Jullien, suggested that Pestalozzi's institute should be combined with Fellenberg's as in the past. Fellenberg's educational enterprise had grown considerably since then. It consisted of several branches, each organized for a particular social class and its appropriate type of education. There was an institute for young gentlemen which had won great fame, and a 'School of Industry' run on Pestalozzian principles which attracted attention. The Yverdon institute was to supply the hitherto missing middle-class element. The financial arrangement was to be such that Pestalozzi would be enabled to open his own poor-school and be relieved of all economic worries for the rest of his life. He let himself be persuaded to sign an agreement while, as he puts it later, he was 'in a weak state of mind' (at Bulet). Schmid, too, was induced to give his consent. But no sooner was the contract completed than Swiss newspapers published reports of it which highly offended Pestalozzi. They implied that the efficient and successful Fellenberg had come to the rescue of the old and enfeebled Pestalozzi out of pity, as an act of kindness. Whether the notices were inspired by Fellenberg himself or by Schmid who naturally disliked the idea of having his influence reduced—the fact is that Pestalozzi would not share his authority with another man of equal status. What had not been possible in 1804 could not be made to work now. Pestalozzi broke the agreement and wrote to Fellenberg in an almost insulting tone. 'I would rather spend my last days in the Zurich almshouse than accept at your table the place of honour given to the patriarch of education forced into retirement in a princely way.' No, he continued, he was not a patriarch but a soldier who must not leave his post. 'I wish to have the honour and the disgrace of my campaign for myself. I am not proud, but I know my worth and my merits and must know them for the sake of my purpose.'

The institute in Yverdon was run by Schmid for several more years. He was practical and energetic and obtained good results especially in the teaching of mathematics. A considerable number of new pupils enrolled; some came in groups, the largest from England. This was the time when Pestalozzi's name became increasingly known in Great Britain. Educators and social reformers such as Andrew Bell, Robert Owen, Henry Brougham and others dedicated to the education of the poor visited Yverdon to find out what they could learn there. In 1819 Charles Mayo, a young clergyman, arrived from London with a number of boys who were soon followed by others. They stayed for nearly three years, and during that time English, besides French and German, became a medium of instruction in the institute.

(For a more detailed account of Pestalozzi's association with Britain and with America see Appendix I.) The English boys were happy to be with Pestalozzi though they never experienced the carefree atmosphere that had prevailed during the first ten years of the school's existence. Schmid was cold and his rule firm. Pestalozzi gave him complete freedom of action and had in consequence to forgo Niederer's assistance for ever.

This, then, was the state of affairs in Yverdon at the close of the year 1817: The famous institute was rent with internal strife. The renowned educationist had been publicly declared to be past his best. Three rival institutes stood close together in one small town, for besides Niederer's girls' school and Krüsi's boys' school there was an institution for deaf and dumb children run by another former assistant of Pestalozzi. And the municipality were bombarded with contradictory applications from opposing parties. All this made an unfavourable impression on the public. Pestalozzi withdrew more and more from active participation in the management of his institute. He lived for one thing only, the establishing of a poor-school, now or never.

The changed political situation, Napoleon's fall and Switzerland's independence, his approaching death, and, most important of all, the prospect of being able to finance the poor-school himself, held for Pestalozzi the long-delayed promise of his life-dream's realization. 'If I don't manage at least to prepare during my lifetime the application of the idea of elementary education in poor and elementary schools, and to secure, in however small a way, its application after my death, the essential part of my service to mankind will be lost,' he wrote to Nicolovius. And he prayed, 'O God, don't let me die until I have fulfilled my vow to you.' All the appeals to 'patrons and philanthropists', to kings and states, which he had sent out at various times during his life had met with little response. Now he thought he held in his own hands the means of obtaining his heart's desire. The necessary funds were to come from the edition of his Collected Writings.

In his gratitude for the achievement of his aim Pestalozzi later described the proceedings in such a way as to attribute the idea of dispensing with outside help and of relying on the subscription to his works to Schmid, and to Schmid alone. In him he saw the kind of level-headed associate whom Menalk, fifty years earlier, had advised him to consult before entering into far-reaching enterprises. In actual fact Pestalozzi had been in communication with Cotta, the Stuttgart publisher, for several years, but it was owing to Schmid's business acumen that a favourable agreement was now reached. In January 1817 on behalf of Pestalozzi he signed a contract arranging for an edition of Pestalozzi's Collected Writings in twelve volumes. A thirteenth including the *Swansong* was later added, and was followed by a further two volumes under Pestalozzi's name but containing Schmid's essays on the method of teaching mathematics.

This Cotta edition of Pestalozzi's works is not by any means representative of his writings as they were available at that time. It contains his previously published principal works, viz. the *Inquiries*, *How Gertrude*, the *Innocence* etc., *Leonard and Gertrude* in a new (third) version, and some hitherto unpublished writings, e.g. an essay called *Views on Industry, Education, and Politics* (part of a long memorandum on orphanages, written in 1807 and not yet published in its entirety even to this day). In the additional volume are the works of his old age, the *Swansong* and the Langenthal Address. But surprisingly it does not contain the *Evening Hour*, nor the *Swiss Journal*, nor all the works written during the periods of the Revolution and Helvetian Republic—this for political reasons. Those essays which Pestalozzi had not yet finished are, naturally, not included. These have added greatly to our knowledge of Pestalozzi since their recent publication in the Critical Edition. The Cotta *Collected Writings*, then, are, like all Pestalozzi's publications in his lifetime, incomplete and unreliable, in selection as well as in production, although it took several years for the thirteen small volumes to come out (1819–26).

But the financial terms were favourable. The publisher agreed to pay Pestalozzi three Louis d'ors for each sheet of 16 pages and to let him share equally the sum resulting from the subscription. The latter amounted to 50,000 francs, as yet, it is true, merely on paper. Many subscribers later withdrew because they were dissatisfied with the pace and the quality of the production. Pestalozzi did not receive the first instalment until three years later. But in view of the favourable prospect and in great exultation at having reached his life's goal, he settled on his seventy-second birthday (12th January 1818) the whole of the expected sum as 'an inalienable capital' for the realization of his idea. The annual interest was to be used 'to all eternity' for 'the extension of popular education in the spirit of the home, through the fourfold pursuit of a further investigation into its principles, the training of elementary teachers, the establishment of experimental schools, and work on a manual for mothers'. The existing institute as well as the prospective poor-school were no longer to be regarded as private property but as 'an enterprise dedicated to the country, to education, and to the poor'.

Since all but one of Pestalozzi's nearest relatives had died it was only this one grandson's future which he had to consider. Gottlieb possessed no particular intellectual abilities. In order not to repeat the mistakes made in his father's education Frau Pestalozzi and her friends had seen to it that he was given a sound manual training. He was apprenticed to a tanner. His craft, his grandmother's legacy, and his ownership of the Neuhof ensured him a good livelihood. And so Pestalozzi felt justified in leaving his capital to the community; for, in his opinion, 'not money but his own effort' would bring his grandson success and satisfaction. However, he was greatly pleased when Gottlieb after the completion of his apprenticeship came to him and said, 'I want to become what you are.' He was made an assistant in the institute, and Pestalozzi saw in his mind's eye Gottlieb and Schmid standing together at the head of a poor-school. But it never came to this. The two men so dear to his heart, on whom he set all his hopes, were to be linked only by family bonds. In 1822 the marriage took place of Schmid's sister Katharina (1799–1853) and Gottlieb, an alliance cleverly contrived by the Schmid family, probably more in their own economic interests than for the sake of helping the poor.

Pestalozzi's famous Birthday Address of 1818, in which he announces his endowment for the furthering of popular education, contains in its theoretical part a review of the 'artificiality' of the times and a proposal for combating the resulting corruption. The ideas are, in essence, the same as those expressed in the *Innocence*, and they culminate, as in the previous work, in a veritable hymn of praise on 'the sanctity of the home'. Pestalozzi contrasts the home with the licentiousness of 'the world', calling it 'a bird's nest' or 'the Christ-child's manger' to bring out fully its smallness and warmth. It is for him 'the centre where lies united all that is divine in nature's educative powers'; 'the only firm ground on which we must seek to stand with regard to popular education, national culture, and the welfare of the poor'.

The Address differs from the *Innocence* in that it lays more stress on the conception of natural growth. Development is likened to a growing tree, and the educator to a gardener. But since the corruption of the times has interfered with organic development, the latter must be supported by the art of education. Pestalozzi therefore distinguishes three processes. First there is the natural growth of a human being; here he continues to waver between an optimistic concept of 'good nature' and a realist view of 'corrupt nature'. Then there is the formative influence of the child's relationships and circumstances, the 'individual condition' which, at its best, provides his 'natural' training. And finally there ought to be the education of his powers and faculties with the help of 'art'. All three should exist in a good home. The more, however, this 'natural nursery of humanity' has lost of its original goodness, the more must wisdom and art be brought in to save, or renew, its true spirit.

All previous attempts to improve popular education, including his own, so Pestalozzi ends his Address, have had only a limited effect. Even the bequest he is making this day can be only 'an insignificant mite', for it is not given to man to accomplish his task save only 'in part'. Others must join in the effort, expand the work, and bring it to perfection. In a vision resplendent with hope, Pestalozzi sees his life-work completed as the achievement of a united community. Only a few months after Krüsi's and Niederer's departure he is able to say, 'The end of my life is happy. Except for a few moments during my latter days of despair, I have never lost faith and hope.' So he invites all 'noble men and youths' to take part in this effort. First and foremost, he asks Niederer and Krüsi, his first assistants, to return to his House and to rejoin in his purpose. He calls upon all friends of the institute with 'the words of a father approaching the grave'. 'Remember that the home is the focal point of our endeavours. Investigate its truth and teach the means of its salvation. Renew in these pursuits my House in its old spirit. Unite in love. For love is long-suffering and kind; it bears all things, it believes, hopes, and endures all things; it never fails!'

But Niederer and Krüsi remained adamant and refused to be associated with Pestalozzi as long as Schmid was by his side.

Pestalozzi was determined not to lose any time in opening his poor-school. Indeed, he was thinking of establishing two: one in the Neuhof, the place of his early dreams and disappointments, which he had always kept against his friends' advice in the hope of the day of fulfilment to come; the other in Yverdon whose accommodation and staffing he thought suitable for the purpose.

The fate of these poor-schools was decisively influenced by the contradiction between Pestalozzi's theories on education according to social classes which was in accordance with contemporary thought, and his actual practice which was the result partly of necessity and partly of his humanitarian views. Human nature and consequently education according to nature are the same with every man, he had just pronounced in his great Birthday Address; 'in all stations man should be educated to be religious, knowledgeable, kind, and useful in home and community'. But divergences in their circumstances necessitate differences in the education of children from various homes and with disparate prospects. The child of 'the rich' must be stimulated to greater effort by greater knowledge, while the poor child must be guided to greater knowledge through need and work. The same aim of a balanced use of all their powers must therefore be pursued by different means and in opposite ways. The children most readily educable are, in Pestalozzi's view, those of the middle classes, i.e. of people who have only a small share in the goods of this world but a high degree of working and staying power, and on whose endeavours the national well-being depends. For the children of well-to-do parents the method of teaching various school subjects was to be further developed; their place was the Yverdon institute. For the very poor Pestalozzi hoped to found as soon as possible a school in the Neuhof in which book-learning was to be combined with industrial and agricultural work. For some carefully selected boys and girls from the lower middle class he opened in Clindy, within a twenty minutes' walk from Yverdon, a training-school for teachers of the people, 'not only for their own sakes but because of their usefulness to the country' (September 1818).

At first there were twelve pupils. They were to be 'educated as poor children and trained for the education of poor children'. These were soon followed by a number of paying boys and girls who, however, had to come from 'simple homes' and be 'uncorrupted by the manners of the times'. The educational aim was the development of their sense of duty and the transmission of the knowledge and skill necessary for their future domestic and civil occupations. The house was run by Schmid's elder sister Marie and the lessons given by the teachers of the Yverdon institute.

Pestalozzi felt that after a long life of frustrated attempts he was suddenly transported to this school 'as if by a miracle'. 'I have won through,' he exclaimed, 'I have achieved my aim! I am again the loved father in the midst of poor children and can before my death bring nearer to fruition my life's purpose, the education of the people, the training of the poor.' These children of Clindy, he said in his New Year Address of 1819, were not there to receive benefits. 'You are here to become benefactors of mankind, fathers of the poor and mothers of their children. . . . You are destined to unfold, strengthen, and revive in the poor, the destitute, and the weak, those powers for self-help which God has laid universally in human nature. Children, your destiny is great.' He felt that only through God's mercy had it become possible for him to be with these children. 'There is perhaps no other case in history', he wrote to Nicolovius, 'of a man in his seventy-fifth year experiencing such a change from a situation bordering on despair to the sudden fulfilment of his highest hopes. . . . I am happy.'

If Pestalozzi had died in that year, his troubled life would have ended in contentment. But he was not granted final success and a peaceful death. Greater suffering than ever was still ahead of him, and like King Lear he found himself, after having given away all he possessed, destitute and forsaken at the close of his life.

Because of the children's predominantly middle-class origin Clindy had from the beginning not entirely been the poor-school which Pestalozzi had had in mind, and as time went on it developed more and more into a training-college in which instruction in definite school subjects was of first importance. There were various reasons for this trend. First, Schmid did not look favourably on education of the poor because, in his opinion, it cost money and brought in nothing. But young teachers trained in the Pestalozzian method would provide the staff so urgently needed in the main institute. He therefore advised the old man to devote his last years to the completion of his educational theory rather than to 'the application of its incomplete method in one single poor-school'. Second, an enthusiastic Englishman had come to stay in Yverdon, and his teaching further increased the intellectual bias of Clindy. J. P. Greaves, the same to whom Pestalozzi wrote the *Letters on Early Education* previously mentioned, was a London business man deprived of his career through the Continental Blockade and now devoting himself to philanthropic pursuits. He was greatly impressed by Pestalozzi's endeavours, and Pestalozzi set great hopes on Greaves' attempts to make his method known in Britain (cf. Appendix I). Meanwhile Greaves taught with notable success the English language according to Pestalozzi's principles not only in the Yverdon institute but also at Clindy, so that, among other things, three languages were taught in Clindy, with Latin added later. In fact, identical instruction was given by the same teachers in two places; two high schools were run, but no poor-school. And since financial considerations played an important part, the Clindy institute was combined with that of Yverdon after an independent existence of about one year.

In a public report Pestalozzi was anxious to show, and to convince himself, that the results of the union were favourable. The poor children, he says, enjoy all the advantages of the rich children's means of education, and they are treated in the same way; only, 'as poor', they must get used to great self-denial and 'forgo with calm and equanimity much, very much, that the others enjoy daily before their eyes'. For instance, in their spare time, when the rich children play games, they must serve in the House, 'but this is really only a service which children owe to their parental home'. With equal naïveté he defends the living together of boys and girls in the same house as being comparable to life in a real family; it gives education a freer, even more innocent bent. 'And so the possibility of running a good educational institute with children from different social classes has been made clear in its essentials.'

But he was mistaken. Public opinion was against a joint education of boys and girls (that is, if they belonged to the middle classes; it did not matter in the case of the poor). And the children themselves contributed to the growing decline of the institute. Some of them, Pestalozzi tells in *The Story of my Life*, 'craved for knowledge with a greed similar to that with which Eve brought sin into the world'. And with their increased knowledge developed their increased demands. Now well educated, they no longer considered themselves 'as poor' and assumed an attitude which, in Pestalozzi's opinion, was the exact opposite of that befitting their station and destiny. So the living-together of children from different social classes, in the same house but under different conditions, proved to be impracticable. The class distinctions had begun to disappear. Pestalozzi with his humane educational principles had himself brought about the process.

He, however, thought that the children were incited from without and his institute undermined by Niederer and his clique. Indeed, these people broadcast widely that Pestalozzi's establishment had greatly deteriorated and that they could supply a better education than he. Thereupon anxious parents took their children from Pestalozzi's institute and sent them to theirs. Elder pupils and student-teachers also withdrew their loyalty from Pestalozzi and went over to the other camp. The reasons for their discontent were laid down in a pamphlet written by one of them under the title *How Herr Schmid manages the Pestalozzian Institute*.

Events occurred in 1821 which exacerbated the situation. Pestalozzi applied to Yverdon town council for an extension of the rent-free use by the institute of the castle to fifteen or twenty years after his death instead of the five already granted. This was to secure the succession, ostensibly for Gottlieb, in actual fact for Schmid. At once the rival party protested; actions and counter-actions multiplied. Because of a technical error which he was alleged to have committed when publishing his book *Truth and Error in Pestalozzi's Life* (1822)—a far-fetched pretext which had nothing to do with the present case—Schmid was brought to court. His enemies even accused him of offences against public morality. All this roused Pestalozzi's wrath. He felt in honour bound to share in the penalties inflicted on Schmid during the following years, and every time Schmid had to appear in court Pestalozzi went with him and sat in the dock beside him. He refused the suggestion made by the harassed town council to dismiss Schmid in order to save his institute and secure peace in his old age. He wrote heart-rending letters to Niederer and his wife imploring them 'for God's and his mercy's sake to make an end to this torment'. Frau Niederer replied in the same vein but did not give in. When finally the government, tired of this litigation, expelled Schmid as an 'undesirable alien' (he was Austrian) from the Canton of Vaud, Pestalozzi was resolved to share this fate also with him. Thus after an existence of nearly twenty years the Pestalozzian institute in Yverdon came to an inglorious end.

The plan of opening a mixed industrial and agricultural school for the poorest of the poor in the Neuhof had meanwhile been progressing, and a suitable house was in course of erection. Pestalozzi therefore hoped to transfer the remnant of the Yverdon institute to the Neuhof. But, as he puts it, 'this dream also faded'. The young people's hearts were so 'hardened' that they refused his urgent appeal to help him to continue his educational work on his estate. They made it quite clear that they thought it beneath them to work in a poor-school, and that their excellent training qualified them to look for better positions. They did not think they owed it to Pestalozzi to sacrifice their careers.

So the possibility of building up again in the Neuhof what had been begun in Yverdon with such high hopes, only to end so pitifully, was entirely gone. Pestalozzi was at last brought to the point of pronouncing his goal 'completely unattainable'. In March 1824 he published the following statement: 'I am obliged to declare that the foundation I planned and from which I hoped to see so much good emerge has been completely frustrated, and that I am entirely incapable of fulfilling the obligations which I have taken on in this respect.' 'Indeed', he says in *The Story of my Life*, 'I felt as if I were taking my own life with this withdrawal. It hurt so much. Under these circumstances my life was no longer worth living.'

However much personal rivalries and petty jealousies had contributed to the fall of the institute, they cannot be taken as the sole causes of its ruin. The malicious allegations spread by its enemies would not have met with public response if the political atmosphere had not been unfavourable to Pestalozzi's ideas. These were the years in which the Metternich System held down liberal movements and free enterprises everywhere in Europe, and its repercussions influenced the turn of events even in a small Swiss town. How much it bore upon the Pestalozzian movement can be seen in a few examples. Schmid was under observation by the police for several years because of alleged demagogic activities. Schools run according to Pestalozzi's principles in various European countries were closed. Pestalozzi himself thought it wise to omit a considerable number of his more revolutionary writings from his *Collected Writings*. His opponents did not, as yet, dare to attack him personally. But by making his principal assistant their target, they hit at the institute itself.

If he had been able to foresee the consequences of his assistants' quarrels, Pestalozzi wrote later, he would have restricted his life's endeavours to that part which he could have carried out without anyone's help. This sounds right in theory but was not possible in practice. For if he had been capable of planning his enterprises carefully, of acting wisely, and of keeping the reins in his own hands, everything would have been different. But then he would not have been Pestalozzi. The poor-school would have been his life; but to bring it into being required men and means. For the sake of these he allowed the Yverdon institute to become too big for his personal direction. In a community of fellow-workers he hoped to find those qualities which he himself lacked. He was deeply disappointed. His 'spiritual heirs' not only failed to continue his work, they were, in fact, the instruments of its destruction. The harm they wrought was, however, only temporary; they could not destroy Pestalozzi's influence on future generations.

It was not in Pestalozzi's nature to place the blame for any failure on other people or untoward circumstances. Always his own severest judge, he attributed it to a complicated trait in himself which made it at once necessary and impossible for him to work with others. He was, he said, unable either to dominate or to submit. 'I cannot rule and I cannot serve. Must I do the one, I am lost; must I do the other, I am unhappy.' Or the same confession expressed differently, 'Although I was certainly not born to dominate and to rule, I need, perhaps more than most people, a measure of assured independence in order to do my best work, and what makes this circumstance somewhat difficult is the fact that I, despite my demand for independence, require more help and assistance than do other people with their rightful claims.' This contradiction in his character explains his stubborn refusal of Niederer's influence as well as his exaggerated regard for Schmid's efficiency. But from it derived also his conception of personal freedom, his own as well as that of others.

However great was Pestalozzi's despair at the failure of his life's purpose, however unjust the report which he gave in his first excitement—his energy was certainly not exhausted by the events. He decided 'no longer to try to do the impossible' but to retire at last and to devote the rest of his life to writing. In March 1825 he left Yverdon, accompanied by Schmid and four boys of whom two were Spaniards, and returned to the Neuhof, the place of his early struggles. His mood was one of humble resignation, but he still believed that his work was not yet lost.

III THE LATE WORKS

The works of Pestalozzi's old age, *Leonard and Gertrude*, third version, and especially the *Swansong*, are not, as the latter title suggests, new creations of the years in which they were published. Yet they present his ideas on popular education and national culture in their final form. A systematic treatment of Pestalozzi's educational thought would have to take them as its point of departure. A genetic account like the present has had to consider his ideas and their later development or changes at the time and place in which they first occurred. For this reason Pestalozzi's most mature writings must now receive comparatively brief treatment, an apparent contradiction which must be expressly mentioned.

The *Swansong* (published 1826) consists of two main parts: an account of 'the idea of elementary education' which probably contains the unfinished essay on 'natural education' written in 1812, and the story of Pestalozzi's life as a psychological justification for the success and failure of his enterprises, which also makes use of earlier notes but presents them in a way and tone obviously influenced by the harassing experiences of the last few years. A plea to the public for the examination and continuation of his endeavours provides a loose framework and makes, more or less successfully, a single work out of the two parts. Whatever the genesis of the book may be, the fact remains that Pestalozzi himself published it in its present form. It must therefore be considered as a whole and taken as his 'swansong' in keeping with his intention.

The outstanding characteristic of this work is that, compared with earlier writings on the method, the importance of synthesis is brought out more strongly than ever before. Pestalozzi admits that the various branches of education are severally important and that specialized training of the mind, the heart, and the hand are necessary, but he regards them mainly as parts of a general education. Having drawn a parallel between the course of nature in the development of man and the course of art in education (in *How Gertrude*), and shown the unity of human nature (in the *Views and Experiences*) and its dangers through the corruption of the times (in the *Innocence*), he now stresses the necessity of maintaining, or restoring, this unity. Having, further, declared education to be an aid to the development of nature, a help to the unfolding of powers inherent in the child, he now not only distinguishes separate powers of thought, will, and 'being able to do', but treats of a superior power uniting them all, which he calls a 'general power'. The task of education is, then, to develop and strengthen this general power, or to achieve a balance between the various powers, to attain a 'harmony of powers'.

Such a harmony can only be achieved if the educator draws on life. The fundamental theme in the *Swansong* is 'Life itself educates'. Education must use the resources of real life, the activities of a father and a mother in their actual homes. The home is for Pestalozzi the ideal starting-point for education because on the one hand, the fundamental human relationships existing there are the same for all men, and on the other, the particular social conditions prevailing in each are the formative influences decisive for the development of the individual. Thus the home is at once of universal and of individual importance and is, therefore, the prototype of 'real life' in its most concentrated form.

But however formative the natural course of family life may

be, the art of education must go beyond it. Instinctive care must become conscious guidance. This prescription applies universally but it is of especial importance in times of corruption when the true spirit of the home no longer exists. Man must be helped, otherwise he falls to his lowest level, to animal nature. Only if his reason and his experience are fully developed, will he reach human, i.e. moral maturity. The art of education must therefore guide the child to a higher state, to a 'second nature', to true humanity. This task is feasible because the potentiality of a 'second nature' is implanted in man. It is, in fact (as had been shown in the *Inquiries*), this potentiality which makes him human and distinguishes him from all other living beings. If, then, education brings out this 'good nature' it revives the divine spark inherent in every human being. If the method used in this process is in agreement with this better part of human nature, it is 'natural' or 'elementary', which for Pestalozzi mean the same.

The sections of the *Swansong* dealing with the various branches of education assign the first importance to the training of the moral powers. The significant demand here is that any rupture between higher and lower nature should be carefully avoided. In these works of his old age Pestalozzi emphasizes in ever-increasing degree what he had propounded in his earliest works, namely that the child's development should proceed continuously and uninterruptedly from the sensory to the moral plane. It is, he says, 'the assured and continued satisfaction of his physical needs' through 'the God-inspired care of his mother' which unfolds the child's moral powers naturally from the day of his birth. To maintain this undisturbed satisfaction in the infant and the young child is therefore of utmost importance for man's development to true humanity.

The 'power of thought' (as the intellectual powers are called here) originates in 'the impression which objects of the outer world make on our mind. In affecting our inner and outer senses, objects stimulate and activate the impulse towards thought which is inherent in our mind.' But the mental powers by themselves would remain abstract if they were not combined with the practical powers, those faculties which translate into actions the knowledge attained by the mind. The trained physical powers provide the skill necessary for the individual's particular occupation and condition of life. All specific powers are interdependent and must be related to one another. Their true balance is the aim of a 'harmonious education'.

In speaking of the method of instruction Pestalozzi now distinguishes between 'exercises designed to unfold the child's fundamental powers' and 'exercises designed for him to practise and apply his skills'. The latter are as various as are the objects to which they can be applied and the conditions and circumstances of the individuals who apply them. But the former are the same for all men in all circumstances. Therefore it is the task of elementary education to give preference to exercises devised to strengthen the fundamental powers over those which help to achieve specific skills.

Rather than repeat what has already been said about the method of instruction (even though its treatment in the *Swansong* contains in many respects a correction of previous errors) we shall examine further the concept of 'general power' so characteristic of this book. For, says Pestalozzi, although well-thought-out specific teaching aids strengthen the child's partial powers of perception, language, thought, will, and skill, they do not meet the essential needs of his true inner self. On the contrary, they have a tendency to develop one power more than another, and the consequent lack of balance is the cause of the hardening of men in the mass, the corruption of the world, the war of all against all. 'General power', on the other hand, comes from a striving for balance, a wish to blend the powers of feeling, thinking, and acting, and thus leads towards an inner unity which brings all man's actions to a higher (or deeper) level. It is the aim to be attained in the mature personality—true and full 'humanity'.

A balance of powers cannot be achieved without effort; in fact, it can never be fully achieved, only approached. But an approach is as possible with restricted as with wider powers. Pestalozzi claims to have shown 'the maximum of this balance and the general power ensuing therefrom existing with the minimum of worldly means and specific powers' in the character of Gertrude, almost half a century before. The degree of balance attainable, i.e. of true humanity, depends on the degree of love and faith existing in the individual. For love is for Pestalozzi the essential means of unfolding the general power.

Although love, he says, is a divine power and requires as such no human art for its coming into being, it requires the art of education for its practical application, to help man to give priority to the needs of his spiritual nature, or 'individual existence', over those of his physical nature, or 'collective existence'.

Pestalozzi reminds his readers, however, that true love and true faith can only be attained by a general striving for truth, from which it follows that moral education must be closely connected with intellectual education. Again, knowledge without action is only a vain pretence. Therefore a true education of the mind must be connected with a training of the practical powers necessary for man's occupation and position in life. Thus, in the familiar circular way of argument, we are back again to the statement made before that a close interrelation of moral, mental, and practical education is necessary to achieve, or to restore, the balance of powers in man.

Having set forth his theory of education from a psychological point of view, Pestalozzi now turns to its sociological aspect, applying his principles to men's various conditions and circumstances. The kind as well as the degree of education must be different in different 'stations', he says, for a child would be burdened and confused if he were taken above the needs of his particular social class. Only if his education is related to his home conditions will he be prepared naturally for the tasks awaiting him in his special sphere. He will thus be saved from succumbing to superficiality and mere pretence and led to attain sound craftsmanship and an honest character.

These virtues of soundness and honesty, constituting the independence of the individual which Pestalozzi values so highly, are, he thinks, a special characteristic of the middle class. As in the *Innocence*, he is most emphatic about the necessity to restore a vigorous middle class, since rising industry with its mass demands and mass organization threatens its very existence. He thinks that the middle classes are more in need of a training in observation ('Anschauung') than in abstract thinking which is of more use to the upper classes. On the other hand he reminds his reader over and over again that the child of even the lowest class needs the training of all his powers. He solves this 'apparent contradiction' by referring to his concept of the unity of human nature and his principles of continuity, completion, and perfection; every single skill, even the simplest, if soundly developed and so perfected in itself, can be a means to the acquiring of wider skills and so to the perfection of the self.

The striving for perfection is by the aged Pestalozzi related to the seeking of God's mercy. An art of education in agreement with the unity of nature is, he says, not attainable without God's help. This is the point where elementary education coincides with Christianity; it is the 'natural' manifestation of the doctrines of religion and morality. The art of education cannot, of course, give rise to religion but it can, as far as is humanly possible, help to put into practice and to 'make habitual' the demands of religion. Or again, religion cannot initiate human actions but it can, by reason of its divine origin, purify them and purge them of sensuality and selfishness. Religion 'completes what it does not give, it sanctifies what it does not create and it blesses what it does not teach'. It raises all human endeavours, even love, from the realm of the flesh to that of the spirit. It unites all separate pursuits into one harmonious whole and promotes that 'general spirit' which is the result of the striving for perfection.

The presentation of 'the idea of elementary education' in the *Swansong* is Pestalozzi's last attempt to synthesize all the aspects of education. Although it is a great work of educational thought, it does not succeed in offering a consistent theory. In trying 'to make art natural, and nature artificial' and to solve all 'apparent' contradictions he does not escape entanglement, for the effort to reduce life's manifold to a unity cannot fail to violate reality. His whole edifice rests on a dual conception of 'nature' signifying, on the one hand, the divine in man, and on the other, his animal instinct. These he tries to reconcile. Perhaps it is just this ambiguous conception of man which brings Pestalozzi's observations nearer to the understanding of modern students than to that of his contemporaries, because they do justice to the complexities of real life. For this reason his idea of 'natural' education remains of value. It means (expressed in modern terms) that the child, especially the infant, must be given security and love as a basis for his healthy development; that these can best be supplied by his mother; that the educator can do little more than prepare the ground best suited for the growth of the child's own powers, but that he should guide these powers, as long as they need help, along lines commensurate both with the general ideal and the child's individual circumstances. The phrase 'life itself educates' indicates that the child's immediate environment provides the first means of education which by their very existence and inevitable use foster his growing powers. They are most effective if made to affect not only certain sides of the child but his whole being. For in this way will be developed what is called a 'general power' which unites the faculties of knowing what is right, willing what is good, and being able to do what has been found right and good. The place where personal guidance, environmental influences, and inherent powers can most satisfactorily work together is the home. The soundness of the home is therefore the most important condition in education.

Pestalozzi ends his explanation of 'the idea of elementary education' in the *Swansong* with the expression of his firm belief that its success would be 'infallible' if the necessary conditions for carrying it out existed. And foreseeing that his readers might be surprised at the contrast between his confident tone and the actual fact of the institute's downfall, he feels obliged to explain this contradiction, so that the consequences of outward failure should not overshadow the true value of his idea.

The obstacles lying in the way of his enterprises, he says, consisted, first, in 'the high degree of corruption' which has its origin 'in our animal nature'. Man's 'worldly' attitude had prevented an understanding of a true art of education. For this reason his ideas had not had a fair chance of falling on fertile ground where they could have grown and flourished. The obstacles consisted, further, in faults of his own ('lying in myself') and in the special circumstances prevailing in Burgdorf and Yverdon. The story of the institutes was to be published separately (*The Story of my Life*). The justification of his work through a psychological account of his own character and personal life story forms the second part of the *Swansong*.

Pestalozzi's autobiography in its details has already been extensively used in the present study. It is the richest source for the story of his life, if it is used with discretion. The question now is how far the particular kind of work done by Pestalozzi was a necessary outcome of his individual character and circumstances and how far, therefore, he himself was, as he maintains, responsible for its failure.

Pestalozzi judges severely both himself and his life's 'conditions'. Looking back at his development in its special circumstances he dwells more on its defects and weaknesses than on its positive side. In his maternal home as well as in his college days, he says, he had lacked the firm discipline and practical training which might have supplied the curb necessary to his emotional nature. Consequently, his inclination towards 'dreaming' had been encouraged and an education for 'real life' denied. His tendency to attempt more than he was able to do had first shown itself in the Neuhof enterprise which had been planned on too large a scale. Later, in Burgdorf, his undertakings had again been too bold and 'highflown' and had led, in Yverdon, to the building of a 'Tower of Babel' with the result that he lost sight of his original purpose. Now he can see that the running of such institutes requires qualities which he did not possess, and that it was wrong to begin a work, however necessary and philanthropic, which one could not carry out oneself.

But this is not all. 'The most important cause of its inevitable miscarriage is our enterprise itself.' It was bound to fail because 'it set out to do on a large scale, without preparation and suitable means, something which can only be done in a small way, developed through time and care to a healthy growth in an individual place, and brought by slow degrees to maturity and perfection in a whole community'. It is not possible to establish in one single house a method of education satisfying all human conditions and all educational principles. The institutes in Burgdorf and Yverdon had special merits but no 'general power'. They could not have it because something unnatural was being attempted there.

'Is, then, my life's purpose entirely lost?' Pestalozzi's answer is that the institutes and the experiments carried out there are not really his life's most cherished aim. Their temporary failure, he insists, is not a proof of their low value but the result of his individual defects. His true purpose, 'the simplification of popular education in its most important aspects and especially in its beginnings' has been kept alive ever since the times of the

Neuhof poor-school and the writing of *Leonard and Gertrude*, and will not be defeated even by the most adverse circumstances. On the contrary, the late intrigues have created the 'happy necessity' to re-build his enterprise on 'sounder foundations'.

'I have got over what lies behind me.' 'It is a fact that the results of my endeavours in their original and individual form are still unshaken and intact.' Even as nature herself cannot perish, so an attempt to relate the art of education to the course of nature cannot entirely disappear. Admittedly, it has until now produced but few results, which however have been proved practicable and sound. This shows that a natural method of education is no 'castle in the air'. Pestalozzi considers it his 'most sacred duty to live, to fight, and to die for it until his last breath'.

The great idea of elementary education, he concludes, is, of course, not yet attained. We must constantly strive for it. The work which has been begun must be examined and continued. Every single individual in his particular position can contribute to a strengthening of man's higher powers. The fundamental means of elementary education are, therefore, 'within ourselves'. Their use depends only on our own free will. However small an individual contribution might be—if it is perfect in itself it cannot fail to affect the whole. Pestalozzi ends the *Swansong* with the same words with which he had begun: 'Examine everything, retain what is good, and if you have found something better, add it in truth and love to what I have tried to give you in truth and love in this book.'

To the question of how to evaluate Pestalozzi's assessment of his individual contribution to 'elementary education' and of his faults as causing the institute's downfall the answer may be made that his own judgment in the *Swansong*—as opposed to that in *The Story of my Life*—is on the whole fair. It is an example of true self-knowledge and genuine humility given by a man who has risen above life's afflictions. At the same time it is the testimony of his unbroken faith in the permanent value of his work and, as he is not too modest to say, of his belief in its originality. This balance between admission of fault and knowledge of strength makes the autobiography both objective and moving. Never is he concerned with mere self-justification but always with the vindication of his work. This he recommends to the care of everyone who may be better qualified than he to carry it out, 'and certainly not for my sake or because of my request'.

The *Swansong*, like all Pestalozzi's theoretical works, is very difficult and, as he admits himself, diffuse. But, like the *Evening Hour* and the *Inquiries* earlier, it has a narrative counterpart. This is *Leonard and Gertrude*, third version. Throughout his life Pestalozzi had a special preference for his novel and therefore attempted in various phases of his development to bring its implicit doctrine up to the corresponding stage of his theory. Thus he worked at it, off and on, for forty years. If the second version reflects his economic materialism and political paternalism, the third expresses the final aim of his method, education of the people through self-activity. Although the work, even in its last edition, has not become 'A Book for the People', it presents Pestalozzi's ideas in narrative form and plain language. The words 'method' or 'elementary education' do not occur once.

Pestalozzi had begun work on a new edition as early as 1805. In contrast to the shortened second version the third was to be greatly extended. At the time, however, when his *Collected Writings* began to appear (1819/20), only four of the six volumes originally intended were ready for publication. Of the fifth and sixth parts large sections must have been written in these or the following years, but they were never finished. Unfortunately, before being printed they were lost during the transport of Pestalozzi's manuscripts from the Neuhof to Schmid in Paris (1845, after Pestalozzi's death). Only a few fragments which happened to be in other hands remain to indicate Pestalozzi's intentions.

The experiences of four decades which went into the making of the new edition result in a very different attitude to education, politics, and religion from that to be found in the original version. Education is no longer regarded with youthful enthusiasm but is shown as a slow process involving great difficulties. Religion plays a more important part, and reforms are not introduced from above but initiated by the people themselves.

The book's main theme is, of course, as always an attack on all one-sided, mechanical routine work and the recommendation of a well-balanced, comprehensive education to be achieved not through words, but through action. 'Life itself educates' is the maxim which, as in the *Swansong*, pervades the book. Again it is Gertrude who carries out this life-resembling form of education. 'Life itself in its full range, as it affected her children, was the starting-point of all her doings. . . . She never spoke to the children like a school teacher or a mother intent upon instruction. She never said, "Child, this is your head," or "This is your nose", or "Where are your eyes?" On the contrary, she would speak as does a mother tending her children and say, "Come, child, I want to wash your hands," and "I want to comb your hair" etc.' (Here Pestalozzi corrects the mistakes made earlier in his writings on teaching language.) And just as learning to speak is drawn from 'life', so also are learning to count and learning to work (i.e. spin) accomplished through natural situations. Gertrude's way of educating her children, the author asserts, has a particularly formative influence also for the reason that it is done in love and faith, and received in freedom and joy. The children realize that they play a part in the family's well-being and therefore contribute their share gladly, even though it may cost them an effort.

Gertrude's help to lieutenant Glülphi the teacher and her participation in the actual school-work are increased in comparison with the former editions. Glülphi himself with his noble intentions, but also his scruples and his 'dreaming', is drawn more vividly and resembles Pestalozzi more obviously than before. The opening day of school is now by no means so successful as it was in the first version, in spite of Gertrude's presence. On the contrary, the lieutenant is shocked by the children's impudence and ignorance, and he finds it extremely difficult to apply in school the ways of domestic education observed in Gertrude's 'living-room'. For, he argues, a schoolmaster confronting pupils stands in a very different relation to them from that of a father and mother to their children. If in a home the moral qualities develop naturally through the obligations existing between members of the family, in a classroom discipline and effort must be achieved through an interest in the subject and a belief in God. Only after having learned to know each individual child can the teacher succeed in educating all in a paternal spirit.

After the model of Gertrude Glülphi educates his children

to lead 'an active life of love'. He encourages their good will but finds that this alone is not enough. It must be accompanied by a training of those powers which can translate good intentions into good deeds. He draws their attention to the need and suffering in their neighbourhood and enables them to alleviate these ills. He accustoms them to unceasing activity and sympathetic helpfulness in an ever-widening sphere of life. 'Every day it became clearer to him that the will to work, man's practical activity, was the true, sacred, and eternal means of uniting the whole range of his powers into one single general power, the power of true humanity.' With these words the aged Pestalozzi has come full circle to the same conclusion which the young man had reached half a century before: the humanizing value of vocational training.

Thus the lieutenant attempts to restore the spirit of the 'good old times' in which, he held, honest work played an essential part in every man's life. Since honesty was based on the Christian faith, religion is introduced again into the classroom. A word spoken almost casually by Gertrude makes a deep impression on the schoolmaster and directs his attention to himself: 'Any teaching or attempt at education, she said, which originates in our sin is as if cursed.' He ponders over it and finally decides that what she probably means is that both good and evil lie in the educator's hands. If he is not pure in spirit and if his teaching comes from a selfish heart, the bad within him will appeal to the bad in the children, and his influence will not be a blessing but a curse. After that Glülphi is no longer angry or impatient with the village children but filled with love and sympathy. For without these qualities, the author remarks, it would not be possible to be schoolmaster in Bonnal.

An even greater change is to be noticed in the squire's attitude towards his village. Arner has found in Bonnal 'individual people of such wisdom and strength in everything concerning human affairs' that he refuses to impose reforms from above but accepts the suggestions coming from the people themselves. Although he alone, as the executive power, has the means of carrying these proposals into effect, it is Cotton Meyer who advises him because he knows what the people really need. Some highly respected villagers, together with the squire and the pastor, now form a 'governing council' and confer about improving their affairs. They decide to build on the good which still exists in some households and to exercise their influence only by slow degrees in this or that individual matter. There is no talk of extensive reforms. Arner prefers to take counsel about Bonnal's business with Cotton Meyer and his fellows in the pastor's house to 'racking his brains about State affairs with the minister in his cabinet . . . I do in my own corner, as well as I can, what seems to be right, and leave the consequences beyond my domain to Him who governs us all.'

The minister informs Arner that there is no hope of the Duke's supporting his schemes. But this is perhaps to the good. For 'anyone who is not of our station does not know our ins and outs'. So the only help against the evils prevailing in the community must come through education.

The obstacles lying in Arner's way consist not so much in the Duke's passive attitude as in the active opposition of a powerful court party who do not care for the improvement of popular education at all. Sylvia, the product of bad natural tendencies and a faulty education, and Helidor 'who is in the duchy what Hummel was in the village' slander and thwart Arner in his endeavours. Pestalozzi attributes their 'heathen view' that 'the people must remain without rights, and the heads of the poor as empty as their purses' to their lack of religion. 'They have no faith in anything divine, neither in themselves nor in others.' And their contempt for all that is good and true goes with an admiration for mere appearances, a craving for the luxuries of the world and for the satisfaction of their animal desires.

'But was it really necessary to picture so many scenes of degradation?' Pestalozzi asks himself, and answers, yes, the evil had to be painted black so that the heart, startled by the portrayal of corruption, may become strong enough to resist the bad and assist the good. An actual attack on Arner's endeavours is not described in the incomplete third version although it was probably intended to come in (cf. *Leonard and Gertrude*, first version). It can be conjectured that the struggle between good and evil and the final victory of light over darkness provided the content of the lost fifth part.

The extension of reforms beyond the village into the whole country (part VI) was probably intended to be treated as plan rather than fact. For the ageing Pestalozzi was becoming ever more modest. Education of the people was for him now the concern of individuals, of the best in a small circle, and not any longer of States. He was too realistic to believe in the possibility of a Utopia on earth. On the other hand he could not leave off 'dreaming'. At the end of the fourth part he gives—but, as he expressly says, only as 'fragmentary ideas of a man searching for truth'—the views on the education of man which Glülphi tries to make clear in his mind during sleepless nights. It can truly be said that in these few chapters (§§ 79–87) Pestalozzi's theory of education is stated in its most concise form. It culminates in the 'dream' not only of introducing the principles of Gertrude's 'living-room' into schools but also of reintroducing through well-educated children, the good spirit into the homes of future generations. 'He thought that this aim was the highest for which one could strive in popular education and national culture.'

The views on political economy which did not find expression in the fragmentary third version of *Leonard and Gertrude* are expressed in the Langenthal Address (1826) which Pestalozzi at the age of eighty worked out for the 'Helvetic Society'. It links up with his *Views on Industry* of 1807 but treats the subject with an up-to-date knowledge of economic conditions and an astounding foresight of future problems.

Pestalozzi believes the contemporary situation to be full of dangers. These he recognizes in the change, brought about by the greater facility in money-making, from an earlier 'spirit of earning' into a 'spirit of spending'. He observes widespread carelessness and extravagance, and also increased demands which, however, go hand in hand with a reduced energy and skill to satisfy them. Although he detects these indications of a dangerous trend in both social classes affected by the new industrial development—i.e. factory masters or 'capitalists' and factory workers or 'the growing number of people without property'—he finds the gulf between them growing ever wider. For, he says, the middle class which formerly bridged it has no share in the new prosperity and has, therefore, lost its traditional importance. Thus financial gain and economic well-being are no longer based on effort and honest work, and even the sense of order and security is disappearing.

In this predicament Pestalozzi does not recommend the arrest of the spread of industry. He admits that industry has done much to improve the standard of living, the intellectual awareness, and the technical skill of the people. But he thinks it necessary to find means to halt the decline of morals and to restore the 'essential foundations of industry'. This can be done, first, by recognizing the causes of the prevailing situation, and second, by applying the proper remedies.

It is a sad fact, says Pestalozzi, that the majority of people are thoughtless and almost blind to the dangers around them. Therefore it is for the clear-sighted and noble-minded to see and to act. For 'at a time of apparent peace and quiet we are, perhaps, on the eve of events which may decisively cut off our self-help for the future'. All States of Europe which have experienced this sudden influx of money, ill-suited to existing conditions, suffer from the same consequences of expanding industry. Even England 'in the midst of her immense achievements in skill, politics, and isolation' must take measures to prevent the riches of a few from becoming harmful to the many, and 'the unlimited increase in the number of people without property' becoming 'a public menace'.

The means to halt the ruinous trend of the 'spirit of the time' consist not in petty economies but in a more serious attitude and a simpler way of life. What the country needs before everything else is solidity and inner strength. A limitation of unnecessary demands must be accompanied by an extension of working power and skill. In short, the people must be educated to greater diligence, so that they may be willing and able to work according to the higher demands of this industrial age.

The growing number of factory workers, he concludes, presents a problem formerly unknown and not envisaged. Today, it is a public duty to meet this situation and to provide education for all classes—recognizing, on the one hand, their differences, and on the other, the equality of all human beings—so that economic security may be achieved 'through an equilibrium between productivity and demand'. The lowest class has particular need both of a general education and a specific training (Pestalozzi's favourite theme), and this for various reasons. Their fathers once belonged to the middle class who laid the country's foundations; their own importance is growing;

and there is the possibility, even certainty, that their sons will one day hold the country's fate in their hands. After all, the mass of poor people consists of individuals; each of them has the right to education. What ought to be given to them is small compared to what they possess in themselves and what they can give back to the country. They are not really so poor; 'their wealth lies within themselves'. It consists in their physical and intellectual faculties which are capable and worthy of training, in their power to work.

In however critical a mood Pestalozzi may begin any survey, he will always finish on a note of hope; for his belief in man is unconquerable. What makes this, his last completed major work, particularly remarkable is his shrewd assessment of the social change taking place in Europe at that time. He foresaw the dangers of capitalism and proletarianism in the early machine age and therefore pressed for education of the masses to counterbalance their mechanical occupation and moral decline. Anticipating later theories, he recognized the wealth of nations as lying in their productivity. He also showed—in a sociological survey of the Reformation period at the beginning of the Langenthal Address—a strikingly modern awareness of a connection between Protestant religion and economic success. It was perhaps in these matters of political economy that Pestalozzi was furthest ahead of his time.

IV HEINRICH PESTALOZZI (3)

Pestalozzi was in his eightieth year when he returned to the Neuhof, apparently beaten and forsaken, without followers or institute, but not without courage and faith. As on his first arrival in the neighbourhood of Birr half a century earlier, a new house was being built, but this time he was not to see its completion. He was glad, however, that he had retained the Neuhof in the family against frequent advice to the contrary, and he hoped that it would be kept by his descendants as 'a place of wise welfare and philanthropy'. In actual fact it changed hands as early as 1833. At the time of the centenary celebrations of Pestalozzi's birth (1846) some Swiss education-ists planned to buy the estate to use it according to Pestalozzi's wish, but the necessary money was not forthcoming. The plan was realized in 1909 when, with the help of the Swiss government, the cantons, and an extensive collection made in schools, an approved school for boys was opened there which is still running successfully. The boys are trained in agriculture or handicrafts and educated in the spirit of Pestalozzi to become self-reliant and useful members of the community.

When Pestalozzi had come to the Neuhof as a young man, he had been accompanied by a 'noble young wife' ready to share with him the vicissitudes of life. Now he was alone. Gottlieb and Katharina showed little interest in the concerns most dear to his heart. But he was grateful for their physical care and happy about the birth of his great-grandson, 'a strong boy with a head as round as the full moon'. This Karl Pestalozzi (1825–91), later a professor at the Technical University of Zurich, remained unmarried and thus was Pestalozzi's last descendant.

Schmid had been refused permission to stay in the Aargau and had gone to Paris and London to make the method known there. Pestalozzi set the greatest hopes on his future career. Schmid, he believed, would bring the science of education to a point far beyond that attained by himself. After his return from abroad Schmid would start the proposed industrial school in the Neuhof. 'What I only dreamt about the combination of agriculture, industry, and education, you will establish as a well-founded, practicable fact.' He wrote him the most affectionate letters and longed for his answers and his return. Schmid on his part remained cool and wrote but seldom. That Pestalozzi retained unswerving faith in him until the end was incomprehensible to the rest of his friends. They held Schmid responsible for the latest failure, but refrained from undeceiving the old man to save him further disappointment. Schmid did not fulfil any of Pestalozzi's expectations. He lived a lonely and undistinguished life and died, a forgotten man, in Paris in 1850.

Though Pestalozzi no longer lived among a large number of people, he often had visitors coming to see him from far or near, old friends, or their children, or new acquaintances. They found him as he had always been, lively and affectionate, interested in human affairs, modest in his wants, and as neglectful of his appearance as ever. When they had to leave him again, he would accompany them part of the way to prolong their talk on educational questions. On one such occasion, in the last month of his life, having walked out as usual without a hat and in worn-out shoes, he was caught in a snowstorm. He obstinately declined his friend's offer to take him home or to lend him his umbrella and sat down on a boundary stone from which he refused to budge before his friend reluctantly moved off. When he told this story to his next visitors, he concluded with the words 'I am as strong as a horse'. A few weeks later he was dead.

He would call on his neighbours, the governors and pastors, to talk about matters of politics and education. But what he liked best was to look in at the village school. There he would show the teachers how to attract the children's interest and how to make them think, and often he would take over himself, talking or chanting in his peculiar way. Then the children would laugh at his strange behaviour. In the last summer of his life he visited an orphanage near Basle and was given a wonderful reception. The children presented him with a crown of oak leaves (a symbol of greatness), but he would not accept it and put it on the head of one of them. 'This honour is due to innocence, not to me', he exclaimed. When the orphans sang Goethe's song 'Thou who art in Heaven' which is quoted in *Leonard and Gertrude*, he was moved to tears.

As in his youth he took part again in the annual conferences of the 'Helvetic Society'. To his great surprise he was elected president for the following year (1826). This meeting held in Langenthal, the last Pestalozzi attended, was made into a great occasion. His long address which lasted three and a half hours was read out for him. At the end he rose and promised to contribute a paper every year, as long as God granted him health and life. At the banquet that followed three cheers were given for 'the patriarch of education', and the hundred confederates present—'the noblest and best of the nation'—sang a song specially composed in his honour. When Pestalozzi rose to say a few words of thanks, he could not speak for emotion and sank back into his chair.

He last appeared in public at the meeting of the 'Cultural Society' in Brugg. After his paper on education in earliest childhood had been read out for him, he himself made some additional remarks on his favourite subject, education in the home. He spoke with such enthusiasm that he appeared to his audience 'as if transfigured with the powers of youth'. In the ensuing discussion he answered questions precisely and convincingly.

All this time he was still occupied with writing; his mind was as active as ever. He had a devoted servant and secretary in A. Steinmann who wrote down his ideas to dictation. Often he got up to work during the night, or would dictate while lying in bed during the day. He was still attempting to 'simplify' the teaching of language and to prove the similarity in the construction of ancient and modern languages. He concluded the edition of his *Collected Writings* with the *Swansong* and the Langenthal Address and produced the last chapter of his life's story which in fact led to his death.

Pestalozzi had written *The Story of my Life as Head of the Institutes in Burgdorf and Yverdon* in 1824, at the time when unhappy events had brought about the closing down of his school. It was therefore hardly surprising that his account had become the story of the quarrel between the two factions and, because of his overwrought state, had turned out to be far from objective. It had been intended to be part of the *Swansong*, but Cotta would have nothing to do with these personal contentions. Instead of heeding this warning, Pestalozzi made the grave mistake of having the book published independently, perhaps from a desire to vindicate himself before the world or to defend the honour of his friend Schmid. The latter who was on a short visit to Pestalozzi in the spring of 1826 recognized the dangers of publication. He even approached Niederer and suggested a meeting in order jointly to prevent it. But Niederer refused to co-operate although this would have been in his own interest. The book came out and brought disaster.

The Story of my Life is the self-condemnation of an old man who beholds his life's work in ruins. It is the outcome of deep despair turning into self-reproach. It reads so pathetically because Pestalozzi in his anguish does not blame anyone but himself and the wrong direction of his own endeavours for the failure of his enterprise. The old charges of proneness to dreaming, carelessness, thoughtlessness in times of fortune, and incapability in times of difficulty, recur in a magnified form. If on previous occasions they were to a certain extent justified, they are now highly exaggerated, and Pestalozzi must be defended against himself. The denigration of all previous achievements and depreciation of his oldest assistants are as unjust as the high praise bestowed on Schmid. The picture of himself is darker than his worst enemies had ever painted it.

Pestalozzi's friends abroad were gravely saddened by the book. They were familiar with the persons and circumstances and knew that the institute had not been such a 'monstrosity' as Pestalozzi described it. Mieg, in an affectionate but frank letter, pointed out that through these misrepresentations Pestalozzi had played into the hands of his opponents and at the same time disparaged the efforts of all those who had for many years given their best for his cause. He regarded the publication of the book as most unfortunate.

Nabholz reported later that Pestalozzi had said shortly before his death that the state of agitation in which he had written *The Story of my Life* had made it impossible for him to give a correct account of things; looking back at the events more calmly he felt obliged to retract some assertions as 'opinions not his own but forced upon him against his conviction'. But this withdrawal came too late. The book was distributed and attacked. Fellenberg rushed to confute Pestalozzi in Zurich newspapers. Niederer believed it to be his 'moral duty' to defend 'the idea' which in his opinion Pestalozzi had betrayed, and prepared a counterblast which brought Pestalozzi to his death.

This former disciple induced a teacher at the girls' school, Eduard Biber, to compile a book designed to give the answer to Schmid's *Truth and Error* and Pestalozzi's *Story of my Life*. It contained personal letters, legal documents, and financial accounts from Niederer's files which were genuine enough in themselves; but the use made of them—the raking up of long-settled financial quarrels, the imputing of low motives to the enemy while at the same time stressing his own moral superiority, the malicious interpretation of certain intimate traits in Pestalozzi's character—all this was an outrage to Pestalozzi's feelings. If Pestalozzi's friends had deplored the publication of *The Story of my Life*, they were even more shocked by Biber's fabrication; if Schmid had never enjoyed wide approval, Niederer, too, had now lost all sympathy.

Pestalozzi received the book in the second week of February. He fell into a state of extreme agitation. He could not control his nerves and was unable to rest either day or night. He wandered aimlessly about the house and estate muttering to himself. Then he began to write with his own hand—something he had not done for a long time. But his eyes failed him; he could no longer see what he wrote. He forgot to dip his pen in ink and went on writing nevertheless. Steinmann who stood by his side had to remind him, 'Dip, Herr Pestalozzi, dip!' After a few days he succumbed to the strain. He was attacked by a bilious fever and had to give up the struggle.

He knew he was dying and yet longed to live on for a few more months to refute the shameful slander. But seeing his time running out he sent for his friend the pastor of Birr so as to give him his last will and testament. This consists mainly in a justification of Schmid. Schmid, he declared, had done everything to save his House and his work; to him he entrusted his defence. To his opponents he addressed the request that they should bring their accusations to court for investigation and judgment according to law. He hoped, however, that the peace which was descending on him would also bring peace to them. In any case he forgave his enemies and blessed his friends in the hope that 'they may think with love of him who is gone and further his aims to the best of their abilities even after his death'.

As his strength was visibly failing his doctor advised that he should be taken to the town of Brugg where more medical aid would be at hand. Pestalozzi was unwilling to leave the Neuhof, for he wished to be buried in the Birr village churchyard, beside the school. Only when he was given assurance that his wish would be carried out did he consent. An open sledge was lined with cushions to protect him against cold and wind. When he was carried out of the house he wept, saying that he would never see his Neuhof again. He shook hands with everyone on the estate and made his grandson promise to make over the new building as a gift for educational purposes.

A warm room and a good bed had been prepared in the 'Red House Inn' at Brugg. Gottlieb and Katharina remained with him till the end. Friends visited his bedside to exchange many an affectionate word with him. But his illness made rapid progress. His pain became more severe, and his hands and lips were in restless movement. On the evening of the second day he became calmer, and on the morning of February 17th, 1827, he died peacefully. 'His face had the expression of one waking up from his sleep, smiling gently, and intending to tell his children his pleasant dream.'

The day of the funeral was bright and very cold. The churchyard was covered with deep snow, but the sexton had swept the paths and cleared a large space around the grave, for he expected a great number of mourners. Relatives and friends, followers of the method and teachers from far and near gathered in the Neuhof. They were joined by the people of the neighbourhood and the village schoolchildren. The oldest assistants were absent. The nearest relatives had long since gone. Many true friends were abroad. But the procession from the Neuhof to the churchyard in Birr was so long that no one could remember ever having seen the like. The coffin was carried by the teachers of the neighbouring villages. Before it was lowered the children sang specially composed hymns. The pastor gave a moving account of Pestalozzi's life and character and said the prayer. Then Pestalozzi's body was given back to earth. All present expressed their sympathy and voiced their esteem for the man who had been so violently attacked, and the day passed in quiet solemnity.

A rosebush was planted on Pestalozzi's grave as he had wished. 'Its blossoms will make eyes weep that remained dry at my sufferings', he had said. For many years his burial place was marked only by a rough stone. But when a new school was built as part of the centenary celebrations in 1846, the Aargau government made the gable side which faces the churchyard with Pestalozzi's grave into a monument. It carries this inscription:

'Here lies
Heinrich Pestalozzi,
born in Zurich on 12th January 1746,
died in Brugg on 17th February 1827.
Saviour of the Poor in the Neuhof,
Preacher of the People in 'Leonard and Gertrude',
In Stans Father to Orphans,

In Burgdorf and Münchenbuchsee
Founder of the new Elementary School,
In Yverdon Educator of Mankind.
Man, Christian, Citizen.
All for Others, Nothing for Himself.
Blessed be his Name.'

A long life was at an end; a great variety of factors had contributed to its formation. Its course had included the end of the *ancien régime* and the beginning of the machine age; it had witnessed very different forms of political constitution, economic systems, and social order. People from many countries had played a part in it, men and women, distinguished and ordinary people, princes, citizens, and peasants. Yet Pestalozzi, the centre of these relationships, had moved in a comparatively narrow circle, crossing the borders of his country only rarely, and regarding himself as a plain man. His life presents an 'apparent contradiction', but his struggle to overcome this gives it some claim to unity.

Pestalozzi's character reveals marked contrasts: delicacy and strength, blindness and vision, vacillation and determination, restlessness and inner security, daring and humility. Each of his traits extended over the whole range of its possibilities; along with its positive quality it had the corresponding negative side. His outward peculiarities, so obvious to every observer, came only from his unconcern for worldly appearances and his own welfare; his obstinacy and single-mindedness from his love and his faith. The same complexity existed in his opinions: he was at once a Swiss patriot and a world citizen, an upholder of tradition and an apostle of freedom, a good Christian and an exponent of humanism. Clearly as each single feature appears in this or that action and is a characteristic part of him, it is difficult to see them together and to draw a coherent picture of the man as a whole. For Pestalozzi was not a 'harmonious personality'; he was not an example of that desirable 'balance of powers'.

Not only his natural endowment and convictions, but also the events of his life—which certainly were largely influenced by his own inclination and choice—went to the shaping of his character. That Pestalozzi with his carelessness managed to

accomplish so much; that with his tendency to self-abandonment he yet retained a feeling of self-esteem; that his 'dreami-
ness' was accompanied by a knowledge of the world 'as it is';
and that this knowledge did not destroy his belief in the better
powers of man—all this was the fruit of bitter experience, hard
struggles, and his power to overcome outer and inner obstacles.
His inborn benevolence towards all men would have remained
ineffective, had it not been accompanied by awareness of the
evil in human nature and raised to true love by action in spite
of it. That he succeeded in making 'the spirit govern the flesh'
without being false to his own true self he ascribed to his misfortunes. An easier life, he declared, would not have produced
in him this power of endurance and self-denial—a power which,
transmuted into faith, hope, and charity, gave him true unity
and greatness.

His own person was of no importance to him; it was merely
the vessel of his mission. The older he grew the stronger became
his feeling of dependence on a will other than his own. He
called it 'God's hand' and humbly accepted from it success and
failure. He endeavoured to walk in the footsteps of Jesus and
believed true Christianity to be 'not only a doctrine but also a
way of life'. He practised in deed what he preached in words,
and this sincerity was the secret of the impression he made.

He regarded himself as only a forerunner, as one who cried
in the wilderness, preparing the way for those coming after him.
He tried to make of others what he knew he himself was not.
Like Socrates he stirred consciences and asked questions so that
others would have to answer them. He made the impact and
set the example of a man who, trying and erring, struggling and
failing, loving and suffering, was for ever reaching upwards and
sacrificing himself.

Pestalozzi certainly attempted more than one single man can
achieve. His aim was not merely to establish a new method of
teaching, not even to educate children, or to improve the lot of
the poor. His dream was to promote the well-being of all men
through the strengthening of their own better powers and
thereby to bring peace and security to the world—a goal
certainly not unlike the Abbé St. Pierre's 'paix perpétuelle' with
which it had been compared. In his 'most ambitious days', as
he called them, he tried to achieve no less than a harmony

between a complete theory of education and a practical policy for the happiness of mankind. This goal he failed to reach. Nor did he succeed in realizing either part of it. His practical enterprises miscarried, and his theoretical system remained fragmentary. At the end of his days he felt compelled to say, 'My life has produced nothing whole, nothing complete.' And yet it was more fruitful than appeared to him in retrospect. What is the lasting value of his endeavours?

In an age when 'enlightenment' made great strides but was still confined to the upper and middle classes, Pestalozzi discovered 'the people'. He drew attention not only to their needs, but also to their capacities which had hitherto remained unknown and neglected, and claimed that it is not only possible but necessary to cultivate their powers, and this not only for their own sakes, but for the benefit of all. Believing as he did in the higher potentialities of every human being, even the lowest, he advocated every man's right to education and society's duty to implement that right. He thus conceived a new idea of democratic culture and paved the way for universal national education.

In giving pre-eminence to man's 'better nature' or his moral powers, Pestalozzi propounded a theory of education based on moral principles. Asserting that morality is the prerogative of man as opposed to the animal and of the individual as opposed to the mass, he made 'ennoblement' of every single individual the goal as well as the starting-point of all education. He certainly considered a sound training of man's intellectual and practical faculties necessary for his satisfactory and useful position in society, but insisted that these must always be related to the inmost centre of man's being which he called moral, or religious, or sometimes 'love', or 'the divine spark'.

The place from where he wished education to issue is the home. He pleaded, like none before him, for the safeguarding or, if necessary, the restoration of the good spirit of the home and the enlightening of the mother. He endeavoured to 'simplify' the means of education so that they could be used in every 'simple home' and in every elementary school. Again, he admitted that schools are necessary for a more expert training in special subjects but stressed that they, too, must be filled with a parental spirit. For the most powerful stimulus to the development of a child's moral qualities being love, and love possible only between individuals, he demanded the utmost support for the natural relationships and, in their absence, conditions which would approach these as nearly as possible.

The task of education, according to Pestalozzi, is to be found not in imposing on the child fixed doctrines and alien concepts, but in helping him to develop his own constructive powers and conquer his own corrupting tendencies. Its way lies in the establishing of his inner security by rooting him firmly in his family and giving him a sure place in society. Its means consist in the training of all his faculties through a combination of moral, mental, and practical activities. The child being, like nature, conceived as an integrated whole, education, too, becomes something single and complete in itself. The aim of a 'harmonious education' is, however, not an aesthetic ideal but the morally balanced personality.

In formulating fundamental principles Pestalozzi made education an independent branch of knowledge alongside religion, ethics, and politics. He declared its essence to be not an engendering of something new but the fostering and developing of powers inherent in human nature. With the creation of a new science of education he raised the status of the educator, especially that of the elementary teacher. He initiated the founding of teachers' training colleges and thus made possible popular education. He invented a new method of teaching, abolishing the old way of making the child learn by rote incomprehensible material and replacing it by leading him to think for himself; and he applied this method also to practical and moral subjects.

Pestalozzi recognized the necessity of establishing a close link between education in the home and education at school. He emphasized the immense importance of the mother in the child's early upbringing and the influence of his first emotional experiences on the rest of his life. He laid the foundations for the study of psychology. He pointed out the inter-relationship between family life and public morality, and between the people's well-being and the trend of politics. He recognized the importance of healthy working conditions and good workmanship and was much concerned for the maintenance of a sound middle class. Thus he brought out the interdependence of politics, economics, and education, and saw the true art of government in a due regard for the related interests of the three, based on ethics and religion.

Pestalozzi's limitations arose from the defects of his qualities. His greatest fault, his inability from sheer magnanimity and trustfulness to control institutions and people, was the main reason for the collapse of his enterprises. Since he would not curtail the freedom of anyone in his community, he let discipline, financial order, and even the original spirit of his creation go to the winds. Thus it happened that others who were far less original but more efficient and who owed the fundamental principles of their work entirely to him (e.g. Fellenberg) reaped the success and the glory which he threw away with both hands.

His love of the people left him no time for the education of the upper classes; he thought these could look after themselves. He took no interest in, and his work is not concerned with, wide fields of culture—literature, music, fine art. His conception of history was antiquated even by the end of his own life, remaining untouched by the newly developed genetic method of historical thinking. He looked at developments in 'time' as being bound up with 'the world' and 'society', concepts which on the whole he depreciated. With his static view of society, as well as of nature, he saw social differentiation mainly in divergences between classes belonging to an unchangeable order. Thus poverty was for him an established 'estate'.

Many of his notions are, of course, the outcome of contemporary views and conditions. This is true for his constructive as well as his negative conceptions. His belief in the dignity of the individual is the fundamental principle of German idealist philosophy, while the notion of unchangeable nature comes from eighteenth-century rationalism. The idea that the order of social classes and the station of 'the poor' were unalterable facts established by God was generally held far into the nineteenth century. The home was in his time the centre of domestic and even of occupational activities; his demand for a close-knit social community was, therefore, still practicable, although signs of its dissolution were beginning to appear.

It is all the more remarkable that in some fields, especially in economics, he was considerably ahead of his time. He foresaw the consequences of the industrial revolution, the impact made by large cities, machines, capitalism, and the proletariat. If he indicated the dangers, he was also able to suggest the remedies; and although he knew the iniquity of men and the world, he remained firm in his belief in positive values. The significance of his work lies therefore in this combination of realism and idealism. While the German classical philosophers tried to solve their problems by shunning this world and soaring into the purer realm of the spirit, Pestalozzi chose to compromise by recognizing man's membership of both worlds.

Because of its ambivalent quality his work can be understood in many ways. During the hundred and thirty years since his death its interpretation has changed several times and the emphasis been laid on different aspects. In the nineteenth century the creation of a method of intellectual education was taken as his main achievement, and he was then regarded as the celebrated schoolmaster who had introduced universal elementary education. (Incidentally, a similar error was made in the case of Fröbel whose founding of the Kindergarten has been held to be the whole of his educational design.) At that time school education was, however, predominantly regarded as an imparting of knowledge, and critics ignored too much Pestalozzi's demand that it should be based on moral principles and linked at one end with the home upbringing and at the other with vocational training.

In connection with the centenary celebrations of his death (1927) the study of Pestalozzi has been stimulated in Switzerland and Germany. A substantial number of hitherto unknown writings have come to light, and new points of view have been applied to their interpretation. Since then the awareness of his importance not only as an educationist, but also as a philosopher and social reformer has steadily grown. At the beginning of this revival Pestalozzi's ideas on social and moral education attracted the main interest. Then the modernity of his sociological and political writings was discovered. And during the last years it has become possible, through experience gained in interpreting other complex and 'obscure' existentialist writings, to give new meaning to his dialectic philosophy. Of all this development the English reader has so far had no knowledge.

However interesting his written work may be, it has at all times been Pestalozzi the man who has made the strongest impression. He lives in his portraits, his mask, and his writings, most immediately in his addresses and letters. The goodness, loving-kindness, and marks of suffering which are revealed in them, the humanity which seems to proffer love and sympathy to all who approach them—these cannot but touch the heart even of twentieth-century man so that he feels a breath of the Pestalozzian spirit.

What is Pestalozzi's significance today? In an age of increasing specialization and State intervention, growing demand and diminishing effort, a general levelling in all human affairs, and man's progressive separation from nature, he proclaims the value of independent thinking, constructive work, and individual moral responsibility; also the necessity of secure natural relationships between mother and child, members of the family, and of the immediate working community. He asserts that nothing in the world is more important than the physical, mental, and moral well-being of each individual man. His educational aim, the 'ennobling' of all men through the cultivation of their own powers, has proved to be of perennial value and may even claim to remain unsurpassed. More than by his writings he convinces by his life that it is possible to put an ideal into practice, however great the obstacles, if there is a willingness to pay the price in personal sacrifice. Thus Pestalozzi is in line with those earlier and more recent teachers of humanity—Socrates, Gandhi, Schweitzer—who have chosen the same goal and trodden the same path of tireless devotion and self-sacrifice.

Appendix I

PESTALOZZIANISM IN BRITAIN AND
THE UNITED STATES[1]

PESTALOZZI had friends and followers in various European countries, and schools run according to his principles were founded in many and widely separated places. But because of the Napoleonic Wars and the Continental Blockade Pestalozzi's connections with English people were not established until late in his career. Yet at the end of his life he hoped that it would be from England and America that his method would spread.

There had, of course, been cultural relations between England and Switzerland before the Revolution, for ideas and visits had been freely exchanged. English gentlemen on their grand tour were almost bound to pass through Switzerland on their way to Italy, and ever since Milton's stay at Geneva and Gibbon's residence in Lausanne these two places in particular were favoured by Britishers. In Geneva, there existed something like a British colony even during the Napoleonic régime, the important link between the two nations being the *Bibliothèque Britannique*, founded in 1796 by the brothers M. A. and C. Pictet. When the Romantics discovered the beauty of nature and the grandeur of the mountainside, and when after the wars travelling to Switzerland became fashionable, a veritable stream of visitors poured into the country. Lord Byron's and Shelley's

---

[1] While the treatment of the main part of this book has aimed at condensing an enormous material, Appendix I deals with all the available sources in greater detail because of the subject's special relevance. It is based to a large extent on hitherto unpublished letters.

visits to Geneva (1816) and their literary outcome are only the best known of many.

As has already been mentioned in the main part of this book, English ideas had influenced Swiss thought during the eighteenth century: Milton's *Paradise Lost* had inspired Bodmer to compose his epics on biblical themes, Addison's *Spectator* had become the model for Swiss Moral Weeklies, and the 'natural' trend of English literature had won final victory over the formal French style in the literary controversy between Bodmer and Gottsched. Hobbes', Locke's, Shaftesbury's and Hume's philosophies were part of Swiss higher education, and the Habeas Corpus Act remained the Swiss ideal of personal freedom.

By all these factors Pestalozzi was consciously or unconsciously affected in his thinking. He took more active steps to inform himself about conditions in England when, in the seventeen-eighties and nineties, he read widely on constitutional questions. In later years, he was mainly interested in England's industrial development and sought to learn more about it through Swiss newspapers and personal contacts. He had perceived at an early stage that the problems of England, the country furthest advanced in industrial development, were significant and instructive for other lands; and considering the isolation of the island and the difficulties of communication at that time, he was remarkably well informed. On the other hand, there was in England only sporadic knowledge about Pestalozzi's activities during the time of French hegemony in Europe, and the little that became known there was conveyed through books rather than through people.

It seems fitting that it was women writers who were among the early advocates of Pestalozzi's method. Although her book *Hints addressed to Patrons and Directors of Schools*[1] was not published until 1815, Mrs. Elizabeth Hamilton, a Scotswoman, had, as early as 1801, written *Letters on the Elementary Principles of Education* and, in 1808, *The Cottagers of Glenburnie*, a novel with a strong educational bias whose action takes place in rural

---

[1] 'Principally intended to show that the Benefits derived from the new modes of Teaching may be increased by a Partial Adoption of the Plan of Pestalozzi.' Edinburgh, 1815. Cf. *Hints to Mothers on the Cultivation of the Minds of Children in the Spirit of Pestalozzi's Method*. By a Foreigner, three years resident at Yverdon. London, 1823. The authorship cannot be established.

Scotland and whose characters speak in the Scots tongue. The style of the latter and the form of the earlier are strongly reminiscent of *Leonard and Gertrude* and *How Gertrude teaches her Children*, but direct dependences were unlikely at that time. A similar correspondence exists in the case of Maria Edgeworth, the Irish novelist. Although she did not visit Pestalozzi personally until 1819/20, she collaborated with her father R. L. Edgeworth in the writing of *Essays on Professional Education* (1809), and her didactic novels and moral tales have a strong local flavour, like Pestalozzi's. The third, very different, woman writer to make Pestalozzi known to the English reader was Mme de Staël. Her *De l'Allemagne* (1810) was prohibited in France and reprinted in England in 1813. This book which informed the educated Briton about the German philosophical and literary movements, contains in its nineteenth chapter a warm appreciation of Pestalozzi's work in Yverdon, based on her own observation. It was widely read and played an important part in publicizing Pestalozzi's ideas in England.

It was, indeed, in the French language and through French connections that Pestalozzianism was introduced to the British. Pestalozzi's old friends P. A. Stapfer (Helvetian Ambassador to France) and F. C. Laharpe (former Tutor to the Czar of Russia) recommended him to M. A. Jullien (general in Bonaparte's army and officer of the Légion d'honneur), and he in his turn became a mediator between Pestalozzi and English-speaking people. He had studied 'the method' from eight to ten hours daily for several months and published a *Précis sur l'Institut d'Education d'Yverdon* (Milan, 1810). His larger work *Esprit de la Méthode d'Education de M. Pestalozzi* (Milan, 1812) was read in many European countries and was for a long time considered to be the best contemporary description of the Pestalozzian method. It surpassed an earlier work by Daniel-A. Chavannes: *Exposé de la Méthode Elémentaire de M. Pestalozzi* (1805). The brothers Pictet in Geneva were instrumental in directing foreign visitors to Pestalozzi; they pointed out the Yverdon institute as one of the sights of Switzerland worth seeing.

When after Waterloo travelling on the Continent was easier, educationists and philanthropists went to European countries seeking both pleasure and information. There was at that time in England a strong awareness of the need for improvement of the condition of the poor, activated by religious motives and promoted by such religious groups as the Evangelicals, the Methodists, and the Quakers. The Anti-Slave-trade movement, connected with the name of William Wilberforce, set the ways and the means for other enterprises to follow. Infant school and elementary school societies sprang up, and their mode of organization was in the first place determined by the religious denomination of their founders. The well-known Bell–Lancaster controversy about who originated the teaching method used by both developed into a struggle for supremacy in the organization of British primary education.

Joseph Lancaster, a Quaker, and Andrew Bell, a Church of England clergyman, had introduced the monitorial system simultaneously and independently, although even contemporary critics were of the opinion that Lancaster was first in the field.[1] Its chief object was to give the rudiments of education to masses of poor children as cheaply as possible, employing one qualified teacher to several hundred or even one or two thousand pupils and making the more advanced of these pass on their knowledge to their less developed fellows. In the Lancastrian schools the three R's were taught, while Dr. Bell, at least in the beginning, taught writing only so as not to raise the poor above their station. Learning was purely mechanical, superficial, and by rote. Neither method aimed at the formation of character or the development of the child's own potentialities. The singling-out and endowing with authority of the abler boys encouraged favouritism and conceit; the lack of contact between master and pupil prevented the operation of any truly educational process. The system was a practical expedient at a time of acute shortage of teachers. The Royal Lancastrian Society, later called British and Foreign School Society, was based on religious principles common to all Christian denominations; it was patronized mainly by Nonconformists and Whigs; while the National Society for the Education of the Poor according to the Principles of the Church of England was, as the name suggests, under the direction of the Established Church and consequently was superior to the other in influence and in numbers. It was

[1] [Henry Brougham]: 'On the Education of the Poor'. In: *The Edinburgh Review*, 1810, p. 58 ff.

the supporters of the former who tried to combine its method with the Pestalozzian, those of the latter who saw to it that Pestalozzianism did not take a firm hold in England.

A young German, W. H. Ackermann (1789–1848), assistant master in Yverdon for two years before joining in the Prussian War of Liberation, had gone to London in 1814 to stay with his uncle, the art dealer Rudolph Ackermann (whose prints of Oxford and Cambridge colleges are still well known), and to teach in Lancastrian and National schools. There he made the acquaintance of old Dr. Bell (1753–1832) himself. What a difference he experienced between him, an imperious man generally dreaded and disliked, and Father Pestalozzi, universally loved; also between 'this mechanism, this merely passive memory work and the Pestalozzian active developing of the young mind from the first sensory perception to the highest intellectual conception!' [1] Ackermann is probably the first who tried to introduce the Pestalozzian method into English schools; but he failed to convince Dr. Bell of its superiority to Bell's own. He succeeded, however, in kindling an interest, and in the autumn of 1816, when Ackermann was back again in Yverdon, Dr. Bell visited Pestalozzi in order to see the method for himself.

He was present at a public examination and was invited to conduct a lesson, always using Ackermann as his interpreter, for he did not understand either German or French. But he failed to be impressed even by witnessing the boys give as many as twelve different demonstrations of the Pythagorean proposition. He insisted that the one used in English schools was different and better. On the second day of his stay a colloquium was held between the two world-famous educationists in front of teachers, strangers, and town notabilities in which each expounded his principles as clearly as was necessary for translation into a foreign language. Pestalozzi explained that to stimulate the child's activity he never appealed to ambition, but rather to the child's love of his parents or teachers, his sense of duty, and his interest in the subject. Bell declared he 'went further' by founding his system on emulation, 'that powerful engine' of human achievement. There was no possibility of mutual understanding. When Bell left he said to Ackermann: 'I have

[1] W. H. Ackermann: *Erinnerungen aus meinem Leben bei Pestalozzi*. Frankfurt a.M., 1846, p. 12.

now got to know your Pestalozzi's method. Believe me, in twelve years' time nobody will speak of it, while mine will have spread all over the earth.' [1]

Pestalozzi's friends Stapfer and Laharpe, however, seeing what rapid progress the monitorial system was making in England, were much in favour of amalgamating Pestalozzi's 'psychological' method with the 'military-hierarchic exercises' of the Englishmen Lancaster and Bell. 'The latter as vehicle for your system of education, thought out so much more deeply and aimed at complete development of the human powers, would be an excellent means of spreading and popularizing your method.' [2]

Another meeting might have brought about a fruitful blending of two rather similar educational schemes—which indeed was achieved later for a short while in the United States of America (see p. 301). This was the visit of Robert Owen (1771–1858) who in the company of Professor Pictet went to the Continent in 1818. At this time Owen was a successful factory owner, a model employer, a social reformer, and the originator of a new system of community life and infant education put into practice in his cotton mill village of New Lanark, Scotland. [3] What was being done there was like a realization of what Pestalozzi had proposed in *Leonard and Gertrude*, part III. For Owen, having abandoned the Bell–Lancaster method of instruction as wholly inadequate, had evolved, it appears independently of Pestalozzi, a more humane method of education than that of his fellow-countrymen, coming in many respects close to that of the Swiss reformer. Like Pestalozzi, he held that the fundamental task of education was the development of the child's intellectual, moral, and practical faculties, and its aim the improvement of the adult population's living standard. He also employed similar means by which he hoped to attain this end: he began education at an early age, adapted it to the child's level of understanding, attracted his interest and active co-operation, and engaged the whole child. He used natural objects for teaching purposes in preference to books, introduced physical exercises (dancing!), and abolished punishment. He

[1] Morf IV, 340.   [2] P.B. X, 38.
[3] Robert Dale Owen: *An Outline of the System of Education at New Lanark.* Glasgow, 1824.

wished the child to enjoy his lessons, to take a pride in his work, and so to be happy. Owen was indeed a Utilitarian as well as a rationalist; the greatest happiness of the greatest number was his ideal. 'The essence of national training and education', he says in his *New View of Society*, 'is to impress on the young ideas and habits which shall contribute to the future happiness of the individual and the State; and this can be accomplished only by instructing them to become rational beings.' [1]

This emphasis on reason points to the differences between the two reformers. Owen was an atheist and Utopian who believed in the immediate perfectibility of this world. He was convinced that once the reasonableness of a social scheme had been accepted, it could be established at once. Pestalozzi had a deeper respect for the slow and gradual progress of individual and social life as well as for the moral and religious forces in human nature. He went no further than trying to assist and to safeguard nature's own development, while Owen, like a bene-volent despot, did not hesitate to impose his ideas on the community. Owen admitted to his Institute for the Formation of Character children from the age of one 'to take them away from the erroneous treatment of untrained parents', while Pestalozzi believed in the formative influence of the mother and the home. Owen had, of course, vast means at his disposal—which he had earned by his own successful efforts—in compari-son with which Pestalozzi was like a poor church mouse. Owen was more practical in conduct but less realistic in outlook than Pestalozzi; and although in the end it seemed as if the schemes of both had failed, they brought about reforms which, though carried out without any formal acknowledgement of their initiators, have become widely accepted with the passing of time. Owen's ideas have been a driving force in the socialist and co-operative movement, while Pestalozzi's have permeated educational theory and practice.

The only record of Owen's visit to Pestalozzi in 1818 is that given in his *Autobiography*. [2] This was written when Owen was

[1] Robert Owen: *A New View of Society*, London, 1813 (reprinted in Every-man's Library), Essay IV, p. 74.
[2] *The Life of Robert Owen by Himself* (reprinted from the original edition of 1857/8). London, 1920, p. 244: 'Our next visit was to Yverdon, to see the advance made by Pestalozzi—another good and benevolent man, acting

an old man and contains many slips of memory[1] apart from the fact that he, even at the time of his European journey, was far too convinced of the excellence of his own scheme to appreciate those of others. The tone of his report is, therefore, slightly condescending. Indeed, wherever he went, he urged his ideas on his hosts and, at least according to his description, left them admiring disciples of the 'new views'. Pestalozzi for his part also believed his method to be the best and would not have accepted suggestions from others. Besides, he was an old man at the time, and his institute was in the throes of an unfortunate struggle. This is an important factor which has to be kept in mind when the reports of English visitors are being assessed.

They always called on Fellenberg as well and—at least the casual visitors—were more favourably impressed by Hofwyl than by Yverdon. There was there a younger man in full control of his establishment, able to maintain order, discipline, and success. His House of Industry, a school for poor children based on agricultural and home-industrial labour, caught their particular attention as the most suitable model for their own domestic needs. His rigid segregation of social classes also seemed more acceptable to British views. They did not realize that the principles underlying this enterprise were originally Pestalozzi's, and that it was due to the age, liberality, and kindness of the one and the vigour, organizing ability, and practical efficiency of the other that Yverdon went down and Hofwyl flourished. Owen thought Pestalozzi 'one step in advance' of ordinary school routine, and Fellenberg 'two or three'. Yet although the impression Pestalozzi's institute gave may have been imperfect

for the benefit of his poor children to the extent of his knowledge and means. He was doing, he said, all he could, to cultivate the heart, the head and the hands of his pupils. His theory was good, but his means and experience were very limited, and his principles were those of the old system. . . . His school, however, was one step in advance of ordinary schools. . . .'

[1] e.g. it was probably not 'Father Oberlin' whom he visited in Fribourg, as he asserts, but Father Girard, the same who had given the report on the Yverdon institute in 1810 (see p. 220). J. F. Oberlin, a visit to whom should have been interesting to Owen, for he had founded the first infant schools in Germany, as Owen had in Scotland, was a Protestant pastor living in Waldersbach, in the Vosges mountains, while Father Girard was a Jesuit. See R. R. Rusk: *A History of Infant Education*. London, 1933, p. 119 f.

because it had passed its best, the impact his person made on his English visitors was strong and lasting. 'His goodness of heart and benevolence of intention were evident in what he had done under the disadvantages which he had to encounter', is Owen's patronizing comment.

At least two more well-known British travellers interested in social reform visited Yverdon at about that time (in 1816), Henry Brougham and William Allen. Henry Brougham (1778–1868), afterwards Lord Chancellor, had already made a name for himself as an outstanding lawyer, orator, and member of Parliament. He was a contributor to *The Edinburgh Review* and a successful agitator in the cause of liberalism. He had drawn the attention of Parliament to the sad state of popular education and procured the appointment of a general commission of enquiry into the misappropriation of endowed charities which ultimately led to the reform of many charitable organizations. In 1816, while on the Continent to restore his health, he visited Pestalozzi in Yverdon and Fellenberg in Hofwyl. The impressions and suggestions he received are expressed in his evidence before a Select Committee of which he was chairman, and in several articles in *The Edinburgh Review* which are partly identical with his Parliamentary Report.[1]

From the Pestalozzian point of view it is sad to see here, too, the highest praise reserved for Fellenberg's establishment and Yverdon mentioned only as an afterthought, as 'another institution' which Brougham 'also visited'.[2] Fellenberg's School of

[1] Third Report of the Select Committee appointed to inquire into the Education of the Lower Orders, 3rd and 8th of June 1818; *The Edinburgh Review*, No. LXI, December 1818, Art. 7: 'Mr. Fellenberg's Establishment at Hofwyl'; No. LXIV, October 1819, Art. 13: 'Establishments at Hofwyl'.

[2] Henry Brougham: *Evidence before the Education Committee of the House of Commons*, given on June 5th, 1818, p. 197: 'There is another institution for education at Yverdon which I also visited in August 1816. It is under the direction of Mr. Pestalozzi, and consists of above a hundred boys, who are taught every branch of learning, by different masters, upon a principle quite new and deserving of notice. Mr. Pestalozzi observes, that the received methods of instruction are too mechanical; that children are taught by rote, and that their reasoning faculties are not sufficiently called into action. Accordingly all his pupils are taught in a way that excludes mere mechanical operations, and certainly tends greatly to exercise their mind. No books are allowed . . . [The pupils] had certainly a very accurate knowledge of the rationale of all the operations which they had learned, and their minds

Industry in which thirty to forty poor boys were taught while working in agriculture, thus almost supporting themselves, is described in great detail and considered worth copying in England. In the debate which followed Brougham recommended the introduction of the Fellenberg system into country districts, while declaring 'Mr. Owen's Plan' more suitable for industrial centres. What he said about Pestalozzi is mainly concerned with the new teaching method, especially of mathematics; and although it is much more objective and appreciative than Owen's report, it does not mention the fundamental ideas of 'the method' or the humane spirit of the institute. This, however, could hardly have been felt on a short visit, and Brougham expressly 'wished to be understood as speaking with diffidence on this subject from my imperfect examination of it'.

Ten years later, when much more about Pestalozzi and his principles was known in England, Brougham did more justice to Pestalozzi. He now credited him with having adopted the method of mutual instruction in Stans before Dr. Bell and Joseph Lancaster had invented it and introduced it to this country, each without knowing what the other had done. Of Pestalozzi's system as a whole[1] he said, still omitting any reference to its moral implications, 'It is certain that the plan strengthens the faculties of the mind in an extraordinary degree; . . . and it is equally certain that no other teacher in modern times has duly perceived the importance of carrying on bodily training with mental instruction. . . . Nor can any one doubt, that to him is due the praise of first presenting the grand truth, now the foundation of all the efforts, making with such signal success, for the improvement of our kind,—that the pleasures of science are the inheritance of the poor, as well as the patrimony of the rich.' Yet he still believed that Fellenberg had 'improved the system prodigiously' and 'practised its principles upon a magnificent scale'. He admitted that without the experiments of Stans and Burgdorf Hofwyl would not have been possible, but thought it 'equally true that

were strengthened, I doubt not, by the constant exercise of thought unconnected with notation . . .'

[1] 'The great system of general instruction of which I look upon Pestalozzi to be the originator' (from a private letter, the manuscript of which is in my possession).

without Fellenberg the illustrious Pestalozzi would have lived in vain'. [1]

William Allen (1770–1843), a scientist (founder of the chemical firm of Allen & Hanbury's) and Quaker philanthropist, was a supporter of many good causes and the friend of many distinguished men. With Wilberforce he worked for the abolition of the slave trade, with Brougham for the improvement of the conditions of the poor. With Jeremy Bentham and Robert Owen he was a partner in the social experiment of New Lanark, though an uneasy one on religious grounds. Because of his great knowledge, business experience, moral integrity, and wide connections he would be made secretary or treasurer of as many charitable societies as he had time to serve. When a few years later Pestalozzi's friends agitated for the introduction of his method into England, the discussions took place in Allen's house in Plough Court. His preoccupation with religion and self-examination made him more sensitive to personal qualities and spiritual atmosphere than Pestalozzi's visitors previously mentioned. He found Fellenberg's 'countenance and manner indicative of great mental power, openness of character, and benignity'. The affection he felt for Pestalozzi was instantaneous and was obviously returned. 'He saluted me', Allen noted in his journal (6th September 1816), 'with two kisses, one on each cheek: he is a lively old man, rather below the middle stature, and thin; some of the pupils were examined in our presence, solving, by mental calculation, a variety of difficult questions in algebraic equations, etc. It is pleasant to see the terms upon which the pupils live with Pestalozzi and the tutors—a spirit of harmony seems to pervade the whole establishment. I took an affectionate leave of the old man, who again saluted me three times at parting; I was much pleased with my visit.' [2]

'I shall be happy to promote thy views', Allen wrote to Pestalozzi from London, 'and indeed have already thought of a Plan which I have suggested to Dr. Orpen. I purpose to form a small committee in London of Gentlemen known to the Public

---

[1] *The Edinburgh Review*, No. XCIII, January 1828, p. 142 ff. See also the Preface to this book, p. ix.

[2] *The Life of William Allen, with Selections from his Correspondence*, in three vols. London, 1847. Vol. 1, p. 283.

—for considering the whole subject.' [1] (For what became of the project, see later.)

If these established politicians and successful businessmen were interested in Pestalozzianism as one of many good causes, young men coming to Yverdon by accident or design became devoted to Pestalozzi and made the introduction of his ideas into their own countries the purpose of their lives.

The first to come upon Pestalozzi's method by chance was the 'Irish Traveller' John H. Synge (1788–1845, grandfather of John M. Synge, the dramatist).[2] After having gone through Trinity College, Dublin, and Magdalen College, Oxford, he went in 1812 on his Grand Tour to Portugal and Spain 'to watch the war'. He reached Switzerland on his way back through Italy in the autumn of 1814. Unfortunately, his detailed diary and charming sketch-book break off at exactly this point—be it that he now had to observe more than he was able to record, or more likely that his notes were incorporated in his printed books and were afterwards destroyed.

In the Preface to his *Biographical Sketch of the Struggles of Pestalozzi*[3] John Synge gives the following description of his introduction to the new teaching method. When advised to visit Pestalozzi's institute as 'among the objects of curiosity pointed out to travellers', he had actually refused 'as being a sight not likely to interest him, feeling no small degree of prejudice against schemes of education from the little he had seen of the mechanical systems practised at home'; but when at last persuaded to enter the establishment, 'the intelligent countenances of the children and the energetic interest which they appeared to take in their studies forcibly attracted his attention, although the lesson was in German with which he was, at that time, quite unacquainted'.

He had meant to spend two hours there and, instead, he stayed for three months,[4] making himself familiar with the new

[1] 17th April 1818 (MS. Pest. 50/5, Zentralbibliothek Zürich).

[2] Biographical information from Mrs. L. M. Stephens, Dublin, widow of Edward M. Stephens, great-grandson of John H. Synge and nephew of John M. Synge.

[3] *A Biographical Sketch of the Struggles of Pestalozzi*, to establish his System of Education; compiled and translated chiefly from his own works, by an Irish Traveller. Dublin, 1815, p. v ff.

[4] S XII, 225.

principles of teaching 'in order to bring home as much as possible of what appeared so intrinsically valuable'.

Although, like the rest of the visitors, he was impressed in the first place by the method of teaching arithmetic, he perceived, unlike them, that Pestalozzi's principles 'are applicable not to the science of numbers only, but to every branch of knowledge which can be acquired by the human mind', and that they are suitable for all ranks of society. But the great point of Pestalozzi, he continues, is 'the removal of all that misery and compulsion which, till now, has clouded the acquirements of our juvenile years. He insists on the master never losing sight of his responsible position, viz. that he has undertaken to represent the parent of his pupil; that, as a parent, he must watch over his morals as well as his literary acquirements; he must awaken reflection before he can hope for application; he must suit his labours to the taste of his age, and partake with him in those labours in order that he may enjoy them; in short, the heart of the master must be warm in the cause he has espoused, or success cannot be hoped for.' [1]

With this knowledge and in this spirit he returned home to Ireland in 1815, opened on his father's estate in Roundwood, Co. Wicklow, a school for the village children, and set up a printing press to publish his 'tracts' on Pestalozzi's method.[2] He took infinite pains to translate (or to have translated?) Pestalozzi's and Schmid's works on the Relation of Numbers and the Relation of Forms and to adapt them to British measures; similarly he prepared masses of reading material in the phonetic and elliptic methods. Since cheap books for poor children were not available, he had large wall charts printed which could be held up before the whole class.[3] Not

[1] *A Biographical Sketch*, p. xv f.

[2] *A Sketch of Pestalozzi's Intuitive System of Calculation*, compiled and translated by an Irish Traveller. Dublin, 1815, p. 1 f.: 'It is not rules, not understood, though blindly followed, which serve for the foundation of these [arithmetical] operations: it is intuition the most distinct and complete respecting the relations he calculates; intuition in which his imagination finds an immense latitude, and where it may take widest range.' *Pestalozzi's Intuitive Relations of Numbers*. Parts I, III, IV. Dublin, 1817/19 (part II missing). *The Relations and Descriptions of Forms* according to the Principles of Pestalozzi. Part I (only). Dublin, 1817.

[3] e.g. Alphabet, Spelling and Reading Lessons in carefully graded stages

content with the teaching of the mother tongue, he later wrote a Hebrew grammar based on the principles of Pestalozzi.[1] All these books into which had gone an immense amount of labour and enthusiasm now seem exceedingly dull; for the warm heart and the love of men that inspired them cannot be communicated in printed exercises.

They are more immediately present in the letters John Synge wrote to Pestalozzi after his return home.[2] They report that his poor-school, a House of Industry on a small scale but in the true spirit, was flourishing. The children were taught language, number, and form; they were also reading the Bible, all this for three or four hours a day. For the rest, they were working on the land, making footwear and straw hats. They seemed perfectly happy, and he was satisfied with their progress.

He also made it his business to spread the new method abroad and tells of an English schoolmaster to whom he had lent his material and who had begun to teach according to Pestalozzi's principles. This man's success was so great that the governors of his school objected saying, 'These [poor] children are to be servants to our sons one of these days, and they must not be cleverer than their masters'.

Best of all, some mothers had started to follow in Gertrude's footsteps, and the harmony existing between them and their children could not be expressed in words. The child of one of them, only eighteen months old, already had begun to know the name of Pestalozzi.

Synge was a deeply religious man, a Low Church Evangelical, and he was troubled because some people objected to Pestalozzi's principles on account of his belief that 'l'homme est bon'. He therefore implored Pestalozzi to state clearly that he considered man as corrupt from birth and that, if he speaks in his works of the goodness of man, he only refers to those traces of the image of God which are left in him after his fall and

---

(after the model of Krüsi's *Mother's Book*); Lessons on Scripture, Geography and Natural History; Tables of Money and Measures, etc. (National Library of Ireland).

[1] *An Easy Introduction to the Hebrew Language on the Principles of Pestalozzi*, by Parens. London, 1831.

[2] 3 letters from John Synge to Pestalozzi (written in French). Dublin, 1816–18 (MS. Pest. 55 a/365).

which can be detected in the various faculties with which he is endowed.[1]

This was indeed a serious point on which Pestalozzianism stood or fell in Britain. Pestalozzi's reply to Synge of January 1819[2] is intended to allay his anxiety. Yet although Pestalozzi's personal friends, all devout Christians, were convinced of the genuineness of his Christianity,[3] doubts persisted among the wider public and were largely responsible for the slow progress his method made in this country.

The other young men from Britain who visited Pestalozzi in the next few years came on Synge's advice. It is not quite clear from the sources whether Synge's neighbour, the Lord de Vesci, actually visited Pestalozzi or only was given information by his friend. John, second Viscount de Vesci of Abbeyleix, Queen's Co., Ireland (1771–1855), was Lord Lieutenant of his county and much concerned with the welfare of his people. He was in touch with William Allen about the organization of a society for the suppression of mendicity, and on his advice instituted district visiting associations and soup houses.[4] He opened on his estate a school for 'rich children', his own and those of his friends, in which the teaching was done according to Pestalozzian principles, and he supported Pestalozzi's poor-school in Switzerland by large subscriptions.[5]

[1] Synge to Pestalozzi, 10th December 1818.

[2] 'Religion is the unshakable foundation of all education; this principle I have expressed from my youth. We must correct the bad traits of our nature, and we find the means for that task in the truths of the Christian religion. I am endeavouring to give this idea the greatest importance in the new edition of my Works, especially in the great alterations I have made in *Leonard and Gertrude*, and I have tried to stress this principle as much as possible in a number of letters to Mr. Greaves.' (*Letters on Early Education*, see p. 205.) Isr. II, 284 (translated).

[3] 'The Editor is anxious to express his conviction', says John Synge in *The Struggles of Pestalozzi*, 'that the Bible is, and ever has been, the guide of every thought of Pestalozzi: that when he talks of ennobling the man, and awakening him to the knowledge of the powers he possesses within himself, 'tis with the hope of leading him on to use them to the glory of the Giver, and under the full conviction that this is the surest way of humbling the Christian.' p. xvi f.

[4] W. Allen, op. cit. I, 338 f.

[5] The Abbeyleix school is often referred to in letters from Synge, Orpen, and Mayo to Pestalozzi. See also Pestalozzi's letter to Lord de Vesci (Isr. II, 286), Isr. II, 295, and C. I, p. xv.

No further details can be established about Philip H. Pullen who published two books on the Pestalozzian method (translations and adaptations of Krüsi's and Schmid's works),[1] or about the school in Kildare Street, Dublin, said to have been conducted on Pestalozzian lines.[2] But another Irishman connected with Pestalozzi, Charles Edward Herbert Orpen (1791–1856), is well known as a philanthropist on his own account.

He took his medical degree in Edinburgh and developed an interest in deaf-mutes who had hitherto been considered mentally defective, or heathen, or both.[3] After a startling success, within three months, in the education of a most wretched deaf-mute orphan boy in his own home, Orpen founded a small school for deaf and dumb children in Dublin in 1816, later called the National Institution for the Education of the Deaf and Dumb at Claremont, near Glasnevin. It was the first institution of its kind in Ireland and was supported by voluntary contributions. It is still in existence today.

In 1817/18 Dr. Orpen went to the Continent to visit every institution for the deaf and dumb he could find, and thus came to Yverdon where a former assistant of Pestalozzi conducted a school for deaf-mute children. He remained with Pestalozzi all through the winter of 1818/19 and wrote years later about this visit: 'I can look back with pleasure to the privilege of having lived with Pestalozzi in intimate society and unreserved intercourse for some months, and of having afterwards enjoyed the friendship of one like him—one more truly great and humble, good and noble, as a man and a Christian, never fell under my immediate observation.'[4]

When he returned home he did everything he could to promote Pestalozzi's ideas in Britain. In London he visited everybody likely to be of help: Pullen, Maclure, Greaves, and Allen. Unfortunately, Wilberforce was ill and Brougham out of town

---

[1] Philip H. Pullen: *The Mother's Book*. London, 1820, and *Pestalozzi's Intellectual or Intuitive Arithmetic*. London, 1831.

[2] W. Allen, op. cit. II, 228.

[3] Charles Edward Herbert Orpen: *The Contrast between Atheism, Paganism and Christianity*, illustrated; or *The Uneducated Deaf and Dumb, as Heathens*, compared with those, who have been instructed in Language and Revelation, and taught by the Holy Spirit, as Christians. Dublin, 1827.

[4] Mrs. Le Fanu: *Life of the Rev. Charles Edward Herbert Orpen, M. D.* London, 1860, p. 46.

at the time. But, says Orpen in his first letter to Yverdon,[1] interest in Pestalozzi's work was growing; schoolmasters wanted to know more about it. The plan to form a committee for raising funds is mentioned again; the intention was to have Pestalozzi's works translated into English. They were all waiting for his Collected Works to come out—they were to wait for several years more! Meanwhile substantial collections were made in England and Ireland to support Pestalozzi's poor-school in Switzerland and to have English young men trained in his method.

Like Synge, Orpen alludes to the criticism some people have 'dared' to raise against the Yverdon institute and the Pestalozzian method: Sunday, they say, is not as strictly observed in Switzerland as in Britain, and religion does not play an important part in his system. He urges Pestalozzi, also in the name of Lord de Vesci, to publish a letter refuting these allegations, because much damage has already been done.[2] His letters, again like Synge's, are written in a most affectionate tone. 'Take care of your health', the doctor advises the old man, 'you have still things to do for the welfare of men and the glory of God.'

Orpen, as his biographer reports, saw the Pestalozzian method 'introduced in no long time into almost every infant school in his native country',[3] including the Claremont institution, and he started a school for 'the sons of the higher ranks of society' at Woodside, Birkenhead. The teacher was M. du Puget, a former pupil of Pestalozzi and previously teacher at Lord de Vesci's school.[4] Orpen also wrote a series of small books for parents on the elementary education of their children.[5] These, like Synge's tracts and wall charts, were set up by that first deaf and dumb pupil who had become a skilful printer. 'The beloved physician', as Orpen was called, later entered the

[1] 5 letters from Orpen to Pestalozzi (written in French), London and Dublin, 1818–23 (MS. Pest. 54 a/272).

[2] The same theme is elaborated in a letter to Pestalozzi from the Rev. Francis Cunningham (MS. Pest. 50/58), who visited Continental educationists on behalf of the British and Foreign Bible Society, 1820.

[3] Le Fanu, op. cit. p. 48.

[4] G. H. Orpen: *The Orpen Family*. Frome and London, 1930, p. 200 ff.

[5] Dr. Charles Orpen: *Pestalozzi's System of domestic Education*, 4 parts. Dublin, 1829.

Church and with his family emigrated to South Africa, where he preached the word of God in 'The Wilderness'.

Among the people Dr. Orpen had seen in London on his return from Switzerland was J. P. Greaves who was himself about to leave for Yverdon. James Pierrepoint Greaves (1777–1842) had been a merchant in London from early youth; but when his firm went bankrupt through the Napoleonic blockade of English trade he decided to devote his life to philanthropic pursuits. Informed by John Synge about the activities of Pestalozzi, he went to Yverdon in the summer of 1818 and remained there for about four years.[1] He at once became very enthusiastic about the new method of education and devised various means to introduce it to his country. He undertook to teach English in Yverdon and Clindy (see p. 245) so that Swiss boys might be prepared for teaching in England. He endeavoured to bring English boys to Yverdon that they might be trained on the spot. Seeing that the Prussian government had sent there a number of young men under an official scheme, he addressed a memorandum to Lord Liverpool, the English Prime Minister, suggesting that England should do the same.[2] He advised Pestalozzi (though with little success) to press on with the edition of his Collected Works so that they might be translated into English, and he tried (but in vain) to make him tell the story of his life in a short and clear manner suitable for presentation to the English public. He succeeded, however, in extracting from Pestalozzi a series of Letters addressed to himself, expressing his ideas in concise form and appealing directly to the mothers of Britain. It was these *Letters on Early Education*[3] (see p. 204 f.)

[1] *Letters and Extracts* from the MS. Writings of James Pierrepoint Greaves, 2 vols. Ham Common, Surrey, and London, 1843–45. Vol. I, p. vi ff.

[2] Letter, dated Yverdon, 18th August 1818, from James Pierrepoint Greaves to the 2nd Earl of Liverpool, P.M., 'respecting the advantages of the Pestalozzi's System of Education' (Brit. Mus. Add. MS. 38273). See Appendix II, p. 316 ff. No answer or any consequent official action can be traced. In the spring of the same year Robert Owen had sent his Letter to Lord Liverpool on the Employment of Children.

[3] *Letters on Early Education*, addressed to J. P. Greaves, by Pestalozzi. Translated from the German Manuscript. With a Memoir of Pestalozzi. London, 1827. The German manuscript is lost. The translator and writer of the memoir is C. F. Wurm, later Professor of History in Hamburg, in 1822–5 a student of theology in Tübingen, where Greaves met him and made him interested in Pestalozzi. See P-anum, 1935, p. 5 ff.

more than any writings or deeds of his own that kept Greaves' name from oblivion.

Greaves' activities and the interest shown in the method by those distinguished visitors raised in Pestalozzi, at a time of internal strife at Yverdon, the hope that Britain was the country where his ideas might be most usefully employed. 'There is no doubt that this nation is more advanced and more established in the basic essentials of industry than any other on the Continent,' he wrote to Count Capo d'Istria, minister to the Czar of Russia, in 1818. 'They find that my [principle of] mathematical development can serve as the general and most realistic foundation for their views. They also have entered with rare insight into the main idea that it is necessary to simplify the beginnings of popular education and to restrict it to the essentials so as to give these to the people with solidity and in harmony with their needs.' [1]

In connection with the opening of the poor-school in Clindy (September 1818) an *Address of Pestalozzi to the British Public* was printed in Yverdon for distribution in England, 'soliciting them to aid by subscriptions his plan of preparing schoolmasters and mistresses for the people, that mankind may in time receive the first principles of intellectual instruction from their mothers.' In the following year, notices appeared in Swiss and German newspapers offering training to poor boys and girls with the view to their becoming teachers in Great Britain.[2] They were promised free places in their second and third years if they had done well in their first. Some of these trainees, e.g. J. Heussi and C. F. Reiner, actually went to England to teach according to Pestalozzi's principles, but because of the difficulties arising in Yverdon the plan of sending young men from England to Switzerland was not carried out on any appreciable scale.

During the years of his stay with Pestalozzi Greaves was filled with that spirit of love which was to be the mainspring of his life. 'Remember when I use the word Love, it is the same to me as God, Spirit, or any name others use expressive of Deity', he explained later. He brought away with him from Pestalozzi the conviction that 'but little benefit can ensue from

---

[1] Pestalozzi to Capo d'Istria, 1st September 1818. In French, draft (MS. Pest. 15/2).   [2] Isr. I, 515 f.

any after-education', that 'the sympathies and sensibilities' must be cultivated in infancy, and that mothers must be brought to co-operate in this 'sacred and holy cause'. In order best to promote Pestalozzi's ideas in Britain he became, on his return home, secretary to the London Infant School Society, and, in the absence of training colleges, he was responsible for the training of teachers.[1] 'The great object in all his instruction,' he says of himself, 'was to explain and illustrate the eminent superiority of being to all knowing and doing.'[2]

In 1837 he founded in Ham, Surrey, a Pestalozzian school of his own which he named Alcott House in honour of the American A. Bronson Alcott whose schools for the poor he admired and whose transcendental views he shared.

As he grew older he became more and more of a mystic. His inspiration was the seventeenth century Silesian mystic Jacob Böhme who also influenced Friedrich Fröbel; Greaves' speculations are therefore reminiscent of Fröbel's philosophy. 'Social feelings', Greaves maintained, 'must be submitted to the Spirit. Our efforts must be directed inwards, not outwards. The Divine (not the social) Spirit must be allowed to reign.' Guided by these principles, he attempted to create in Randwick, Gloucestershire, a community centre for the benefit of industrial labourers. It was an Utopian venture similar to that of Robert Owen; but whereas Owen's 'New Moral World' was based on

---

[1] See S[amuel] Wilderspin: *Infant Education*; or *Remarks on the Importance of Educating the Infant Poor*, from the age of eighteen months to seven years. With an account of the Spitalfields' Infant School, and the System of Instruction there adopted. London, 1825 (3rd ed.). Members of the Committee were Henry Brougham and William Allen; among the first subscribers was Dr. Charles Mayo. The influence of Pestalozzi's ideas on British infant schools is evident, especially if the practice in National schools be remembered in contrast: The fundamental principle of instructing is 'love, not fear'; the spirit of the schools is 'reasonable and religious'; children of all denominations are accepted. The method of teaching is 'to follow and assist nature', to use objects of nature, to awake the children's interest and understanding, not to teach words and make them learn by heart, etc. But the name of Pestalozzi is not mentioned at all. Was that in order not to arouse enmity in the presence of strong opposition, and rather to carry out his ideas quietly and anonymously? There was, of course, also the example of Robert Owen's New Lanark schools, which were conducted on principles in many respects similar to those of Pestalozzi.

[2] *Letters and Extracts*, vol. I, p. 2 and p. vi ff.

reason, Greaves' was to be based on love.[1] Neither scheme had a lasting success. Greaves was too unworldly a man to impose his ideas; for the same reason, he was not influential enough to have the Pestalozzian method accepted generally.

The last to be mentioned and perhaps the best-known English follower of Pestalozzi is Dr. Charles Mayo (1792–1846). He came from a distinguished family of professionals and clergymen, took his degrees at St. John's College, Oxford, and was ordained in 1817. He gave up his post as headmaster of Bridgenorth (Shropshire) Grammar School in order to go to Pestalozzi of whom he, like Greaves, had heard from John Synge. He arrived in Yverdon in the summer of 1819, bringing with him a number of boys and young men, among them his brother Richard.[2] His experiences can be gathered from letters which he wrote home while staying with Pestalozzi for the better part of three years (1819–22).[3] Like other reports describing a first meeting with Pestalozzi, his opening letter expresses good-humoured surprise; but as he became better acquainted with Pestalozzi and more familiar with his circumstances, the tone of his letters grows warmer and more appreciative. 'It is delightful to live under the same roof with Pestalozzi,' he was soon able to say. 'Every action of his life is characterized by the most exuberant philanthropy. Had it been checked by a little more prudence, it would perhaps have produced more benefit to mankind.'[4] In the course of time he became a true friend of Pestalozzi and maintained a tactful association with both factions among the old assistants.

For it must be repeated that Mayo—and all the other English visitors—saw Yverdon at an unfortunate time when it was rent

[1] Greaves had a long but gentle controversy with Owen. See *Letters and Extracts*, I, 154 ff.; II, 11.   [2] S XII, 279 f.

[3] Copies (2 complete letters and short extracts from 15 others out of a total of at least 45) were made in 1933 for Miss Mary Mayo, Dr. Charles Mayo's last surviving daughter, then a lady of over ninety years of age. The set given to Dr. R. R. Rusk, at that time Lecturer in Education in the University of Glasgow, was kindly handed on to me in 1958. The original letters have probably been destroyed. Mayo's first letter, written on his arrival in Yverdon (22nd July 1819), has been published in a German translation in P-anum, 1950, p. 5 f. The other complete letter, clearly written for publication, is printed for the first time in Appendix II to this book (see p. 322 ff.).   [4] Mayo, letter 3.

with strife and had passed its best. That they yet were so greatly stimulated by its educational achievements speaks eloquently for its principles. Mayo endeavoured to learn as much as he could in the time at his disposal; he took lessons in French and in German and was instructed in 'the method' by Jacob Heussi, the most gifted of the Clindy pupils. At the same time he taught English and Classics, directed the education of the English boys, and conducted an Anglican Church service on Sundays. In the Pestalozzi–Fellenberg controversy he came down on the side of the former, knowing more intimately the underlying principles and being less easily impressed by outward success than casual visitors. 'His [Fellenberg's] I consider a private institution, Pestalozzi's a public one. The one effects its purpose with the pupils it has, the great advantage of the other is that it fosters a proper spirit—it serves, however imperfect, as a model and may prove the source from which purer streams may eventually flow.'[1]

Pestalozzi formed a high opinion of Mayo as a man and a teacher; as has been said before, he hoped that through his efforts and those of his other British friends his ideas would spread in and from England. 'England is now the country that pays most attention to my endeavours', he wrote to his sister (in 1822). 'We now have in our house over twenty-four people from England, partly pupils, partly adults. Many of them are warmly attached to me and my doings. A Mrs. Hilyard,' he continues, 'has even christened her child whose godfather I am with my name Sybilla Charlotte Pestalozzi.'[2] In the testimonial given to Mayo on his departure he declared that he had co-operated loyally and successfully in the aims of his life and distinguished himself throughout by his calm disposition and the active part he had taken in 'the cause', so that in time he had become a sound counsellor and reliable helper in the affairs of the House. He acknowledged that Mayo had gained a profound knowledge of his educational principles and tendencies and of the practical means of applying them; and he was confident that he would exercise the same generosity and influence in carrying them out in his own country 'which is accustomed to embrace all it has recognized to be good.'[3] He

---

[1] Mayo, letter 14. [2] P. B. V, 91 (translated).
[3] MS. Pest. 5/79.

gave Mayo a *Note* addressed to the 'nobles amis de l'humanité' in England, and another *Aux Anglais généreux qui s'intéressent à l'Éducation* (1823)[1] in which he set out his aims and described his methods. Its purpose was an appeal for funds to be used for a translation of his main works, and the subscription to these translated works was in turn to be used to support his poor-school in Switzerland.

It was the same plan as Allen and Orpen had tried to promote more than four years before (see pp. 288 and 293). As soon as Mayo arrived in London he made strenuous endeavours to bring it off this time.[2] He approached Brougham, Allen, and Wilberforce and prepared a circular letter—based on Pestalozzi's *Note*—to reach a wider circle of people interested in charitable enterprises. He must also have advised Pestalozzi to write direct to influential men, for there are letters from Pestalozzi to Wilberforce and to Canning (just come into office) in which he begs their support.[3] But there is not any evidence that these high personages responded to Pestalozzi's urgent request.

The scheme worked out by a committee to which Allen, Mayo, and 'other gentlemen' belonged, envisaged sending a number of English children to Pestalozzi's poor-school and paying for their maintenance and training. Later it was found to be simpler to support a few Swiss boys and girls if they undertook to become teachers of the poor in England. It seems, however, that Pestalozzi was slow and not very precise in supplying the required information; Mayo, in the name of the business-man Allen, had to ask for definite assurances that he at his advanced age was able to set up his proposed training school. A further difficulty was that the English friends had agreed to support an industrial school for the poor in the Neuhof, but were shocked to hear of a change of plan and its establishment in Yverdon. Such unfavourable reports about the Yverdon institute had reached London, that assistance in that direction

[1] MS. Pest. 5/79 and 464.

[2] 12 letters from Mayo to Pestalozzi (written in French), 1822–4 (MS. Pest. 53/211, Zentralbibliothek Zürich).

[3] Isr. II, 312 f. 'Your Excellency', runs Pestalozzi's letter to the Foreign Secretary, 'You have in the face of Europe supported the independence of States in a way which leaves no doubt in the philanthropist's heart that you will maintain your conviction also in respect of the independence of the individual.' 21st April 1823 (translated).

was flatly declined. In the end, Mayo had to communicate to Pestalozzi the committee's respect for his character and his life's efforts and their interest in his method of education, but at the same time to announce the withdrawal of their support. Mayo had not spared time, money, or health in trying to advance Pestalozzi's aims; nothing, he says, was too much for him to do for Pestalozzi and his 'cause'; but the failure was due, he realized, as is clear from the sad tone of his letters, to the muddle on Pestalozzi's own side.

On his departure from Yverdon Mayo had comforted the old man with the prospect of a possible return. But soon after his arrival in England he started in Epsom, Surrey, a school for boys from the upper classes in which the teaching was done according to Pestalozzian principles. He thought he could help Pestalozzi better in this way than by returning to Switzerland, especially since others in England had already begun teaching in what they claimed to be the Pestalozzian method, but which Mayo considered faulty and in need of correction. His school expanded so rapidly that in 1826 it had to be moved to larger premises in Cheam. Its teachers during the earlier years had all been trained in Yverdon and were mainly Swiss: J. Heussi and a certain Lutener, C. F. Wurm (who had translated Pestalozzi's *Letters* to Greaves) and later Hermann Krüsi jun., son of Pestalozzi's first assistant; also William Brown and Robert Devey. The master whose lessons in mathematics repeated in Cheam the success Schmid, his teacher, had won in Yverdon, was C. F. Reiner, afterwards tutor to Queen Victoria's eldest children. 'His power of teaching was superb', says one of his former pupils.[1]

In the course of the years Cheam School became an English preparatory school like others in its neighbourhood. It had pupils from the highest ranks of society, many of whom took up distinguished careers in the Church, the army, and the professions.[2] In Dr. Mayo's time they were influenced by the headmaster's own generous spirit, lively humour, and simple

[1] *An Account of Cheam School in Dr. Mayo's time,* anonymous (MS. copy in my possession). Charles Reiner published *Lessons on Number.* London, 1831; and *Lessons on Form.* London, 1837.

[2] In 1934 the school moved to Headley near Newbury, Berkshire. It is at present attended by the Prince of Wales.

piety which endeared him to his teachers,[1] colleagues, and pupils alike.

Outside his school Dr. Mayo promoted Pestalozzianism by giving public lectures on the life of Pestalozzi, e.g. at the Royal Institution (1826),[2] and by supporting the teachers' training college which the Home and Colonial School Society had established in Grays Inn Road, London.

This Society was formed in 1836 in order 'to show the application of Pestalozzianism to elementary education'.[3] (The name of Pestalozzi is, however, not mentioned in contemporary records. This must have been considered wise at the time.) The society's institutions were aimed at counter-balancing the influence of the National schools, though stressing the fact that they themselves were based on sound Christian principles. The training college opened with three students but grew very quickly. With its experimental school, it was soon 'a Model School for the instruction of infants and a Normal School for the training of teachers'.[4] It was for many years directed and supervised by J. S. Reynolds, Mayo's close friend, and Elizabeth Mayo (1793–1853), his sister. She had absorbed and applied 'the method' while assisting her brother in Epsom and Cheam, and it was she who had added the chapter on *Pestalozzi and his Principles* to Charles Mayo's book. Her practical experience was recorded in several pamphlets on 'object teaching' [5] (Anschauungsunterricht), that aspect of Pestalozzi's method which was widely taken for the whole of Pestalozzianism in this country.

[1] A draft contract and letter from Pestalozzi to 'a friend', 1824, found in the National Library of Scotland, Edinburgh (MS. 968 f. 82), suggest that Pestalozzi hoped to save the Yverdon institute from dissolution by making Mayo his successor. See K. Silber: 'Ein Nachfolger in Yverdon?' In: *Schweizerische Lehrerzeitung*, Zürich, 11, September 1959.

[2] Published after Pestalozzi's death as *A Memoir of Pestalozzi*. London, 1828; and later, with other papers, as *Pestalozzi and his Principles* (in several editions).

[3] *From the Genealogical Account of the Mayo and Elton Families* by the Rev. C. H. Mayo. Long Burton, Dorset, 1882. (MS. copy in my possession.)

[4] *The Quarterly Educational Magazine* [ed. by Elizabeth Mayo]. London, 1848/9 (2 vols. only), vol. I, p. 44.

[5] Elizabeth Mayo: *Lessons on Objects* as given to children between the ages of six and eight in a Pestalozzian School at Cheam, Surrey. London, 1831 (reprinted in many editions). *Lessons on Shells*. London, 1832; and other works.

Through her training of hundreds of candidates for the teaching profession this method was spread all over the country and overseas (see p. 313 f.), though in later years it was hardly remembered where its origin lay.

Both Mayos stressed the precedence of moral and religious over intellectual education and endeavoured to show that the Pestalozzian method was in harmony with the Christian doctrine.[1] Their own brand of Christianity 'was tinged with the principles of the Evangelical revival of the early part of the nineteenth century'.[2] If after Charles Mayo's death the true Pestalozzian spirit disappeared from Cheam, it lived on in the Home and Colonial Schools, as testified by one who had taught in both.[3]

Besides Cheam, there were other private boys' schools in England which called themselves Pestalozzian because their principals had been educated in Yverdon.[4] Of more interest than a tracing of their history would be an account of Pestalozzi's influence on popular education; but this is almost impossible because it was to a great extent anonymous. Links with the infant school movement have already been pointed out. Influences also could be traced in adult education, e.g. in the teachers' training colleges, in the Mechanics' Institutions, first started by Dr. George Birkbeck in Scotland and spreading in England through Henry Brougham's publicity campaigns (from 1823), as well as in London University, founded in 1827 for the purpose of giving higher education to a larger body of students and offering a more realistic choice of subjects than Oxford and Cambridge, while adopting at the same time more modern methods of presentation.[5] The majority of day schools, however,

[1] *Practical Remarks on Infant Education* by the Rev. Dr. Mayo and Miss Mayo, publ. for the Home and Colonial Infant School Society. London, 1837.

[2] *Genealogical Account* (as above).

[3] Hermann Krüsi jun.: *Erinnerungen* (MS. Kantonsbibliothek Trogen, Appenzell, cop. E. Dejung).

[4] e.g. B. R. F. Heldenmaier had a school in Worksop, Nottinghamshire, in the eighteen-thirties and forties; it made him a rich man (H. Krüsi, op. cit. and P-anum, 1949, p. 19 f.).

[5] 'We understand, instead of getting at a language by rules, acquired by rote, and lost in much less time than acquired, the pupil will have the advantage of some of the recent systems of Pestalozzi, Bell [?] and [Mrs.] Hamilton.' 'London University', in *The Glasgow Free Press*, 24th June 1826.

remained under the supervision of the Established Church and retained Dr. Bell's monitorial system. The only opening for the Pestalozzian method was in the schools supported by Dissenters and Whigs.

It is interesting to note that there was no Pestalozzianism in Scotland. The reason is not that its theory and moral foundation would not have appealed to the Scots. It is that the more democratic constitution of their Church and the great importance they attributed to learning had created a system of education that worked well enough in the beginning of the nineteenth century. Thus there was not the same need as in England and Ireland to seek help abroad. The fact that some of the 'English' pupils in Yverdon were of Scottish birth is irrelevant.[1]

In conclusion, if the impact of Pestalozzianism in England is to be assessed, it must be admitted that it was relatively slight. Most of the reasons have already been stated at various points and may here be summarized thus: Pestalozzianism was brought to England at an unpropitious time; it came, from one point of view, too early, for interest in popular education had just begun and was still bound up with religious education, and from another, too late, for Pestalozzi himself was too old to exert a strong personal influence, and his institute had lost its international reputation. The Yverdon people, by their dilatoriness of dispatch and the confusion in their affairs, can almost be said to have hindered rather than helped its introduction into this country at the very moment of its best chance. Again, the method rested on theoretical foundations, and the English

[1] Four sons of Dr. Charles Badham, M. D., F.R.S., later Professor of Physic in Glasgow University, were at Yverdon for several years. In a letter to John Lockhart, Walter Scott's son-in-law, of 26th July 1825 (Nat. Lib. of Scotland MS. 934 no. 8), Dr. Badham asks whether his eldest son Charles (later Professor of Classics at Sydney, Australia), having been 'substantially educated' by Pestalozzi, may obtain the post of English teacher in Mr. Lockhart's new institution in Edinburgh. An article 'Pestalozziana' in *Blackwood's Edinburgh Magazine* vol. LXVI (1849), p. 93 ff., published anonymously but written by Charles Badham (according to Blackwood's list of authors, Nat. Lib. of Scotland—either the oldest or the second, Charles David, of the four brothers), gives a detailed account of the life in the Yverdon classrooms, dormitories, and refectory as seen by a boy accustomed to the ways of an English Public school (Westminster). It is written in retrospect (thirty years after the experience) in a slightly supercilious tone.

have always been interested in the practical side of education rather than in its philosophy. Pestalozzi's theory, moreover, was expressed in a language not only foreign but exceedingly complicated. Repeated attempts to have Pestalozzi's works translated failed, except for a few individual efforts.[1] And adoption of the teaching technique without knowledge of the underlying principles was like attempting to swim without water; it soon lost its appeal. Furthermore, education was sponsored by private societies, each favouring that teaching method (or its originator) which corresponded with its own religious persuasion. Pestalozzi's friends were all inclined towards unorthodoxy and belonged, spiritually and politically, to the minority. Besides, they were personally too gentle to exert a strong influence. The allegations made against Pestalozzi's method that it was 'not properly Christian' did, perhaps, the greatest harm in preventing its wide acceptance. The fact, however, that all his friends were deeply religious men shows in itself that these accusations were wrong.

[1] *Leonard and Gertrude.* A Book for the Poor, (part I only) was first translated by Eliza Shepherd (of Paddington) who spent long periods at Yverdon during 1818/19 (MS. Pest. 12/132 and Mayo, letter 17). It was published in Geneva in 1824. Another translation appeared anonymously in London in 1825. The question in how far the *Letters on Early Education* addressed to Greaves are a genuine work of Pestalozzi has often been ventilated. The translator admits in the preface that he has availed himself freely of Pestalozzi's permission 'to make any alterations that might become necessary', but points out his familiarity with Pestalozzi's views. In *Letters and Extracts from the MS. Writings* of J. P. Greaves (loc. cit.) vol. I, p. ix ff. a letter from Pestalozzi to Greaves (Yverdon, 1818) is rendered *in extenso*; it is identical in content with the first of the *Letters*, but different in length (!) and parts of the translation. Yet it is obviously the same letter. It shows how freely the text was treated, and also how variously Pestalozzi can be translated. H. Krüsi jun. (*Erinnerungen*, op. cit.) is right when he decides that the answer lies halfway between authenticity and licence.

Some books on Pestalozzi and his plan other than those already mentioned were more critical than commendatory and not calculated to give an unbiased impression of either; e.g.

E. Biber: *Henry Pestalozzi and his Plan of Education.* London, 1831, containing many shortened extracts from Pestalozzi's works, and

K. von Raumer: *The Life and System of Pestalozzi.* Translated from the German by J. Tilleard. London, 1855, which is clearly derogatory.

Herbert Spencer: *Education. Intellectual, Moral and Physical.* London, 1861 (first published in *North British Review*, 1854), refers to Pestalozzi only in relation to the first aspect.

Yet some influence of Pestalozzi's ideas on British education cannot be denied. It penetrated into infant schools and training colleges until it reached elementary education. There it may have worked more powerfully than is commonly recognized. 'It will be seen', says the author of the *Genealogical Account* of the Mayo family, 'that while the name of Pestalozzi has nearly been forgotten, many if not most of his principles have insensibly been adopted and assimilated in the modern system of education'.

Pestalozzianism was introduced into the United States of America much earlier than into England, but was in later years carried on by those trained in this country. As in the case of the 'Irish Traveller', it was by Pestalozzi's French friends that the attention of Maclure, an American traveller, was first drawn to the new method of education. William Maclure (1763–1840), born a Scotsman, had distinguished himself early as a successful businessman. At the age of nineteen he had been sent to America by his London firm; after his second trip to the United States (in 1796) he had become an American citizen. In the course of a few years his wealth had so accumulated that he retired from business and decided to devote his energies, time, and money to scientific and educational work. In 1803 he travelled to Europe to settle the claims of American citizens against the French government for spoliations committed during the Revolution. While in the old world for several years, he studied systems of education, collected objects of natural history for American museums, and made preparations for his life's main achievement, the geological survey of the United States. On his return to America he carried out this immense project privately and singlehanded at a time when scientific method was as yet little known. In 1809 and 1817 he presented his findings to the American Philosophical Society in Philadelphia, and later became the 'father' and first president of the American Geological Society (1828). He was also the moving spirit of the Academy of Natural Sciences (founded 1812 in Philadelphia) and its president from 1817 until his death.

Of particular interest here are his activities in the field of popular education. Having heard of Pestalozzi and Fellenberg, the main figures of European education, he visited their institutes several times (from 1804). In Burgdorf and Yverdon he found the method which, as he wrote later, 'subserved the useful purposes that I had formed to myself of a rational education'. He considered it suitable for introduction into his country 'where the power, being in the hands of the people, through the medium of our popular governments, renders a diffusion of knowledge necessary to the support of freedom'.[1] It is said that he tried to persuade Pestalozzi to emigrate to the new world in order to establish a school in Philadelphia which he was willing to finance. Failing in this, he approached, on Pestalozzi's recommendation, a former assistant, Joseph Neef, who at the request of the French friends was at that time conducting a Pestalozzian school in Paris. Neef accepted the offer and in 1806 set out for Philadelphia to become the first Pestalozzian teacher in American schools.

Education in the United States had suffered severely through the War of Independence and was, towards the end of the eighteenth century, almost non-existent. In colonial times it had mainly been in the hands of the Church; but the new national consciousness and the demand for political equality and religious freedom made necessary a more 'rational' and 'useful' education for all. Private or semi-private philanthropic enterprises were the first to meet an urgent need; city school and infant school societies were formed; the Lancastrian and the Pestalozzian methods were introduced.

Maclure and Neef co-operated for many years in the cause of Pestalozzianism, Maclure as the financial supporter and general superintendent of the schools, Neef as their principal teacher. Joseph Neef (1770–1854), an Alsatian, had been an officer in the French army and had been wounded in the Coalition Wars before joining Pestalozzi in Burgdorf (1801). He is described as a bearded giant, severe in appearance, but with a kind heart and a happy nature; he was a great favourite with his pupils. He had taught for about three years in Paris before accepting the American post.

Neef was allowed to devote three years to the study of the English language and the educational needs of the new country.

---

[1] 'Education and Reform at New Harmony'. In: *Correspondence of William Maclure and Marie Duclos Fretageot*, ed. by Arthur E. Bestor, jr. Indianopolis, 1948, p. 294.

During this time he wrote his *Sketch of a Plan and Method of Education* (Philadelphia, 1808)[1] This is not only the first comprehensive work on the Pestalozzian method in English but 'may be said to be the first strictly pedagogical book written and published in the new world in the English language'.[2] (Some articles on Pestalozzi's principles had appeared earlier in the *National Intelligencer*, Washington, 1806, written or inspired by Maclure, but they were translated passages from Chavannes' book.) In the introduction Neef defines education as 'the gradual unfolding of the faculties and powers which providence bestows on the noblest work of creation—man'. His method is that of developing what lies within the child, his motto 'Festina lente'. His principles are essentially the same as those of his master to whom he pays warm tribute in the preface. Pestalozzi's notion of 'Anschauung' is here called 'object teaching', a term which has too narrowly been identified with the essence of Pestalozzianism in the English-speaking world. It means for Neef that 'all possible knowledge shall be derived from our own senses and immediate sensations', and that books are to be used only at an advanced stage. The idea that the child's interest should provide the motivation for learning, and co-operation be the means to discipline, was, like the rest of the views stated in Neef's book, then quite new in America; as was the suggestion that physical education, based on the child's natural desire for movement, should be included in the school curriculum. Neef applied his method to intellectual and physical education only, considering them to be subjects suitable for school teaching; he left moral education to be conducted in the home.

The first Pestalozzian school in the United States was opened in Philadelphia in 1809. It accommodated over one hundred boys, mostly boarders, from higher class families. Instruction was given orally with the help of blackboards. Physical exercises played an important part. The relationship between Neef and his pupils was entirely free of constraint; there prevailed no 'grave magisterial and dictatorial tone'. 'I shall be nothing else

---

[1] This was later followed by *The Method of instructing Children rationally in the Arts of Writing and Reading*. Philadelphia, 1813, which elaborates the views expressed in the earlier book.

[2] W. S. Monroe: *History of the Pestalozzian Movement in the United States*. Syracuse, 1907, p. 77 f.

but their friend and guide, their school-fellow, playfellow, and messmate', he said.[1] Thus the school differed considerably from other contemporary establishments, and it prospered. After three years, however, it was moved to Village Green in Delaware County, Pennsylvania, to be in the country. Although many boys went with it, its numbers decreased. Another reason for the decline was that Neef, who had liberal ideas on religion, was accused by his neighbours, like Pestalozzi before him, of instilling atheistic views in the boys' minds. A further move to Louisville, Kentucky, proved even more unwise. Neef became discouraged and the school was closed.

Meanwhile Maclure had been keeping in contact with Pestalozzi himself, helping to establish his method in various ways. There is evidence that he financed not only the Pestalozzian schools in America, but also that in Paris, carried on, or re-established, after Neef's departure by Guillaume (later William) S. Phiquepal. He also supported the institute in Yverdon through large sums of money, gifts of books and scientific instruments, and a flow of pupils. For instance, on his recommendation the sons of the American Consul at Paris, Barnet, went to school at Yverdon for several years; at the end of 1811 Pestalozzi mentions four American boys as staying with him.[2] Pestalozzi entertained great hopes that through Maclure's efforts and generosity his ideas would be realized in many lands.

For Maclure had now decided to engage upon the education of the masses on a large scale. In 1819 he returned to Europe, and after having spent some months with Pestalozzi at Yverdon, set out for Spain. That country had at the time a liberal government, the Cortes régime, and seemed to be suitable ground for an experiment in popular education. Maclure bought near Alicante ten thousand acres of land that had been confiscated from the Church, and had the buildings repaired and converted for his purpose. His plan was to found a school of industry such as Pestalozzi had dreamed of all his life and Fellenberg had established at Hofwyl, combining manual labour with intellectual studies and moral training, to educate the masses for self-maintenance and self-government. A few years earlier (1806–8) there

[1] Monroe, op. cit. p. 97.
[2] P-anum, 1944, p. 9 f.; Morf IV, 299; MS. Pest. 5, 73; MS. Pest. 1445, p. 437 f.

had, in fact, been an institution in Madrid in which the teaching followed the Pestalozzian method. It had been under the patronage of King Charles IV and his minister Manuel Godoy, 'the Prince of Peace', and had been attended by high-ranking officers' sons and the Infante himself. But it had to be closed when its protectors were forced to abdicate and to go into exile. No better fate was in store for Maclure's enterprise in that land of violent changes. The liberal government was overthrown (1823), the Church re-instated, and Maclure had to flee the country, losing all his property.

He was, however, not to be defeated and determined to establish a similar institution in his own country. To be sure that it would be run on Pestalozzian lines, he arranged for an expert, M. Phiquepal, to go to Philadelphia, there to join Mme Marie Duclos Fretageot, another trained Pestalozzian teacher from Paris whom Maclure had brought over a few years earlier to continue, or re-open, Neef's original school.

On his way home Maclure visited London and noticed 'the immense progress made in civilization' there in contrast to 'the political and religious obscurity of the Royal French Kingdom' whose consequences he had just experienced. He observed two 'moral improvements' worth transporting across the Atlantic: the mechanics' institutes and cheap periodical publications for disseminating useful knowledge to the mass of the adult population (Brougham's scheme), and the infant schools (Greaves' concern), 'an establishment that lays the ax to the root of all evil by fixing a solid foundation to the future superstructure of men's moral and physical comforts'. He also spent a few days with Robert Owen at New Lanark, Scotland, and liked the way in which similar projects were being carried out there.[1]

At that time Robert Owen prepared, and soon after put into practice, his experiment in co-operative socialism in New Harmony, Indiana. Urged on by the enthusiasm of his assistant teachers rather than convinced himself of the soundness of Owen's social ideas, Maclure invested a considerable sum in the enterprise and transferred his Philadelphia school to New Harmony. The understanding was that Maclure was to be responsible for the educational side of the colony, while Owen carried out his plan of a co-operative society. According to Owen's

[1] Correspondence Maclure–Fretageot, p. 302 ff.

statement 'the avowed intention of Mr. Maclure was to make New Harmony the centre of American education through the introduction of the Pestalozzian system of instruction'.[1] For this purpose Maclure called to New Harmony Joseph Neef who, he had 'reason to believe by experience, has taught it in greater perfection than ever it was taught before'.[2] Neef's wife, a sister of one of Pestalozzi's earliest assistants, J. C. Buss, herself trained in the Pestalozzian method, took over the teaching of girls and of infants.

It was a characteristic feature of New Harmony education that it began at the age of two, and that girls received the same instruction as boys, though in separate groups. In accordance with Pestalozzi's principles the teaching at all stages was adapted to the children's level of understanding, and no subject was pursued for too long at a time to avoid fatigue. Thus the infant school was a mere play centre; and beside the boys' school there were workshops for various crafts to be practised as recreation from mental exertion, while the girls were allocated to help alternately in the cotton and wool mills and in cooking, washing, and sewing. Maclure, like Pestalozzi, had no doubt 'that children, under proper management, can feed and clothe themselves by the practice of the best and most useful part of their instruction; and in place of being a burden, they would be a help to all concerned with them. The schools here', he continues in his 'Notice of Mr. Owen's Establishment in Indiana', 'will be on such a scale, as to location, men of talent, and perfection of machinery, as to constitute them the first in the Union, for every species of useful knowledge.'[3]

The last sentence refers to Maclure's other interest, scientific research, for which he also made arrangements on a lavish scale. He equipped New Harmony with a substantial library, made an extensive collection of natural history and mineralogical objects, and engaged distinguished scientists for teaching and research. These included Thomas Say, 'the father of American zoology', Alexander Lesueur, a well-known French botanist, C. S. Rafinesque, 'the first teacher of natural history in the West', and

---

[1] Monroe, op. cit. p. 50 f.
[2] Corresp. Maclure–Fretageot, p. 367.
[3] In: *American Journal of Science*, XI (1826), p. 189 ff. See Corresp. Maclure–Fretageot, p. 331.

Gerard Troost, a Dutch geologist—a 'Boatload of Knowledge' coming to Indiana in 1826.

Both Owen and Maclure agreed in the positive view that the diffusion of 'useful knowledge' was an essential means to improving the social order, and in the negative, that no doctrinaire teaching of religion should be given, but that morals should be taught by example and precept. They differed widely, however, on other aspects of education. Maclure believed from experience that the adult mind was too inflexible to admit of change, and built his plans for social reform on the teaching of children. Like Pestalozzi, he insisted that education was a slow process, demanding patience and care, while Owen hoped to transform society in a short time and to found Utopia in New Harmony there and then. Maclure accused Owen of favouring the Lancastrian method which he called 'the parrot system of New Lanark', while he followed Pestalozzi in trying to develop the child's own powers and faculties. Thus harmony between the two men was not possible, and after some litigation Maclure withdrew from the partnership with heavy financial losses. As is well known, the community experiment in New Harmony collapsed after existing for only two years; but the School of Industry was carried on independently for several years more. It was transformed into Schools for the Instruction of Orphans in all useful Knowledge as well as in the useful Arts, and its aims were elaborated in Maclure's essay *On Education*, published in the New Harmony Gazette (1827). The scientific programme also went ahead with the aid of a Press established that same year, and important works on natural science were published until the eighteen-forties. The geological survey which Maclure had started was continued by David Dale Owen, Robert Owen's son, between 1837 and 1860. In 1838 Maclure founded a Working-men's Institute, the other 'moral improvement' he had observed in England a decade earlier and found worth while transplanting across the ocean; and although he himself had, for health reasons, to spend the last years of his life in a warmer climate (in Mexico), the Institute flourished and has remained in existence to this day.

Maclure introduced Pestalozzianism into the United States because he was convinced of 'the sanity and efficiency of Pestalozzi's doctrines'. He had found people trained in them 'greatly superior, in all useful accomplishments, to those educated by other methods'.[1] 'One of the most beneficial consequences' of this method, he says in an essay called *The Advantages of the Pestalozzian System of Education* (New Harmony, 1831), 'is the pleasure all Pestalozzian pupils take in mental labour and study.' Thus from early youth learning and thinking can be made 'an enjoyment instead of a drudgery', and any occupation useful to oneself or to others, hitherto regarded as beneath one's dignity, 'can be transformed into an amusement by early habit.'[2]

Of later American Pestalozzians only one or two had been in direct contact with Pestalozzi. William C. Woodbridge (1794–1845) visited Yverdon and Hofwyl twice (1820 and 1823) and introduced music and geography according to Pestalozzian principles into the curriculum of New England schools. He published many articles on Pestalozzi in the American Annals of Education. Solyman Brown, though lacking personal acquaintance with Pestalozzi, examined the Pestalozzian and the Lancastrian methods in *A Comparative View of the Systems of Pestalozzi and Lancaster* (New York, 1825) and decided in favour of the former. Amos Bronson Alcott (1799–1888), father of Louisa M. Alcott of *Little Women* fame, was a Pestalozzian in spirit rather than in name: he introduced a 'natural' system of instruction, adapting it to the needs of the children, and substituted affection for punishment and freedom for rigidity. He was in touch with Pestalozzi's English friend J. P. Greaves, who named his school in Ham Alcott House in appreciation of his principles (see p. 297). Henry Barnard arrived in Europe only after Pestalozzi's death, but was the most active Pestalozzian of that generation: his articles on the method and his translated selections of Pestalozzi's writings were collected in his book *Pestalozzi and Pestalozzianism* (Syracuse, 1859). It was the most widely used handbook on the subject in English for a long time, though the information it provided was second-hand, and even the translations were taken over from other authors.

The movement with which Pestalozzianism is generally connected in America spread from Oswego, New York; it is identified with 'object teaching' (Anschauungsunterricht) as it was first practised in the Home and Colonial Training College,

---

[1] Monroe, op. cit. p. 57 f.
[2] Corresp. Maclure–Fretageot, p. 379 f.

London, under the direction of Elizabeth Mayo (see p. 303). It was introduced into the United States by E. A. Sheldon in an Orphan and Free School in Oswego. He used natural objects as his means of instruction and found the Pestalozzian method (as interpreted by his English followers) most suitable for his purpose. He was anxious to secure a trained Pestalozzian teacher able to train others in America in that method, and brought over Margaret E. M. Jones who had for many years worked in the Gray's Inn Road Training school. Oswego later became one of the State Normal Schools of New York from which Pestalozzianism spread through the country.

Miss Jones' student in London and successor in Oswego was Hermann Krüsi jun. (1817–1903). He had been educated by his father, Pestalozzi's first assistant, and had taught in Cheam, Surrey, and in the Home and Colonial Training College, London. Before transmitting the Pestalozzian method to several generations of prospective teachers in Oswego, he had worked at various other American schools. In 1853 he presented to the American Institute of Instruction an essay on the Pestalozzian method for which he received an Honorary Degree of Master of Arts from Yale College, and later he published a more comprehensive account on *Pestalozzi: His Life, Work and Influence* (New York, 1875). Because of the dates of his life he can hardly be called a direct disciple of Pestalozzi, but he carried on the tradition in which he had grown up.

Although the Oswego movement made the name of Pestalozzi known to the American public, it restricted 'the method' to the mere teaching of school subjects based on the observation of natural objects. It thus unduly stressed the sensory side of education without giving sufficient emphasis to its other aspects. The idea that the child is a whole and that his experiences are indivisible—that part of Pestalozzi's work which at the end of his life he summarized in the slogan 'Life itself teaches'—was neglected at Oswego and kindred institutions.

This conception of wholeness seems to have been more alive in the Philadelphia and New Harmony schools, perhaps because in Neef they had a more direct and truer disciple of Pestalozzi. That neither of these schools had a profound influence on American education has been explained by the circumstance that Neef had merely transplanted the Pestalozzian system failing to

'Americanize' it, and that it reached the United States too early, before an interest in educational reform was fully awake.

Yet although one cannot point to a direct succession of Pestalozzi followers in American schools, his influence, not only in matters of method but also in fundamental theory, has remained alive, even if unidentified. John Dewey incorporated in his system of education many ideas first expressed by Rousseau, Pestalozzi and Fröbel and made them common knowledge to all Americans interested in education.

Appendix II

PESTALOZZIANA

(*Hitherto Unpublished Manuscripts*)

A

Mr. J. P. Greaves
respecting the advantages of the Pestalozzi's System of
Education,
18 Aug[ust] 1818
To the Right Honble Lord Liverpool, London.[1]

My Lord, Stranger, as I am I cannot but believe the subject
of my letter will be a sufficient appology for me, in addressing
you. I have been at this place and Mr. Pestalozzi's establishment five weeks for the purpose of studying his new system of
Education. The more I observe its effects on the children the
more I am forced to confess that it has in it a solidity which is not
to be shaken, nor when seen and understood to be question'd.
This manner and method is altogether different to any thing we
have in England, at least I judge from the Schools that are call'd
Grammar, or national, it is from the knowledge that I have of
them that I form my conclusions. Pestalozzi declares the Laws
of nature are so uniform that however Man may for a while impede them, he cannot alter them, but they will alter him, that is,
they will change him from a sensible corporal to an intellectual
spiritual being if he lets them act on him, and devellope him
internally, in the same manner as every flower, plant or fruit is
develloped. His aim, his object, his end is man's happiness. He

[1] Liverpool Papers, Vol. LXXXIV. Official Correspondence of Second
Earl, Aug.–19 Oct. 1818 (Brit. Mus. Additional MS. 38273, fol. 48–51).

does not arrive at this point by making him a great scholar, a great reader of other men's ideas, in Books, but by teaching him to know himself, the first and last lesson that should be taught every individual, without this knowledge he absolutely knows nothing and by it he knows all that can be known. His means are very simple, his progress towards his object as far as one sees by it[s] effect on the children in the institution is very evident, therefore we may presume at any rate that he has not been mistaken in his measures, as far as he has been able to carry them. To give a detail that will be clear to you is impossible. Truth like light must be its own manifestor, it must be seen or felt, to be understood, in the same manner the interior devellopement which is going on here with children from 7 to 12 years of age must be seen by its result on the children themselves, a description would, by some, be only considered as possible, by a great number as nothing but theoretical; some might go as far as to beleve it probable but very difficult to accomplish. What I wish my Lord to call your attention to, and what I hope will be done to give the nation some views that they may act upon, is to send out to this institution 2 properly qualified persons, who understand the German language, also the mathematics, to remain in it for a year, to examine into the whole system, by attending the exercises daily given, to watch the opening minds of the children, and to receve from Mr. Pestalozzi verbally all his ideas on the subject ⟨as he sees it⟩ of Education.

[If] many persons of this kind were fixed upon by the Government and their reports laid before parliament, or in any other way that would give publicity to them, the nation would soon be awakened by this impulse, and a measure of good would follow to the rising generation of which I dare not allow myself the extent, fearing that many would consider it as impossible.

Persons who ought to fill this sacred trust, and a sacred trust most assuredly it would be found must be qualified for the duties by having hearts and heads that can embrace the subject in all its extent.

Pestalozzi is now near 80 years of age, he is a man of whom it may be said with certainty, that he has feelings with less of Earth in them than Heaven, he is one of those mortals to whom such are given, therefore he would if met by any persons so commissioned pour out his whole soul, and exhibit some sketches,

317

that would bespeak the divine source from whence he draws all his ideas. His character life and conduct his whole being, is a living witness of his internal rectitude, his mind, his heart, his hands though on Earth, have nothing earthly in them, his personal influence is that which a good man sheds around him, to be within the sphere of his mind, is to be warm'd by Love. Such a man then who is progressing daily on the path to heaven, has much to unfold, a man who has devoted half a century to one subject, and that object so essential to the human race, cannot speak in vain, therefore I would gladly that what he could communicate on a subject so near and clear to every man, who bears the human form, and the divine likeness in it, that it should be snatch'd as it were from the borders of the Tomb and given to the world.

He sighs ardently that what he has been devoting a life to should be transplanted to the English shores. He is very well aware that what we adopt we improve. It is with this candid confession on his lips that he has only seen the dawn of his system yet in act, and that he never expects to be able to behold more in his own Institution, on account of impediments which are not to be overcome, the want of sufficient means, and for lack of these, he cannot retain under his roof men who are capable of trying if there is a limit, or point to stop at or not. His masters as fast as they are grounded in his principles, into the practice of his method, discover that they are so improved, as to be more valuable to other Seminarys, than they are to him, that they can get a greater remuneration than he can afford to give them. His institution is calculated for numbers, his feelings are for mankind in general, for those more particularly who are to earn their livelyhood by industry, and who depend on good character, those who have all their riches in their bosoms, and who manifest them outwardly by patience in well doing, those who have but their integrity to depend on, therefore his yearly stipend is but £30 and this cannot be increased, as it would prevent many sending their children to the Institution who at this time struggle to do it.

I must again repeat that it is by the means of the German language Mr. Pestalozzi will be best approached. He speaks French but not with anything like that clearness, that is necessary on this subject, that the persons who should approach him ought to be men who have somewhat of similar feelings, (a Mr. Steinkopft or such) who can respect age and listen with patience to the emanations of an overflowing heart, on a subject about which it delights to dwell, the time that such a measure would require would be a year, less would not do, the detail would be voluminous, and of course necessary so that all who are willing to examine into the plan may receive at least the main outline.

Many English Travellers call to see the system which is so much spoken of, *and known in its intrinsic worth to so few*, they are excessively struck with the happiness of the Boys, the intelligence that they manifest in their countenances, they of course observe the lessons that are going on at the time, but when you are inform'd that the whole lessons change every hour, and the Boys are devided into 6 school rooms, and that there are 12 Masters for them in the course of the day, you may fairly infer that those who are only in the School for a passing glance, cannot form any opinion with great clearness, either in favour, or against the system.

The generality of persons express themselves well satisfied with what they do see, but this does not go far enough, if the System is good enough for devellopeing the minds of the Swiss and foreign children it is so for English infants. You will no doubt have heard of the method, and perhaps it may have pass'd under your consideration, if so I cannot but [express] my hope you will continue to reflect on it, and in due time take such measures as may appear most adviseable.

As I said before to go into any detail that would be satisfactory to you is past my power, I am not equal to the task. I know but little of French and only a few words in German but I will just remark on some of the heads I have gathered together to get them and leave them to be made clear to you by a more ample detail. Pestalozzi's whole aim is at the mind and not at the memory, he uses the memory only as a servant, his instruction is intuitive instead of being abstract, he cultivates as well as disciplines, he shews the difference between the province of the mind and the imagination, he brings the intellectual forward by intellectual means and the sensible by mechanical, he shews were man as Man should begin to act and where man as animal should obey. He declares that education must precede instruction, that you must elicit the faculties before you begin to exercise them, as you must find the matter before you attempt to give it form, that signs are of no use till the child has learnt the thing signified, that Books and the dead Languages are both hinderances untill proper periods. That the Latter should never be taught if the Infant's peculiar calling in Life does not demand it. That the living Languages should take the place of what is useless, and destructive to the faculties of the Child, because they are exercised on a subject, it does not comprehend, and at a period, when true cultivation should go on; That there is no cultivation where there is no comprehension; that words alone are not the food of the mind; that thought alone is the food, that can satisfy an intellectual being.

That the heart must be warmed by spiritual means, that the truths of Gospel must be grafted in it, but not by precepts alone, not by definition of word, not by teaching the derivation of words but by example, every day, every hour, in short in every act, that the precepts which are done unto each other, as you would, they should do unto you, may be made living witnesses, of a right direction of mind, a right end, a right object. Example is the Life in act, precepts are a kind of abstraction which deaden when they are not followed up by some corresponding manifestation.

When the Golden rule is daily and hourly practised before a child it imbibes its influence in the same manner as it does the rays of the Summer Sun—and finds as much internal warmth from the one, as external from the other. That the head the heart and the hands must be taught to act and assist each other, that the entire Man Soul and Body conjointly must be develloped, not in parts, or in an isolated manner, that every School master must first learn *to know himself* before he attempts to instruct youth, that they must consider their occupation as a religious one, as a holy duty, as a sacred duty they have bound themselves to perform, and not as is now the custom to look upon it only as a means of livelyhood.

That mothers must resume their places in nature and become what heaven designed them to be, instructresses of their children, as well as companions and bosom friends of man. Number and form are the first means used in this Institution to cause reflection in the mind and the simplicity with which this is done is the great beauty of the System; The Boys are interested and instructed at one and the same time, they are acting and acted upon in a manner that pleases both master and Scholars, the faculties are always kept awake ready to receive the impression and delighted to communicate it, to learn is agreeable to them, to explain it is more. To hear them to give their reasons why 6 times 4 is 24 is interesting to all who are present, that is why 2 quantities multiplied together produce a third, and when they explain why 2 lines will only make one point of reunion, or one of intersection and will do no more, the anxious mind then begins to observe that a child is an intellectual being and not altogether a sensible one, that he is a tender, but dear, and heavenly plant well worth watering with care, that the seed of the eternal nature may burst its prison of sense and be refined in the heat of the celestial Sun, that Sun which sheds its divine rays on every mind that is open to its influence, and in due time makes it blossom and bring forth fruit.

A Heart opened by Truth, feels truth, and feeds on it it is the cause of the existence of the mind, as well as the subsistance, it is that alone which cloaths the soul with calmness and peace, it is what we are all in search of, let our actions put on what shape they may; but how few are instructed in the nature of the road, and the ease by which the end is to be attain'd. How few are told if they gave one half of the time and care to themselves and their *real* wants, that they do to their *imaginary ones*, they would possess all they are in search of, that is they would possess their true selves, the nature within, and without this possession all the external world is useless—, My Lord if the measure that I solicit you as an unknown individual to do, does not appear at first sight to belong to Government, let me recall to your mind, that you have sent an expedition to the north pole to find a new course through the frozen part of the world, for the benefit of external traffic, of the sensible Life, of the Egotism of man. Can it be said the road of truth is less frozen than the way to the Icy pole, is there not as much reason to hope and to desire that one should be opened as well as the other, is there not full as much probability of the former as the latter, is there not more, if you can remove the winter's barrier from the mind at an expence of which the amount will be as nothing in comparison of the two objects. I would ask which end is most worthy the cost, which will produce the most human happiness—.

Again My Lord if I fail in my object in engageing you as head of the Government to take some active measures in this business, Let me call on you as a Father, as a Husband, as a Christian as an individual Englishman, in every one of these characters, in the whole combined, not to let the time run on and the good man sink into his Sepulchre before some steps are taken, as it were, to engrave on Tables of Stone, his last legacy to mankind. He has nothing else to offer to the World, nor to present to Britton than a description of his labour of love to man, and the exercises he has made in the experiences of it. My Lord the subject that I write upon is an interesting one, it interests many greatly, and this alone must excuse me in addressing you as a stranger perhaps in an uncourtly-like manner. I lack in every thing that is due to your high personal worth, as well as your rank, therefore if I have erred in any want of form, or want of words, I do intreat you to take my motive for my act, and believe me with the highest consideration

I am Lordships

Most hble Servant

J. P. Greaves.

Castle Yverdon, 18th August 1818

To the Right Honble Lord Liverpool
  of his Majestys principle Secretarys of State,
    London.

B

Letters from Yverdon by a Clergyman of the
Church of England
[Dr. Charles Mayo] [1]

Letter No. 28

Yverdun, Jan. 12th, 1821.

to I. L. A. Esq.,

My dear Friend,

Pestalozzi completes this day his 76th year. His grey hair, his care-worn countenance, his hollow eye and bent figure, proclaim that many days, and those days of trouble, have passed

[1] From the collection of Mayo Papers (in my possession).

over his head. His heart, however, seems still young; the same warm and active benevolence, the same unconquerable hope, the same undoubting confidence, the same generous self-abandonment animate it now, that have led to the many sacrifices and have supported him under the many difficulties and trials of his eventful life.

In a thousand little traits of character which unconsciously escape him, I read the confirmation of his history. It is an affecting sight when the venerable object of the admiration of Emperors and Princes appears in the midst of his adopted children.

Rich and poor, natives and foreigners, share alike his paternal caress and regard him with the same fearless attachment.

From the sacrifice of time, property and health for the benefit of a people who knew not how to value his merit, to the picking up of a child's plaything for the soothing of an infant's sorrow, Pestalozzi is ever prompt to obey the call of humanity and kindness. The sentiment of love reigns so powerfully in his heart that acts of the highest benevolence, of the most condescending good nature seem to require no effort, but appear the spontaneous manifestations of one over-ruling principle. I must tell you an anecdote, which, simple as it is, shews at once the warmth and weakness which characterize his benevolence.

He was going to visit some friends at Berne, furnished with as much money as he was likely, under the circumstances, to want.

According to his usual practice, he falls into conversation with the first peasant to whom he has the opportunity of speaking.

He enquires into his means of subsistence, the number of his children, the wants and distresses of his family and so forth.

Becoming interested in the man's little story, Pestalozzi gives him the larger portion of the money which he has about him.

A similar case soon afterwards presents itself and the second rencontre drains his pockets of the last Kreutzer. He had nearly reached Berne when a wretched-looking mendicant comes up to him soliciting relief. Again he fumbles in his pockets; but it is now in vain—what is to be done? He remembers that his buckles are of silver; he hastily takes them from his shoes, thrusts them into the beggar's hand and drives off.

Though regarded in Germany as the most extraordinary luminary and the profoundest practical philosopher of the age, though honored with the most flattering testimonies of esteem and approbation by courts and universities, Pestalozzi is the most modest and unassuming of men. To all who take an interest in his method of education he addresses himself in the most touching expressions of gratitude, as if they conferred the greatest obligation by examining into the truth of his opinions and the utility of his plans. Never shall I forget my first introduction to him. He had been long expecting me and his lively imagination had anticipated in different manners the probable results of our connexion.

Will he like me? do you think I shall suit him? were questions he was perpetually putting to our common friend. I had no sooner arrived than he hurried to meet me, and though I understood not the words he uttered, yet the tone of kindness, the affectionate pressure of the hand, the expression of benignity which lit up his countenance, all assured me I was welcome. Twenty times he rose from his seat, paced with quick but shuffling steps across the room, then, as if suddenly recollecting himself, hastened to place himself near me, to press once more both my hands in his and to mutter some unintelligible expressions of goodwill.

In one of the first conversations we had together, he told me how delighted he was that the English began to pay attention to his system, remarking that that union of exalted sentiments with practical good sense which characterizes the nation, renders it the most competent to appreciate and execute his plans.

'Examine my method', continued he with his noble candour, 'adopt what you find to be good and reject what you cannot approve.'

'We are doing something here towards the execution of my principles of education, but what we do is still very imperfect; it is in England that my views will be eventually realised.'

You cannot conceive the interest which Pestalozzi awakens or the influence he insensibly acquires. All the little barriers behind which reserve or suspicion teach us to entrench ourselves, fall before the child-like simplicity, the unaffected humility and the feminine tenderness of his heart. Self-interest is shamed into

silence, while we listen to the aspirations of his boundless
benevolence, and if one spark of generous feeling glows in the
bosom, the elevated enthusiasm of his character must blow it
into a flame. The powers of his original mind serve to maintain
the interest which his character first excites. In conversation,
however, he is most frequently a listener. Towards those with
whom he lives in perfect intimacy he sometimes indulges in a
playful but forcible raillery, careful meanwhile to avoid giving
the slightest pain or uneasiness. He is peculiarly successful in por-
traying some great character by two or three masterly strokes;
in marking either in retrospect, or by anticipation, the influence of political events on national character or national
prosperity; in characterizing the different methods of education
in vogue, or in tracing the difference between his views and
those of certain philosophers with which they have been con-
founded. There is nothing studied about him. Often as I have
heard him enter on the subject of his system for the information
of strangers, I do not recollect him to have taken it up twice
from the same point of view. When we have conversed on these
subjects, I have sometimes thought his ideas wild and his views
impracticable. The faint and misty but still beautiful light
which emanated from his mind I have regarded with a feeling
of melancholy delight, for it seemed to indicate that the sun of
his genius had set. Still I have been unable to dismiss from my
mind his loose and ill-digested hints. After frequent reconsidera-
tion of them they have appeared more clear and more feasible
and I have subsequently traced their influence on the opinions
I have adopted or on the plans of instruction which I have
pursued.

Pestalozzi once known is never forgotten. I have talked with
men who have not seen him for years or whom the current of
events has separated from all intercourse with him. His honored
image lives as fresh in their memory as if their communication
had never been suspended or broken. Anecdotes illustrating his
benevolence are current in their families and their children
anticipate the delight of one day receiving the parental caress
of good father Pestalozzi. Many of my own countrymen who
have enjoyed the privilege of his society will I am sure carry
the remembrance of him to their graves. For myself—his un-
wearied kindness, his affectionate solicitude for my health and

comfort, the numberless testimonies of his esteem and regard which I daily receive, are engraven on my heart in characters which can never be effaced.

It will ever be a source of proud satisfaction to me that Pestalozzi has honored me with the title of friend, and should I attain myself to a good old age, my decline will be cheered with the remembrance that I have contributed, as he himself declares, to shed a happy serenity over this evening of his days.

Pestalozzi Foundation
of America

I T is perhaps of interest to note that in our own day Pestalozzi
is mentioned more often in connection with practical welfare
organizations than with the theory of education. Swiss, English,
American, even World Foundations have been created in his
name to carry out what he endeavoured to achieve during his
lifetime: to alleviate the misery of underprivileged people,
especially children, and to give them the chance of a normal
development. The schemes in question are non-political and
non-sectarian, give help where help is needed without regard
to nationality or race, and promote tolerance and international
understanding.

The American Foundation[1] began during the last war and is
due to the energy and generosity of one man, H. C. Honegger.
Moved by the exigencies of the war which had not then touched
the United States, and possessed of a great fortune acquired by
his own business acumen, he devised a scheme by which goods
superfluous in America would be dispatched to war-wrecked
areas in Europe in order to save the lives of innocent children.
Thus in 1942 he created the Pestalozzi Foundation of America;
it soon grew into a worldwide welfare organization. In the face
of rigid wartime restrictions it succeeded in shipping, first to
Finland, then to the South of France, food and medicine,
clothing and screening, tools and books, making sure that they

[1] Pestalozzi Foundation of America, 41 East 57th Street, New York 22,
N.Y., U.S.A.

reached their proper destinations. Helped by the International Red Cross in the distribution of the goods but kept going and maintained largely by its creator, the Pestalozzi Foundation of America continued the shipments until the end of the war; hundreds and thousands of cases of clothing and shoes, milk and honey, vitamin tablets and cash were placed where the need was greatest.[2]

But not only material goods were considered important to sustain the lives of needy children. As soon as the war ended the movement's aim was prevention rather than cure. That is why it was given the name of Pestalozzi. In accordance with his teachings it was felt that the social security, sound education and vocational training of young people are the best means of promoting a better future and of averting a recurrence of horrors recently experienced.

In order to attain these ends in an even wider field, a Pestalozzi World Foundation[3] was formed in 1947, with headquarters in Zurich. Its Council consists of prominent men in government, education and business. Its basic capital is a gift from the American sponsors; according to the constitution it must not be touched. Since, however, the interest is as yet not sufficient to meet the ever-growing need, the World Foundation has, during the first years of its existence, been supported by the Pestalozzi Foundation of America. Its aims are threefold: to help in times of need where help is required most urgently; to support measures which are calculated to prevent future states of emergency; and to work together harmoniously with other existing organizations and institutions in order to avoid duplication and waste of effort.

The activities of the Pestalozzi Foundation are varied and extend all over the world. They comprise the support or the creation of children's homes in places as far apart as the South of Europe and the Indian subcontinent. In these homes not only material help but a good education is provided, so that the spirit of Pestalozzi is communicated to receptive minds, and useful members of a Commonwealth of Nations grow up.

Grants are awarded to students and teachers, pastors and

[2] See Ruth Carson: 'The Man who works Miracles for Children'. In: *The Parents' Magazine*. New York, 1953.

[3] Pestalozzi World Foundation, 41 Talacker, Zurich, Switzerland.

missionaries of all lands to enable these to introduce Pestalozzi's ideas to their own native countries. Immediate help in cases of emergency like the Holland flood can be given as the result of a special appeal. Otherwise, the regular source of income is large donations, Easter collections, and annual subscriptions. Ever new ways of raising funds which afford as much pleasure and satisfaction to the giver as to the receiver are devised by the Honorary President's unflagging ingenuity.

For his outstanding service to the cause of children's welfare the highest honours have been conferred on H. C. Honegger by thirteen governments and eleven institutions. In the same way, the World Youth Welfare Prize founded by the Pestalozzi Foundation has been awarded annually since 1949 to great educationists such as Maria Montessori and Eduard Spranger, and to U.N.I.C.E.F., the United Nations International Children's Emergency Fund.[4]

[4] From the printed material supplied by the Pestalozzi Foundation of America.

Select Bibliography

Note

The Bibliography is not a record of works consulted by the author but a guide to further study to the reader.

Editions of Pestalozzi's Works
(in the original German)

For research work K A is the indispensable source (expensive, recommended for libraries). For those later works not yet included in K A, S (2nd edition) must still be used (out of print, available in a few libraries). R and Ro are popular editions of selected works (obtainable through booksellers at reasonable prices). Kü and Kr are one-volume editions suitable for students.

(in English)

The only work in modern translation published separately and un-abridged is *How Gertrude. The Evening Hour* (complete) is included in Green's selection of 'Pestalozzi's Educational Writings'; the whole *Letter from Stans* can be found in Green's 'Life and Work of Pestalozzi'. Green's selection also contains *New Letters to Gessner* (letters 3–8) under the old title 'Views and Experiences', passages from *My Inquiries*, from the *Birthday Address*, 1818, and from the *Swansong*. Anderson's selections are mainly from the same works but include also a chapter from *The Swiss Journal* and the first (narrative) part of *Views and Experiences*. Most English books on Pestalozzi contain extracts from some of his works, known at the time of their publication. Abridged versions and collections of aphorisms are not quoted here.

Literature on Pestalozzi
(in German)

Of the vast number in existence only modern books of outstanding value are listed. It will be noted that most are devoted to special aspects of Pestalozzi's work, hitherto neglected.

(in English)

Contemporary and early works are dealt with in the essay, and its footnotes, under Appendix I. Some of them are difficult to obtain. For later works not the same method of selection as for German literature has been employed; all complete books are mentioned. They are of varying quality; and since all, including the latest published, have used old editions of Pestalozzi's

SELECT BIBLIOGRAPHY

works, they are confined to 'education' in too narrow a sense and have been
superseded by modern research.

A. IN GERMAN

I Works and Contemporary Sources

C   = *Pestalozzis Sämtliche Schriften.* Stuttgart and Tübingen,
            1819/26. 15 vols. (Cotta)
S   = *Johann Heinrich Pestalozzi. Sämmtliche Werke*, ed. L. W.
            Seyffarth. Liegnitz, 1896 ff., 2nd edition, 12 vols.
K A   = *Pestalozzi. Sämtliche Werke*, ed. Buchenau, Spranger, and
(e.g. II, 87) Stettbacher (Critical Edition). Berlin and Leipzig, 1927
            ff., Zürich, 1956 ff. (vols. I–XIX, except VI and XVII;
            still in progress).
B   = *Johann Heinrich Pestalozzi. Sämtliche Briefe*, ed. Pestalozzianum
            and Zentralbibliothek Zürich. Zürich, 1946 ff. (vols.
            I–IV, still in progress).
R   = *Heinrich Pestalozzi. Gesammelte Werke*, ed. Emilie Bosshart,
            Emanuel Dejung, Lothar Kempter, Hans Stettbacher.
            Zürich, 1945. 10 vols. (Rascher).
Ro   = *Pestalozzi. Werke*, ed. P. Baumgartner. Erlenbach—Zürich,
            1945–9. 8 vols. (Rotapfel).
Kü   = *Pestalozzi. Ausgewählte Schriften*, ed. Wilhelm Flitner.
            Düsseldorf/München. 2nd ed., 1954. 1 vol. (Küpper).
Kr   = *Pestalozzi. Grundlehren über Mensch, Staat, Erziehung*, ed. Max
            Zollinger and Hans Barth. Stuttgart 1956. 1 vol. (Kröner).
Isr   = August Israel: 'Pestalozzi-Bibliographie.' In: *Monumenta
            Germaniae Paedagogica*, ed. Karl Kehrbach. vols. XXV,
            XXIX, XXXI. Berlin, 1903–5.
Klinke   = Willibald Klinke: 'Pestalozzi-Bibliographie' (continuation).
            In: *Zeitschrift für Geschichte der Erziehung und des Unterrichts*,
            vols. XI–XIII. Berlin, 1921–3.
Morf   = H. Morf: *Zur Biographie Pestalozzis.* Winterthur, 1868 ff.
            4 vols.
Korr. Bl. = *Korrespondenzblatt des Archivs der Schweizerischen permanenten
            Schulausstellung in Zürich.* 1878–9.
P.B.   = *Pestalozzi-Blätter*, ed. Kommission des Pestalozzi-Stübchens
            in Zürich. 1880–1906.
P-anum   = *Pestalozzianum. Beilage zur Schweizerischen Lehrerzeitung.* Zürich,
            1922 ff. (continuing).
P.St.   = *Pestalozzi-Studien*, ed. L. W. Seyffarth. Liegnitz, 1896–1904.
Z.St.   = Josephine Zehnder-Stadlin: *Pestalozzi. Idee und Macht der
            menschlichen Entwicklung.* Gotha, 1875.
Dejung   = Emanuel Dejung: *Pestalozzi im Lichte zweier Zeitgenossen*:
            Henning und Niederer. Zürich, 1944.
Beg.   = Willibald Klinke: *Begegnungen mit Pestalozzi. Ausgewählte
            zeitgenössische Berichte.* Basel, 1946.
Anek.   = Adolf Haller: *Pestalozzi-Anekdoten.* Basel, 1946.

SELECT BIBLIOGRAPHY

II Modern Biographies and Interpretations

Bachmann, Werner: *Die anthropologischen Grundlagen zu Pestalozzis Soziallehre* Bern, 1947.

Ballauf, Theodor: *Vernünftiger Wille und gläubige Liebe. Interpretationen zu Kants und Pestalozzis Werk.* Meisenheim, 1957 (with extensive bibliography).

Barth, Hans: *Pestalozzis Philosophie der Politik.* Zürich, 1954.

Delekat, Friedrich: *Johann Heinrich Pestalozzi. Der Mensch, der Philosoph und der Erzieher.* Leipzig, 1928 (2nd ed.).

Guyer, Walter: *Pestalozzi.* Frauenfeld, 1932.

Hoffmann, Heinrich: *Die Religion im Leben und Denken Pestalozzis.* Bern, 1944.

Heubaum, Alfred: *Johann Heinrich Pestalozzi.* Berlin, 1920 (2nd ed.).

Hunziker, Otto: *Pestalozzi und Fellenberg.* Langensalza, 1897.

Litt, Theodor: *Der lebendige Pestalozzi.* Heidelberg, 1952.

Löhrer, Alfred: 'Pestalozzi in England'. In: *Schweizerische Pädagogische Zeitschrift.* Zürich, 1924.

Medicus, Fritz: *Pestalozzis Leben.* Leipzig, 1927.

Müller, Karl: *Johann Heinrich Pestalozzi. Eine Einführung in seine Gedanken.* Stuttgart, 1952.

Rupprecht, Heinrich: *Pestalozzis Abendstunde eines Einsiedlers.* Leipzig, 1934.

Schönebaum, Herbert: *Der junge Pestalozzi.* Leipzig, 1927.

  Pestalozzi. Kampf und Klärung. Erfurt, 1931.

  Pestalozzi. Kennen, Können, Wollen. Langensalza, 1937.

  Pestalozzi. Ernte und Ausklang. Langensalza, 1942.

Silber, Käte: *Anna Pestalozzi—Schulthess und der Frauenkreis um Pestalozzi.* Berlin, 1932.

  Pestalozzi. Der Mensch und sein Werk. Heidelberg, 1957.

Spranger, Eduard: *Pestalozzis Denkformen.* Heidelberg, 1959 (2nd ed.).

Stein, Arthur: *Pestalozzi und die Kantische Philosophie.* Tübingen, 1927.

  Pestalozzi und Leibniz. Basel, 1945.

Werner, Gertrud: *Die Symbole Pestalozzis.* Bern, 1954.

Wernle, Paul: *Pestalozzi und die Religion.* Tübingen, 1927.

Zander, Alfred: *Leben und Erziehung in Pestalozzis Institut in Iferten.* Aarau, 1931.

B. IN ENGLISH

I Texts

Pestalozzi: *Leonard and Gertrude. A Book for the Poor.* (Transl. by Eliza Shepherd.) Vol. I (only). Geneva, 1824.

Pestalozzi: *Leonard and Gertrude, or A Book for the People.* (Transl. anonym.) 2 vols. (Part I only). London, 1825.

Pestalozzi: *Letters on Early Education.* Addressed to J. P. Greaves. London, 1827 (and further editions).

Johann Heinrich Pestalozzi: *How Gertrude teaches her Children.* Transl. by Lucy E. Holland and Francis C. Turner. Edited with Introduction and Notes by Ebenezer Cooke. London, 1894 (and further editions).

329

SELECT BIBLIOGRAPHY

Pestalozzi's Educational Writings. Ed. by J. A. Green with F. A. Collie. London, 1912.

Pestalozzi. [Selections ed.] by Lewis Flint Anderson. New York and London, 1931.

II Literature

Payne, Joseph: *Pestalozzi. The Influence of his Principles and Practice on Elementary Education.* London, 1875.

Russell, John: *The Students' Pestalozzi.* (Based on R. de Guimps' 'Histoire de Pestalozzi'.) London, 1888 (and further editions, later under the title *Pestalozzi. Educational Reformer*).

Quick, Robert H.: *Essays on Educational Reformers.* London, 1890.

Pinloche, Auguste: *Pestalozzi and the Foundation of the modern Elementary School.* London, 1902.

Hayward, Frank H.: *The Educational Ideas of Pestalozzi and Fröbel.* London, 1904.

Green, John Alfred: *The Educational Ideas of Pestalozzi.* London, 1905.
Life and Work of Pestalozzi. London, 1913.

Compayré, Gabriel: *Pestalozzi and Elementary Education.* (Transl. by R. P. Jago.) London, 1907.

Monroe, Will Seymour: *History of the Pestalozzian Movement in the United States.* Syracuse, 1907.

Holman, Henry: *Pestalozzi. An Account of his Life and Work.* London, 1908.

Rusk, Robert R.: *Doctrines of the Great Educators.* London, 1918.

Pestalozzi and his Time. A Pictorial Record. Zürich and London, 1928.

Walch, Sister Mary Romana: *Pestalozzi and the Pestalozzian Theory of Education.* Washington, 1952.

Index

Note: The Index contains names of contemporary and historical persons only. Fictional characters are not included. Places and subject matter can be ascertained in the detailed table of contents.

331